CONTESTING THE FAR RIGHT

New Directions in Critical Theory

NEW DIRECTIONS IN CRITICAL THEORY
Amy Allen, General Editor

New Directions in Critical Theory presents outstanding classic and contemporary texts in the tradition of critical social theory, broadly construed. The series aims to renew and advance the program of critical social theory, with a particular focus on theorizing contemporary struggles around gender, race, sexuality, class, and globalization and their complex interconnections.

For a complete list of books in the series, please see the Columbia University Press website.

Contesting the Far Right

A PSYCHOANALYTIC AND FEMINIST CRITICAL THEORY APPROACH

Claudia Leeb

Columbia University Press
New York

Columbia University Press
Publishers Since 1893
New York   Chichester, West Sussex
cup.columbia.edu
Copyright © 2024 Columbia University Press
All rights reserved

Library of Congress Cataloging-in-Publication Data
Names: Leeb, Claudia, author.
Title: Contesting the Far Right : a psychoanalytic and feminist
critical theory approach / Claudia Leeb.
Description: New York : Columbia University Press, 2024. |
Series: New directions in critical theory | Includes bibliographical references and index.
Identifiers: LCCN 2023043168 (print) | LCCN 2023043169 (ebook) |
ISBN 9780231213066 (hardback) | ISBN 9780231213073 (trade paperback) |
ISBN 9780231559706 (ebook)
Subjects: LCSH: Right and left (Political science)—Psychological aspects. |
Right and left (Political science)—Economic aspects. | Political psychology. |
Group identity—Political aspects. | Critical theory.
Classification: LCC JA74.5 .L427 2024 (print) | LCC JA74.5 (ebook) |
DDC 320.01/9—dc23/eng/20231102
LC record available at https://lccn.loc.gov/2023043168
LC ebook record available at https://lccn.loc.gov/2023043169

Cover design: Milenda Nan Ok Lee
Cover image: Kwangmoozaa / Shutterstock

In memory
an meinen Papa, Anton Leeb (1944–1990)
Ein Schlosser in der Papierfabrik Lenzing, in Oberösterreich.
Seine Abenteuerlust und seine Verspieltheit sind immer mit mir.
Er war ein Sozialdemokrat, aber wechselte gegen Ende seines kurzen
Lebens zur extrem rechten Freiheitlichen Partei Österreichs über.
Ich wollte immer verstehen warum.

of my father, Anton Leeb (1944–1990)
A Schlosser in the paper factory Lenzing, in Upper Austria.
His adventurous spirit and playfulness is always with me.
He was a Social Democrat but changed to support the far-right
Freedom Party of Austria toward the end of his short life.
I always wanted to understand why.

Contents

Acknowledgments

I want to acknowledge all those who helped me finalize this book. I am grateful to Matt Stichter for his ongoing and unwavering support of my intellectual endeavors. He read each chapter (and at different stages) carefully, and his thoughtful and insightful feedback brings out the best in me. He also helped me adjust the book to the publisher's guidelines in the final stages. I am also thankful to David Plotke for his feedback on the general theoretical framework I am developing in the book and his detailed comments on chapter 6 and chapter 7. I also thank Amy Allen for her support of my overall theoretical framework and her feedback on earlier versions of chapters 2 and 3 and for inviting me to present chapter 5 at the Philosophy Department at Penn State University. I would also like to thank Joan Braune for her feedback on the conclusion and for discussing the theoretical aspects of the book with me. Our biweekly meetings and laughter helped me debrief when engaging with difficult material. I also thank Samir Gandesha for inviting me to present chapter 5 at the Institute for the Humanities at Simon Fraser University, Canada. I am also thankful for Wendy Lochner's feedback on chapter 5 and her unwavering support for this project. I also would like to thank my research assistant, Arin Mitchell, for her research on secondary literature and far-right material. I am grateful for the ongoing support of my small check-in group at the Faculty Success Program, which kept me on track. I am also thankful for Linda Braune's diligent and precise editing work, which helped me strengthen each chapter. I also would like to thank Monica Vilhauer for her insightful feedback on the book's first four chapters and her editing work. I also would like to thank the members of the Sigmund Freud Institute in New York City for their support and for granting me access to their Freud archives. I also thank Karl Fallend for inviting me to the University of Vienna, Austria, and supporting the book. I also would like to thank Sebastian Brameshuber for granting me access to his documentary on neo-fascism in Austria, which I analyze in chapter 6. Finally, I would like to thank the members and participants of the many conferences where I presented different stages of the book's chapters. Their feedback made this a stronger book. Also, many thanks to the Columbia University board members for trusting my abilities. Lastly, I would like to thank the Washington State University Arts and Humanities Fellowship, in particular Todd Butler, and the ADVANCE Washington State University External Mentorship Grant, which provided me with some of the resources to accomplish this book.

Introduction

Precise and undiluted knowledge of Freudian theory is more necessary and relevant today more than ever. The hatred of it is directly of a piece with anti-Semitism, by no means simply because Freud was a Jew but rather because psychoanalysis consists precisely of that critical self-reflection that makes anti-Semites vivid with rage.

—THEODOR W. ADORNO, *GUILT AND DEFENSE*

W hy have millions of subjects worldwide responded to the adverse effects of precarity capitalism—growing exploitation, economic insecurity, isolation, and alienation—by supporting far-right leaders, parties, and movements? This book draws on psychoanalytic and early Frankfurt School Critical Theory to help explain this phenomenon. I develop a dialectical relationship between the psychological and the socioeconomic, which means that psychological and socioeconomic factors are equally important to grasp the rise of the far right.[1]

In addition, the dialectical relationship is broader than its contents. As Adorno points out, "The name of dialectics says no more than that objects do not go into concepts without leaving a remainder."[2] The remainder refers to the moment of nonidentity in any concept and outlines that attempts to reduce the psychological to the socioeconomic (or vice versa) cannot fully succeed. It underlines that the psychological and socioeconomic are interconnected and thus dependent on each other. Nevertheless, they retain a moment of independence from each other.

However, contemporary scholarship often reduces the psychological to the socioeconomic, thereby missing the dialectics between the two. Those scholars who provide a socioeconomic analysis of the rise of the far right often do not (or not in detail) elaborate on the psychological factors, thereby reducing the psychological to the socioeconomic.[3] And scholars who attempt to incorporate sociopsychological explanations do so often without any in-depth engagement with (Freudian) psychoanalytic theory.[4] Furthermore, there is also a growing problematic chorus of thinkers of the early Frankfurt School kind who reject applying the insights of Freudian psychoanalytic theory to the study of the far right.[5]

While I consider Freudian psychoanalytic theory as central to grasping far-right propaganda techniques, the rise of the far right today is not *only* a psychological problem. It is also a socioeconomic and political problem. However, insofar as the far right's irrational objective aims *contradict* the material interest of most subjects whose support they aim to win, subjects do *not* join the far right because of rational economic or other self-interests, and the far right cannot win the support of the masses through rational arguments.[6] Instead, as Adorno noted, fascist (and today far-right) propaganda "must necessarily be deflected from discursive thinking; *it must be oriented psychologically*, and has to mobilize irrational, unconscious, regressive processes" in the masses to win their support.[7]

In this book, I show that Freudian psychoanalytic theory and terminology remain indispensable today to understand the psychologically oriented propaganda techniques the far right uses to turn subjects into followers of leaders and movements whose objective goals contradict their economic and other self-interests.[8] I draw on Freud and Adorno to show that far-right propaganda techniques function akin to hypnosis, which mobilizes unconscious and regressive processes in subjects, allowing the far right to manipulate them to support their irrational goals.

However, I go beyond Freud and Adorno in significant ways, allowing me to better explain the dialectics between the psychological and the socioeconomic. To begin with, I show that we must attend to questions of *subjectivity* in order to grasp how far-right propaganda techniques become effective.[9] I do not propose any notion of a "whole" subject here. Instead, I start from the assumption that subjects are fundamentally nonwhole, which generates anxieties and desires (the desire to achieve "wholeness") in subjects.

I show that far-right propaganda techniques are particularly effective in precarity capitalism because precarity capitalism heightens subjects' anxieties and desires around their nonwhole subjectivities. The reason for this is the prevalence of the fetish of "success" in capitalist societies, which implies (classed, raced, and gendered) economic, interpersonal, and bodily "success" standards for subjects living in such societies.

However, objective conditions of suffering in precarity capitalism (the threat of declassing, the inability to get or keep a job, exploitation, alienation, and isolation) make it difficult if not impossible for subjects to live up to such standards. As a result, objective conditions of suffering generate subjective forms of suffering, which people experience in the form of heightened castration anxieties and desires around their nonwhole subjectivities.[10]

Furthermore, I connect such socioeconomic conditions in precarity capitalism with the psychological processes engendered by far-right propaganda techniques. In psychoanalytic thought, the ego initially believes itself to be perfect and "whole" (the narcissistic state). However, when confronted with societal demands the ego cannot fulfill, it splits part of itself off—the ego ideal. The ego ideal is composed of people's ideal view of themselves and what they aspire to be like. In capitalist societies, a subject's ego ideal arises from classed, raced, and gendered economic, interpersonal, and bodily "success" standards.

Since most people cannot live up to their ego ideal in precarity capitalism, they experience a sharp tension between the ego and the ego ideal, with accompanying feelings of anxiety and failure. The core psychological mechanism in far-right propaganda techniques allows a subject to undo the split between their ego and their ego ideal. Once their ego coincides with their ego ideal, they can feel "whole" as a subject again and eliminate uncomfortable feelings of castration anxiety and failure.

The psychologically oriented far-right propaganda techniques are effective because they allow subjects to feel "whole" while leaving intact the objective conditions in precarity capitalism that generated their subjective suffering (feelings of failure and anxieties). Only a psychoanalytically inspired theoretical framework can explain how economic problems can influence people to turn to far-right actors who do not offer reasonable economic solutions (and who may even be responsible for perpetuating the economic problems).

Also, I show that in a far-right mass with an identifiable leader (such as the Trump mass or the Austrian Freedom Party), the leader (the hypnotist) enables the followers to replace their ego ideal with that of the idealized leader, which undoes the split between their ego and their ego ideal, and so they feel "whole" again. In contrast, in a far-right mass without an identifiable leader figure (such as the alt-right and the identitarian movement), the movement and its use of specific propaganda techniques (such as racist and sexist jokes) fulfill a similar function.

In addition, the theoretical framework I develop in this book shows how far-right propaganda techniques engender in subjects not only a sleep state (as in hypnosis) but also a dream state, where the followers can experience an "ecstatic high" that allows them in a dreamlike hallucinatory manner to feel they have economic, interpersonal, and bodily "success," even though nothing in their lives has objectively changed (or their socioeconomic conditions have become even worse). Since the far right does nothing to change the objective conditions of suffering in precarity capitalism, the followers remain vulnerable to far-right propaganda techniques that allow them to feel as "whole" subjects again.

Furthermore, my book contributes to resolving the current literature controversy concerning why white male subjects (of all classes) in particular support the far right. On the one side, we find those scholars who foreground economic suffering and not racist attitudes as a core reason white men turn to the far right.[11] On the other side are those thinkers who argue that economic suffering has nothing to do with why white men support the far right. Instead, they say it results from long-standing racist attitudes, which the far-right leaders and movements bring to the foreground.[12]

My approach in the book shows that far-right propaganda techniques can prey on unconscious racist and sexist attitudes in the context of precarity capitalism. Objective conditions of suffering in precarity capitalism (and here particularly the threat of declassing or being unable to "class up") also affect white, male subjects of all classes. To the extent that white men believe that they ought to be on the top of the economic hierarchy, they experience heightened castration anxieties around their nonwhole white, male subjectivities in precarity capitalism, which far-right propaganda techniques exploit.

To explain why white men might think they ought to be on the top of the economic hierarchy in both the U.S. and European contexts, I draw on decolonial theory. White European colonialists introduced the idea of whites and men being naturally "superior" to all other races and women to justify colonial violence toward and capitalist exploitation of the indigenous population and enslaved Africans, in particular colonized female subjects. Such racist and sexist classifications engendered a supposedly "natural" raced and gendered division of labor, which is still in effect worldwide today.[13]

Because whites in the U.S. and European contexts failed to work through their violent colonial pasts, such racist classifications were passed on from one generation to the next, and they continue to circulate in the unconscious of white men (and women) today. Such colonial classifications were used by fascist propaganda during the National Socialist era, and they continue to be used by the far right today. My theoretical framework explains that the same psychological processes that allow far-right followers to feel "whole" again also bring their repressed racist and sexist attitudes to their conscious.

The propaganda techniques that allow the followers to undo the tension between their ego and their ego ideal also put their superego[14] out of action temporarily (or for prolonged periods)—as a result, the followers can consciously express not only their repressed aggressive and libidinal drives (which enhances their pleasure) but also their unconscious racist and sexist attitudes. Since the unconscious attitude predominates among followers, the far right can now redirect the followers' aggression and resurfacing hatred of racial minorities and women toward its chosen foes.

Lastly, when I argue that far-right propaganda techniques engender in subjects regressive and unconscious psychological processes, I do not mean to pathologize those caught by far-right propaganda techniques, a risk Amy Allen recently worried about. Also, I do not want to suggest that those who are critical of such psychological processes or outline how far-right propaganda devices work are somehow, as she puts it, "more psychologically mature than our political opponents. Although this can be satisfying, we should be wary of the comforts and seductions of those satisfactions."[15]

One comfort of such a view is that it assures us we could never fall for far-right propaganda techniques. However, we all suffer in precarity capitalism and struggle with feelings of nonwholeness (albeit to varying degrees). In addition, most of us have had experiences in our childhoods[16] and from living in nations with violent colonial and fascist pasts that we have not worked through, which generate disturbances in our subjectivities upon which far-right propaganda preys. Therefore, we are not protected from getting caught by far-right propaganda techniques and the illusory promise of the wholeness it offers.

Also, far-right agitators do not necessarily have any theoretical knowledge of psychologically oriented devices. Instead, agitators resemble their followers psychologically. As Adorno puts it, they are distinguished from their followers only "by a capacity to express without inhibitions what is latent in them, rather than by an intrinsic superiority."[17] In other words, the agitators help foreground the unconscious state in the followers, which is the state they operate in themselves, allowing them to manipulate them for their own political and economic gains.

Context and Theorists

This book establishes the dialectics between psychological and socioeconomic factors by discussing the rise of the far right in the United States and Europe today. In the United States, I discuss Trump's rise and the growing appeal of the alt-right (alternative right). In Europe, I outline the ever-increasing electoral success of Austria's Freedom Party (Freiheitliche Partei Österreichs, FPÖ) and the growing appeal of the Austrian identitarian movement (Identitäre Bewegung Österreich, IBÖ).[18]

Here I would like to briefly outline the use of the term *far right* and the choice of context. I use the term *far right* to refer to *both* established far-right leaders and parties and growing neofascist (youth) movements to underline that today, as Herbert Marcuse puts it, the demarcation between the outsider agitator and the legitimate politician has been blurred if not obliterated, as the agitator has been introjected from "the fringe" into the legitimate political machine.[19]

However, to outline the (dis)connections between "legitimate politicians" and the "outside agitator," I discuss the rise of Trump and the alt-right in the United States and the growing appeal of the Freedom Party of Austria and Austrian identitarian movement in *separate* chapters. While the (political theory) literature on the rise of Trump mentions the alt-right (or vice versa) and the literature on the Freedom Party of Austria sometimes mentions the Austrian identitarian movement, such literature does not explore their (dis)connections, which I pursue in this book.

Although the literature on "populism" contributed significantly to explaining the rise of the far right, I do not employ such terminology in this book for two core reasons. Such literature often tends to treat "right-wing populism" as the same species as "left-wing populism," which distracts from the noticeable difference between them—the far right seeks to retain the objective conditions causing suffering in precarity capitalism and exploit such suffering with its psychologically oriented devices to catch followers. In contrast, left movements seek to remove such objective conditions of suffering.

Second, the literature on populism tends to make a sharp distinction between right-wing populism and fascism, which is problematic on two fronts. First, it suggests that an analysis of fascism (such as provided by early Frankfurt School Critical Theory) does not shed much light on today's problems of the resurgence of the far right. Second, it closes our eyes to the fascist elements in established politicians and parties and how the far right can slide into fascism.[20]

My analysis shows a (dis)connection between the far right and fascism on various levels. First, on a theoretical level, I draw on psychoanalytically inspired early Frankfurt School Critical Theory, which explains the rise of fascism in Europe and the protofascist elements in the United States to analyze the rise of the far right today. I show that the far right today uses psychologically oriented propaganda devices to manipulate the unconscious of potential followers for its destructive purposes, which brings back the specter of fascism that some of the literature on populism aims to ignore.

Second, I analyze the (dis)connection between the far right and neofascism in the United States and Europe. In the United States, I examine Trump as an example of "legitimate" far-right politics and the rise of the alt-right as an example of a (neo)fascist movement. Here I challenge theorists such as George Hawley, who make a sharp distinction between the alt-right and Trump followers (and claim that Trump has nothing to do with fascism), because I show that Trump and the alt-right use similar devices, namely, ones that allow their followers to eliminate the split between their ego and their ego ideal and feel as "whole subjects" again.[21]

Trump initiates processes that allow his followers to replace their ego ideal with the idealized leader figure, which in turn allows the followers' ego ideals coincide with their egos and so allows them to feel better about themselves. The alt-right instead uses racist and sexist jokes to achieve the same effect. In both mainstream Trump followers and alt-right followers, such processes can lead to violent behavior. In the attack on the U.S. Capitol in 2021, in which mainstream Trump followers, the alt-right, and other (neo)fascist groups participated, we can see that the boundary between the far right and neofascism has been obliterated.

In Europe, I focus on the Austrian Freedom Party as an example of "legitimate" far-right politics and the growing Austrian identitarian movement as an example of a (neo)fascist youth movement. My analysis shows how Austria's failed working-through of its feelings of loss and guilt about its recent National Socialist past makes people vulnerable to the propaganda techniques the FPÖ uses, which are particularly effective in the context of precarity capitalism and enable their followers to close the books on the past.

My analysis of the psychologically oriented propaganda tactics of Identitäre Bewegung Österreich shows that the IBÖ also employs tactics to attract new followers that exploit repressed feelings of guilt and loss and anxieties generated by precarity capitalism. I also outline how the IBÖ's "movement trick" and the "indefatigability" propaganda device engender in its followers sleep and dream states that are akin to hypnosis, which engenders not only an ecstatic "high" in the followers that makes them feel "whole" again but also leads them to engage in violent behavior toward vulnerable migrant and immigrant populations in Austria.

I chose the United States and Austria as examples of the far right because I have an "outsider-within" perspective in both countries. I was born and grew up in Austria and spent part of my adulthood there, which provides me with insight into the specifics of Austria's culture and the language skills necessary to analyze the deeper and unconscious content of the materials of far-right agitators (some of which are only available in German) in the European context.

At the same time, I have already lived a large part of my adulthood in the United States, which affords me some distance to analyze challenging topics, such as Austria's failed working-through of its past and its connection to a (neo-)Nazi present. Furthermore, I am not dependent on Austria for my livelihood, so I can discuss topics that generate strong resistance reactions in Austrians.[22]

I also have lived in the United States long enough to understand the details of its culture and politics enough to analyze the far right in this context. Nevertheless, at the same time, I remain an "outsider," which provides me with the necessary distance to outline the dangerous potential of that culture to allow what happened in Europe not too long ago to also happen in the United States.

This book brings core concepts coined by German critical theorists, mainly Karl Marx and Theodor W. Adorno, into conversation with the psychoanalytic theory of Sigmund Freud to outline the dialectics of economic and psychological forces that help explain the rise of the far right in Europe and the United States. However, German critical theory does not neatly stand for the economic and Freud for the psychological in the dialectics I aim to establish.

I draw on central concepts coined by Marx, including exploitation, alienation, and isolation, to outline the objective conditions of suffering in precarity capitalism, which helps me explain the economic forces in the socioeconomic/psychological dialectics. However, I also show that Marx helps us shed light on how economic forces interact with psychological ones because his theory relates to questions of subjectivity.[23]

Regarding the early Frankfurt School Critical Theory tradition, I focus on Adorno because his work assists me in advancing my overall methodological framework, which outlines the dialectics between the socioeconomic and the psychological. Furthermore, I focus on those texts of Adorno in which he drew on psychoanalytic theory to study fascism, since such texts are more helpful than others in grasping psychologically oriented propaganda tactics and their effects.

While there has been a recent return to the *Authoritarian Personality* (AP) study, to which Adorno contributed and which draws on Freudian theory to explain the rise of far right, my approach differs from the AP study.[24] The AP study is an empirical look at the consumer at whom fascist propaganda is directed and whose character structure (a product of society) can make them susceptible to fascist propaganda.

In contrast, Adorno's texts, which draw on Freudian psychoanalytic theory, aim to provide a theoretical foundation for the functioning of psychologically oriented techniques that (proto)fascist agitators use to capture vulnerable people. It is these latter texts that I draw on to analyze the (online) texts, writings, and speeches that today's far-right leaders, parties, and movements use to catch followers. Adorno is helpful because he takes up and further theorizes Freud's concept of ego ideal replacement as the core mechanism that holds various propaganda techniques together.

I draw on core concepts coined by Freud, including his concept of the ego ideal and his notion of libidinal and aggressive drives and how they are connected to forming far-right masses. Throughout the book, I also return to Freud's theory of the unconscious and his theory of dreams and hypnosis to explain sleep and dream states, in which the follower's unconscious predominates and that agitators induce in their followers to make them submit to their arbitrary will.

Also, this book is *not* primarily about the early Frankfurt School and psychoanalysis more generally.[25] Instead, I draw on Freud and psychoanalytically inspired texts by Adorno because these theorists provide the most insightful framework to theorize the mediation between the socioeconomic and psychological in the rise of the far right in today's U.S. and Austrian contexts.

However, drawing on Adorno and Freud does not mean that I arrive at the same points Adorno and Freud were making, as my book aims to go *beyond* mere exegesis of early Frankfurt School Critical Theory and Freudian psychoanalytic thought. I intend to analyze the current recruitment tactics used by the far right so that we can figure out how to counter them. Other early Frankfurt School critical theorists and psychoanalysts offer some helpful concepts to theorize the rise of the far right today, which I draw on in this book.[26]

However, these authors do not provide a theoretical framework to understand what holds different propaganda techniques together. This framework is what I am delivering by drawing on some concepts from Adorno and Freud. Beyond Adorno and Freud, I make the more general argument that to understand the rise of the far right today we must foreground questions of subjectivity and feelings of nonwholeness in precarity capitalism and how recruitment tactics generate sleep and dream states in followers. Such states allow the followers to feel "whole" on a subjective level, while the objective conditions of suffering in precarity capitalism remain intact. Furthermore, such states generate the conditions for the followers' violent behavior toward the far right's chosen foes. Therefore, I hope to offer a robust theoretical framework to study and contest the far right today.[27]

Chapter Outline

In chapter 1, I mostly outline the socioeconomic aspects (while also discussing psychological aspects), and in chapter 2, I mostly outline the psychological aspects of the socioeconomic/psychological dialectics (while also discussing the economic aspects). In chapter 3, I further detail such dialectics by discussing Adorno and by introducing my account of how propaganda techniques introduce sleep and dream states in the followers of far-right movements. Chapters 4 (the rise of Trump) and 5 (the alt-right) elaborate on the far right in the United States. Finally, chapters 6 (the

Freedom Party of Austria) and 7 (the Austrian identitarian movement) explain the far right in the European (Austrian) context.

In chapter 1, "Castration Anxiety and Capitalism," I introduce the theoretical distinction between objective conditions and subjective forms of suffering. I show that subjects in capitalist societies are expected to live up to economic, interpersonal, and bodily "success" standards that are classed, gendered, and raced. However, objective conditions of suffering in precarity capitalism (the threat of declassing, the inability to get or keep a job, exploitation, alienation, and isolation) make it difficult if not impossible for subjects to live up to such standards.

As a result, the objective conditions generate subjective forms of suffering that people experience as castration anxieties, which refers to their fears about being nonwhole subjects. Castration anxieties appear in three forms: economic, interpersonal, and physical. Propaganda devices allow people to quell their castration anxieties and experience themselves as "whole" subjects. Such devices do away with subjective forms of suffering without removing the objective conditions of suffering in precarity capitalism that generated the subjective forms of suffering in the first place.

Chapter 2, "Psychoanalytic Concepts," introduces the reader to the core psychoanalytic theoretical concepts that I will be using throughout the book to establish the dialectics between the socioeconomic and the psychological: the unconscious, repressed libidinal and aggressive drives, the superego and its relationship to the id (the unconscious) and the ego ideal, as well as ego ideal replacement. I then outline how the unconscious and the libidinal and aggressive drives help integrate what Freud determines as the "psychological mass."

Here I also go beyond Freud in innovative ways. While Freud (and critical theorists who draw on Freud) mainly foregrounded the centrality of the libidinal bond between the followers and the leader, I foreground the centrality of the aggressive drive to integrate the (fascist) masses. To support my argument, I discuss Freud's *Civilization and Its Discontents* in connection with *Group Psychology and the Analysis of the Ego* because in the former text the aggressive drive is more central.[28]

Chapter 3, "Sleeping and Dreaming While Awake: Adorno Revisited," draws on Adorno to further detail how the (fascist) agitator, or the movement, functions akin to a hypnotist who induces archaic regressions that generate a passive-masochistic attitude that makes followers submit to the arbitrary will of the agitator or movement. Here I also challenge the chorus of contemporary critical theorists of the early Frankfurt School who aimed to distance Adorno from Freudian psychoanalytic theory, as I explain how Adorno's focus on Freudian psychoanalytic theory allows us to further theorize the dialectics of the socioeconomic and the psychological in the rise of the far right today.

I also go beyond Adorno (and Freud) in innovative ways: First, I outline how propaganda techniques put the followers into a sleep state, which makes them subject themselves to the leader's or movement's irrational aims, which are irreconcilable with their rational economic and other self-interests. Second, the sleep state induces in the followers also a dream state, in which their ego ideals of having "success" on the economic, interpersonal, and bodily levels are fulfilled in a hallucinatory manner. Third, the followers' unconscious dominates in the sleep and dream states, which the far right manipulates for political and economic gains.

Chapter 4, "From Melancholia to Mania: The Rise of Trump," details how far-right propaganda techniques use the melancholia/mania complex, which Freud merely hinted at but did not develop further in *Group Psychology and the Analysis of the Ego*. The chapter outlines the objective conditions that suffering people in the United States experience and the effects on their subjectivity, which set the stage for the effectiveness of Trump's propaganda techniques. First, I outline how precarity capitalism generates in people a melancholic state, in which they feel worthless and experience a sharp tension between their egos and ego ideals.

I then explain how Trump's propaganda techniques undo the tension in his followers between their egos and their ego ideals, allowing them to oscillate out of the melancholic state into a state of mania. In mania, they can experience the dream hallucination that they are now (via the idealized leader figure) "whole subjects" and "successful," which allows them to shed their self-depreciation. At the same time, the ecstatic Trump festival makes the followers regress to the "primal horde," where they are more likely to take out their aggression toward Trump's targets of hatred. I analyze interviews with Trump followers and a Trump rally, Trump's handling of the COVID-19 pandemic, and references to the 2021 attack on the Capitol.

Chapter 5, "The Culture Industry of Jokes: The Recruitment Tactics of the Alt-Right," brings Freud's *Jokes and Their Relation to the Unconscious* into conversation with his *Group Psychology and the Ego* to theorize the role of tendentious jokes in far-right propaganda technique.[29] While Freud hinted at such a role, he did not further theorize it. I analyze the growing appeal of the alt-right, an internet-focused (neo)fascist movement in the United States. Alt-right figures link jokes, pleasure, humiliation, and (potential) violence in a circuit illuminated by Freud's account of jokes as antagonism.

The yield of pleasure a joke produces bribes predominantly young white men into becoming co-haters, allowing them to undo the split between their egos and ego ideals and feel like "whole white male subjects" again. At the same time, the jokes lift the inhibition of the repression of hostility against the jokes' targeted groups and reduce barriers to committing violence against them. To ground my theoretical elaborations, I analyze alt-right jokes, a neo-fascist alt-right online publication, as well as alt-right outlets that aim to make the alt-right acceptable to a mainstream audience. I also outline how Trump uses tendentious jokes targeting women and minorities to appeal to his audience, connecting the alt-right's recruitment tactics to Trumpism.

In chapter 6, "Austria's Far Right: A Failed Working-Through of the Past," I analyze the documentary *Und in der Mitte, da sind wir* (And in the middle we are) (2014) to explain how taboos around Austria's violent National Socialist past have become a barrier to a successful working-through of the past over several generations. Furthermore, I show that the (grand)parents' failure to work through the past and confront difficult feelings of guilt and loss and patriarchal family structures make their children susceptible to far-right propaganda devices.

I also outline the devices the Austrian Freedom Party uses to tap into the vast pool of Austrians who aim to keep feelings of loss and guilt repressed in their unconscious. I trace the historical roots of the Freedom Party in Austria's recent Nazi past and show how its attempts to close the book on the past assisted the party's early rise. Finally, I outline how the Austrian Freedom Party aimed to deride and minimize the opening of a "House of History" museum in Vienna, which would have exposed Austria's violent past, to tap into the vast pool of Austrians who aim to keep difficult feelings of guilt and loss repressed in their unconscious.

In chapter 7, "Gratifications of Terror: The Austrian Identitarian Movement," I analyze the writings of Martin Sellner, one of the core leaders of the power-seeking (neo)fascist Austrian identitarian movement (IBÖ), which is part of the pan-European (neo)fascist identitarian movement (IM). The IBÖ has backing from those in power in Austria and connections with and support from other (neofascist) movements in Europe. It also has connections to the alt-right in the United States. I group the psychologically oriented devices that Sellner uses to catch followers in sections to show how they reinforce one another.

I explain how the "movement trick" and the "indefatigability device" work together to undo the followers' split between their egos and their ego ideals. Such undoing generates euphoria in the followers, eradicating their feelings of failure and anxieties around their male subjectivities in precarity capitalism. I also discuss how Sellner uses a series of tricks (the "terror strategy") that generate in the followers' negative feelings (mostly anxiety) while simultaneously promising them unconscious gratifications. Finally, I elaborate on how the IBÖ's tactics aim to stimulate and rationalize violence in their followers.

In my concluding remarks, "Suggestions for Undermining the Far Right Today," I outline how far-right propaganda techniques prey upon our wounds and our scars, generated in our childhoods, in our daily (work-) lives in precarity capitalism, and through living in nations with violent histories. They can catch us because they allow us, through generating an "ecstatic high" in the sleep and dream states, to (temporarily at least) forget and not feel such scars. Insofar as we want to remain in such a state (as it allows us to avoid touching painful wounds), we keep returning to and supporting the far right to get "high" again. To become less vulnerable to far-right propaganda techniques, we must work through the past and touch our scars.

I outline how "embodied reflective spaces" can assist us to work though our past and touch our scars and how the "subject-in-outline" that embraces nonwholeness can assist in the painful process of working-through one's past and not falling for far-right propaganda that promise us the illusion of wholeness.[30] I also explain why far-right followers who commit atrocities under the "spell of hypnosis" remain morally and legally responsible for such acts. Finally, I suggest that we must reintroduce the notion of the revolutionary proletariat-in-outline to overthrow capitalism and create a better society, one in which all subjects have a chance to thrive, and hence do not need illusions provided by the far right that make them feel better about themselves.

CHAPTER I

Castration Anxiety and Capitalism

Fear of castration is one of the commonest and strongest motives for repression and thus for the formation of neuroses.

—SIGMUND FREUD, *NEW INTRODUCTORY LECTURES ON PSYCHO-ANALYSIS*

Castration in the age of concentration camps is more characteristic for social reality than competition.

— THEODOR W. ADORNO, "DIE REVIDIERTE PSYCHOANALYSE"

The far right, I will argue, does not appeal to rational economic interests. Instead, it taps into deeper anxieties, particularly castration anxieties, around people's subjectivities. The distinction between *objective* conditions of suffering and *subjective* experiences of suffering is my innovative theoretical approach, which I use to build up the dialectic of the psychological and socioeconomic sides of the rise of the far right.

Contemporary capitalism engenders two interconnected forms of suffering: The first results from the objective conditions of capitalism, such as the threats of declassing, exploitation (e.g., lengthening of the working day, an intensification of workload via new technology), alienation, and isolation. The second, less obvious form of suffering refers to how objective forms of suffering in capitalism generate castration anxieties and affect subjectivity.

The objective conditions of suffering in capitalist societies generate castration anxieties in three related areas: first, in economic security; second, in interpersonal relationships; and, third, on the bodily level. People experience castration anxieties as a threat to their "whole" subjectivity—these make them feel "nonwhole" or in danger of becoming nonwhole (that is, castrated) as subjects. Also, castration anxieties manifest differently along class, gender, and "racial" lines.[1]

I understand the subject as fundamentally and irrevocably nonwhole. Such fundamental nonwholeness generates anxieties and the desire to attain (or restore) an impossible wholeness. Objective conditions of suffering in capitalism heighten the castration anxieties of nonwhole subjectivities and further strengthen the desire to reach wholeness. Far-right propaganda techniques are effective because they provide their followers with the illusion of being "whole" subjects again, which allows them to quell their castration anxieties.

I do not aim at a "wholesale" explanation of the source of the far right in castration anxieties.[2] Instead, I want to draw attention to how the socioeconomic conditions of precarity capitalism generate castration anxieties in people, which the far right exploits for its own purposes. I argue that objective conditions of suffering in precarity capitalism make it difficult, if not impossible, for people to live up to economic, interpersonal, and bodily "success" standards, which result from classed, raced, and gendered ideologies of what it means to be a "whole" subject.

As a result, objective conditions of suffering generate subjective forms of suffering, which people experience as castration anxieties and that I theorize as their anxieties about being "nonwhole" subjects. Psychologically oriented far-right techniques prey on such anxieties because they offer the hope that people can experience themselves as "whole" subjects again.

However, the far right does nothing to change the objective conditions of suffering in capitalism that generated such anxieties in the first place. To the extent that subjects are satisfied with the illusion of wholeness the far right provides, this cycle can be perpetuated without capitalism's objective conditions changing. So, subjects keep being made miserable by their objective conditions in capitalism. As a result, they keep wanting the far right to put them into states where they can enjoy the illusion of being whole subjects, without the objective conditions of suffering that generated their subjective forms of suffering changing.[3]

In "The Threat of Declassing," I explain the classed, raced, and gendered elements of economic castration anxiety. In "Castration Anxiety of White Subjects," I introduce decolonial feminist theory to explain why white men believe they should be at the top of the economic hierarchy. In "Exploitation and Subjectivity," I demonstrate how capitalist exploitation generates bodily and interpersonal castration anxieties. In "The Alienated Subject," I explain the connection between alienation in capitalist societies and the far right. In "The Castrating Conditions of the Culture

Industry," I outline how the culture industry of mass media and its technology generates subjectivities susceptible to far-right propaganda.

The Threat of Declassing

In *Aspekte des neuen Rechtsradikalismus* (Aspects of new right radicalism), Adorno warns us not to resort to easy economic explanations for the rise of the far right, because fascism, once it has established itself as the dominant political force, "always has a tendency to become independent of the existing economic interests." Furthermore, since fascism needs a mass base but favors the few over the many, it cannot sustain itself by appealing to and satisfying its subjects' rational economic interests. Instead, it must appeal to its subjects' emotional needs and irrational anxieties and wishes.[4]

In "Die revidierte Psychoanalyse" (The revised psychoanalysis), Adorno further explains the anxieties and wishes to which fascist propaganda appeals. Here he reiterates that it is *not* rational economic interests, such as competition for resources (money, jobs, housing, etc.), as suggested by the neo-Freudians, that activate the antidemocratic potential in the great mass of people. Instead, the antidemocratic potential is activated because people live in a capitalist society held together by indirect threats of physical violence—threats of castration, which Freud, according to Adorno, clearly understood.[5] Furthermore, he points out that the neo-Freudians, who aim to do away with the "terrible and unmistakable phenomena such as the threat of castration," castrate psychoanalysis itself because they do away with its critical *Stachel*—its sting.[6]

Adorno, in *Aspekte des neuen Rechtsradikalismus*, points out that the preconditions for the reemergence of far-right movements remain in the Germany of the 1960s intact, because of the concentration of capital, which implies "the possibility of a permanent declassing of those layers of society, who were in their subjective class-consciousness bourgeois and who want to hold on to their social status and perhaps even strengthen that status."[7]

The threat of declassing generates economic castration anxiety (the first of my three forms of castration anxiety) for those subjectively identified with or objectively part of the bourgeois class.[8] This anxiety is the result of capitalist ideology, which generates the standard of "economic success." This standard implies that in capitalist society, to be a "whole" and noncastrated subject you must have "economic success." A failure to live up to that standard generates castration anxiety on the economic level, which takes on different forms along class, gender, and "racial" lines. A bourgeois subject (particularly if this subject is also white and male) who fails to hold on to or strengthen their bourgeois class position experiences economic castration anxiety, which the far right taps into to catch followers.

As Albena Azmanova points out, today's neoliberal capitalism has transformed into precarity capitalism, where everybody faces the threat of declassing, even "labor market insiders" who have well-paying jobs. Precarity capitalism has created economic and social insecurity among most of the population, including the bourgeois class. Through offloading social risk to society, precarity capitalism, as she puts it, has "created a condition of generalized precarity from which the labor-market insiders—those who are skilled and have well-paying jobs—are not sheltered." She further argues that generalized precarity has generated heightened competition among people (for jobs, resources, etc.) and anxieties, which the far right has exploited.[9]

I agree with Azmanova's argument that the far right today is "an expression of a broadly shared and lasting anxiety" generated by precarity capitalism. However, as Adorno has emphasized, the rise of the far right is not the result of heightened competition in capitalism. Instead, it results from the threat of declassing, which generates economic (as well as interpersonal and bodily) castration anxieties.[10] For subjects identified with or objectively part of the bourgeois class, precarity capitalism has heightened their castration anxieties because it has made the threat of becoming declassed a reality. Such potential or actual declassing means the potential or actual loss of their class privileges and the social status associated with it. Precarity capitalism also has made it more difficult for subjects of the bourgeois class to strengthen their class position.

For example, one means by which the bourgeois classes aim to secure their class position is by sending their children to the "right schools" to secure bourgeois jobs. However, it has become more difficult for young adults from the bourgeoisie to meet their parents' class standards and positions despite holding advanced degrees from such schools and universities. As a result, instead of securing or keeping a bourgeois job, they are not landing their first job or are losing their jobs and not finding new ones.

The possibility of declassing within the constraints of precarity capitalism generates subjective forms of suffering, making bourgeois subjects experience their subjectivities as nonwhole, with accompanying castration anxiety. In particular, young white male bourgeois adults who are, despite the class and racial privileges they enjoy, not economically "successful" are often viewed as failures in the eyes of society and their parents.

As I will show in chapters 5 and 7, the alt-right in the United States and the identitarian movement in Europe tap into the economic castration anxieties of young male bourgeois adults. Its propaganda specifically targets a college-educated audience, and its psychologically oriented techniques allow frustrated young white male subjects from the bourgeois class to experience an illusory wholeness that quells their economic castration anxieties. Unfortunately, these same techniques also unleash the subjects' antidemocratic potential.

The threat of declassing means something slightly different for the poor and working classes. To be a "whole" and noncastrated subject from the poor and working classes, you need to be able to secure a job that pays a living wage and possibly offers an opportunity to "move up" the economic hierarchy. Here the threat is not so much of declassing but of not being able to "up-class," or live up to the capitalist standard of "economic success."[11]

As a result of precarity capitalism, many of the poor and working classes either have lost their jobs or cannot get a job that allows them to "up-class" and secure a decent livelihood; more acutely, often they cannot even ensure their current survival. However, the bourgeois ideology of "upward mobility" (particularly in the United States) promotes the fantasy of rising from dishwasher to millionaire, from janitor to CEO. This ideology ignores existing class, gender, and racial barriers that make such "mobility" difficult, if not impossible, to achieve. It's all up to the individual to succeed or fail. This ideology makes all those not living up to the capitalist standard of "economic success" individually responsible, which further heightens the castration anxieties of poor and working-class subjects. In reality, working-class hopes to move "higher" up the economic hierarchy, either through their efforts or their children's efforts, have been mainly frustrated.[12]

The capitalist ideology of "upward mobility" also hides the fact that children of the working classes rarely find themselves in elite institutions of higher education. As Louis Althusser has shown us, the reason for this is not their incapacity to succeed in such institutions but because they are sub-tly pushed into education destined for the working classes (such as voca-tional training), because capital needs a new generation of "fresh blood" for exploitation.[13]

Those children from the working classes who pursue higher education find themselves often not in the "right kind" of institutions, that is, those that could increase their chances of securing a job and making a decent livelihood. Moreover, in contrast to their bourgeois peers, they cannot rely on their families to pay the expenses of higher education—tuition, hous-ing, etc. and must take out loans to finance their education. And unlike their peers from the bourgeois class, they lack the necessary social connec-tions that would enable them to secure a decent job to pay back their col-lege debts.[14]

Also, for many subjects of the poor and working classes, the specter of becoming homeless and living on the streets has moved closer to reality or has already become a reality. Since the COVID-19 pandemic, more and more people live on the streets in tents in urban centers in the United States, which underlines the inhumanity of a capitalist system that insists that each individual rely on themself and has done away with most social safety net-works. Insofar as becoming homeless is a core expression of finding one-self "economically castrated" in capitalist societies, precarity capitalism has heightened such castration anxieties, particularly for the poor and work-ing classes.

Current economic conditions in precarity capitalism have also height-ened economic castration anxieties around subjectivities in a gender-specific way. Capitalist ideologies that propagate the idea of "economic success" interconnect with patriarchal ideologies of masculinity and man-hood: They expect men of all classes, and more so than women from the same class, to have "economic success." Not being able to live up to such standards has heightened particularly males' castration anxieties around their subjectivities.

Capitalism has heightened the threat of declassing for all subjects of the bourgeois class. However, castration anxieties are more substantial for men from this class because the bourgeois class expects them to be responsible for maintaining or strengthening the privileges and social status associated with it (although more and more, women are also taking on this function). Thus, the threat of declassing heightens castration anxieties particularly of bourgeois men.

All subjects from the gendered and raced proletariat experience economic castration anxieties around their subjectivities. However, such anxieties are heightened for proletarian men particularly, as there is still the expectation that as males they are the "breadwinners" (even though more and more women from the poor and working classes are carrying out this function). Not "making it" heightens the castration anxieties of proletarian men.

These class- and gender-specific threats of declassing (or threats against "up-classing" for the poor and working classes) have created subjective forms of suffering in men of all classes. They express themselves in anxieties that one is not a "whole" person or not a "real man"—that is, a castrated subject. Thus, it is no surprise that far-right propaganda techniques effectively win over men across the class spectrum.

Far-right propaganda techniques are effective because they allow men to feel like "real men" again. But again, as I will emphasize throughout this chapter, these techniques tap into subjective forms of suffering (castration anxieties and the threat to manhood) and offer so-called relief without doing anything substantive to eradicate the objective conditions in capitalism and patriarchy that created such forms of suffering in the first place.

For example, such techniques generate in the followers a process that allows them, via the idealized "whole" leader figure, to feel themselves as "real men" again and quell their economic castration anxieties.[15] In chapter 4, I show how Trump's self-styling of himself as a "self-made man" (which hides the class, racial, and gender privileges that made him "economically successful") allows his male followers to feel via the leader figure the illusion that they are themselves "economically successful" or on the way to become so (if they support Trump).

Castration Anxiety of White Subjects

Some scholars have examined how economic suffering and racial attitudes have contributed to whites supporting the far right today. For example, Wendy Brown suggests that the rise of white nationalist authoritarian political formations results from the socioeconomically aggrieved white working- and middle-class populations and their racial attitudes. For her, such rise is "animated by the mobilized anger of the economically abandoned and racially resentful, but as contoured by more than three decades of neoliberal assaults on democracy, equality, and society."[16]

Similarly, Johanna Fernández details how economic suffering and racial attitudes are interconnected in the rise of the far right today. She points out that while workers of color in the United States have always been exploited, white workers have seen their livelihoods decline significantly too. Such decline created a "social injury" for white workers, which they perceived as a fall from the top of the country's racial hierarchy. Furthermore, their economic suffering went hand in hand with the growing presence of people of color, gays, lesbians, and women in public, economic, and political life, and "the perceived rising fortunes of these Others flouted their sense of white superiority."[17]

White working classes have relied on their "white superiority" to compensate for their economic status—that is, they might not be able to feel good about their economic status but instead could emphasize their "white superiority." With the advent of precarity capitalism and the contemporary focus on multiculturalism, neither their economic status nor their privileged racial status enables them to feel good about themselves. According to Fernández, the far right has channeled white subjects' "social injury" by blaming Black Americans and immigrants from Mexico and Latin America for the social (and, I would add, economic) problems.[18]

While both thinkers (Brown and Fernández) suggest that economic suffering is interconnected with racial attitudes, they do not further explain why whites of all classes believe they should be on the top of the economic hierarchy and why they become "racially resentful" or experience a "social injury" if they are not (an "injury" the far right exploits). Furthermore, both thinkers do not (or only marginally) discuss the psychologically oriented techniques far-right leaders and movements use that allow them to exploit white supremacist attitudes in the context of their economic suffering.

The Peruvian decolonial thinker and sociologist Annibal Quijano helps us understand why whites believe they should be at the top of the economic hierarchy. He explains it as being the result of the legacies of a global model of power he calls the "coloniality of power."[19] This model of power had a specific geopolitical location—it was initially established through the European colonization of the Americas, and from there it expanded through further European colonial projects over the entire world.

The coloniality of power also has a specific rationality—Eurocentrism, which assisted the social classification of the world's population around the idea of "race."[20] Through Eurocentric knowledge production that exclusively associated white Europeans with modernity and rationality and dismissed knowledge productions of the colonized as "premodern," such rationality situated colonized peoples in a natural position of inferiority to white Europeans, which allowed the conquerors to feel naturally superior.

The new global model of power also allowed the assignment of all forms of unpaid labor to the colonized and the assignment of salaried labor to the colonizing whites in Europe and the colonies only. Given their "racial inferiority," the colonized were not considered worthy of wages and were naturally obliged to work for the profit of the colonizers. The exploitation of natural resources in the colonies and colonized people (enslaved Black people, the indigenous population, and mestizos) allowed the colonizers to produce profitable goods for the world market, which established world capitalism with Europe at the center.[21]

The coloniality of power engendered a global raced division of labor, where racialized subjects were relegated to the most degrading, dangerous, and underpaid jobs. This division is still in place worldwide today. Maria Lugones further expands upon Quijano's theoretical coloniality of power. She shows us that European colonialists not only introduced the hierarchical classification of whites as "naturally" superior to all other races but also the idea that women are "naturally" inferior to men. The colonialists enforced rigid gender and sexual roles, which led to the devaluation and disempowerment of indigenous women and those that did not conform to such roles.[22]

While Quijano and Lugones allow us to understand how capitalism and colonialism are intrinsically connected, they did not theorize the connection between colonialism and fascism. However, other thinkers have. For example, George Padmore coined the term "colonial fascism" and explained that settler-colonial racism was the breeding ground for the European fascist mentality. Furthermore, he considered England's criticism of Nazi Germany hypocritical "when fascism and racial terrorism are flourishing within their own Colonial Empire."[23]

Similarly, Aimé Césaire explained that European colonial imperialism generated fascism and that Hitler's crimes were the enactments of "colonialist procedures" on the European continent. These provoked international outrage only because Hitler applied to Europe procedures that until then had been reserved exclusively for colonized subjects in their colonies.[24] More recently, James Whitman argues that the brutal history of legally sanctioned and codified antiblack racism in the United States may have served as a model for the Nazis' antisemitism.[25] Also Anne Spice points out that expressions of fascism today are nothing but "timeless colonial techniques." As she puts it, "neofascist and white supremacist movements also attempt to make a deeply hierarchical social order appear to be the natural order of things. This is an old colonial trick, and one that Indigenous people know about."[26]

So the feelings of whites in both the U.S. and European contexts that they ought to be on the top of the racial hierarchy are a continuation of colonial-era racial classifications in which whites appear naturally superior and more "deserving" of the best jobs. At the same time, people of color are supposedly "inferior," which makes them "naturally" fit for the most degrading, dangerous, and underpaid jobs.

Since the United States and Europe have largely failed to work through their violent colonial pasts, such classifications got passed on from one generation to the next, and they continue to circulate in subjects' unconsciouses. Fascists used such classifications during the National Socialist era, and the far right continues to use them today in their propaganda techniques.

In the context of precarity capitalism, white men (and women) from all classes are threatened with objective conditions of suffering (such as the threat of declassing and the impossibility to "up-class"), which heightens their castration anxieties and desires around their nonwhole subjectivities. Far-right propaganda techniques exploit these anxieties to win their support. The same techniques that allow them to feel better about themselves on a subjective level (although nothing has objectively changed) also permit colonial-era classifications to resurface in their consciousnesses, which the far right redirects toward its targets of hatred.[27]

Exploitation and Subjectivity

It is the objective conditions of suffering, in particular exploitation, as one cause of our subjective forms of suffering in precarity capitalism, that engender castration anxieties on the bodily level, not the scapegoat causes that the far right comes up with (immigrants, foreigners, and refugees). Adorno in *Aspekte des neuen Rechtsradikalismus* points at another precondition for the emergence of new right extremist forces in Germany in the 1960s: "Despite full employment and despite all the prosperity symptoms, the specter of technological unemployment is going around to such an extent that in the age of automation . . . also those people who are in the production process must feel themselves already as potentially superfluous . . . as potentially unemployed."[28]

In today's capitalist societies, full employment and prosperity are scarcer than they were during the postwar economic boom, which Adorno is referring to. Precarity capitalism has generated precarious work conditions for all sectors of society. Furthermore, we are now fully living in the age of automation, which heightens castration anxieties (expressed in the fear of being already potentially superfluous) even in subjects that still have jobs.

As society elevates technological advance and automation, there is a concomitant increase in exploitation. Marx in the first volume of *Das Kapital* shows us how the age of automation engenders exploitation, which he explains to us with the metaphor of the "vampire Capital": "Capital has only one life-drive, the drive to exploit itself, to create surplus value, with . . . the means of production, to suck the greatest amount of surplus work in. Capital is dead work that only enlivens itself through the vampire-like sucking in of living work and that lives the more it sucks in from it."[29]

Through sucking in unpaid surplus work, which is the time the worker works beyond the necessary time they need to sustain themself yet for which they are not paid wages, the vampire Capital generates surplus value, which facilitates the accumulation of capital. For example, in today's capitalist societies, the automated cell phone (really, a pocket computer) has made us 24/7 on-call workers without pay, instead of "freeing" us (as the ads claim). This surplus work time, for which we are not paid wages, generates surplus value. Unpaid surplus work is invisible. The "boss" does not acknowledge that you are doing work after hours and not getting paid.

To satisfy its life-drive to create surplus value, capital aims to suck in the greatest amount of bodily and mental energies from the workers possible in a twenty-four-hour day; this encapsulates bodily (and mental) castration. So, while capital, through the eating up of workers' bodily and mental energies, becomes a more potent force, the workers' bodies and minds become ruined, or nonwhole. Capital eats "holes" into the minds and bodies of w/hole subjects to enliven itself. Exploitation (an objective form of suffering in capitalism) implies the threat of castration.

It generates subjective forms of suffering—heightened castration anxieties on the bodily level.

However, the vampire Capital encounters physical and moral barriers to its bloodsucking enterprise. Marx explains the physical barriers to exploitation thus: During a twenty-four-hour day, the worker can only "expend a certain amount of life-energy. A horse can only work day in, day out, for 8 hours. During a part of the day it must conserve its force [Kraft], sleep, and satisfy other needs, eat, clean up, and put on clothes."[30]

Besides these physical barriers, the vampire Capital also encounters moral barriers to exploiting the workhorse: "The worker needs time for the satisfaction of mental and social needs."[31] However, since "both barriers are of elastic nature," the vampire Capital can issue its own interpretation of them. It aims to circumvent these barriers through two means: the extension of work hours and the intensification of work through improved machinery.

Thus, the vampire Capital extends the limits of the natural workday into the night through the introduction of shift work. But the lengthening of the workday "does not fully satisfy the thirst of the vampire for living work blood."[32] To further quench its thirst, capital introduces improved machinery (Adorno's specter of technological unemployment). In this way, capital gains sustenance even while seeming to improve the workers' conditions.

However, Marx clarifies that the introduction of improved machinery is not in the service of reducing the worker's hardships. Instead, it serves as "a medium of greater sucking out [Aussaugung] of labor power."[33] In other words, technological "progress" serves only one aim: to do away with the physical and moral barriers to exploitation as a means to accumulate ever more capital. Throughout Das Kapital, Marx outlines the castrating consequences of such a bloodsucking enterprise on workers' bodies (and minds), such as chronic illness and premature death.

Louis Althusser in his "Preface to Capital" applies Marx's elaboration of exploitation through the lengthening of the working day ("relative surplus value") and the introduction of new technology ("absolute surplus value") to modern-day capitalist societies. The top form of exploitation in modern capitalist societies, absolute surplus value, is a more subtle and less visible form of exploitation than relative surplus value. Beyond Marx, Althusser points out that workers on all levels of the work hierarchy experience exploitation through the lengthening of the working day, either despite existing legislation (the forty-hour week, which is never enforced) or via existing legislation (mandated overtime bonuses). Furthermore, overtime pay is never provided to please workers but rather to run the machines continually—to be able to suck the living work blood twenty-four hours a day.

The introduction of new technology heightens productivity, as the worker can produce the same amount in a shorter time. However, it also leads to the

> aggravation of the exploitation of labour power (speed-up, the elimination of blue- and white-collar jobs) not only for proletarians but also for non-proletarian wage-labourers, including certain technicians and executives, even in the higher grades, who can no longer "keep up" with technical progress and therefore have no more market value, hence the subsequent unemployment.[34]

Althusser here is coming quite close to the idea that introducing new technology implies economic castration through the threat of technological unemployment. Althusser (like Marx) also foregrounds the fact that technological progress leads to heightened exploitation during the production process, which implies the threat of the worker's castration on the bodily level. Thus, all levels of the work hierarchy (albeit to varying degrees) face the threat of castration on the bodily level.

Again, objective forms of suffering in capitalism, here exploitation through the lengthening of the workday and technological progress, engender subjective forms of suffering (the threat or actual economic and bodily castration). In terms of the first and more obvious form of exploitation, workers on all levels (albeit to varying degrees) in today's capitalist societies (both in the United States and Europe) experience the fangs of the vampire Capital through the lengthening of the working day and working week. They are expected to work overtime, remain in their workplace until late, and continue their work at home in the evenings and on weekends, often without pay. In addition, before getting a paid position in a bourgeois job, one must often spend years in unpaid training or internships, with long working days and long working weeks with low or no compensation, to prove oneself "worthy" of full employment.

Relative surplus value (the lengthening of the workday and workweek) leads to a disregard of physical barriers to exploitation, including rest, sleep, and the time to satisfy other essential needs, such as taking in nourishment.[35] Thus, the lack of rest and sleep and the lack of time to satisfy one's essential needs generate subjective forms of suffering experienced by the exploited as overwork and exhaustion. It is overwork and exhaustion, caused by exploitation, that are the causes of the problems of the workers, not immigrants or the other scapegoats that the right uses to explain the suffering of workers.

The work of Paul Apostolidis helps detail further how capital enlivens itself through exploitation in today's precarity capitalism. He points out that precarity capitalism "exceptionalizes and generalizes, such that even as precarity singles out specific groups for especially harsh treatment, it also spreads throughout the working world."[36] His empirical work on Latina migrant day laborers in the United States exposes how precarity capitalism singles out this group of workers and other vulnerable migrant workers for particularly harsh treatment, which leads to their feelings of desperation—including desperation to find work and to survive daily. Their desperation also stems from occupying the position of "illegality" in the United States, which renders the "migrant subject as perpetually deportable, hyperexploitable, and available for the most hazardous jobs."[37] However, while precarity capitalism exceptionalizes certain groups, similar dynamics of precarity extends across society as a whole.[38]

Far-right propaganda techniques prey on these subjective forms of suffering generated by relative surplus value. It is easier to win over subjects to one's irrational aims if they are exhausted, desperate, and half-asleep from overwork. Also, a half-asleep state makes it easier for such techniques to induce in the potential followers a hypnotic state, which, as I will show in the next chapter, is essential for manipulating them.

Relative surplus-value leads also to the disregard of the moral barriers to exploitation and the workers' inability or reduced ability to satisfy their mental and social needs.[39] Such disregard leads to subjective forms of suffering for all workers on two levels. First, they cannot satisfy their mental needs (which are different from sleep and rest), which adds to their exhausted state. Second, the reduced ability to satisfy their social needs makes them feel isolated and disconnected.[40]

While the first level refers to the threat of bodily castration, the second level refers to interpersonal castration. I consider the inability to satisfy one's mental needs as a threat of castration on the bodily (or physical level), since mental needs have to do with the body: thinking is a form of bodily activity. Workers on all levels of the work hierarchy who cannot satisfy their need for intellectual stimulation and feel disconnected are a more accessible target audience for far-right propaganda than workers who think critically and foster connections with other workers.[41]

Further, exploitation through absolute surplus value (the introduction of new technology) also contributes to the disregard of physical and moral barriers to exploitation, which leads to subjective forms of suffering, which far-right forces utilize in their propaganda techniques. An example is an introduction and further investment in robots by Amazon, which employs hundreds of thousands of workers in its massive warehouse networks.

Amazon did not introduce robots to ease the plight of the workers. Instead, the introduction of robots led to the aggravation of the workers' exploitation. The workers are now required to speed up their tasks even more than before.[42] Furthermore, robots allowed Amazon to disregard the physical barriers to exploitation—quite simply, the robots are not flesh and blood—which also heightened the threat of bodily castration for their human coworkers; one effect of this is in the fact that the number of work-related injuries of warehouse workers has risen.[43] Robots are, then, nothing else, as Marx would say, but "a medium of greater sucking out [*Aussaugung*] of labor power"—an *Aussaugung* that heightens the worker's castration anxieties on the bodily level.[44] Furthermore, insofar as workers now work with robots, their ability to satisfy their social needs through interacting with other people in the workplace is reduced, increasing their isolation and the threat of castration on the interpersonal level.

Insofar as the employment of robots could one day lead to the complete elimination of warehouse worker jobs, the specter of technological unemployment and the threat of economic castration has materialized. Since being a "whole" subject in capitalism implies being employed, exploitation in the sense of absolute surplus value (the introduction of new technology) heightens subjects' anxieties about being nonwhole.

The objective conditions of suffering (the introduction of new technology and the lengthening of the workday and workweek) heighten castration anxieties around nonwhole subjectivities and accentuate the desire to become "whole." These subjective forms of suffering set the stage for the successes of the far right today because far-right ideologies promise their followers that—again, even though leaving the castrating conditions of capitalism intact—they will become "whole" subjects again.

The Alienated Subject

Alienation is another central aspect of suffering in capitalism, contributing to the rise of the far right today. Marx characterizes nonalienated labor as productive work that allows workers to develop their bodily and mental powers and energies. However, in its quest to make more profit, the vampire Capital depletes workers on all levels of the work hierarchy (albeit to varying degrees) of such energies.[45]

Marx outlines four forms of alienation. The first form is alienation from the product of one's work. Here, "the life which [s/]he (the worker) has conferred on the object confronts [her/]him as something hostile and alien."[46] The outcome of alienated labor is the creation of capital (the object) itself. The vampire Capital enlivens itself (i.e., produces more capital) by sucking out the greatest amount of the worker's surplus work. Then, once it has done so, it turns into something hostile and alien—a castrating force that confronts the worker.

Such confrontation heightens the workers' castration anxieties around their nonwhole subjectivities at all levels of the work hierarchy (in a class, gender, and race-specific way). Again, far-right forces exploit such anxieties for their own economic and political interests. For example, by constructing the image of foreigners as a castrating force that threatens to castrate whites (by doing better than them economically), they individualize and cover the real threat of declassing and alienation engendered by the vampire Capital.

The second form of alienation is alienation in the act of production. It means that "labour is external to the worker; i.e., it does not belong to [her/]his essential being; that in [her/]his work, therefore [s/]he . . . does not feel content but unhappy; does not develop freely [her/]his physical and mental energy but mortifies [her/]his body and ruins [her/]his mind." As a result, the worker feels "at home" only when they do not work, and whenever they leave their work, "labor is shunned like the plague."[47]

Today workers on all levels of the work hierarchy find themselves in jobs where they do not freely develop their physical and mental energies. Instead, their jobs mortify their bodies and ruin their minds. For example, most "white-collar" workers mortify their bodies by sitting in front of the computer in a tiny cubicle for long workday stretches. They also often ruin their minds through the performance of numbing, banal tasks. It does not take too much imagination to realize why such workers feel alienated and shun their work whenever they are away from it.

Far-right propaganda techniques utilize the subjective forms of suffering (feelings of unhappiness and being "not at home" at work) generated by alienation in the act of production. For example, as I will further discuss in chapter 7, the identitarian movement in Europe aims to recruit followers by offering subjects "meaningful work" for their movement, in which alienated young men (and some women) can feel "at home" and overcome their alienation in the act of production.

Alienation from the product of work and in the act of production leads to the alienation of the worker from their "species-being," which is the third form of alienation Marx outlines.[48] The term "species-being" refers to the idea of "conscious life activity," which is a work activity that allows the worker to produce freely and beyond a mere means of existence and survival. However, in capitalist production such conscious life activity is denied to most workers at all levels of the work hierarchy.

In today's precarity capitalism, most people do not have jobs that allow them to produce freely and beyond a mere means of existence. Instead, they perform meaningless and often exploitative work to pay their bills. Insofar as engaging in conscious life activity contributes to peoples' feelings of "wholeness" on a subjective level, alienation from one's species-being also heightens castration anxieties around their nonwhole subjectivities. Far-right forces exploit such anxieties by making it seem that joining them will allow the followers to engage in a conscious life activity; in reality, their tactics aim to make their followers' unconscious attitudes predominate to better manipulate them.

All three forms of alienation, alienation from the product of work, alienation in the act of production, and alienation from one's species-being, lead us to the final form of alienation that plagues capitalist societies— "estrangement of [wo/]man from [wo/]man."[49] This form of alienation underlines that we are all fundamentally isolated from one another. Our fundamental alienation from other subjects in capitalist societies refers to the threat of interpersonal castration in today's capitalist societies.

In "Die revidierte Psychoanalyse," Adorno connects people's fundamental alienation from one another to Freud's theory of narcissism.[50] He points out that in capitalism, relationships between humans are the result of economic conditions that "sich über ihre Köpfe durchsetzen" (prevail above their heads). Here Adorno implicitly refers to the vampire Capital (Marx's first form of alienation), to which people of all classes (albeit in different ways) are subjected and that they cannot control.

Adorno also points out that Freud clearly understood how we are atomized and divided from one another by an unbridgeable gap, which connects to Marx's notion of our fundamental alienation from one another.[51] Because of the almost insurmountable difficulties encountered in establishing spontaneous and direct relationships, we must direct our libidinal energy toward ourselves, pointing at the sociological origins of narcissism.[52]

As I will show in the coming chapters, far-right propaganda techniques prey upon the followers' narcissistic libidinal energy and their inability to fulfill their narcissism (by living up to economic, interpersonal, and bodily "success" standards) by redirecting such energy toward the leader or the movement, which establishes the libidinal bond between the leader (or the movement) and the followers, which the far right then exploits for its purposes.

In *Guilt and Defense*, Adorno further theorizes how our alienation from one another (Marx's fourth form of alienation) creates a coldness in capitalist societies, which fascists utilize in their propaganda tactics. As he puts it, the

> organizational tightening of the weave in the societal net that encompassed everything, also afforded protection from the universal fear of falling through the mesh and disappearing. For countless people, it seems that the coldness of social alienation had been done away with thanks to the warmth of togetherness, no matter how manipulated and contrived.[53]

National Socialists caught people in a "societal net" and tightened that net around them, so that they could counter the fear that they might disappear and "not matter." As an example, once the Austrian Adolf Eichmann, who was responsible for administering the murder of millions of people in Auschwitz during the Nazi regime, escaped to Argentina after Hitler lost the war, he became afraid of "falling through the mesh" and disappearing. He gave himself up voluntarily so that at least he would be a "famous criminal" tried in Jerusalem rather than disappearing in anonymous exile.

Today's far-right movements promise their followers a manipulated and contrived "warmth of togetherness" to cope with the coldness of social alienation. For example, the identitarian movement's propaganda tools, which I discuss in chapter 7, offer young alienated men (and women) something akin to a *Wohngemeinschaft* (living community), in which the followers can counter their alienation and feel themselves as "whole subjects" and experience a warmth of togetherness, however contrived.

Here a vicious cycle can be perpetuated: If people are being satisfied with such illusory "togetherness," they will continue to support the far right because it offers them illusions of wholeness, which assuage their subjective forms of suffering without changing the objective conditions that created the suffering in the first place.

In *The Authoritarian Personality*, Adorno outlines the concept of "intellectual alienation," which makes people susceptible to fascist propaganda techniques. He points out that the core thesis of that study is that "the objectification of social processes, their obedience to intrinsic supra-individual laws, seems to result in an intellectual alienation of the individual from society. This alienation is experienced by the individual as disorientation, with concomitant fear and uncertainty."[54] Here, Adorno's "objectification of social processes, their obedience to intrinsic supra-individual laws" again refers to Marx's notion of alienation from the product of work. The vampire Capital, once it is alive through having sucked out the blood of the workers, develops its own supraindividual laws, to which the worker (and the capitalist) is subjected to and which they cannot control, creating their intellectual alienation from society.

Adorno points out how fascist propaganda uses stereotypes, such as the highly stereotyped and irrational imagery of the Jew, to help followers deal with their alienation (and so turn them into followers). As Adorno puts it, the Jew's "alienness seems to provide the handiest formula for dealing with the alienation of society. Charging the Jews with all the existing evils allows the followers to penetrate the darkness of reality like a searchlight and allow for quick and all-comprising orientation."[55]

Fascist propaganda uses stereotyped and irrational images about Jews, which make Jews responsible for the exploitation and alienation workers (and capitalists) experience in capitalism. Such stereotypes provide the followers with quick and all-comprising orientation in a world where they feel disorientated, anxious, and uncertain. However, this "searchlight" blinds them about the real state of affairs—that it is the vampire Capital and not Jews or other stereotyped groups that makes them suffer.

Today, the far right continues to offer the stereotyped and irrational image of "the Jew," to which it adds other irrational and highly stereotyped images, including the images of "the Moslem," "the migrant," and the "illegal alien" to its followers as beacons in a disorienting society that induces castration anxieties and uncertainty.[56] Stereotyping is also what Adorno calls "identity thinking," a form of thinking in fixed and rigid categories, which eradicates the moment of nonidentity in identity. For example, far-right propaganda constructs racialized Others as both "castrating Others" (they come to destroy us or to take away our jobs) and as "castrated Others" (they are nonwhole). Such techniques make racialized Others responsible for the ills of precarity capitalism.

The Castrating Conditions of the Culture Industry

The "culture industry," a term coined by early Frankfurt School critical theorists, helps explain an element in capitalism that centrally contributes to "castrate" people's bodies and minds beyond the production process, which makes them susceptible to fascist propaganda techniques.

In "Culture Industry Reconsidered," Adorno replaced the concept of "mass culture," which he used in earlier works, with the concept of the "culture industry," to make clear that such culture does not arise spontaneously from the masses themselves. Instead, the culture industry, which is dominant in capitalist societies, erases any spontaneity in the masses— for the sake of profit, it produces cultural goods according to plan, and people subject themselves to it.[57]

In the mid-twentieth century, the culture industry referred to Hollywood films, television shows, radio broadcasts, and print periodicals. Today, it predominantly refers to the internet and social media. Capitalism's expansion of consumerism went hand in hand with the expansion of mass media and its technologies, enabling the culture industry to influence every aspect of our lives. In addition, many people spend most of their days on the internet for work and to meet their social needs (heightened during the COVID-19 pandemic).

As a result, the culture industry has an even stronger and more intrusive presence in our lives than Adorno could have ever imagined.[58] Moreover, the more substantial exposure to today's culture industry on the internet accentuates the culture industry's castrating capacities. In the *Dialektik der Aufklärung*, Adorno and Horkheimer further elaborate on how the culture industry produces subjects easily deceived by fascist propaganda. They point out that "the threat of castration" is the essence of the culture industry, which functions as a tool to keep subjects of late capitalist society in line. The culture industry produces castrated subjects who become easily susceptible to fascist propaganda because it massacres and dismembers thought, leading to the *Verkümmerung* (atrophy) of the imagination and spontaneity and the *Verstummung* (silencing) of language.[59]

Insofar as an intact imagination and the ability to think coherently and speak effectively are central to resist the culture industry and the psychologically oriented propaganda tools fascists use to acquire followers, the culture industry produces subjects that are susceptible to fascist propaganda. The culture industry entices them to believe that consuming its products will satisfy their unmet needs. However, it deceives them: consuming its products generates nothing but a profit for capitalists and a pseudosatisfaction of the customer's mental and social needs.

Furthermore, the culture industry serves as a "medicinal bath" to adjust consumers to the castrating conditions of capitalism. Adorno provides an example: He analyzes a TV comedy where a young, underpaid schoolteacher has no money to pay for her meals and is starving. The "funny" situations of the comedy consist of her trying to hustle food from various acquaintances, regularly without success. The humor lies in the humiliation of the schoolteacher. For Adorno, "the script is a shrewd method of promoting adjustment to humiliating conditions by presenting them as objectively comical and by giving a picture of a person who experiences even her own inadequate position as an object of fun apparently free of resentment."[60] Laughing about the schoolteacher's desperate attempts to hustle food from her colleagues allows us to put a castrating capitalist system that pays schoolteachers a starving wage out of mind.

The script tells us that even if we experience humiliating conditions of capitalism in our daily lives, such experiences are not genuinely objectionable as long as we can laugh about them. Since humiliation is not truly objectionable and everybody experiences the same humiliation, we do not need to change capitalism. Furthermore, the comedy offers us the chance to feel as "whole" or noncastrated subjects through the promise of pleasure generated by the laughter.

However, the culture industry offers us nothing but a pseudopleasure. It aims to diffuse any insight into the castrating conditions of capitalism and the subjective forms of suffering they create. As a result, we give up the thought—if we are even capable of formulating it in the first place— that it is desirable or even possible to resist or radically challenge the system that is castrating us on the economic, bodily, and interpersonal levels.

Today the culture industry has more opportunities to mutilate our critical thinking, atrophy our imagination, and silence our critical voice so that we cannot imagine anything beyond what the culture industry demands us to want and buy. However, most importantly, it stifles us from imagining another system beyond capitalism, one in which everybody can freely develop their bodies and minds.

Furthermore, the salience of the culture industry of the internet heightens the opportunities of the far right, which is internet savvy, to catch new followers, particularly on social media. It is no coincidence that they aim to capture people's minds (and bodies) precisely with the technology (the internet) that contributes to stifle critical thought.

In capitalism there are objective conditions that make people suffer (so it's not just the far right claiming, falsely, that you suffer and need a remedy). However, the far right then points to a *made-up cause* for the suffering (such as women, minorities, and immigrants) and provides a solution. But while capitalism provides the objective conditions of people's suffering, it's the far right that *conceals* the actual causes, distracts with other made-up causes, and then provides the solution to the made-up causes.

Löwenthal's and Guterman's concept of "malaise" helps explain further how the far right, like the culture industry, conceals the actual causes of suffering in precarity capitalism. Feelings of malaise (which they theorize as feelings of distrust, dependence, exclusion, anxiety, and disillusionment) are the result of the socioeconomic conditions in capitalism, which "reflect the permanent insecurity of modern life."[61]

The agitator distorts the objective condition of his audiences' suffering in capitalism to trick the audience into accepting the very situation that produced their malaise. The agitator tricks his audience by not providing any understanding of the roots of their malaise and avoiding talking about the objective conditions that generated the audience's malaise (or suffering). Instead, the agitator "grovels in it, he relishes it, he distorts and deepens the malaise to the point where it becomes almost a paranoiac relationship to the external world."[62]

Once the malaise is turned into a paranoid relationship to the external world, the agitator can channel malaise into a stream of hate, which "paves the way for the relief of the malaise through discharge of the audience's aggressive impulses; but simultaneously he perpetuates the malaise by blocking the way toward real understanding of its cause."[63]

To better understand how the far right can channel the followers' aggression into a stream of hate and how they redirect the follower's libidinal energy toward the leader or the movement, in the next chapter I will work through core psychoanalytic concepts introduced by Freud. Understanding core psychoanalytic concepts will allow us to understand how propaganda techniques can make subjects believe that they can relieve their malaise if they become followers. However, the economic conditions that generated their malaise and their suffering remain intact or actually worsen because of the destructive policies of the far right.

CHAPTER II

Psychoanalytic Concepts

What is conscious could never prove so fateful as what remains unconscious, half-conscious, or pre-conscious.

—THEODOR W. ADORNO, *GUILT AND DEFENSE*

I n this chapter, I outline the core psychoanalytic concepts I will use to set up a theoretical framework that can identify and describe the functioning of the psychologically oriented propaganda techniques that the contemporary far right uses to catch new followers. The concepts include libidinal and aggressive drives; the ego, superego, and id; the ego ideal and ego ideal replacement; and narcissistic love.

Freud's *Group Psychology and the Analysis of the Ego* foregrounds how *libidinal* drives establish the ties between the leader and their followers and maintain the cohesion of what he termed the "psychological mass (in short: the mass)."[1] Early Frankfurt School thinkers, including Adorno and Margarete and Alexander Mitscherlich, draw on this text to explain the rise of fascist masses in Europe and protofascist elements in the United States. They follow Freud in that they mainly foreground the centrality of libidinal drives in how fascist masses form.

In this chapter, I go beyond Freud and early Frankfurt School Critical Theory to explain that libidinal *and* aggressive drives are both implicated in the cohesion of far-right masses today.[2] While Freud at certain points in *Group Psychology and the Analysis of the Ego* hinted at the importance of the aggressive drive in integrating the mass, he did not outline this in more detail. In this chapter, I discuss Freud's *Civilization and Its Discontents*, in which the aggressive drive is more central, in connection with *Group*

Psychology and the Analysis of the Ego to foreground the centrality of the aggressive drive in the formation of fascist masses.

I also draw on Freud's *New Introductory Lectures on Psycho-Analysis*, a later text, in which we find Freud's final view on certain core concepts, which he developed throughout his life, including the aggressive drive; the superego and its relationship to the ego ideal; and the relationship between the ego, superego, and id. I furthermore draw on "On Narcissism: An Introduction" to further explain the centrality of narcissism in psychological masses. Finally, I draw on *Totem and Taboo* to describe the processes of regression that occur in a mass.

The chapter comprises six sections, excluding the introduction and conclusion. "The Struggle Between Eros and Death" explains the concepts of libidinal and aggressive drives and the functions of the ego and the superego. "The Unconscious" outlines the meaning of the unconscious. "Libido and Aggression in the Masses" outlines how libidinal and aggressive drives hold the masses together. "Ego Ideal Replacement and Narcissism" explains the concept of the ego ideal and its connection to narcissism. "Narcissistic Mass Love" explains processes of ego ideal replacement through the concept of narcissistic love; "Hypnotic Regression" outlines the centrality of regressions in a mass.

The Struggle Between Eros and Death

Freud distinguishes two primary drives: the love drives (Eros) and the death drives (Death). "Libido" refers to the manifestation of the power of Eros, that is, the energy of love drives, with sexual love as its nucleus and sexual union as its aim.[3] However, Freud conceptualizes "love" in a broader sense, which includes not only sexual love for others but also self-love, friendship, and the "devotion to concrete objects and to abstract ideas."[4]

The aggressive drive is the derivative and the main representative of the death drive. It manifests itself in a primary mutual hostility between and among people, which Freud terms "the hostility of each against all and of all against each."[5] The death drive opposes civilization and threatens it perpetually with disintegration. The meaning of civilization is the struggle between Eros and Death, between the drives of life and death. The most critical task of civilization is, for Freud, to set limits to the aggressive drive.[6]

In 1929 Freud ended *Civilization and Its Discontents* with the assertion that Eros "will make an effort to assert [her/]himself in the struggle with his equally immortal adversary." However, in 1931, when the menace of Hitler became all too apparent, Freud was less sure that Eros will succeed in asserting itself against the aggressive drive and added the following sentence: "But who can see with what success and with what result?"[7] The millions of victims of the National Socialist regime warranted Freud's hesitation about the success of Eros's struggle against the aggressive drive. Ninety years after the menace of the National Socialist regime, with the global rise of the far right, whether Eros can successfully assert itself in its struggle with the aggressive drive has again become a pressing question. And it has again become necessary to take a closer look at the methods civilization uses to assert itself in its struggle with the aggressive drive.[8]

The "program of civilization" is a process in the service of Eros, whose purpose is to combine single individuals, and after that families, peoples, and nations, "into one great unity, the unity of 'mankind,'" to curb our desire for "cruel aggressiveness."[9] Civilization curbs that desire by creating *aim-inhibited* libidinal ties between us. It inhibits the aim of libido (sexual union) and instead fosters affectionate ties between people.

However, it is difficult for us to give up our desire for cruel aggressiveness because the satisfaction of the aggressive drive "is accompanied by an extraordinarily high degree of *narcissistic enjoyment*, owing to its presenting the ego with the fulfillment of the latter's old wishes for omnipotence."[10] Therefore, our aggressive drive opposes the program of civilization.[11]

Furthermore, although love drives have been diverted from their sexual origins in aim-inhibited love, they do not operate with any less energy. Also, the sexual drives "remain more or less strongly preserved in the unconscious, so that in a certain sense the whole of the original current continues to exist." So, insofar as we preserve the sexual drives in the unconscious, they can always be "put into activity by means of *regression*."[12]

Civilization binds people together through aim-inhibited libidinal ties, for which it employs large amounts of psychical energy, which it draws from people's sexuality. Here Freud points out that "civilization behaves towards sexuality as a people or a stratum of its population does which has subjected another one to its exploitation. Fear of a revolt by the suppressed elements drives it to stricter precautionary measures."[13] Civilization aims to hinder sexuality's revolt against its repression by restricting its expression toward only the opposite sex. It further limits heterosexual love to monogamy and legal, religious, and cultural legitimacy. However, since the satisfaction of our sexual drives is a potent source of happiness, civilization's "precautionary measures" result in our "cultural frustration."[14]

One way to counter this cultural frustration is to tame our libidinal drives through processes of sublimation. For example, when people engage in intellectual work, they can redirect their libidinal drives toward expressions of thought and creativity, providing them with some pleasure and happiness. However, Freud makes clear that a tamed drive has much less intensity than an untamed one: "The feeling of happiness derived from the satisfaction of a wild instinctual impulse untamed by the ego is incomparably more intense than that derived from sating a drive that has been tamed."[15]

In brief, civilization establishes libidinal ties between people to counter their desire for cruel aggressiveness. However, cultural frustration dominates because it can only accomplish such a task by suppressing people's sexuality. The suppression of people's sexuality is the cause of new forms of hostility between people, against which all civilizations have to struggle.[16]

Another method civilization employs to buttress Eros's struggle with the aggressive drive is to establish a superego within our psyches. The superego allows us to master our aggressive drive by weakening and disarming it.[17] Although Freud does not further detail the superego's role concerning the repressed sexual drives in *Civilization and Its Discontents*, in Freud's *Jokes and Their Relation to the Unconscious* it is implicit that the superego is also central to monitoring our sexual urges repressed in the unconscious.

The superego is the part of the ego that observes, monitors, and criticizes the ego. In the *New Introductory Lectures*, Freud points out that the ego is both a subject and an object: "[It] is in its very essence a subject." However, the ego can also take itself as an object and treat itself like other objects by observing and criticizing itself. In Freud's words, "In this, one part of the ego is setting itself over against the rest. So, the ego can be split; it splits itself during several functions—temporarily at least. Its parts can come together again afterward."[18] The superego is the part of the ego that sets itself over against the rest. It is the instance in which civilization aims to master what Freud calls our "dangerous desire for aggressiveness." The superego aims to weaken and disarm our aggressive drive by constantly watching it, "like a garrison in a conquered city." Furthermore, the superego takes over our desire for aggressiveness and directs it back to where it came from—the ego.[19]

The superego, which acts as our conscience, "is ready to put into action against the ego the same harsh aggressiveness that the ego would have liked to satisfy upon other, extraneous individuals." The superego takes over every piece of aggressiveness we give up and directs it toward the ego. This is why we fear the superego.[20]

However, the superego does not bind *all* of our desire for aggressiveness and turn it against the ego. Instead, a part of the aggressive drive is "carrying on its mute and uncanny activity as a free destructive drive in the ego and the id."[21] Here it becomes evident that the sexual and aggressive drives remain active forces in the unconscious (and the ego) and that the superego is necessary to monitor both.

The ego's task is to satisfy the divergent and often incompatible demands of its "three tyrannical masters"—the superego, the unconscious (the id), and the external world. The ego aims to represent the demands and standards of the external world to the id while also carrying out the id's intentions. At the same time, the strict superego observes the ego at every step it takes and lays down definite standards for its conduct.[22]

Freud points out that the harsh superego does not take into any account the ego's perpetual dilemma—that it has to satisfy the often incompatible demands of both the unconscious and the external world. If the ego does not fulfill the standards laid down by the superego, the superego punishes the ego "with tense feelings of inferiority and of guilt."[23] Here we can see how the superego interconnects with the ego ideal (in that the ego ideal is composed of standards set by the outside world, and the superego monitors whether we fulfill such standards), which I will further detail in the fourth section of this chapter. Furthermore, insofar as feelings of nonwholeness relate to failing to meet standards of "success" in a capitalist society, we can see how not living up to the strict demands of the superego is connected to the psychological senses of inadequacy, what I have been calling "nonwholeness" and "castration," that far-right propaganda techniques prey on.

Even if we give up our desire for cruel aggressiveness, we cannot conceal from the superego that unconsciously we continue to desire to express our hostility should the occasion allow it. Here a tension between the ego and the superego, what Freud calls "a sense of guilt," arises in us. We experience this sense of guilt as permanent internal unhappiness, an *Unbehagen* (discomfort), which remains unconscious mainly. This *Unbehagen* refers to the book's original title in German, *Das Unbehagen in der Kultur* (Discomfort in culture). For Freud, the price of civilization is "a loss of happiness through the heightening of the sense of guilt."[24]

Akin to the superego, which civilization sets up in each subject to curb our desire for cruel aggressiveness to allow Eros to assert itself in its struggle with Death, civilization also sets up a "cultural superego" in the larger cultural community. Although Freud distinguishes between the individual and cultural superego, they are interconnected because the culture's commands are expressed in our individual superegos. The cultural superego is composed of strict ethical demands, and "disobedience is visited with 'fear of conscience.'"[25]

At the core of the cultural superego we find the ethical command of "Thou shalt love thy neighbor as thyself," which is, according to Freud, older than Christianity. The problem with this command is that the neighbor inspires my hostility more than my love. For Freud, humans "are not gentle creatures who want to be loved . . . they are, on the contrary, creatures among whose instinctual endowments is to be reckoned a powerful share of aggressiveness."[26]

The subject's desire for cruel aggressiveness creates a scenario where instead of loving their neighbor, "their neighbor tempts them to satisfy their aggressiveness on him[/her], to exploit his[/her] capacity for work without compensation, to use him[/her] sexually without consent, to seize his[/her] possessions, to humiliate him[/her], to cause him[/her] pain, to torture and to kill him[/her]. And thus, *Homo homini lupus* (Man is wolf to man)."[27]

The problem with the cultural superego is that when it issues the commands such as "Love thy neighbor as thyself"—akin to the standards issued by the individual superego—it does not trouble itself with the question whether humans can obey them. Freud suggests that it is difficult, if not impossible, for us to obey this command because it runs counter to our primary aggressive drive, and we cannot control our unconscious.[28]

The ego faces resistances against obeying the (cultural) superego's commands, first and foremost the instinctual strength of the unconscious, insofar as we find in the unconscious the energy of repressed aggressive (and sexual) impulses that lie in wait to unleash themselves, and second the difficulties presented by the external environment.[29] Furthermore, "in circumstances that are favorable to it [our aggressive drives], when the *mental counter-forces which ordinarily inhibit it are out of action*, it also manifests itself spontaneously and reveals [wo/]man as a savage beast to whom consideration towards [her/]his own kind is something alien."[30]

As I will show in the coming chapters, psychologically oriented propaganda techniques put those counterforces that inhibit our desire for cruel aggressiveness out of action. The far right activates and channels the aggressive drive that waits in the unconscious to unleash itself on extraneous subjects. Such unleashing spares us from our aggressiveness being turned against our egos and provides us with narcissistic enjoyment.

The Unconscious

Because the unconscious is an inaccessible part of us, Freud terms the unconscious also as the id, which refers to the German impersonal *Es*, "it." For Freud, there are two kinds of the unconscious. The first is the latent unconscious, which he terms the "preconscious." The preconscious can be easily and is often transformed into something conscious. The second unconscious takes a lot of effort to change into something conscious, or such transformation is never possible at all. Freud reserves the term "unconscious" for this second kind of the unconscious.[31]

In the course of our mental development, we affect a separation of our mental existence, our psyche, into an ego and an unconscious and repressed portion, which is left outside the ego. However, any notion of a stable ego is deceptive. As Freud asserts, "We know that the stability of this new acquisition is exposed to constant shocks. In dreams and in neuroses, what is thus excluded knocks for admission at the gates, guarded though they are by resistances."[32]

The ego establishes the resistances (the gatekeepers) and allows only portions of the repressed material, often in disguised form, to enter our consciousness (such as in dreams). When we are awake, we make use of special artifices to allow what is repressed to circumvent the ego's resistances so that we can receive it "temporarily into our ego to the increase of our pleasure. Jokes and humor, and to some extent the comic in general, may be regarded in this light."[33]

However, there are no sharp frontiers between the ego, the id, and the superego, and the development of these divisions varies in different subjects. Furthermore, the conscious part of the ego is nothing but a portion of the unconscious modified by its proximity to and influence by the external world. Large portions of the ego (and all of the superego and id) are unconscious and remain so.[34]

We do not know when unconscious processes are activated; we can only infer these processes from their effects. Freud aims to make the unconscious understandable to us with the assistance of analogies: "We call it a chaos, a cauldron full of seething excitations . . . it has no organization, produces no collective will, but only striving to bring about the satisfaction of the instinctual needs subject to the observance of the pleasure principle." While the ego stands for reason and good sense, the id stands for untamed passions. In the id, there are no logical laws of thought. As Freud puts it, "the logical laws of thought do not apply in the id"; contrary impulses can exist side by side without canceling each other out.[35]

The unconscious follows the "pleasure principle" and strives to bring about an immediate satisfaction of our instinctual impulses (our sexual and aggressive drives), which generate pleasure in us. There is no morality in fulfilling the "pleasure principle": the id neither knows good nor evil. Also, the id has no notion of the passage of time: "Wishful impulses which have never passed beyond the id, but impressions, too, which have been sunk into the id by repression, are virtually immortal; after the passage of decades they behave as though they had just occurred."[36]

In the ego, we also find the origin of the idea of time, a synthesis of contents, and a combination and unification of mental processes not existent in the id.[37] The ego dethrones the pleasure principle in the id and replaces it with the "reality principle." The ego is the component of personality that deals with the demands of reality. It makes sure that the id's desires are met in appropriate ways. For example, rather than taking your desire of aggressiveness out by hitting somebody who has upset you in some minor way, it will force you to step back and redirect your anger in a way that does not hurt the other person.

The ego aims to represent the demands of the external world to the id, while also carrying out the id's intentions. Freud points out that this is fortunate for the id, "which could not escape destruction if, in its blind efforts for the satisfaction of its drives, it disregarded that supreme external power." It seems that Freud refers here particularly to the aggressive instinctual wishes, whose satisfaction would lead to the id's (and civilization's) destruction. At the same time, the ego is observed at every step it takes by the strict superego, which lays down definite standards for its conduct.[38] But the ego is also weak and derives its energies from the unconscious, so the ego aims to be on good terms with the unconscious and tries to find ways to carry out the id's intentions.

In the *New Introductory Lectures*, written a year before Hitler became chancellor of Germany, we get several glimpses into how the mental geography of the id, ego, and superego are interconnected with the sociopolitical context. Freud uses the following example, where the horse stands for the unconscious and the rider for the ego, to explain the relationship between the two: "The horse supplies the locomotive energy, while the rider has the privilege of deciding on the goal and of guiding the powerful animal's movement. But only too often there arises between the ego and the id the not precisely ideal situation of the rider being obliged to guide the horse along the path by which it itself wants to go."[39]

While the pleasure principle rules the unconscious (the horse), the ego (the rider) is ruled by the reality principle, in that it deals with the demands of reality. The ego guides the horse to make sure that its desires are satisfied in ways that are effective and appropriate to the ego's goals. However, in certain circumstances, a not-so-ideal situation arises, where the pleasure principle dethrones the reality principle and the rider can no longer guide their powerful horse (the unconscious). This is the case in fascism.

Freud also points out that today (both in his age of fascism and ours) we must reorganize the diagram Freud has drawn depicting the structures of the psyche. Although in the figure he includes in the text of the *New Introductory Lectures* the ego takes up more space than the unconscious, "the space occupied by the unconscious id ought to have been *incomparably greater* than that of the ego or the preconscious. I must ask you to correct it in your thoughts."[40] In a scenario where the unconscious can take up an incomparably greater space than the ego, fascists will be able to manipulate their followers better.

Finally, in Freud's depictions of the id and ego, we *also* see the superego, which furthermore "merges into the id" and as a result has an "intimate relationship" with the unconscious.[41] The intimate relationship between the superego and the id, which does not allow the superego to control unconscious impulses anymore, together with the greater space the unconscious occupies, created a not-so-ideal situation where the horse (the unconscious) obliged the riders (the National Socialist followers) to go down the destructive paths of the National Socialist regime. Today, with the global rise of the far right, we are again in a situation where the unconscious occupies more space than the ego. Furthermore, the superego (as the vehicle of the ego ideal) is more and more merged with the unconscious. We again need to attend to how the far right uses unconscious forces to direct their followers down its destructive paths.

Freud in *Group Psychology and the Analysis of the Ego* outlines the centrality of *unconscious* processes in the "psychological mass (in short: the mass)."[42] For Freud, mass psychology is concerned with an individual (which I call a subject), who is "part of a crowd of people who have been organized into a group at some particular time for some definite purpose."[43] Here he characterizes the mass using similar analogies to those he used to describe the unconscious in the *New Introductory Lectures.*

The core question Freud aims to answer in *Group Psychology* is why the subject, once they find themself submerged in a mass, thinks, feels, and acts quite different than when they are on their own. For example, the subject, once submerged in a mass, becomes spontaneous, violent, enthusiastic, and heroic, and the mass "has a sense of omnipotence; the notion of impossibility disappears for the individual in the (mass)."[44] The core reason for this change in the subject is that in a mass "the individual is brought under conditions *which allow him[/her] to throw off the repressions of his[/her] unconscious instinctual impulses.*" A mass is attractive because it brings us under conditions that allow us to throw off the repressions of our sexual and aggressive drives. The supposedly "new" characteristics the subject displays in the mass are nothing but the manifestations of the subject's unconscious.[45]

In a mass, the unconscious predominates, and the mass (akin to how Freud describes the unconscious) is "impulsive, changeable and irritable. It is led almost exclusively by the unconscious."[46] In a mass, the pleasure principle dethrones the reality principle. The critical faculties and reason are pushed to the background or disappear completely, and the wishful unconscious instinctual impulses dominate. Like in the unconscious, the most contradictory arguments can exist side by side in a mass, without any conflict arising from the logical inconsistencies between them. Furthermore, the mass thinks in images, which call one another up by association "and whose agreement with reality is never checked by any reasonable agency."[47] Akin to the unconscious, passions dominate over the rational element in a mass. And the feelings of a mass are always very simple and very exaggerated, so that it knows neither doubt nor uncertainty. It goes directly to extremes, and "if a suspicion is expressed, it is instantly changed into an incontrovertible certainty; a trace of antipathy is turned into furious hatred."[48]

The mass is subject to the magical power of words and formulas, which reason and arguments cannot combat. Anyone (such as those who wish to become mass leaders) who wishes to produce an effect upon the mass does not need to draw upon logic or rational argument. Instead, "he must paint in the most forcible colours, he must exaggerate, and he must repeat the same thing again and again."[49] Also, the masses do not want the truth from those that want to produce an effect upon them. Instead, "they demand illusions, and cannot do without them." Masses constantly give what is unreal precedence over what is real, and they are almost as strongly influenced by what is untrue as by what is true.[50]

To underline the centrality of the unconscious in the mass, Freud also discusses the mass in connection with hypnosis and dreams. "Just as in dreams and in hypnosis the reality of things falls into the background in comparison of the strength of wishful impulses with their affective cathexis."[51] While Freud hints here at the centrality of the dream in masses, he does not go into any more detail; I will expand on this in the next chapter. However, Freud further details the centrality of hypnosis in his discussions of how the libidinal ties between the mass followers and the leader are established, which I will further outline in the sixth section of this chapter.

Libido and Aggression in the Masses

In *Group Psychology*, Freud points out that a mass is held together by the power of Eros, that love relationships constitute the essence of the mass, and that Eros means nothing else but the German word *Liebe* (love).[52] Although Freud foregrounds the centrality of *Liebe* to create lasting bonds between the mass leader and the followers, he does not further elaborate on what happens with the aggressive drive in a mass. Nonetheless, at a certain point, the aggressive drive does enter the text.

Akin to the "program of civilization," which uses aim-inhibited sexual drives to bind people together with affectionate ties into ever-larger units, in the mass aim-inhibited sexual drives create lasting ties between the mass followers and their leader and among the mass followers themselves. Also, the love drives are diverted from their sexual origin in the mass, but they do not operate with less energy or intensity. On the contrary, for Freud, it is "precisely those sexual impulses that are inhibited in their aims which achieve such lasting ties between people."[53]

A group of subjects only emerges as a mass once the libidinal ties between the mass followers and the leader and among the followers have been established. Once submerged in a mass, a subject is bound by intense libidinal ties in two directions: the libidinal tie to the mass leader and the libidinal ties to the other followers. However, Freud points out that the libidinal tie between a follower and the leader is more central than those between and among the mass followers. The former allows the mass followers to unite through *identification*. The unity formed among the mass followers is mediated through a common element that they share with all the other mass followers, which is the libidinal tie with the leader.[54]

Although Freud in *Group Psychology* does not elaborate on the centrality of the aggressive drive in unifying the mass followers, he points out that love need *not* be the central element that unifies the mass followers. Instead, "the leader or the leading idea might also, so to speak, be negative; hatred against a particular person or institution might operate in just the same unifying way, and might call up the same unifying emotional ties as positive attachment."[55]

In *Civilization and Its Discontents*, it becomes clearer how hatred against a particular person or group can unify a mass. Here, Freud states that the mass followers can *only* be bound together in love, so long as there are other people left over to receive the manifestations of the mass member's desire for aggressiveness. As he puts it,

> the advantage which a comparatively small cultural group offers of allowing this drive [the aggressive drive] an outlet in the form of hostility against intruders is not to be despised. It is always possible to bind together a considerable number of people in love, so long as there are other people left over to receive the manifestations of their aggressiveness.[56]

Nothing binds people together in love like a common hatred. The mass leader provides an outlet for the mass followers to satisfy their aggressive drive, which tightens the libidinal ties within the mass. Freud also adds that "in this respect the Jewish people, scattered everywhere, have rendered most useful services to the civilizations of the countries that have been their hosts."[57] The massacre of the Jews in the Middle Ages (and the recent pogroms) shows that the cohesion of their Christian fellows bound together in love was made possible through their ability to unleash their aggressive drives toward those designated as "intruders"—the Jews.

Here it becomes clearer than in the earlier *Group Psychology* that the unleashing of the aggressive drive on people outside the mass is a precondition for the libidinal ties between the mass followers to emerge. Mass followers can only be bound to the leader and to one another by love if they can take out their aggression against those people the mass leader designates as outlets for their aggressive drives. So, if a mass leader provides the followers with targets of hatred and does away with those mental counterforces (the superego) that inhibit the mass followers' desire for cruel aggressiveness, the mass can easily turn into a violent mob.

What happens to the fundamental hostility (and envy) between the mass followers? Here identification with one another allows them temporarily or permanently to counter "their readiness for hatred."[58] Freud explains the vanishing of hostility between the mass followers and the emergence of the *Gemeingeist* (group spirit, or communal or social feeling) with the notion of *primary envy*, which the group members do away with through identification.

In primary envy, the older child envies the younger one and wants to keep them away from the parents and rob them of their privileges. However, since the older child cannot maintain the hostile attitude without damaging themselves, they are forced to give up their hostility and instead identify with the younger child. Here the *Gemeingeist* develops between the siblings, which is further developed in the nursery and at school.[59]

Here Freud also provides the example of a group of women jealous of one another because they are all in love with the same pianist (I would add here that the same phenomenon is possible with a group of men). Since it is impossible for them to reach the aim of their love because of their numbers, they renounce that aim. Instead of fighting with one another, they identify with one another's love for the pianist and act as a united group. Freud states it this way: "Originally rivals, they have succeeded in identifying themselves with one another by means of a similar love for the same object."[60]

Likewise, the mass followers are jealous of one another, because they are all in love with the same object (the mass leader). Since their numbers make it impossible for them to reach the aim of their love and a hostile attitude would be damaging to them in the long run, they are forced to give up their hostility and identify with one another, which happens through their shared love for the leader. Here the "social feeling is based upon the reversal of what was first a hostile feeling into a positively-toned tie in the nature of an identification."[61]

Ego Ideal Replacement and Narcissism

Freud employs the idea of *ego ideal replacement* to describe the processes that establish the libidinal ties between the mass followers and the leader. The ego ideal is differentiated from the ego and serves as the repository of standards of perfection of various sorts. It represents the ideal toward which we aspire. Throughout Freud's works, the evolving concept of the ego ideal is closely connected with the concept of *narcissism.*

When Freud introduces the ego ideal in his paper "On Narcissism: An Introduction," he points out that it opens important avenues for understanding mass psychology. He describes the ego ideal as a substitute for the original lost narcissism of childhood, in which the ego is its own ideal. In this "blissful state of mind," the ego believes itself to be perfect and omnipotent and, as a result, enjoys a high self-regard.[62]

When the ego has to contend with the demands from the environment, which it cannot always meet, it faces the reproaches of others and its own awakening critical judgment. However, the ego is unwilling to give up the original narcissism of childhood and seeks to recover it.[63] Here the ego sets up an ego ideal that differentiates itself from the ego to recover the original narcissism. Once the ego sets up the ego ideal, the ego transfers narcissistic libido (or self-love) onto the ego ideal. Like the infantile ego before, the ego ideal now "finds itself possessed of every perfection that is of value."[64] In other words, in the narcissistic state, the child finds itself to be "whole." Although the ego may not be satisfied with itself, it can now find narcissistic satisfaction through its ego ideal.

In the following chapters, I will detail how our ego ideal in capitalist societies results from specific environmental demands—to meet raced, gendered, and classed standards of "success" on the economic, interpersonal, and bodily levels. Since most people cannot live up to their ego ideal in precarity capitalism, failure to live up to ego ideal standards generates feelings of nonwholeness.

I will also outline how far-right propaganda techniques prey on such feelings. They allow the followers to transfer their (disappointed) narcissistic libido not so much onto the ego ideal (as happens with the original split between the ego ideal and the ego) but onto the idealized leader figure or the "movement." As a result, the followers can "return" to the narcissistic state of "wholeness," where they have the illusion of being "perfect" again.

The evolving concept of the ego ideal is also closely linked with the evolving concept of the superego.[65] The superego is the psychic structure that monitors the ego to keep it in line with the ego ideal. In "On Narcissism," Freud points out that the superego "performs the task of seeing that narcissistic satisfaction from the ego ideal is ensured and which, with this end in view, constantly watches the actual ego and measures it by that ideal."[66] In brief, the superego punishes the ego for not living up to the ego ideal. Similarly, in the *New Introductory Lectures*, Freud designates the superego as "the vehicle of the ego ideal by which the ego measures itself, which it emulates, and whose demand for ever greater perfection it strives to fulfill."[67] The superego constantly watches the ego to ensure it lives up to the ego ideal and demands ever-greater perfection from it.

This demand for ever-greater perfection, which the ego cannot fulfill, leads to repression. As Freud puts it, the ego ideal "heightens the demands of the ego and is the most powerful factor in repression." Therefore, in *sublimation*, the libidinal drives are deflected or redirected from their sexual aim. In contrast, when the ego generates an ego ideal, it can only meet the increased ego ideal demands through *repressing* the libidinal drives.[68] Thus, the difference between sublimation and repression is that in sublimation libido still gets an outlet, so the ego is not entirely frustrated, but in repression, there's no outlet, producing lots of cultural frustration in the ego.

Repression is either carried out by the superego or by the ego in obedience to its orders.[69] Since the ego ideal is bound up with repression and implies for the subject being constantly measured by the ego ideal and criticized for not living up to it, it is no surprise that the "separation of the ego ideal from the ego cannot be borne for long either, and has to be temporarily undone. In all renunciations and limitations imposed upon the ego a periodical infringement of the prohibition is the rule."[70]

When the separation between the ego and the ego ideal becomes undone—that is, when what the ego *is* temporarily overlaps with what the ego ideal dictates the ego *should be*—the subject finds themself relieved from the feelings of low self-regard for not living up to the ego ideal's demands. Freud points out in *Group Psychology* that in festivals, the separation of the ego ideal from the ego is temporarily undone, and festivals' cheerful character signifies a release from ego ideal demands. As he earlier explained in *Totem and Taboo*, "A festival is a permitted, or rather an obligatory, excess, a solemn breach of a prohibition . . . the festive feeling is produced by the liberty to do what as a rule is prohibited."[71]

In a mass, the followers can replace their ego ideal with the leader figure, which creates conditions for the mass followers akin to festivals, allowing the mass followers a more permanent undoing of the separation between the ego and the ego ideal. A mass is composed of "a number of individuals who have put one and the same object in the place of their ego ideal and have consequently identified themselves with one another in their ego."[72] Ego ideal replacement allows the far-right mass followers to circumvent their ego ideal, which leads to a "magnificent festival" for the mass followers. As Freud puts it, insofar as "the ego ideal comprises the sum of all the limitations in which the ego has to acquiesce . . . the abrogation of the ideal would necessarily be a magnificent festival for the ego, which might then once again feel satisfied with itself."[73]

In a (far-right) mass, the libidinal bond between the mass followers and the leader is established through *introjection* and not through identification. Introjection (*Verinnerlichung*) is when a subject takes an object from the external world (in the mass, the leader figure) into the ego. In a mass, the subject internalizes the leader figure, whereby the distinctness of the object disappears and the subject experiences herself and the object as the same. In contrast, *identification* is the process that establishes a tie between the followers through the shared love for the leader.

When a person identifies with another person, they mold their ego ideal after the object they have taken as their role model. As a result, the person has enriched themself with the properties of the model. In contrast, when one introjects an object, the ego is not enriched as in identification. Instead, the "ego is impoverished, it has surrendered itself to the object, it has substituted the object for its own most important constituent."[74]

People who support a (far-right) leader do not identify with them or take them as their role model. Instead, they introject the leader into themselves, which means that they have replaced their ego ideal with the figure of the leader, which allows them at the same time to identify with other followers. Once the mass followers substitute their most important constituent, their ego ideal, with the leader, their egos become impoverished. Followers with an impoverished ego surrender themselves to the (destructive) will of the leader (the object). As Freud puts it, "There is always a feeling of triumph when something in the ego coincides with the ego ideal. And the sense of guilt (as well as the sense of inferiority) can also be understood as an expression of tension between ego and the ego ideal."[75] Once the tension between the ego and the ego ideal vanishes in the mass followers, which happens through the replacement of their ego ideal with the introjected leader, the followers experience a feeling of triumph because they can get rid of feelings of guilt and inferiority for not being able to live up to their ego ideal.

Here I would also like to introduce how ego ideal replacement connects with the melancholia-mania complex, which I will detail further in chapter 4, with reference to the rise of Trump. In melancholia, the subject introjects a lost object (a lost ideal or a lost person), and as a result, the ego divides into two pieces, the first of which rages against the second. The misery of the melancholic is the "expression of a sharp conflict between the two agencies of the ego, a conflict in which the ideal, in an excess of sensitiveness, relentlessly exhibits its condemnation of the ego in delusions of inferiority and self-depreciation."[76] That sharp conflict between the two agencies of the ego (one of which is the ego and the other the ego ideal) is resolved when the subject oscillates from melancholia into mania. In mania, "the ego and the ego ideal have fused together, so that the person, in a mood of triumph and self-satisfaction, disturbed by no self-criticism, can enjoy the abolition of his inhibitions, his feelings of consideration for others, and his self-reproaches."[77]

Ego ideal replacement in a mass allows the mass followers to eliminate the tension between the ego and the ego ideal, which plagues them with feelings of inferiority and guilt of not being able to live up to their ego ideal. Such an undoing of that tension generates narcissistic pleasure on two levels. First, it allows the mass followers to experience (temporarily or more permanently) repressed libidinal impulses. Second, it enables them to live out their desire for cruel aggressiveness and, with that, do away with the sense of guilt.

Narcissistic Mass Love

In "On Narcissism," Freud points out that when the ego faces hindrances in fulfilling its ego ideal, a love object enters into an "interesting auxiliary relationship" with the ego ideal.[78] In *Group Psychology*, Freud further details how in a mass it is the mass leader who enters into that auxiliary relationship with the ego ideal of each of the mass followers. He refers here to ego ideal replacement, which establishes a narcissistic love bond between the leader and the followers and allows the followers to identify with one another.

Freud distinguishes two forms of narcissism: complete object love and pure narcissism. In complete object love, the ego "will love in conformity with the narcissistic type of object-choice, will love what [s/]he once was and no longer is, or else what possesses the excellence which [s/]he never had at all . . . what possesses the excellence which the ego lacks for making it an ideal, is loved."[79] The love between the mass followers and the leader entails complete object love. Here the mass followers choose a leader who can substitute for their ego ideal and offer all the excellence they never possessed.

In *Group Psychology*, Freud describes that such a narcissistic object choice occurs as an ego ideal replacement. In a mass, the love object (the leader) "serves as a substitute for some unattained ego ideal of our own. We love it on account of the perfections which we have striven to reach for our own ego, and which we should now procure in this roundabout way as a means to satisfying our narcissism."[80] The mass followers transfer their narcissistic libido and fall in love with an idealized "whole" leader who allows them, by replacing their ego ideal with the "whole" leader figure, to feel "whole" and perfect again, providing them with the illusion of being "successful" on the economic, interpersonal, and bodily levels. The followers' transfer of narcissistic libido to the leader underlines that it is narcissistic love that characterizes the relationship between the leader and his followers. Such narcissistic love also engenders a regression to a sleep and dream state, which I will further detail in chapter 3.

However, the leader does not need to possess the perfections the mass followers seek to attain through him, nor does he need to be "whole" himself to engender ego ideal replacement in his followers. Freud explains this with the peculiar "phenomenon of sexual overvaluation," which implies the idealization of the love object. When we idealize a love object, our judgment is impaired. We value the love object's characteristics more than those of objects we do not love, and we abstain from criticizing its less desirable features. The reason for such sexual overvaluation is that when we are in love, a considerable amount of narcissistic libido "overflows" to the love object.[81] As a result, the "object, without any alteration in its nature, is aggrandized and exalted in the subject's mind."[82] Because such an aggrandized and exalted love object serves to satisfy our narcissism, we at the same time conceal or forget any of its flaws and shortcomings.

Freud points out that parents' affection toward their children is nothing but a revival of the parent's own abandoned narcissism. The parents "are under a [neurotic] compulsion to ascribe every perfection to the child—which sober observation would find no occasion to do—and to conceal and forget all [her/]his shortcomings."[83] The parents aim through the idealized child to fulfill their wishful dreams, which they never carried out.

In a mass, a similar neurotic compulsion prevails. The mass followers ascribe every perfection to the mass leader, to which in reality he has no claim, and they overlook his shortcomings and flaws. The mass followers aggrandize and exalt him because he allows them to undo the separation between the ego and the ego ideal through ego ideal replacement. The abrogation of the ego ideal, as mentioned, enables them to get rid of nagging feelings of guilt and inferiority and feel satisfied with themselves again.

Freud also points out that the selection of a leader in a mass is facilitated by the circumstance that in many subjects, the separation between the ego and the ego ideal is not very far advanced, and "the two still coincide readily; the ego has often preserved its earlier narcissistic self-complacency."[84] Since many subjects have preserved their narcissistic self-complacency, the leader's function as a replacement for their ego ideal is made easier.

Here the mass leader "need only give an impression of greater force and of more freedom of libido; and in that case the need for a strong chief will often meet him halfway and invest him with a predominance to which he would otherwise perhaps have had no claim."[85] The mass followers, whose separation between the ego and the ego ideal is not far advanced, invest the leader with the perfections they seek to obtain through him in ego ideal replacement.

The other members of the mass, "whose ego ideal would not, apart from this, have become embodied in his person without some correction," are then "carried away" with the rest of the mass through identification. In the mass, we find a libidinal structure that "leads back to the distinction between the ego and the ego ideal and to the double kind of tie which this makes possible—identification and putting the object in the place of the ego ideal."[86]

In "On Narcissism," Freud also explains that besides complete object love, there is another form of narcissism, which he denotes as a "pure" form of narcissism. This form of narcissism intensifies the original narcissism and is unfavorable for the development of object love and idealization. In *Group Psychology*, it becomes clear that while complete object love characterizes the bond between the mass followers and the leader, pure narcissism is characteristic for the mass leader.

Pure narcissism characterizes a subject who only loves themselves, with an intensity comparable to the love brought towards them from complete object love. The subject does not love but needs to be loved, and the one who fulfills this condition is the one who finds favor with the subject. The completely narcissistic subject has a great attraction for those who have renounced part of their narcissism and are searching for an object to which they can transfer their renounced narcissistic libido. The narcissistic leader, therefore, attracts followers. Freud points out that "even great criminals and humorists, as they are represented in literature, compel our interest by the narcissistic consistency with which they manage to keep away from their ego anything that would diminish it. It is as if we envied them for maintaining a blissful state of mind—an unassailable libidinal position which we ourselves have since abandoned."[87] A purely narcissistic leader who manages to keep away from his ego anything that could diminish it and only loves himself has, akin to the great criminals and humorists, a great attraction for those who are in search of transferring their renounced narcissistic libido. The transfer of their narcissistic libido to the purely narcissistic leader and the replacement of their ego ideal with him allow them to regain the "blissful state of mind" of the original narcissism.

The problem of complete object love is that the transfer of the narcissistic love, or self-love, of the ego results in an impoverishment of the ego in favor of the love object, which leads to the subject's neurotic compulsion to ascribe perfection to the love object.[88] Furthermore, when the love object gets in possession of the entire self-love of the ego, at the end, "the object, has, so to speak, *consumed* the ego."[89] The problem with an impoverished ego is that it completely *surrenders* itself to the love object and fails to be critical of its deeds and demands on the ego. A mass is composed of followers whose egos are so impoverished that the mass leader consumes them. As a result, the mass followers uncritically surrender to the mass leader and cease to see anything wrong with the deeds of the mass leader or what he wants them to do.

The mass followers uncritically surrender themselves to the mass leader because, once the love object has been put in place of the ego ideal, a core function of the superego, which is moral conscience, ceases to operate.[90] Once the function of the superego, which is to keep the ego in line with the ego ideal, ceases to operate, the subject is no longer critical of the love object. As Freud puts it, once "the criticism exercised by that agency is silent everything that the object does and asks for is right and blameless. Conscience has no application to anything that is done for the sake of the object; in the blindness of love remorselessness is carried to the pitch of crime."[91]

The "remorselessness" in this citation hints at something else, which Freud did not further elaborate on in *Group Psychology*. As outlined earlier, the superego is the chief influence that monitors and our desire for cruel aggressiveness, redirecting that cruelty against the ego as a means to weaken the aggressive drive and punish the ego.[92] In a mass, once the superego ceases to function, the mass followers can no longer keep their desire for cruel aggressiveness as well as their libidinal impulses in the unconscious in check.

The mass leader directs the mass followers' no longer repressed sexual drives toward himself to strengthen the libidinal ties between him and the mass followers. At the same time, he directs the no longer repressed aggressive drives toward designated targets of hatred, which also helps unify the mass. Both processes generate different kinds of narcissistic satisfaction for the mass followers.

The transfer of (aim-inhibited) sexual impulses onto the mass leader allows them to eliminate nagging feelings of inferiority and regain their original narcissistic blissful state. Taking out their desire for cruel aggressiveness on designated targets allows them to obtain a high degree of narcissistic enjoyment because it fulfills their infantile wishes for omnipotence.

In summary, in a mass, three things come together that allow the mass followers to throw off the repressions of their unconscious instinctual impulses: First, ego ideal replacement weakens the mass followers' capacity to keep their aggressive drives in check because the superego functions cease to operate. Second, in a mass, the followers are encouraged to receive their repressed aggressive and libidinal drives in the ego. Third, the mass leader provides the followers with objects of hatred outside the mass, upon whom the mass followers can satisfy their aggressiveness, which helps unify the mass "in love."

The undoing of the split between the ego and the ego ideal and the abrogation of the ego ideal make the mass followers blind to the wrongness of the leader's deeds and susceptible to his encouragement to take out their desire for cruel aggressiveness against designated targets of hatred. Since the function of criticism, both in the form of self-criticism and in the ability to criticize the leader, ceases to be operative, remorselessness can be easily carried to the level of criminal and violent behavior.

Hypnotic Regression

In *Group Psychology*, Freud discusses narcissistic love also in connection with hypnosis.[93] Narcissistic love and hypnosis are for him intimately connected, and from being in love to hypnosis it is only a short step: "there is the same humble subjection, the same compliance, the same absence of criticism, towards the hypnotist as towards the loved object." Hypnosis is identical with mass formation, and the conditions of a subject in a mass are hypnotic.[94]

However, there are slight differences among narcissistic love, hypnosis, and the psychological mass. Being in love is based on the simultaneous presence of direct sexual drives and aim–inhibited sexual drives. The love object draws a part of the subject's narcissistic ego libido to itself. Here there is only room for the object and the ego. Hypnosis resembles being in love insofar as it is limited to two people, but it is based entirely on sexual drives that are inhibited in their aims.[95]

Furthermore, in hypnosis, the subject puts the object (the hypnotist) in place of their ego ideal, and here "the hypnotist has stepped into the place of the ego ideal." The mass multiplies this process. Like in hypnosis, direct sexual drives are absent, and only aim–inhibited sexual drives hold the mass together. In addition, the mass is also held together by aggressive drives that are directed toward a target outside it (which Freud did not note here). Furthermore, akin to hypnosis, the mass leader steps into the place of the ego ideal of the mass followers. However, unlike in the hypnotist-hypnotized dyad, in the mass we also find the identification of the mass followers with one another.[96]

Finally, both mass formation and hypnosis have the character of a *regression*, which does not take place in being in love. Regression makes its appearance whenever the advance from directly sexual drives to aim-inhibited sexual drives has not been wholly successful. It represents a *conflict* between the aim-inhibited sexual drives that have been acted upon by the ego and those that remain repressed in the unconscious and still strive to attain direct satisfaction.[97]

Given the centrality of aggressive drives to unify the mass, it seems that regression also makes its appearance when the suppression of the aggressive drives has not been wholly successful. Regression also represents a conflict between aggressive impulses that remain in the unconscious and those that the mass leader has allowed to surface in the ego of the mass followers by providing them with an object of hatred outside the mass upon which they can satisfy their desire for cruel aggressiveness.

In both hypnosis and in the mass, through regression, the conscious personality of the hypnotized mass followers vanishes, and their unconscious personality predominates. Through replacing their ego ideal with the leader (the hypnotist), the mass followers find themselves in a hypnotic state of "fascination" with the leader, in which all feelings and thoughts are bent in the direction determined by the hypnotizer (the mass leader), in whose hands they find themselves.[98]

In a state where the conscious personality disappears and the unconscious personality predominates, the hypnotized is no longer entirely conscious of their acts. The hypnotist asserts the power to rob the hypnotized subject of their own will, and as a result "[s/]he is no longer [her/]himself, but has become an automaton who has ceased to be guided by [his/]his will." Also, in a mass, once the hypnotized mass followers cease to be guided by their own will, they follow the will of the leader (the hypnotist).[99]

Freud also points out that the uncanniness of hypnosis "suggests something old and familiar that has undergone repression." What has undergone repression is the oldest form of human psychology, which implies that we are members of the "primal horde," which refers to Freud's theory of an earlier form of human society that was ruled despotically by a powerful and threatening male, the *primal father*.[100] The experience of the primal horde is part of our inheritance; it has left traces in all of our psyches.

In *Group Psychology*, Freud outlines how in hypnosis and in the mass, regression to the stage of the primal horde takes place. In a mass, through regression, a revival of this oldest form of human psychology occurs. The mass leader, akin to the hypnotist, awakens in the followers a portion of this repressed archaic heritage, which makes them experience the leader as the primal father, with a dangerous personality to whose will they must surrender. In the mass, we find the same dwindling of consciousness and the predominance of the unconscious personality and the affective side of the mind, the carrying out of intentions whenever they occur, and the focusing of thoughts and feelings into the direction of the leader.[101]

The repressed archaic heritage is the revival of the psychology of the "primal horde." As Freud puts it, "the leader of the group is still the dreaded father; the group still wishes to be governed by unrestricted force; it has an extreme passion for authority. . . . The primal father is the group ideal, which governs the ego in the place of the ego ideal." Here Freud returns to what he had argued in *Totem and Taboo* and points out that totemism, which is the beginning of religion, morality, and social organization, is "connected with the killing of the chief by violence and the transformation of the paternal horde into a community of brothers."[102]

In *Totem and Taboo*, Freud outlines that in the archaic primal horde, the brothers had contradictory feelings toward their father. The brothers hated him because he was an obstacle to their cravings for power and sexual partners, but they also loved and admired him. None of the brothers individually could topple and replace the father, which was why they banded together to kill him.

When they killed him, they satisfied their hatred, but the affection toward him, which had been pushed aside, made itself felt. Here a "sense of guilt" made its appearance, which coincided with the remorse felt by the whole group. Here the father whom they murdered was elevated into a god, and the brothers again submitted to him as an attempt to atone for that deed.[103]

The totemic system was an attempt to bring about a reconciliation with the murdered father, so they could expect protection from him (the totem animal, which is a substitute for the father), in exchange for the commitment that they would not repeat the deed, which destroyed the father. As Freud puts it, "totemic religion arose from the filial sense of guilt, in an attempt to allay that feeling and to appease the father by deferring obedience to him."[104]

With the introduction of the patriarchal system, the deposed father took harsh revenge, as here "the dominance of authority was at its climax." The patriarchal family restored the former primal horde, and "it gave back to fathers a large portion of their former rights."[105] As time went on and the totem animal lost its sacred character, the brothers offered sacrifices to the father for the outrage they inflicted upon him.

Freud's outlining of the "primal horde" in *Totem and Taboo* allows us to grasp further why the mass followers wish to be governed with unrestricted force by the dreaded father: It is a means of assuaging their "sense of guilt," which reminds them of the use of violence against the father.

Akin to the primal horde, we find pure narcissism on the leader's side (the primal father) and complete object love on the side of the followers (the primal horde members) in a mass. Whereas the members of the primal horde were subject to libidinal ties with one another, the primal father "had few libidinal ties; he loved no one but himself, or other people only in so far as they served his needs." Akin to the primal horde, in a mass, the members need the illusion that their leader equally loves them, "but the leader himself need love no one else, he may be of a masterful nature, absolutely narcissistic, self-confident and independent."[106]

However, the leader does not need to be self-confident and independent, as the mass followers readily ascribe characteristics to him to which he has no claim. Akin to the primal father, the mass leader "need only give an impression of greater force and of more freedom of libido; and in that case the need for a strong chief will often meet him halfway and invest him with a predominance to which he would otherwise perhaps have had no claim."[107] The followers can meet the chief halfway through idealizing him and transferring their (disappointed) narcissistic libido to the leader. As a result, they can love themselves via the idealized chief again.

Conclusion: The Socioeconomic Dimension of Mass Psychology

How can we counter the formation of psychological masses, which lead to a scenario where the followers satisfy their desire for cruel aggressiveness upon targets of hatred determined by the mass leader? The National Socialist regime and the new forms of cruelty encouraged by new global far-right forces reveal that normative, ethical commands are not effective enough to prevent us from turning into wolves and satisfying our aggressive drive on our neighbor.

Early in *Civilization and Its Discontents*, Freud suggests that to deprive a drive of satisfaction is not without danger, and that "if the loss is *not compensated for economically*, one can be certain that serious disorders will ensue." Later in this work, he reiterates that only "a real change in the relations of human beings to possessions" can counter the aggressive drives.[108] Here Freud provides us with a glimpse of how the psychological is connected to the socioeconomic.[109] In a capitalist society, large sectors of the population are not compensated economically for being deprived of the satisfaction of their sexual and aggressive drives, which, however, remain forces in the unconscious. Such a situation, assisted by the heightened senses of guilt, inferiority, and cultural frustration, creates a fertile ground for far-right forces to attract new followers.

Such techniques, as I will show in the following chapters, put the mental counterforces that repress our desire for cruel aggressiveness out of function. Such techniques exploit the followers' cultural frustration (which is a result of the repression of sexuality), their *Unbehagen* (which is the result of the repression of aggressive drives), and their feelings of inferiority (from not being able to live up to their ego ideal). They also affect their followers' regression to the unconscious, which allows them to channel their sexual and aggressive drives for their own political and economic interests.

Given the high degree of narcissistic enjoyment that expressing their aggressive impulses and directly acting out libidinal impulses has in store, it is not a surprise that the mass is attractive particularly (but not only) for those people who are not compensated economically for the renunciation of their aggressive (and sexual) drives. While economic compensation for giving up our libidinal and aggressive drives directs our attention to the socioeconomic dimension that could help us tackle far-right forces, other elements in Freud's psychoanalytic theorizing allows us more directly to relate mass psychology to precarity capitalism.

As I will further develop in the coming chapter, the socioeconomic aspect that intersects with the psychological is the heightened tension between peoples' ego and their ego ideal. Such a tension is the result of narcissistic ego's inability live up what Freud calls the "demands of the environment." I call the "demands from the environment" the capitalist standards of economic, interpersonal, and bodily "success." Such tension results from challenges to living up to economic, interpersonal, and bodily success standards in precarity capitalism. Since in precarity capitalism most subjects cannot live up to these standards they can no longer retain the original narcissism, and their self-regard diminishes.

As I will show in the following chapters, the "animal" that holds psychologically oriented far-right propaganda techniques together is that they allow the followers to undo the tension between their ego and their ego ideal. In a far-right mass, the followers can replace their ego ideal with the leader figure, which creates conditions for the mass followers akin to festivals, allowing the mass followers a more permanent undoing of the separation between the ego and the ego ideal. Here mass followers don't have to feel bad when they can't live up to economic, interpersonal, and bodily success standards because their leader is doing it for them.

In the far-right mass, where there is no salient leader figure, other techniques (including the use of racist and sexist jokes) allow the undoing of the split between the ego and the ego ideal, which allow followers to create a "festival" that allows them to get rid of feelings of low self-regard that are the results of not being able to fulfill standards of "success" in precarity capitalism. When the separation between the ego and the ego ideal becomes undone, the subject finds herself relieved from feelings of low self-regard for not living up to the ego ideal's demands. However, such a "blissful" state also sets the stage for the followers' regression to an older form of psychology: the psychology of the primal horde, in which the followers are ready to carry out the violence demanded by the threatening chief.

CHAPTER III

Sleeping and Dreaming While Awake

Adorno Revisited

> Although the fascist agitator doubtlessly takes up certain tendencies within those he addresses, he does so as the mandatory of powerful political and economic interests. Psychological dispositions do not actually cause fascism; rather, fascism defines a psychological area which can be successfully exploited by the forces which promote it for entirely non-psychological reasons of self-interest.
>
> —THEODOR W. ADORNO, "FREUDIAN THEORY AND THE PATTERN OF FASCIST PROPAGANDA"

This chapter outlines the psychoanalytic theory that Adorno picks up from Freud's *Group Psychology and the Analysis of the Ego* and other texts to explain the functioning of fascist propaganda techniques. I extend Adorno's ideas to more fully theorize the process by which sleep states and dream states, as defined by psychoanalysis, are exploited by fascist propaganda.

I show that Adorno pursued close textual reading of Freudian psychoanalytic theory to explain the rise of fascism in Europe and protofascist elements in the United States, and I thereby challenge the suggestions of contemporary critical theorists of the early Frankfurt School kind that Adorno distanced himself from Freudian psychoanalytic theory. However, while Adorno's focus on psychoanalytic theory allowed him to theorize what holds different fascist propaganda devices together, he also went beyond Freud. More so than Freud, he established a dialectics between the socioeconomic and the psychological, which I further develop in this chapter.

I also go beyond Adorno in innovative ways. I outline how propaganda techniques put the followers into a "sleep state," which makes them subject themselves to the irrational aims of the leader or movement, aims that are irreconcilable with the subjects' rational economic and other self-interests. The "sleep state" induces in the followers also a "dream state," in which their latent wishes become fulfilled. Both states foreground the unconscious in the followers.

This chapter has five sections. In "The Repression of Psychoanalysis in Critical Theory," I outline and challenge contemporary critical theorists' attempts to distance Adorno from Freudian psychoanalytic thought. In "The Libidinal Bond and Aggression in the Fascist Mass," I detail how Adorno takes up Freud's theory of libido and the aggressive drive to explain fascist mass formation. In "Narcissistic Regressions," I explain how Adorno takes up Freud's theory of narcissism and archaic regressions to explain fascist propaganda techniques. In "Race in Adorno's Work on Fascism," I outline how Adorno relies on psychoanalytic theory to explain how fascists draw on the pseudonatural category of "race" in their propaganda devices to capture followers. In "Sleeping While Awake," I draw on Freud and Adorno to theorize how far-right propaganda techniques induce a sleep state in followers. Finally, in "The Dream State," I explain how fascist agitators induce a dream state in their followers, which allows the followers, in a hallucinatory manner, to live up to the economic, interpersonal, and bodily standards of "success" in precarity capitalism and feel themselves as "whole" subjects again.

The Repression of Psychoanalysis in Critical Theory

> But above all one should think about psychoanalysis, which is still being repressed today as much as ever. Either it is altogether absent, or it is replaced by tendencies that while boasting of overcoming the much-maligned nineteenth century, in truth fall back behind Freudian theory, even turning it into its very opposite.
>
> —THEODOR W. ADORNO, *GUILT AND DEFENSE*

Adorno wrote these lines in 1955 in his reflections on how we can counter a return of fascism.[1] He argued that we must turn to the insights of psychoanalysis. However, psychoanalysis's crucial potential in understanding and countering the return of the fascist threat has become less available because of its repression in society. Today, we continue to encounter much repression of Freudian psychoanalysis, even by thinkers who draw on early Frankfurt School Critical Theory, and particularly on Adorno, to study the resurgence of the far right.[2]

For example, Peter Gordon suggests that any turn to psychoanalysis to grasp the rise of the far right leads to a reduction of sociopolitical phenomena to the psychological, which was, according to Gordon, supposedly also Adorno's view. "According to Adorno, it would be mistaken to explain fascism by appealing to psychological categories, not least because psychologism carries a serious threat of depoliticization."[3] However, Adorno never argued that psychoanalysis carries "psychologism" and "a serious threat of depoliticization." Instead, Adorno consistently argued that we need Freudian psychoanalysis to understand and counter the threat of a return to fascism. Here Gordon invokes the authority of Adorno as a mere tool for his aim—to repress psychoanalysis as a critical tool to study the far right today.

Gordon aims to achieve such a goal also with the argument that Adorno suggested in "Freudian Theory and the Pattern of Fascist Propaganda" that psychoanalytic theory has no value in explaining the threat of a return of fascism because nineteenth-century psychological thought still assumed the autonomy of the subject, which has vanished in a thoroughly reified society.[4] Gordon conveniently ignores that Adorno draws on Freud precisely to challenge the notion of an autonomous subject. Adorno argues that Freud's concept of an impoverished subject who has surrendered themself to the idealized leader and who has substituted their most important constituent (the superego or, more precisely, the ego ideal) with the leader figure "anticipates almost with clairvoyance the post-psychological deindividualized social atoms that form the fascist collectivities."[5]

Gordon also cites a letter from Horkheimer to Marcuse in which Horkheimer questioned academic psychology as relevant for critical theorizing.[6] However, Gordon ignores that Adorno did not contribute to this letter and that Horkheimer was questioning academic psychology and its focus on quantitative research and not psychoanalysis as relevant for critical theorizing.

Gordon also aims to suppress the critical insights of psychoanalysis by returning to Adorno's remarks in the *Authoritarian Personality* (AP) study, which examines the potential for fascist victory in the United States in the 1940s.[7] Here Gordon fabricates the idea that Adorno had a conflict with the psychoanalysts and psychologists of the research team because while Adorno aimed at a dialectics between the social and psychological, the research team's one-sided focus on the psychological generated a breakdown of such dialectics.[8] Here Gordon conveniently leaves out those aspects of

Adorno's remarks that counter his claim of a conflict. For example, Adorno states that their study is in "full harmony with psychoanalysis in its more orthodox Freudian version." Adorno's remarks are in line with his colleagues, who point out in the introduction to *The Authoritarian Personality* that their theory of personality "leaned most heavily upon Freud."[9]

Furthermore, Adorno's argument that the authoritarian personality is nothing but a "generalized feature of the social order itself" is not in conflict with (as Gordon argues) but is also in line with the other researchers' general definition of personality. In the introduction, the researchers argue that "far from being something which is given in the beginning [and] which remains fixed," personality is something that "evolves under the impact of the social environment and can never be isolated from the social totality within which it occurs."[10]

Furthermore, Adorno also points out that because "prejudice may be pre-conscious or even unconscious," it is not advisable (as Gordon seems to advise us) to approach such attitudes as clear-cut issues. For him, "all aspects of anti-minority prejudice are so affect laden, so deeply involved with irrational urges and mechanisms, that a rational approach must necessarily remain superficial and fallacious." Here Adorno is in line (and not in conflict) with the core argument of his research team, who points out that since fascism needs a mass base but favors the few over the many, it cannot appeal to rational economic and other self-interest but must appeal to "emotional needs—often to the most primitive and irrational wishes and fears."[11] For Adorno, only a psychoanalytic approach, which examines the unconscious, can help us understand how propaganda techniques appeal to irrational wishes and fears.

Robyn Marasco rightly points out that Gordon's assumption that Adorno distanced himself from the AP study is incorrect because "far from disavowing or distancing himself from the project, Adorno invoked the idea of the authoritarian personality on several occasions after the book's publication in the 1950s."[12] For example, Adorno, in his *Aspekte des neuen Rechtsradikalismus*, repeatedly reinvokes the AP study and points out that new right extremist propaganda is nothing but a mass psychological technique, which appeals to the authoritarian-bound personality.[13]

Furthermore, he argues that to understand how fascist propaganda techniques capture people, we must have a conception of the unconscious. As Adorno puts it: "The unconscious tendencies, which feed this authoritarian personality, are not made conscious by this propaganda, but on the contrary, they are pushed more into the unconscious, they are kept unconscious by artificial means." Psychoanalytic theory helps us understand how fascist propaganda techniques feed on the unconscious to function and how, to keep functioning, it must counter any methods that make the unconscious conscious. In this text, Adorno also points out that "especially the hatred of psychoanalysis and anti-intellectualism, the fear that the unconscious becomes conscious, and the authoritarian character are all part of a syndrome."[14] It seems that the attempts of numerous thinkers who draw on the early Frankfurt School critical theorists to explain the far right and who dismiss Freudian psychoanalysis are also part of this syndrome.

For example, Federico Fichtelstein, drawing on Gordon as an "authority," suggests that the AP study's fusion of political analysis and psychoanalysis "does so at the risk of separating politics from context."[15] Similarly, Apostolidis rejects psychoanalytic theory with the timeworn charge that any drawing on psychoanalytic theory reduces the socioeconomic to the psychological, an argument I challenge in this book.[16] In addition, Martin Jay warns us about the danger of "psychoanalyzing" political behavior, which he sees particularly salient in "orthodox Freud."[17]

Gandesha contributes to such a syndrome in his repeated dismissive statements about "orthodox Freud" and his attempt to distance Adorno from Freud by turning Adorno into an object-relations theorist, a characterization Adorno would have strongly objected to. Although Gandesha in a more recent work acknowledges that Adorno draws on "orthodox Freud" in his "Freudian Theory," he considers such an engagement problematic because Freud supposedly relied on a Hobbesian account of civilization.[18]

However, as my careful reading of Freud's account of civilization in chapter 2 shows, we do not find any such notion in Freud. Instead, we find it in Gandesha, who seems to project his Hobbesian view on capitalism onto Freud. According to Gandesha, because subjects find themselves in a Hobbesian "state of nature" in the "war of everybody against everybody" in precarity capitalism, they identify themselves with the aggressor, which entails making themselves competitive concerning other individuals, leading to a scenario where they subordinate themselves to an economic system (and far-right leaders who support such system) that is bad for them.

However, as outlined in chapter 1, it is *not* competition but the threat of castration on the economic, interpersonal, and bodily levels in precarity capitalism that helps explain the rise of the far right. Furthermore, while "identification with the aggressor" as a theoretical concept might help explain some aspects of fascist propaganda techniques, it does not allow us to understand why subjects support leaders and movements that *contradict* their rational economic interest and other self-interests. Only a theoretical account, which I develop in this book via Freud and Adorno, that explains how far-right propaganda techniques engender in their followers regressive and unconscious processes can explain such a phenomenon.[19]

And although Robyn Marasco defends Adorno's closeness to the AP study against Gordon, she also contributes to the suppression of Freudian psychoanalytic thought. Like Gordon, she downplays the use of Freudian psychoanalytic theory for early Frankfurt School critical theorists in her assertion that the "Freudian treatment of group psychology . . . is rather marginal to their work."[20] Here Marasco ignores that Adorno makes clear in "Freudian Theory" that since it would be impossible for fascism to win over the masses through rational arguments it must be oriented psychologically and has to mobilize unconscious and regressive processes. As Adorno points out, to understand fascist propaganda techniques we need "the application of a more comprehensive, basic psychoanalytic theory to the agitator's overall approach. Such a frame of reference has been provided by Freud himself in his book *Group Psychology and the Analysis of the Ego*."[21] As such, Freud's *Group Psychology* is central to Adorno's work on fascism.

The Libidinal Bond and Aggression in the Fascist Mass

At the beginning of "Freudian Theory," Adorno asserts that although Freud's *Group Psychology* was published long before German fascism became acute, Freud "clearly foresaw the rise and nature of fascist mass movements in purely psychological categories."[22] Adorno is correct that Freud delivered the psychological or, more accurately, psychoanalytic categories that allow us to grasp the rise and nature of fascist (as well as new far-right) movements.

However, Freud not only foresaw fascism in "purely psychological categories," as Adorno suggests. He also provides some entry points to theorize further how the psychological interacts with the socioeconomic. For example, Freud points out that we must economically compensate people for the deprivation of the satisfaction of their drives. Not compensating them is dangerous and leads to "serious disorders"—the disorder of the National Socialist regime.[23] Furthermore, Freud provides theoretical concepts, such as the ego ideal, allowing me to theorize further why people become vulnerable to fascist propaganda in precarity capitalism.

Adorno's reading of Freud provides me with further entry points to theorize the dialectics between the psychological and the socioeconomic in the rise of fascism and the current far right; his reading also counters the argument that drawing on Freudian psychoanalysis necessarily leads to a breakdown of such dialectics. As outlined in the previous section, Adorno repeatedly states that it would be impossible for fascism to win over the masses to fascism's irrational aims through rational arguments. Because of that, fascist propaganda must be oriented psychologically "and has to mobilize irrational, unconscious, regressive processes." Adorno argues that only a return to Freud allows us to grasp how psychologically oriented propaganda techniques mobilize irrational, unconscious, and regressive processes. However, he also outlines how socioeconomic forces play into mobilizing such processes. Adorno goes on to state that manipulating the unconscious is "facilitated by the frame of mind of all those strata of the population who suffer from senseless frustrations and therefore develop a stunted, irrational mentality. It may well be the secret of fascist propaganda that it simply takes [wo/]men for what they are: the true children of today's standardized mass culture, largely robbed of autonomy and spontaneity."[24]

Although Adorno hints here that the suffering in capitalism generates a "stunted mentality," he does not further elaborate on what such suffering implies. As I outlined in chapter 1, the objective conditions of suffering in capitalist societies (exploitation, job insecurity, alienation, and isolation) generate subjective forms of suffering (or make people suffer senseless frustrations) and, assisted by the culture industry, generate a mentality that can be exploited by psychologically oriented fascist propaganda techniques.

It seems that what Adorno means by "those strata of the population" that suffer from senseless frustrations is the working classes. However, as I have discussed, the objective conditions of suffering in capitalism generate subjective forms of suffering at *all* levels of the work hierarchy in precarity capitalism (albeit to varying degrees). Furthermore, capitalism's culture industry today, mainly social media and the internet, contributes to the production in all classes of subjectivities that are susceptible to far-right propaganda tricks.

Adorno draws on Freud to explain that fascist propaganda techniques engender irrational, unconscious, and regressive processes by creating a libidinal bond between the fascist demagogue and the mass followers. "The fascist demagogue, who has to win the support of millions of people for aims largely incompatible with their own rational self-interest, can do so only by artificially creating the bond Freud is looking for . . . in fact, *that is the unifying principle behind his various devices.*"[25]

Adorno also draws on Freud's concept of ego ideal replacement, which states that the followers replace their ego ideal with the introjection of the leader and that this allows them to identify with one another, to explain how fascist demagogues artificially create the libidinal bond between themselves and the mass members. "The fascist community of the people corresponds exactly to Freud's definition of a group [mass] as being a number of individuals who have substituted one and the same object for their ego ideal and have consequently identified themselves with one another in their ego."[26]

Unlike Freud, Adorno suggests that the mechanism that generates the libidinal bond between the demagogue and the followers is identification.[27] However, as outlined in chapter 2, Freud shows us that introjection and not identification is what generates the libidinal bond between the leader and the followers.[28] Fascist propaganda techniques make the followers "fall in love" with the fascist demagogue through a process whereby they incorporate the idealized leader into themselves, replacing their ego ideal with the internalized leader figure. Their shared love for the leader allows the followers to "fall in love" with one another and (temporarily) suppress their feelings of envy and hostility.

In chapter 2, I noted that the difference between introjection and identification is important. When the followers introject the leader figure, they are not enriched by his qualities, as happens in identification. Instead, introjection generates deindividualized subjects with impoverished egos, who completely surrender themselves to the love object. Such subjects cease to be critical of anything the leader does and willingly carry out his commands.[29] This difference is critical to keep in mind, as it shows us how Freud challenged any notion of a mass as composed of "free individuals," that is, as autonomous subjects who carry out their own wills.

Adorno considered the creation of a libidinal bond between the fascist demagogue and the mass followers through ego ideal replacement and among the mass followers themselves through identification as the ultimate goal behind every fascist propaganda technique. He also points out that the bond between the followers and the demagogue is based on "narcissistic love," since ego ideal replacement entails a process of idealization, where the follower, "by making the leader [her/]his ideal," will love "[her/]himself, as it were, but gets rid of the stains of frustration and discontent which mar [her/]his picture of [her/]his own empirical self."[30]

As I have outlined in chapter 1, the subjects' ego ideal is generated through economic, interpersonal, and physical "success" standards in capitalist societies. However, objective conditions of suffering make it impossible to live up to these standards, and this failure to do so generates subjective forms of suffering—castration anxieties and feelings of failure about their "nonwhole" subjectivities. Adorno is speaking of these anxieties and feelings when he notes that ego ideal replacement allows the follower to get "rid of the stains of frustration and discontent which mar [her/]his picture of [her/]his own empirical self."

Freud expresses these subjective forms of suffering as arising from the sharp tension between the subject's ego and their ego ideal, with accompanying feelings of failure, guilt, and inferiority. Far-right propaganda techniques successfully capture subjects who subjectively suffer because they allow people to undo this tension. Once the tension is undone, people can experience themselves as "whole" subjects again and get rid of Adorno's "stains of frustration and discontent."

Adorno also reiterates Freud's argument that hatred against a particular person or institution can unify a mass. "This negative integration feeds on the drive of destructiveness to which Freud does not explicitly refer in his *Group Psychology*, the decisive role of which he has, however, recognized in his *Civilization and Its Discontents*."[31] However, Adorno does not further discuss these two texts together to foreground the role of the aggressive drive in the integration of fascist masses, which I undertook in chapter 2.

Nonetheless, Adorno provides insights into how fascist propaganda techniques utilize the aggressive drive to integrate fascist masses. Since there are few positive contents available in fascist ideology and because libido is solely invested in the leader figure, fascist propaganda techniques utilize negative contents to integrate the followers. He provides the example of the "sheep and bucks" (that is, good and evil) propaganda device. This device allows the followers to bond together and find love for one another via having a common enemy. As Adorno puts it, "Freud has succeeded in identifying the libidinal function of this device. It acts as a negatively inte-grating force."[32]

In *The Psychological Technique of Martin Luther Thomas' Radio Addresses*, Adorno further explains the functioning of this device. Here Adorno exam-ines the radio addresses of the U.S. Christian fascist agitator Martin Luther Thomas in the 1930s during his work with Paul Lazarsfeld on the radio's culture industry. He points out that Thomas, in his speeches and writings, excludes all the reconciliatory features of Christian teaching (including the idea of *Nächstenliebe* [*caritas*]) but takes in all its negative elements, includ-ing the condemnation of the "sinner," the establishment of an absolute dif-ference between the sinner and the just for all times, the defamation of the intellect, and the exclusivity of Christianity against other religions, par-ticularly Judaism. He uses the "sheep and bucks" device, in which he brands an enemy who is a priori "damned" and declares that only his followers belong to the noble and admirable group. Such construction allows the fol-lowers to bond in love through their shared hatred of a common enemy.[33]

Furthermore, because the fascist agitator provides the followers with a target of hatred (all those "damned") upon whom to unleash their desire for cruel aggressiveness, their hostile feelings toward other mass members can remain repressed. As Adorno points out, the "sheep and bucks" device suggests to the followers that simply through belonging to the "in-group," they are "better, higher and purer than those who are excluded. . . . Con-comitantly, the concentration of hostility upon the out-group does away with intolerance in one's own group to which one's relation would other-wise be highly ambivalent."[34]

Adorno considers Freud's theory of libidinal (and aggressive) drives vital because it allows us to explain fascism in terms of the pleasure prin-ciple, which shows that subjects join fascist masses because of "the actual or vicarious gratifications individuals obtain from surrendering to a mass."[35] As an example, as I will further detail in chapter 7, one core propaganda device the identitarian movement Austria (IBÖ) uses to acquire follow-ers in the European context is the "terror strategy," which promotes the idea of impending catastrophes such as the threat of a migrant invasion.

While such a device generates in the followers irrational, unconscious processes, which the IBÖ uses to manipulate subjects into becoming fol-lowers, it also promises them gratifications—for example, that they can one day (on the day of the pogrom) take out their aggression on those that the IBÖ designates as a threat. This offers the prospect of returning to the narcissistic state of "omnipotence," which, as Freud outlined, generates immense pleasure in us.

Adorno makes clear that a mass is attractive for us because "in a group [mass] the individual is brought under conditions which allow him to throw off the repressions of his unconscious drives."[36] The elimination of repressions generates pleasure by allowing us to receive our repressed libidinal and aggressive impulses in our ego. However, he also makes clear that the throwing off of instinctual repressions alone cannot explain the attraction the fascist mass holds for followers. Something else happens in a fascist mass—agitators induce *regressions* in their followers artificially, through their propaganda techniques.

As Adorno puts it, "It is hardly adequate to define the forces of fascist rebellion [against civilization] simply as powerful id energies which throw off the pressure of the existing social order. Rather, this rebellion borrows its energies partly from other psychological agencies which are pressed in the service of the unconscious."[37] These "other psychological agencies" include the ego ideal, which, when replaced by the introjected leader, induces the followers' regressions to what Freud called the psychology of the "primal horde."

Narcissistic Regressions

What happens when masses are caught by fascist propaganda is not a spontaneous primary expression of instincts and urges but a quasi-scientific revitalization of their psychology—the artificial regression described by Freud in his discussion of organized groups.
—THEODOR W. ADORNO, "FREUDIAN THEORY AND THE PATTERN OF FASCIST PROPAGANDA"

This section further outlines how Adorno draws on Freud to explain how followers in fascist masses surrender themselves to the leader's will, even if such a will contradicts their rational economic and other self-interests. For this to happen, fascist propaganda techniques artificially induce regressions in the followers, which generate a mass's passive-masochistic attitude. As Adorno puts it, "the more [her/]his political behavior becomes irreconcilable with [her/]his own rational interests as a private person as well as those of the group or class to which [s/]he actually belongs," the more must agitators promulgate a passive-masochistic attitude in the followers, which makes them surrender to the will of the leader to the expense of their own interests.[38]

For fascist propaganda techniques to work, the followers' attitude must be passive in the sense that they completely surrender to the leader's will and cease to see anything wrong with it and masochistic because such surrender is irreconcilable with their private and class interests. To explain how the fascist demagogue achieves such an attitude in his followers, Adorno provides a lengthy citation from *Group Psychology*, where Freud explains that the mass leader, akin to the hypnotist, awakens in the mass members their archaic inheritance, which makes them experience the leader as their dreaded primal father, to whose dangerous personality and will they must surrender.[39]

For Adorno, the artificial regression to the "primal horde" is central to understanding why followers surrender themselves to the will of the demagogue, even when this contradicts their private and class interests. Furthermore, Adorno points out that the fascist demagogue's creation of artificial regressions in his followers via his propaganda technique "*actually defines the nature and content of fascist propaganda. It is psychological* because of its irrational authoritarian aims which cannot be attained by means of rational convictions but only through skillful awakening of 'a portion of the subject's archaic inheritance.' "[40] Again, Adorno does not aim to suppress psychoanalytic theory as Gordon and Gandesha suggest.[41]

Instead, we need psychoanalytic theory to understand how fascist propaganda engenders regressions in followers of the far right, which makes them surrender to irrational authoritarian aims against their private and class interests. The same psychological mechanism that allows them to feel better about themselves via replacing their ego ideal with the idealized leader figure (the hypnotist) also triggers their regression to the "primal horde" (discussed in chapter 2), which generates their passive-masochistic attitude.

Adorno explains a core device through which the fascist agitator engenders the regression to the "primal horde," the "great little man" device, which, according to Adorno, Freud anticipates in his *Group Psychology*. Here the leader must appear in the contradictory images of the "great man" and the "little man." Adorno sums up this standard device in the following way: "While appearing as a superman, the leader must at the same time work the miracle of appearing as an average person, just as Hitler posed as a composite of King Kong and the suburban barber." He points out that the fascist agitator promulgates the psychological image as the "superman" through the enigmatic personalization of fascist propaganda. Instead of discussing objective issues in his speeches, he incessantly plugs names of supposedly "great men."[42] Adorno also draws on Freud's theory of narcissism to explain how the "great little man" device induces artificial regressions to the "primal horde" in the followers. He cites where Freud points out that when we are in love, a considerable amount of narcissistic libido overflows to the love object and that we only love it on account of the perfections that we had striven for in our ego (which Freud terms "narcissistic love").

The leader does not need to possess the perfections the followers seek to attain through him. Instead, by idealizing the leader, which happens through transferring their narcissistic libido to him, the leader *appears to possess* all the perfections they strive for themselves (but cannot obtain). Adorno explains that "it is precisely this idealization of himself which the fascist leader tries to promote in his followers, and which is helped by the *Führer* [leader] ideology."[43] The leader ideology promulgates the agitator as the "superman." Hence, the followers "fall in love" with him and can feel themselves via the idealized leader imago as "supermen" themselves.

Another way the agitator promotes the image of himself as the "superman" is by appearing as a "pure narcissist." Adorno points out that Freud's descriptions of the mass leader as a pure narcissist

fit the descriptions of Hitler no less than idealizations into which the American demagogues try to style themselves. In order to allow narcissistic identification [or, more precisely, introjection], the leader has to appear himself as absolutely narcissistic, and it is from this insight that Freud derives the portrait of the "primal father of the horde" which might as well be Hitler's.[44]

To engender a process by which the followers transfer their narcissistic libido to him, the demagogue presents himself as wholly narcissistic, as only loving himself, which is how the threatening primal father presented himself to the primal horde.

Adorno outlines that the agitator's attempt to promulgate of themselves the picture of the threatening primal father explains one of the most central features of the agitator's speeches, "namely the absence of a positive programme and of anything they might 'give,' as well as the paradoxical prevalence of threat and denial . . . the leader can be loved only if he himself does not love."[45] The prevalence of threat and denial in the agitators' speeches generates the followers' passive-masochistic attitude because it reanimates the image of the all-powerful primal father, to whose will the followers must submit.

At the same time, the leader must promulgate the image of himself as the "average person." Here, according to Adorno, Freud's theory of narcissism anticipates the fascist leader's startling symptoms of inferiority and his resemblance to ham actors and asocial psychopaths. "For the sake of those parts of the follower's narcissistic libido which have not been thrown into the leader image but remain attached to the follower's ego, the superman must still resemble the follower and appear as [their] 'enlargement.' "[46] In the next chapter, I will further discuss how Trump uses the "great little man" device in his response to the COVID-19 pandemic as a device to appeal to voters.

Adorno also hints at how socioeconomic conditions advance the idealization of the leader:

> The people he has to reckon with generally undergo the characteristic modern conflict between a strongly developed rational, self-preserving ego agency and the continuous failure to satisfy their ego demands. The conflict results in strong narcissistic impulses, which can be absorbed and satisfied only through idealization as the partial transfer of the narcissistic libido to the object.[47]

I understand the characteristic modern conflict between a rational ego and ego ideal demands to be a result of objective conditions of suffering in capitalism (the threat of declassing and the inability to up-class, job insecurity, exploitation, and alienation), which do not allow us to live up to capitalist standards of economic, interpersonal, and bodily "success." The conflict between the ego and the ego ideal produces strong narcissistic impulses, which means that our self-love suffers—we feel like failures and "nonwhole" as subjects. To get rid of such feelings, we transfer our disappointed narcissistic libido onto a leader figure, who, through internalization processes, makes us feel "whole" again.

Adorno also takes up another aspect of how, in the fascist mass, regressions to the primal horde occur. He draws on Freud to explain that the fascist mass is transformed into the coherence of the "brother horde" through the repression of primary envy. As Adorno puts it, "Their coherence is a reaction formation against their primary jealousy of each other, pressed into the service of group coherence."[48] Since members of the in-group identify with one another by loving the same object (the leader), they cannot admit their contempt for one another. However, their primary jealousy, which the mass members have repressed to secure the coherence of the mass, according to Adorno, reappears in fairy tales, where small animals such as bees and ants signify the brothers (and sisters) of the primal horde, and in daydream symbolism, where insects and vermin signify them. The fascist agitator makes use of the ambivalence toward the brothers (and sisters), and such ambivalence "is expressed by completely negative cathexis of these low animals, fused with hatred of the out-group, and projected upon the latter."[49]

The fascist agitator in his propaganda compares out-groups (foreigners, refugees, and Jews) with low animals and vermin.[50] In other words, he projects the in-group members' primary jealousy and hostility toward hated out-groups. Since the agitator provides them with a different target for hostility, they can now bond together in love. The following chapter will also outline how Trump uses this device to integrate the Trump mass.

Another critical point that Adorno brings up is that the traits that subjects display, once submerged in a fascist mass, are not contradictory to their normal rational behavior. Instead, as he points out, "What is peculiar to the masses is, according to Freud, not so much a new quality as the manifestation of old ones usually hidden."[51] Because in a fascist mass the followers can throw off the repressions of their unconscious drives (their libido and aggression), they display forms of behavior that are usually repressed. Here I would add that the throwing off of repressions also makes unconscious attitudes come to the surface—such as (colonial) hierarchical racial classifications, where whites consider themselves superior to those deemed racially inferior.

However, to grasp how the fascist mass turns into a violent mob, for example, against those classified as racially inferior, fascist propaganda techniques artificially engender a regression to the primal horde. Such regression generates in a fascist mass "the affinity of certain peculiarities of masses to archaic traits. Particular mention should be made here of the potential short-cut from violent emotions to violent actions." For Adorno, the prevalence of this archaic trait shows us that Freud's "assumption that the murder of the father of the primary horde is not imaginary but corresponds to prehistoric reality."[52] As I will show in the coming chapters, such "prehistoric reality" resurfaces in today's far-right masses, where a shortcut from violent emotions to violent actions (such as the attack of Trump supporters on Capitol Hill) remains a continuing threat.

Race in Adorno's Work on Fascism

Thinkers have critiqued the racial bias in Adorno's take on the culture industry in the U.S. context, particularly his views on jazz.[53] However, we find in his writings on fascism a more nuanced view of the category of "race." In this section, I will outline Adorno's view to provide a deeper insight into the functioning of fascist propaganda techniques.

To begin with, in "Freudian Theory," Adorno outlines how fascists used the pseudonatural category of "race" to integrate the fascist mass. Since the followers invest positive libido entirely in the image of the primal father (their leader), fascists needed to establish a negative integrating force. Since fascists do not recognize any spiritual criterion concerning who is chosen into and who is rejected from the fascist mass, "they substitute a pseudonatural criterion such as the race, which seems to be inescapable and can therefore be applied even more mercilessly than was the concept of heresy during the Middle Ages."[54]

For Adorno, "race" is not grounded in any nature. Fascist propaganda constructed this pseudonatural category as "natural" to negatively integrate the fascist mass. All those who were part of the "master humans" (*Herrenmenschen*), German whites, were the chosen ones. And all those classified as "racially inferior" or "subhuman" were rejected from the fascist mass. Such a trick, which dehumanized the prospective victim, generated moral disengagement in fascist followers and allowed the fascists to justify the violence the master humans had in store for those they classified as racially inferior. However, as Zoé Samudzi shows us, and what Adorno did not outline, is that the pseudonatural category of "race" was not a uniquely National Socialist German invention but was already employed by German colonialists to justify and naturalize colonial exploitation and their merciless violence toward colonized subjects.[55]

In his *Guilt and Defense*, Adorno examined the defensive reactions of postwar Germans when confronted with their feelings of guilt about the atrocities committed during the National Socialist past. He argues that given Germany's evading the past, aspects of fascist ideology such as racial classifications did not disappear but survived in postwar German democracy. For example, he found in the interview material residues of racial theories. These repeatedly resurfaced in his interviews, and according to Adorno, they underline the lasting success of the fascist propaganda trick of classifying Germans as the *Herrenmenschen*. As he puts it, "The Germans are still depicted by many as the community of a special king, as more human than other humans, a kind of order of the holy grail."[56]

In chapter 6, I will further detail how Austria's repressed guilt about their involvement in the administrative murder of millions of Jews, Roma, Sinti, and "other" people during the Nazi regime deemed as "inferior" contributes to a scenario where the *Herrenmenschen* ideology continues to live on in people's unconscious. The Austrian far right today exploits such unconscious racial attitudes.

Adorno also outlines how the discussants adapted fascist racial theories when discussing the changed political circumstances of the postwar era. For example, the discussants changed the term "race" into "culture" and "racial inferiority" into "racial foreignness." The discussants used such changed terminology to deny and downplay the hatred of those "races" they continue to consider inferior to themselves. As Adorno puts it here: "The ideology of race helps to deny the hatred and to downplay it into a mere awareness of difference, which is then nevertheless employed in the service of discrimination."[57]

He also outlines how postwar Germans used the pseudonatural category of race as a defense mechanism to keep feelings of guilt concerning their active or passive involvement in the murder of millions of Jews, as well as of Roma, Sinti, and others the National Socialists classified as subhuman, at bay.[58] Here Adorno encountered pathological forms of projection in the interview material, which implies the "obsessive transference of one's own inclinations and urges onto others, on the basis of which one assigns blame."[59]

The topic of lynching in the United States was at the top of the list of the discussant's pathological projections. The basic logic goes as follows: "You murdered Negroes, so you cannot reproach us for having murdered Jews, if not even: You actually showed us how."[60] Here the discussants project their urges to murder and their actual murder of Jews onto the United States' violent practice of lynching African Americans—now it is the United

States that becomes responsible for the National Socialist violence (since they showed them how to murder), and the discussants can evade their guilty conscience and responsibility.

On the other side of the continent, we encounter Adorno's view on race in his discussion of the (interconnection) between antisemitism and racism in his contributions to the AP study. For example, in his discussion of prejudice in the interview material, he points out that while the AP study grew out of specific investigations into antisemitism, they soon found the need to examine the relationship between antiminority prejudice to broader ideological and characterological patterns. Furthermore, antisemitism disappeared more and more from the interview material.[61]

A core thesis of the researchers was the "functional" character of antisemitism, which means that for prejudiced individuals it is accidental against whom they direct their prejudice. Thus antisemitism is not so much dependent "upon the nature of the object as upon psychological wants and needs [*Triebe*]" of the prejudiced subjects.[62] So the primary hostile reaction in prejudiced subjects is directed against foreigners per se, whom they perceive as "uncanny."

Adorno points out that this infantile fear of the strange is only subsequently "filled up" with the imagery of a specific stereotyped group that presents itself as handy for this purpose. While the Jews are favorite stand-ins for such infantile fear, "the transference of unconscious fears to the particular object, however, the latter being of a secondary nature only, always maintains as an aspect of accidentalness." Here the interviewees found numerous replacement objects for the Jews, such as Mexicans and Greeks, who are "liberally endowed with traits otherwise associated with the imaginary of the Jew."[63]

He explains the functional character of antisemitism with persecution mania, which has many structural features in common with antisemitism:

> While the paranoid is beset by an overall hatred, he nevertheless needs to "pick" his enemy, to molest certain individuals to draw his attention upon himself: he falls, as it were, negatively in love. Something similar may hold good for the potentially fascist character. As soon as he has achieved a specific and concrete counter-cathexis, he may "canalize" his otherwise free-floating aggressiveness[64] and then leave alone other potential objects of persecution.[65]

In chapter 7, I will further detail the persecution mania in the functional hatred of the "foreigner," as it appears in the writings of Martin Sellner, one the core leaders of the neofascist identitarian movement Austria (IBÖ). I will also show how Sellner's propaganda tactics aim to generate a regression of his followers into a sleep-and-dream state to manipulate them better.

Sleeping While Awake

In this section, I take Adorno in a direction he did not pursue. I show how fascist (and far-right) propaganda techniques engender a regression that put subjects into a sleep (and dream) state. In such a hypnotic state, the mass followers' unconscious dominates, and they are easier to manipulate. Furthermore, in a sleep state, resistances that keep aggressive and libidinal drives in check are weakened, which allows fascist mass leaders to redirect drives for their destructive aims. Suppose the fascist leader can keep his followers in a sleeplike state. In that case, he can get them to forget the world of the objective conditions of their suffering in capitalism, redirect their rage to "evil" outsiders, and get them to ignore that it is not in their best interest to live in an antagonistic society (that is, the one the fascists are creating).

Freud in *Group Psychology* outlines that the mass leader (akin to the hypnotist) awakens in his followers a portion of their archaic heritage, which makes them experience the leader as the threatening primal father. Such awakening generates a passive-masochistic attitude, which makes them submit to the will of the leader and causes them to act and think in ways that contradict their rational interests. Here Freud also tells us about the technique he uses. He points out that at the beginning of hypnosis, the hypnotist gives a "command to sleep," which implies "an order to withdraw all interest from the world and concentrate on the person of the hypnotist."[66]

Far-right propaganda uses the same technique—it puts people to sleep, so they withdraw their interest from the external world (and the objective conditions of suffering in capitalism) and place it onto the mass leader. Freud continues that "in this withdrawal of interest from the external world lies the psychological characteristic of sleep, and the kinship between sleep and the state of hypnosis is based on it."[67] In sleep and hypnosis, the subject withdraws their attention from the external world, leading to a scenario where the unconscious predominates over the conscious attitude. For this to happen, the hypnotist (the mass leader) avoids directing the subject's conscious thoughts toward his intentions and instead tells the subject "now concern yourself exclusively with my person; the rest of the world is quite uninteresting." The hypnotist (or the mass leader) directs the subject toward his person rather than toward his intentions because the latter would "tear the subject away from his[/her] unconscious attitude and stimulate him [/her] to conscious opposition."[68] To induce regressions in his followers, which generate their passive-masochistic attitude, the hypnotist (the mass leader) must ensure that the unconscious attitude predominates in his followers. He must avoid the stimulation of any conscious opposition to the leader's desires, plans, and projects.

The hypnotist (the mass leader) accomplishes the subject's withdrawal from the external world and onto his person by distracting the subject's attention. He makes the subject sink into an activity that makes the world around them seem uninteresting (such as listening to a monotonous sound). At the same time, "the subject is in reality unconsciously concentrating his[/her] whole attention upon the hypnotist, and is getting into an attitude of rapport, of transference on to him."[69]

Here the hypnotist steps into the parents' place, particularly the threatening father, and the subject transfers their feelings toward the father onto the hypnotist.[70] Through this "measure," the hypnotist activates in the subject a portion of their archaic heritage, "which made him compliant towards his parents."[71] This generates the subject's passive-masochistic attitude, which makes them submit to the hypnotist's (the mass leader's) will.

Freud further points out that "indirect methods of hypnotizing, like many of the technical procedures used in making jokes, have the effect of checking certain distributions of mental energies, which would interfere with the course of the events in the unconscious."[72] Today's far-right propaganda devices employ indirect methods of hypnosis that put their followers to sleep.

As I will show in chapter 5, the alt-right uses an indirect method of hypnosis through jokes. Such a method distracts its followers' attention from the existing objective conditions of suffering in capitalism and the irrational aims of this movement, which are irreconcilable with the followers' rational private and class interests. Since the unconscious attitude prevails, any conscious reflection and the possibility of opposition become difficult, if not impossible.

Adorno touches on the topic of sleep in his discussion of the "indefatigability device" in *The Psychological Technique of Martin Luther Thomas' Radio Addresses*. He points out that Thomas repeatedly tells his followers that he never sleeps but always works and sacrifices himself for the movement, incomparably more so than his followers. "The fascist hatred of sleep . . . is reflected by the fascist leader's emphasis upon his being indefatigable himself, therewith setting an example for his followers."[73] The important thing here is that the hatred of sleep and the agitator's call for the constant work and sacrifice of his followers do not aim to generate a conscious or awake attitude. Instead, it aims at the exact opposite—it aims to bring out an unconscious attitude while they are fully awake. This device is nothing else but an indirect method of distracting attention from the external world, which becomes evident in the highly ambivalent relationship between sleeping and indefatigability. The indefatigability device feeds upon this ambivalence. As Adorno puts it:

> Just because the follower is expected, in a way, to fall asleep and to act while he is asleep, he is told innumerable times that he has to be awake and that he must not sleep. . . . He who is asleep while he is told that he has to be indefatigable and that he is indefatigable, may offer much less resistance to the will of his leader than he otherwise would. He is made to believe himself vaccinated against the very contagion that threatens him.[74]

Telling the follower that they are fully awake and must not sleep distracts attention from the fact that they are, in reality, being asked to fall asleep. However, since they are told not to sleep and that they must constantly work, they falsely believe themself to be fully awake and conscious, and thus nobody can manipulate them—while the exact opposite is the case. Thus, the follower's unconscious (and irrational) attitude prevails in the sleeping state, which the fascist leader can manipulate for his aims.

Adorno further points out that under fascism, nobody is allowed to sleep. For him, "indefatigability is a psychological expression of totalitarianism. No rest should be given, unless everything is seized, grasped, organized. And since this aim will never be reached, the ceaseless efforts of every follower are needed."[75] Also, he points out that one of the favorite torture methods of authoritarian governments is to interrupt the sleep of their victims hourly until they entirely break down.

The fascist leader wants his followers to be active and ready to do things "but only under a kind of spell"—the spell of hypnosis. Adorno points out that the sociopolitical context of capitalism also contributes to generating subjects that engage in an activity of the hypnotized—the praise of indefatigability and the idea that one constantly needs to work is rooted in middle-class capitalist society. However, in fascism, indefatigability has become a fetish, and self-denial turns into an end rather than a means. For him, "This transformation is one of the deepest psychological changes that have taken place in our time."[76]

As outlined in chapter 1, the objective conditions of suffering, in particular, exploitation through the lengthening of the working day and the introduction of new technology (such as robots), refer to the changes in the sociopolitical conditions that made such deep psychological changes possible in our time. Being required to work and speed up one's work process constantly generates a mindset that can be easily captured by far-right propaganda devices that create subjects that sleep while they believe themselves to be fully awake.

It is no coincidence that Adorno comes back here to hypnosis. The indefatigability device distracts attention away from the external world—the objective conditions of suffering in capitalism—but it also provides a narcotic against the subjective forms of suffering generated by capitalism. While there is a highly "rational" element in fascism, insofar as the followers hope for material gains and improved social status, "so much may be safely said: It is the activity of the hypnotized which is expected by fascist propaganda rather than that of responsible and conscious individuals. Thus, the insistence upon indefatigability works as a kind of dope [narkotikum]."[77]

In "Freudian Theory," Adorno applies Freud's discussion on hypnosis to elaborate how fascist propaganda techniques function akin to hypnosis. Here the fascist leader turns into the hypnotist who steps into the ego ideal of his followers and thereby induces archaic regressions in them. "The techniques of the demagogue and the hypnotist coincide with the psychological mechanisms by which individuals are made to undergo the regressions which reduce them to mere members of a group."[78]

Such archaic regressions are central to cover over the contradictions between the irrational aims of the fascists and the rational interests of the followers. The relation of the hypnotist to his subject "defines the nature and content of fascist propaganda. It is psychological because of its irrational authoritarian aims which cannot be attained by means of rational convictions by only through skillful awakening of 'a portion of the subject's archaic inheritance.'"[79]

In *The Psychological Technique of Martin Luther Thomas' Radio Addresses*, Adorno further explains how the "hypnotic" and "rational" elements work together in fascism. Fascism aims to maintain an antagonistic society repressively. However, it is rational only regarding the interests of single groups or individuals, and there exists a discrepancy between the interests of other groups or individuals and the irrationality of the whole. Furthermore, the irrationality of the hidden final goals of the movement produces some sort of bad conscience within each fascist. Adorno points out that "here the hypnotic element comes into play. It helps to overcome the bad conscience. The fascist stops thinking, not because [s/]he is stupid and does not see [her/]his own interest, but he does not want to acknowledge the conflict between [her/]his particular interest and that of the whole."[80]

It is important to reiterate here that Adorno does not think that those who fall for fascist propaganda techniques are stupid or "irrational." Rather they do not want to acknowledge that there is a conflict between their rational interest and the irrational ultimate goals of the fascist movement, which also creates a bad conscience in them. Here the sleep state, which fascist propaganda techniques help engender, makes such conflict (almost) disappear. However, Adorno also points out that the individual fascist has to take measures to remain in such a sleep state, which is why hypnosis in fascism is, in the end, self-hypnosis.[81]

Self-hypnosis makes fascism (as well as the far right today) alluring because it allows followers to overcome their bad conscience and keep their eyes shut; it allows followers to remain in the dark about the salient contradiction between the interest of the whole and their particular interest.[82] Also, when we are asleep, the possibility of a dream enters, and such a dream makes a frustrating life seem "great again," which makes any contradiction vanish.

The Dream State

In this section, I show that far-right propaganda devices induce both a sleep and a dream state in order to capture followers.[83] Such a state allows the followers to cover over the objective conditions of suffering in capitalism and feel as "whole subjects" again. It is no coincidence, then, that when Freud discusses his theory of dreams, he comes back to the topic of sleep, hypnosis, as well as archaic regressions, which are all central elements of the psychological organization of the mass.[84] However, Freud never clarified the connection between the dream state and mass psychology.

In the *New Introductory Lectures*, Freud points at the course of events that engender dream formation. We encounter a wish to sleep and the intentional turning away from the external world, which has two consequences: First, it makes it possible for older methods of working in the mental apparatus, or "archaic regression," to emerge,[85] and second, the strength of repression is lowered, which makes dream formation possible.

Although the level of repression is lowered during sleep to form a dream, a portion remains intact, leading to dream censorship. Thus, resistance is a conflict between the unconscious repressed, which seeks expression, and the "conscious," which aims to prevent its expression. The manifest dream is a compromise between these two tendencies. It communicates what the unconscious wants to say, but only in the dream's distorted and unrecognizable form.[86]

Far-right propaganda techniques engender in the followers' psychological processes something akin to the course of events that engender dream formation: First, they induce a "sleep state" in their followers, turning their attention away from the very much external world. Second, such a turning away engenders archaic regression to an older form of psychology (the primal horde). Finally, a mass allows the followers to throw off the repressions of the unconscious drives, which makes dream formation possible.

Our sleep can be interrupted from three directions: by external stimuli during sleep; interests of the day, which we cannot break off when going to sleep; and repressed drives, which seek expression. Because the repressions are diminished when we sleep, there is a risk that the sleep is interrupted whenever an internal or external stimulus links up with an unconscious instinctual source. Here the dream has a double function: It gets rid of stimuli, which interfere with our sleep, and it allows repressed drives to obtain satisfaction "in the form of the hallucinated fulfillment of a wish" and thereby assures the continuation of sleep.[87]

Through dream-work, the "Oh! If only . . ." is replaced by "It is," and the "It is" is then given a hallucinatory representation. For Freud, in every dream, "an instinctual wish has to be represented as fulfilled." As Freud explains:

> The shutting off of mental life from reality at night and the regression to primitive mechanisms which this makes possible enable this wished-for instinctual satisfaction to be experienced in a hallucinatory manner as occurring in the present. As a result of this same regression, ideas are transformed in the dream into visual pictures.[88]

Fascist propaganda techniques function akin to dream-work. They put the followers into a sleep state and shut them off from reality (the objective conditions of suffering in precarity capitalism) during the day while they are fully awake. Furthermore, as in dream-work, such shutting off enables a regression to the primal horde, making them experience the leader as the threatening primal father to whose will they must submit. The same regression allows them to satisfy their instinctual and other wishes through hallucinatory representation.

The double function of the dream is essential for fascist propaganda techniques: First, it allows the fascist leader to eliminate any external and internal stimuli that could interfere with the followers' sleep state. Any "waking up" could turn the followers' attention away from their unconscious attitude, which propaganda techniques exploit, and back to the external world. Such a turn could make the followers aware that their rational private and class interests contradict the irrational aims of their leader.

Second, the dream state is central for propaganda techniques because it allows the followers to satisfy their strong narcissistic impulses, resulting from not being able to live up economic, interpersonal, and bodily "success" standards, which make them feel nonwhole on a subjective level. Here, "Oh! If I could only have a meaningful job that pays my bills and provides satisfying relationships" turns into "I have a meaningful job and satisfying relationships!" It allows them to feel themselves "whole subjects" in the form of a "harmless hallucinatory experience."[89]

However, in fascism and the current far right, such hallucinatory experience is not that harmless. As Freud points out, the dream itself is a pathological product and is the first member of a class that includes hysterical symptoms, obsessions, and delusions. It is distinguished from the others only by its transitory nature and occurrence under conditions of everyday life.[90] Furthermore, dreaming involves a turning away from the external world, which is also a feature of psychosis. In psychosis, the turning away from the external world is brought about in two kinds of ways: "either by the unconscious repressed becoming excessively strong so that it overwhelms the conscious, which is attached to reality, or because reality has become so intolerably distressing that the threatened ego throws itself into the arms of the unconscious instinctual forces in a desperate revolt."[91]

The ways subjects turn away from reality in dreams differ from psychosis: "The harmless dream-psychosis is the result of a withdrawal from the external world, which is consciously willed and only temporary, and it disappears when the relations to the external world are resumed."[92] However, in fascism (or the far right today), followers do not consciously withdraw from the external world. Therefore, their dream state has more in common with psychosis than with "harmless dream-psychosis." Also, in fascism, the followers' withdrawal from the external world is not temporary but more permanent, as in psychosis. Furthermore, the withdrawal from reality does not disappear when the relations to the external world are resumed but remains intact while awake. The fascist leader does not want his followers to resume their relations to the external world because this could make them see the salient contradiction between their particular interest and the interest of the whole, or of the leader and movement.

In the current far right, we also encounter the two kinds of ways the turning away from reality happens in psychosis. First, as I will show in chapter 6, the Austrian Freedom Party's followers' turning away from reality is the result of the unconscious repressed, which has become "excessively strong so that it overwhelms the conscious, which is attached to reality."[93]

Austrians struggle with unconscious feelings of political guilt about Austria's Nazi past. These unconscious feelings of guilt are overwhelming because Austria has not or has only partly dealt with them. These feelings become excessively overwhelming when somebody tries to make them conscious. Austria's Freedom Party offers its followers a way to turn away from reality to suppress such feelings.

Second, far-right propaganda techniques utilize the second form of turning away from reality in psychosis, particularly in precarity capitalism. Objective conditions of suffering in capitalism have made a reality for most subjects intolerably distressing. Thus, it is no surprise that they are attracted to the fascist mass, where they can more permanently turn away from such reality. Moreover, it is attractive because it allows them to throw themselves "into the arms of the unconscious instinctual forces in a desperate revolt."[94]

The desperate revolt the followers engender is not the revolt that Marx had envisioned, a revolt that would change capitalism into a better society, where suffering would cease to exist for all classes. Instead, their revolt makes them experience a better society merely in a hallucinatory fashion. Such a revolt allows the followers to escape the intolerably painful reality of precarity capitalism without changing the objective conditions of suffering in capitalism that generated their distress.

Freud also points out that forming a dream is subject to the condition of censorship, which is exercised by the residue of the repression still in operation during sleep. During sleep, a part of the repression needed to hold the unconscious down can be lifted, and a dream can be formed. However, enough resistance from repression is retained even during sleep, leading to dream censorship.[95] Therefore, the task of the dream-work is to overcome the inhibition from censorship through dream distortion.

Displacement is one of the two principal means used for dream distortion. Here, dream thoughts are separated from the affects attached to them and then displaced onto something else. It also implies a shifting of accent. Something that may only have played a minor part in the dream thoughts may be pushed into the foreground as the main thing in the dream, while the essence or crux of the thoughts finds only passing representation, which makes the dream incomprehensible to the dreamer.[96]

Also, far-right propaganda techniques utilize displacement to capture followers in their dream-work. For example, the anger of the exploited becomes separated from their bourgeois exploiters and displaced onto objects of hatred (such as migrants). Here something that only played a minor or no part in their exploitation (migrants) is pushed to the foreground, and the essence (capitalist exploitation) is pushed to the background. Such dream distortion circumvents the inhibition from censorship.

However, there is something else that the far right uses in its dream distortion: It (the right) removes the superego from its function of censorship.[97] Since the superego ceases to operate through ego ideal replacement in fascist masses, any prevailing dream censorship caused by repression is further lifted. Thus, the followers can fully indulge in throwing themselves into their unconscious drives' arms and taking out their desire for cruel aggressiveness on the objects of hatred determined by their leader.

Conclusion: The Possibility of Resistance

Is there any hope that the hypnotized can wake from their dream about themselves? Adorno suggests here that "socialized hypnosis breeds within itself the forces which will do away with the spook of regression through remote control, and in the end awaken those who keep their eyes shut though they are no longer asleep."[98]

What forces within socialized hypnosis will achieve this? Adorno suggests a certain "phoniness" in the followers' enthusiastic identification (or, more precisely, introjection) with the leader. The followers are phony because "in the depth of their hearts," they do not wholly believe in their leader or that the Jews are the devil. As a result, they do not *really* identify themselves with the leader but merely *act out* their identification (or, more precisely, their introjection).[99]

Through performing their enthusiasm, the followers participate in their leader's performance. However, the phoniness of the fascist performance has real consequences. As Adorno puts it, "It is probably the suspicion of the fictitiousness of their own 'group psychology' which makes fascist crowds so merciless and unapproachable. If they would stop to reason for a second, the whole performance would go to pieces, and they would be left to panic."[100] In other words, the suspicion that it is all a performance makes the followers even more resistant to any challenges to their complete subordination to the agitator.

Again, Gordon suggests that Adorno's theorizing of the followers' "phoniness" shows us that Adorno disavowed Freudian psychoanalysis.[101] Instead, Adorno argues that "Freud came upon this element of 'phoniness' within an unexpected context, namely when he discussed hypnosis as a retrogression of individuals to the relation between primal horde and primal father." He cites where Freud points out that the hypnotized retain some knowledge that hypnosis is only a game and a deceptive renewal of the old impression of the primary horde.[102]

In today's fascist masses, argues Adorno, the fascist agitator's appropriation of mass psychology and the streamlining of their technique allow them to collectivize and institutionalize the hypnotic spell. However, such collectivization and institutionalization have increased the "phoniness" of the followers' enthusiastic introjection of the leader. The increase of phoniness of the fascist performance "may well terminate in sudden awareness of the untruth of the spell, and eventually in its collapse."[103]

However, Adorno does not further outline how such increased phoniness could generate the possibility for the hypnotized masses to become suddenly aware that they are under a hypnotic spell, which could then lead to the spell's collapse and generate a "waking up" from the sleep and dream state. I will take up this possibility in the conclusion.

CHAPTER IV

From Melancholia to Mania

The Rise of Trump

Those who become submerged in masses are not primitive [wo/men] but display primitive attitudes contradictory to their normal rational behavior.

—THEODOR W. ADORNO, "FREUDIAN THEORY
AND THE PATTERN OF FASCIST PROPAGANDA"

We need a strong leader to get back on track.

—A TRUMP FOLLOWER

In this chapter, I build upon the theoretical elaborations of the previous chapters. I show how the dialectics between the socioeconomic and the psychological led to Trump's rise. I explain that Trump's propaganda techniques are effective because they allow his followers to move from a state of melancholia into a state of mania, where they can get rid of their subjective feelings of suffering produced by precarity capitalism. At the same time, the objective conditions that generated such suffering remain intact.

To support my theoretical analysis, I draw on Arlie Russell Hochschild's in-depth interviews with members of the far-right Tea Party in Louisiana in her *Strangers in Their Own Land: Anger and Mourning on the American Right*. She conducted these interviews over several years, and they provide a rich and respectful account of the far right in the United States today.[1] Whereas Hochschild draws on sociology, here I argue that only an analysis that draws on Marxist and psychoanalytic theory allows us to understand the dialectics between the socioeconomic and the psychological that made people from all classes vote for Trump.

According to Hochschild, people in Louisiana did *not* join the Trump mass out of economic self-interest, as many liberals argued, but because of what she calls *emotional self-interest*. People in Louisiana voted for Trump because he was able to elicit in them an "ecstatic high," which released them from feeling like economic, cultural, demographic, and political "strangers in their own land." As Hochschild puts it, "while economic self-interest is never entirely absent, what I discovered was the profound importance of emotional self-interest—a giddy release from the feeling of being a stranger in one's own land."[2] I agree with Hochschild that economic self-interest was not at the center of the rise of Trump. However, I cannot entirely agree with her for two reasons.

First, Hochschild suggests that people in Louisiana joined the Trump mass because they had a *rational*, emotional self-interest—to do away with feelings of "being a stranger in their own land." However, far-right leaders do not exploit any rational interests, whether emotional or economic. Instead, their psychologically oriented propaganda tools must engender irrational, unconscious, and regressive processes in subjects to cover over the fact that the irrational goals of the far right *contradict* subjects' economic *and emotional* self-interests.

My theoretical framework explains how those who seem to be suffering the most and have the most reason to improve their situation enthusiastically support a leader who does not genuinely care about them and will only make matters worse. For example, it cannot be in the emotional and economic self-interest of people in Louisiana to support Trump, a leader who further entrenches socioeconomic conditions that castrate them on the economic, interpersonal, and bodily levels.

Second, Trump followers' search for an "ecstatic high" in the Trump mass is *not* disconnected from the economy, as Hochschild suggests. Trump was able to capture people in Louisiana because the "ecstatic high" released them on a subjective level from the objective conditions of suffering in capitalism and the effects on their subjectivity, which allowed them to feel "whole" on a subjective level even as the objective conditions that generated their suffering and heightened their feelings of nonwholeness remained intact. Scholars have outlined that Trump exploited the economic suffering caused by precarity capitalism in the United States, which affects workers on all levels of the work hierarchy (albeit to varying degrees), to gain support.[3]

Here it is important to reiterate that Trump did not have or need to have conscious insight into the propaganda techniques he used to attract followers. Instead, he unconsciously guessed the psychological wants and needs of those susceptible to his propaganda because he resembled them psychologically. He is distinguished from them not by some intrinsic superiority but by a capacity to express without inhibitions what lies dormant in his followers' unconscious, which his propaganda tools activated and then redirected toward his irrational goals.[4]

The chapter consists of four sections, excluding the introduction and conclusion. In "Precarity Capitalism," I outline the objective conditions that suffering people in Louisiana experience and what effects they have upon their subjectivity, which set the stage for the effectiveness of Trump's propaganda techniques. In "From Melancholia to Mania," I outline how precarity capitalism generates in people a melancholic state and explain how Trump's propaganda techniques assist his followers in moving from the melancholic state into a state of mania. In "Narcissistic Regressions," I explain the centrality of narcissism to explain the appeal of Trump. In "The Return of the Archaic," I outline Trump's techniques to induce regression to the "primal horde" in his followers. Finally, in the fifth section, "Trump: The 'Great Little Man,'" I outline the "great little man" propaganda device Trump used in his handling of the COVID-19 pandemic. In the conclusion, I give some suggestions on how we can counter the threat of a return of the Trump phenomenon.

Precarity Capitalism

Louisiana is one of the poorest states and the top producer of hazardous waste in the United States. Louisiana attracts oil and petrochemical plants because of low business taxes, cheap labor, and the absence of labor protections and environmental regulations. In Louisiana, precarity capitalism threatens workers on all levels of the work hierarchy (albeit to varying degrees) with castration on the economic, interpersonal, and bodily levels.

As an example, Lee Sherman, an eighty-two-year-old white U.S. male, did dangerous work in the Pittsburgh Plate Glass petrochemical plant for most of his life.[5] He was a pipefitter, installing and repairing pipes carrying lethal chemicals, and his bosses made him dump toxic waste into a nearby canal. Most of Sherman's coworkers died young because of the plant's low safety standards, which underlines how the plant disregarded physical and moral barriers to exploitation.[6]

At one point, Sherman barely escaped death when he was exposed to toxic chemicals during a hydrocarbon burn, which killed five of his coworkers. Although Sherman worked a hard, unpleasant, and dangerous job all of his life, working for the plant generated his "wholeness" as a proletarian male subject. For Sherman, "the workplace had been where he experienced his finest hour, had shown his great skill, his bravery, his endurance, his manhood."[7]

However, the quest of the vampire Capital to enliven itself ate holes into Sherman's proletarian male subjectivity. Having been exposed to toxic chemicals all of his life and after the hydrocarbon burn, he found himself castrated on the bodily level—he could not move his feet anymore and had to go on an eight-month medical leave. When he returned to the plant after the medical leave, the company fired him because it did not want to pay his medical disability.

After the plant had depleted his physical and mental energies (and used him to dump toxic waste), it considered Sherman too nothing but waste it could dump. The vampire Capital, which promised Sherman his "wholeness" as a proletarian man, castrated him on the bodily level (leading to his illness) and then on the economic level, after he lost his job. Moreover, since his job provided him with interpersonal connections, it castrated him also on the interpersonal level. In the end, Sherman held little value for the vampire Capital after it had depleted him of his physical and mental energies.

Those male workers subjectively identified with the middle class also face objective forms of suffering in capitalism that affect their subjectivity. For example, Mike Schaff worked in the oil industry to get himself through college. Later he trained himself as an "estimator," who calculates the size, strength, and the cost of materials needed to construct the large platforms that hold oil-drilling rigs in the Gulf of Mexico and the caverns that store vast quantities of chemicals and oils underground.[8]

In its quest to generate surplus value, the oil industry also disregarded physical and moral barriers to exploit those higher up in the work hierarchy. For example, Schaff likes spending time in nature, but he had no time to enjoy it during his working life for the oil industry. For the first five years in his job, he received only one week off per year, then two weeks for five years, and only after ten years three weeks (sick time and vacation combined). He had hoped to enjoy nature with his new wife and grand-children when he retired, but then the sinkhole came.

When the Houston-based drilling company Texas Brine disregarded safety regulations to drill underneath Bayou Corne, it pierced one of the caverns that Schaff had helped create, triggering one of worst environmental disasters in the United States: a giant sinkhole that swallowed homes, animals, and trees and left 350 members of Bayou Corne homeless.

Although the governor of Louisiana issued an evacuation order for all residents, Schaff refused to leave his disheveled house. Insofar as his house signifies for him that he has "made it" economically, the vampire Capital left Schaff castrated on the economic level. The vampire Capital castrated him also on the interpersonal level because the environmental disaster shattered and displaced the "warm, cooperative" community he had been a part of.[9]

He also feels depressed because his new wife moved out of the house, and his grandchildren are afraid to visit him because the methane gas still bubbling up from the sinkhole does not make it safe—the house might blow up if somebody lights a match. As a result, the threat of bodily castration confronts him daily. Furthermore, Schaff feels depressed because of something else—despite working hard all of his life and giving all of his physical and mental energies to the oil industry, he feels that the American Dream had still to some extent eluded him: "From a shotgun home on the Armelise sugarcane plantation to a college education, a professional career, and a home on Bayou Corne, Mike had done well, but he didn't seem sure it was well enough."[10]

The wealthy people that live nearby, whom he calls "millionaires," remind him of his castrated status as a male subject in the bourgeois class. For example, the wife of a retired Exxon engineer who lives on the other side of the highway, where the what he calls "fancy-dancy" houses are located, "let it slip out" that his house was substandard because the homeowners association allows trailers on house lots, which is not the case on her side of the highway.[11] Here, the devaluing gaze of one of the "real" members of the bourgeois class upon his house forced Schaff to question his belonging to the class he identifies with.

Marx made clear that, in order to make an end to the bloodsucking enterprise of the vampire Capital, which leaves workers on all levels of the work hierarchy economically, interpersonally, and physically castrated, a class must be formed "which has a universal character because its sufferings are universal . . . which cannot emancipate itself without emancipating itself from all the other spheres of society," which is for him the proletariat.[12]

Why did Sherman, Schaff, and other exploited workers in Louisiana's oil and petrochemical industry not form with other mentally and physically depleted workers a revolutionary proletariat to overthrow the vampire Capital to end their objective and subjective forms of suffering? Why did they, like more than half of the population of Louisiana, turn to the Tea Party and to Trump, parties and figures that protect industry and support governmental deregulations of all sorts?[13] Marx explains the overturning power of the money fetish and its effects upon subjectivity. "What money can buy, *I am*, the possessor of money," he explains. "The extent of the strength of money is my own strength."[14] Money allows subjects to cover over the holes in their subjectivities and their weaknesses. A nonwhole or castrated subject, if they possess money, like a mirage, appears as whole and strong.

Hochschild points out that in all of her conversations with members of the Tea Party in Louisiana, "the repeated term 'millionaire' floated around conversations like a ghost."[15] These repeated references to the signifier "millionaire," which results from the capitalist ideology of the American Dream, show that this ideology and its effects on subjects remain salient in the United States today. It also outlines that subjects who are in reality economically, interpersonally, and physically castrated or face the threat of castration are still thinking of themselves as always potentially becoming "whole" subjects—in precarity capitalism of the United States, this manifests through the fantasy of becoming millionaires (or billionaires).

Subjects in Louisiana also believe that with the help of industry they will become rich and "fill their holes": Hochschild points out that "the mention of Sasol [a giant corporation] was often accompanied by the word 'billion,' as in a $7 billion investment for the ethane cracker, a $14 billion investment for the gas-to-liquids plant."[16] Industry provides here subjects, who feel powerless, unimportant, and unable to live up to the American Dream, the illusion, via the money fetish and its association with industry, of feeling powerful, important, and successful.

Industry uses the culture industry to advance the illusion that it will make people rich. As an example, a video of a ceremony celebrating the expansion of Sasol, the South Africa–based petrochemical giant in Louisiana, promises that it will bring an industrial renaissance and "progress" to Louisiana, which would turn Louisiana, like a mirage, from being the poorest state to becoming the most prosperous.[17]

Insofar as the Tea Party supports industry against labor and environmental regulations, it is the chosen party for those who hope to reduce their castration anxieties on the economic level. Furthermore, the Tea Party allows its followers to attenuate their bodily and interpersonal castration anxieties and feel as "whole" and noncastrated proletarian and bourgeois *men*.

Far-right followers perceive the Tea Party as being on the side of "being manly" and as defending men against the "cultural erosion of manhood," while they perceive the federal government as "unmanly," or castrated. Sherman supports the Tea Party because it is on his side, the side of *the Cowboy*, which is one of the figures that dominate the Tea Party in Louisiana. The cowboy is brave and confirms his manhood in taking the risk of being exposed to toxic chemicals. Sherman calls those workers who take precautions and listen to dangers "sissies" or "castrated men." Any concern for the environment is for him a "soft and feminine issue."[18] Since the Tea Party is against the protection of labor and the environment, it confirms his status as a cowboy. Furthermore, it allows him to mitigate his castration anxieties on the economic, interpersonal, and physical levels and feel like a "whole" proletarian man again.

Schaff, subjectively identified with the bourgeois class, was, like Sherman, brought up to admire cowboys and not cry. But whenever he speaks about the environmental disaster, he has to fight back tears.[19] Schaff, is *the rebel*: he joined an environmental group that tells companies to fix what they have broken, but in doing so he has "rebelled" against the Tea Party on this issue of the environment and its association with not being manly.

However, Schaff supports the Tea Party because it stands for free-market capitalism and small government and against paying social security. If he did not have to pay into social security, he argues, he could have invested that money and "would be a billionaire by now."[20] The Tea Party has allowed him to attenuate his economic castration anxieties. It gave him the illusion that he would one day have a house on the right side of the highway and become a billionaire. He could then be a "whole" male, bourgeois subject.

Exploited workers in Louisiana believe that the money fetish will fill the holes they feel. The only way to get more money is through industry, which might give them a chance to become billionaires one day, a hope that sustains them through their suffering. Since they believe that industry will make them "whole" subjects again, they support far-right politicians, who support industry expansion, corporate tax breaks, and the lifting of labor and environmental laws.

They also think it is "manly" to take risks with toxic chemicals and "effeminate" and weak to be concerned about the environment. Their turn to the far right helps them attenuate their subjective feelings of suffering and quells their castration anxieties on the physical, interpersonal, and economic levels. However, it also distracts from the objective conditions of their suffering in precarity capitalism (exploitation, alienation, declassing, isolation) and the subjective forms of suffering such conditions engender.

Furthermore, it distracts from the fact that an increase in unrestricted industry will exploit them even more and not make them rich (it only makes the owners of the means of production rich). Despite the arrival of the oil industry and the "progress" it promised, Louisiana remains the second-poorest state in the United States, and the oil industry only generated a small number of jobs and only on the lower levels of the work hierarchy for Louisianans.[21]

Although industry promised them to become "whole" subjects again, it did the opposite. Industry left people in Louisiana economically, interpersonally, and physically castrated, which generated people's state of melancholia, which they expressed in feeling depressed. The situation was ripe for Trump, the idealized leader figure, to arrive on the stage.

From Melancholia to Mania

The Trump rally that I analyze in this section took place in Louisiana a day before the Louisiana presidential primary vote in 2016. Trump won 41 percent of the Louisiana Republican primary vote, beating his evangelical rival Ted Cruz.[22]

According to Hochschild, Trump managed to attract followers in Louisiana because the Trump crowd acts as a "great antidepressant. Like other leaders promising rescue, Trump evokes moral conscience. But what he gives participants, emotionally speaking, is an ecstatic high."[23] I agree with Hochschild that the Trump crowd, or more precisely Trump himself, serves as an "antidepressant" and that he elicits in his followers an "ecstatic high." However, Hochschild's lack of psychoanalytic background means that she misses that the basis of the depression is not mourning, which she also foregrounds in the subtitle of her book, but *melancholia*, which is generated through the *absence* of mourning for the losses people in Louisiana faced as a result of the bloodsucking enterprise of the vampire Capital—the loss of their health and limbs, jobs and income, homes, a clean environment, and community.

Furthermore, Hochschild's theoretical framework (primarily derived from Durkheim) does not quite allow her to explain how Trump evokes moral conscience in his followers and elicits an "emotional high" in them. I will show that Trump's propaganda tools engender in his followers' processes of ego ideal replacement, which allow them to move out of the melancholic state (the state of depression) and into the manic state, where they can feel like "whole," or noncastrated, subjects again.

Freud points out in "Mourning and Melancholia" that mourning is the reaction to an actual loss, such as the death of a beloved object. In contrast, melancholia is the reaction of a loss of a "more ideal kind," which means that the object has not perhaps actually died but has become lost *as an object of love.* In other cases, melancholia is the result of a loss that one has experienced, "but one cannot see clearly what has been lost."[24] While in mourning there is nothing unconscious about the lost object, melancholia is related to an *unconscious* loss of an object.

The losses people in Louisiana faced as a result of the bloodsucking enterprise of the vampire Capital are actual losses. Furthermore, they also faced losses of an ideal kind—the losses connected to not being able to live up to the ideals (or standards) of capitalist society—to have economic, interpersonal, and bodily "success." Both kinds of losses (the actual and the more ideal ones) generated a structure of melancholia.

The capitalist ideology of the American Dream, which people hope to achieve through industry (and politicians who support industry), contributed to imposing a structural amnesia around real and ideal people's losses, which did not allow them to pursue the work of mourning and instead generated a state of melancholia. Also the capitalist ideology that industry will bring "progress" to the people in Louisiana imposed structural amnesia around the losses of an ideal kind—that industry in fact does not enable them to live up to capitalist economic, interpersonal, and bodily success standards (or ideals) but instead castrates them on all three levels. Moreover, the ideology of "progress" prevented them from clearly seeing what was lost, which underlines that these losses remained *unconscious* and, as a result, could not be mourned.

Moreover, the industry and its supporters in Louisiana explicitly aimed to make people's actual losses unconscious. Hochschild points out that local and national political leaders, as well as Christian religious leaders who receive donations from industry, imposed a *structural amnesia* around the loss of a clean environment generated by toxic industrial pollution. Political and church leaders carefully avoided, in their speeches and on their websites, any mention of the environmental disasters.[25] As a result, Louisianans could not mourn the loss of a clean environment. However, Hochschild does not mention that such speeches also avoided mentioning other losses the industry's exploitation of people has generated—the loss of their health and limbs, jobs and income, homes, and community.

In addition, in the United States, the structure of melancholia is also generated through repressed memories of the nation's violent past. As Alyosha Goldstein points out, the United States' violent overseas colonial expansion coincided with the consolidation of its continental colonial control through military force and state-sanctioned and extralegal violence against the Indigenous population and Blacks.[26] Similarly, Alberto Toscano explains that we must establish a link between the normalized classed and racialized violence that accompanies liberal democracies (such as the anti-migrant militarization of the U.S. borders) and the emergence of explicitly fascistic movements and ideologies.[27] However, the United States as a nation and white subjects in particular have not mourned but instead repressed disturbing memories about their white ancestors' genocide inflicted on the Native American population and brutal enslavement of African Americans, contributing to their privileges.[28]

The work of mourning entails a process of grieving in which the ego, at great expense of time and energy, gradually withdraws all libido from the love object and transfers it to another one. When the work of mourning is completed, the mourner accepts that the loved object no longer exists in reality and resumes full relations with the external world.[29] Any ambivalent feelings toward the lost object can become integrated—one mourns the love for the lost object and celebrates its loss insofar as one also hated the love object.

In contrast, in melancholia, the subject does not give up the love relationship with the lost object. Instead of accepting that the lost object no longer exists, she narcissistically identifies with it and *incorporates* it into the ego. The incorporated object serves as a substitute for the lost object.[30]

When she cannot give up the love object and takes refuge in narcissistic identification with it, the subject cannot integrate any ambivalent feelings toward the lost love object, such as hate.

Instead, the subject turns feelings such as hate around upon herself. The melancholic person's reproaches against herself are actually reproaches against the lost loved object that have been shifted onto the subject's ego. Freud provides the example of a woman who loudly pities her husband for being bound to such a poor creature as herself but who is unconsciously accusing her husband of being a poor creature in some sense or other.[31]

The problem of melancholia is that it results in the subjects' loss of self-respect and self-esteem, losses absent in mourning. In melancholia, the loss of the object becomes transformed into a loss in the ego. It leads to "an impoverishment of his ego on a grand scale. . . . The patient represents (her/)his ego to us as worthless, incapable of any effort and morally despicable; (s/)he reproaches (her/)himself, vilifies (her/)himself and expects to be cast out and chastised."[32]

The structural amnesia imposed by capitalist ideologies, industries, and churches did not allow Louisianans (or other Americans) to mourn and accept their actual and ideal losses. Instead, they incorporated these lost objects and ideals into themselves, which allowed them to hold on to (and continue to love) them. As a result, they do not realize that these objects and ideals are lost or impossible to reach, and they keep on loving what is no longer possible or has never been possible.

In melancholia, people cannot integrate ambivalent feelings toward the lost objects and ideals. So instead they turn these feelings against their egos. Such ambivalent feelings are, for example, the result of the frustration and anger people in Louisiana feel because they have been working hard all their lives for industry, which has led to their overexhaustion and the loss of their health, homes, a clean environment, and community—and they still have not achieved the American Dream.

Since they could not mourn the lost ideal, they could not acknowledge and integrate these negative feelings. Instead, they expended their negative emotions (anger and frustration) on the incorporated object, which, now as part of their egos, is effectively an attack from within: "You are such a loser, worthless and despicable for not being (economically, interpersonally, and physically) successful." Instead of giving up on these ideals, by mourning their loss, they continue to hold onto them and so continue to feel bad about not realizing them. People in Louisiana represent their worthlessness through their feelings of being "cast out and chastised" and feeling economically, culturally, demographically, and politically "strangers in their own land."

How is the melancholic state connected to mass psychology? While Freud provides some hints to theorize that connection further, he did not embark on such an enterprise in his work, which I aim to pursue in the remainder of the chapter. For example, a brief passage in *Group Psychology* outlines the centrality of the oscillation between melancholia and mania for mass psychology.[33] Here Freud points out that the misery of melancholia is the *expression of a sharp conflict between the ego and the ego ideal*, which the manic state undoes. The misery of the melancholic "is the expression of a sharp conflict between the two agencies of his ego, a conflict in which the ideal, in an excess of sensitiveness, relentlessly exhibits its condemnation of the ego in delusions of inferiority and in self-depreciation." In contrast, in the manic state, "the ego and the ego ideal have fused together, so that the person, in a mood of triumph and self-satisfaction, disturbed by no self-criticism, can enjoy the abolition of his inhibitions, his feelings of consideration for others, and his self-reproaches."[34] Freud also uses the language of "triumph" when he outlines processes of ego ideal replacement in the mass, which underlines the connection between the melancholia/mania oscillation and the psychological mass.

People in the United States experience a sharp conflict between their ego and the ego ideal, that is, a state of melancholia, because instead of mourning ideal and actual losses in precarity capitalism, they have introjected these lost real and ideal love objects into themselves, which now relentlessly condemn their egos as worthless and as "nonwhole."

Ego ideal replacement with an idealized leader figure such as Trump allows them to move out of the melancholic state and into a manic state where all feelings of inferiority and self-depreciation vanish. Moreover, such a move generates in the followers a sense of "triumph" because, in the manic state, their egos can once again coincide with the ego ideal— they have fused and they can feel "great again" and "whole" on a subjective level although objectively nothing has changed in their lives.[35]

Christina Tarnopolsky, who draws on Freud's melancholia and mania complex to explain the rise of Trump, points out that neoliberal capitalism generated the ideal of economic "success" for people in the United States, which has become the ego ideal for Americans. However, large numbers of the United States' lower and middle classes, who suffer economically in capitalism, feel the loss of this ideal without mourning that loss.[36]

The inability to mourn that loss created a melancholic public with an extensive reserve of inward-directed aggression, which "could then be tapped into and re-directed outwards by Trump's own brand of the politics of demonization."[37] In mania, this aggression is freed up and can be redirected away from the person's ego and outward onto others in the form of aggression and hostility. One can expand on and deepen Tarnopolsky's analysis in several ways.

First, the ego ideal in the United States comprises economic "success" standards and interpersonal and bodily "success" standards. Since most people cannot live up to those standards and cannot mourn such lost ideals, they also become part of the public's melancholic structure, which the far-right leader can exploit for his gains. The far-right leader can continually exploit this melancholic structure because the manic state only temporarily alleviates the melancholy, and the far-right leader is not looking to help them mourn the lost ideals (and without mourning, the followers will only melancholically cling more tightly to those ideals).

Second, the movement out of melancholia into the manic state goes beyond the release of inward-bound aggression, as outlined by Tarnopolsky, although it does that too, which Freud expresses in the quotation just cited that the manic state generates an "abolition of (her/)his inhibitions, his feelings of consideration for others"[38] and allows the mass leader redirect the freed-up aggression toward his chosen foes and the libido toward himself.

However, the throwing off of instinctual and other repressions alone cannot explain the attraction the fascist mass holds for followers and the leader's ability to generate crowds bent on violent action. Something else happens in a fascist mass—agitators induce artificial regressions in their followers (through their propaganda techniques) into a sleep and dream state, in which the contradictions between Trump's regressive political goals and his followers' economic and other self-interests and objective forms of suffering in precarity capitalism magically vanish. Furthermore, such hypnotic state reactivates an archaic or "older form of psychology" in them, which the mass leader manipulates for his purposes.

Freud hints at such a regression in a passage where he explains that the melancholic state leads to people's loss in their ego and to "an impoverishment of his ego on a grand scale."[39] As you might recall from chapter 2, Freud also explains that in ego ideal replacement, where one introjects an object and replaces it with the ego ideal, the ego is not enriched, as in identification. Instead, the "ego is impoverished, it has surrendered itself to the object."[40]

Therefore, the movement out of the melancholic state and into mania through ego ideal replacement, which provides the followers with the illusion of "wholeness" on a subjective level, further impoverishes the followers' egos, which have already been impoverished on a "grand scale" in the melancholic state. For Adorno, subjects with impoverished egos anticipate the deindividualized social atoms that form fascist collectivities.[41] Consequently, such deindividualized subjects fully surrender themselves to the love object—the idealized leader—and willingly carry out his destructive goals, which contradict their rational economic and other self-interests and might even lead to their destruction.

Narcissistic Regressions

How does the mass leader engender a sleep state and dream state in his followers? At the beginning of a hypnosis, the mass leader/hypnotist asks the followers to go to sleep and transfer all attention from the world onto the person of himself.[42] He does so by letting his followers sink into an activity that makes the world around them appear as uninteresting to them, such as repeating the same slogans over and over again.

Such activity prevents the followers from directing their conscious thought toward the leader (which could break the hypnotic spell and wake them from their sleep). However, in reality, the followers' "feelings and thoughts are bent in the direction determined by the hypnotizer."[43] In the hypnotic state, the followers find themselves fascinated with their leader. For example, a man at the Trump rally, in a state of rapture, with arms uplifted, explains to those around him but to no one in particular, "To be in the presence of such a man!"

Adorno explains the techniques far-right leaders use to put people into a state of fascination with the leader: the mass leader puts a hypnotic spell on his followers by speaking incessantly to them, to "befool the others. . . . Language itself, devoid of its rational significance, functions in a magical way and furthers those archaic regressions which reduce individuals to members of crowds."[44] Trump speaks incessantly (both in person and online), and what he says in his speeches is devoid of any rational significance. For example, at the rally in Louisiana, he did not address any of the objective issues that the people in Louisiana and individuals in the crowd face—poverty, exploitation, unemployment, exposure to toxic waste, and the devastating losses caused by industrial pollution.

Instead we find the main technique of fascist propaganda: the incessant reiteration of a small handful of ideas.[45] Trump "befools" his followers by repeatedly and monotonously invoking in his speeches the ideas that he is a "great man" who, if (re)elected, will "make America great again" and that everybody who opposes him in any sense is a "loser." He reiterates these ideas with hats, posters, shirts, and boots that sport the same slogan and that most of his followers wear at his rallies. Through monotonously reiterating that he is a "great man," Trump promotes an idealization of himself, which instigates his followers to transfer their narcissistic libido upon him. The followers think that if their leader is a "great man" or a "whole" subject, they will become more like this if the leader is (re)elected. Certainly, Louisianans would instead feel "greater" than they currently feel in the melancholic state—depressed, helpless, and like "losers"—which helps explain Trump's appeal.

Once idealized as an incarnation of their ego ideal, the followers introject the idealized leader image into themselves, allowing them to replace their ego ideal with the idealized leader image, generating their common narcissistic love bond with the leader. Here Trump turns into the hypnotist who steps into the place of the ego ideal of each of his followers. Furthermore, through their shared love bond with the leader, the followers can now identify with one another, allowing them to repress their feelings of envy (since they love the same love object) and hatred toward one another.

Ego ideal replacement undoes the followers' sharp tension between the ego and the ego ideal, allowing them to move from the melancholic and into the manic state. The manic state and its effects on mass followers are crucial to understanding why Trump's followers support him despite the disaster of his first presidential term. In the manic state, the followers' feelings of failure and inferiority vanish, and they can, in a hallucinatory manner, feel that they are "whole" subjects on the economic, interpersonal, and bodily levels.

However, ego ideal replacement also induces a regression into a sleep state, which makes the followers turn their attention away from the external world and the objective conditions of suffering in precarity capitalism—and from the fact that the irrational aims of the leader (Trump) contradict their rational economic and other interests. Furthermore, the sleep state allows the followers to throw off the repressions of their unconscious drives, which makes dream formation (as a compromise between the unconscious repressed and the conscious, which seeks to prevent its expression) possible.

The dream state allows the mass leader (Trump) to eliminate any external stimuli that could engender the followers' "waking up" from their sleep state—such as "disturbing" intellectuals that critique capitalism and make the followers aware of the contradiction between the mass leader's aims and the followers' interests. Furthermore, the dream allows repressed drives to obtain satisfaction "in the form of the hallucinated fulfillment of a wish" and thereby assures the continuation of sleep.[46] In such a hypnotic state, the followers can, in a dreamlike, hallucinatory manner, feel as if they are now "whole" and "successful" on the economic, personal, and bodily levels. However, in the manic state the followers' unconscious attitude predominates, which the mass leader can manipulate for his sinister purposes.

Freud also points out that melancholia implies a regression into narcissism.[47] The melancholic state generates a basis for what Freud calls complete object love.[48] In complete object love, the followers choose or love a leader through whom they can love themselves again. As Freud points out, the mass leader "serves as a substitute for some unattained ego ideal of our own. We love it on account of the perfections which we have striven to reach for our own ego, and which we should now procure in this roundabout way as a means to satisfying our narcissism."[49]

Trump followers love Trump because he *appears* as a "whole subject" on the economic, interpersonal, and bodily levels, which they have striven to reach for their own egos and which they now aim to procure through introjecting Trump and replacing their ego ideal with him. However, the leader does not need to possess the perfections the mass followers seek to attain through him, because in complete object love, a considerable amount of narcissistic libido (or self-love) "overflows" to the love object. Here the followers aggrandize and exalt (or idealize) the leader and at the same time conceal any of his flaws.[50]

Furthermore, the narcissism of complete object love searches for a love object representing the second form of narcissism Freud outlines: "pure narcissism." Pure narcissism characterizes a subject who only loves herself, and with an intensity comparable to the love brought toward her from complete object love. The pure narcissist has no need for loving but only of being loved, and the one who fulfills this condition is the one who finds favor with her.[51]

While complete object love is characteristic for the mass followers, pure narcissism is characteristic for the mass leader. Trump is a paradigmatic example of a pure narcissist. He appears as absolutely narcissistic, as only loving himself and not anybody else, reiterating that he is a great man and that everybody else (including his followers) are "losers." He also presents himself as the ultimate "free man" who has no restrictions on his sexual or aggressive drives. Trump can say hateful things about women, Mexicans, people with disabilities, and anybody who opposes him, and he presumes there will be no real repercussions.

Trump's insistence on loyalty is another example of his pure narcissism. He requires that everyone serve him and only him, even over the law and doing the job they were hired to do. He expected loyalty from his attorneys general and cabinet members and fired them when they were disloyal. He expected from people that they would love him first and foremost, even if this meant that they would break laws for him (and he rewarded them for it). For example, he expected Mike Pence to break the law for him at the Capitol on the day of the insurrection.[52]

The completely narcissistic subject has a great attraction for people in Louisiana, who are in search of an object onto which they can transfer their renounced narcissistic libido. Trump's narratives about himself assist the followers in transferring their narcissistic libido to him. He portrays himself as a "winner" and a self-made millionaire who has achieved the American Dream; as such, he is a "whole man" on the economic level.[53] As a man who is married and has children, he represents the U.S. white, bourgeois, nuclear family ideal; as such, he is a "whole man" on the interpersonal level. Furthermore, his sexist treatment of women and remarks are "proof" that his male virility is intact, which produces the picture of him as a "whole man" on the bodily level. Through introjecting the idealized leader and replacing their ego ideal with the idealized "whole" leader, the followers can undo the sharp tension between their ego and their ego ideal and, via the internalized leader, feel as "whole" subjects again.

Another example of narcissistic love is an interview with a Trump supporter at a rally in Melbourne, Florida. The follower repeatedly outlines that he is "in love" with the leader, which he underlines by telling us that he salutes a cardboard standup of Trump every day.[54] This love for Trump is not of a mature kind. Instead, it is purely narcissistic, insofar as replacing his ego ideal with the idealized leader has assisted him in getting out of his melancholy state and into a manic one. That Trump represents this follower's ego ideal is evident in his follower's repeated statements that he thinks that "the president is great" and that Trump is a "winner." By internalizing Trump and making him part of himself, the follower has replaced his ego ideal with the idealized leader figure.

Trump assisted this subject's ego ideal replacement when he invited him to join him on stage, where Trump whispered in his ears that he (the follower) "is great." Ego ideal replacement silences the ego ideal, which in the melancholic state relentlessly attacks the followers' ego as a "loser" who is economically, interpersonally, and physically castrated. Instead, the follower can feel, via the idealized leader figure, like a "winner" or a "whole man," that is, a noncastrated subject.

In the manic state, the feelings of inferiority and self-deprecation that characterize the melancholic state turn into the opposite. As the Trump follower puts it, "I am doing fantastic; there are no words to describe it," implying that the follower can love himself again via the narcissistic love bond with the leader. Once the ego and the ego ideal have fused, which happens via the idealized leader, the follower's insignificant and downtrodden life, in a mood of triumph and self-satisfaction, turns into its opposite.

This example underlines the centrality of my theoretical framework to grasp the attraction and growth of the far right. Since entering the manic state, this person's life hasn't changed objectively, and we can see that this state functions as an opiate that makes the followers, via the idealized "whole" leader figure Trump, in a dreamlike manner, feel their lives have significantly changed for the better. In the manic state, through processes akin to dream-work, the Trump follower's wishes to live up to their ego ideal, the "Oh! If only were successful (on an economic, interpersonal and bodily level)" are replaced by "I *am* successful (on all these levels)." Here the "I am" is given a hallucinatory representation.[55] However, since the followers do eventually fall back into their melancholic state (when the effectiveness of the opiate diminishes), where they are again plagued with feelings of inferiority and failure, they keep returning to and supporting their leader to reenter the manic state—even if their leader, on an objective level, worsens their lives.

Here the follower's life becomes the center of attention, much like the leader's life, which the Trump follower underlines with the statement that he "got a lot of media attention." However, the problem is that once the ego and the ego ideal have fused, the superego's critical function and moral compass vanishes. Once the love object has been put in place of the ego ideal, "every command of the idolized object, the leader, becomes ipso facto just, lawful, and true."[56]

No matter what untruths Trump proclaims, the follower maintains that what Trump says "is the truth. It comes from his heart." Like the person in love, who is in a state of fascination with the love object, the Trump follower finds excuses for all the bleak imperfections of Trump and is ready, as he puts it, to challenge any "lies" spread about him. Here we can see that the problem of the hypnotic conditions in the mass is that "just as in dreams and in hypnosis, the reality of things falls into the background in comparison of the strength of wishful impulses with their affective cathexis."[57]

The wishful impulse to become a "whole" subject again leads to a scenario where the reality of the objective forms of suffering in capitalism, which caused the follower's castration and to which the mass leader, Trump, as a policy-enacting member of the exploiting class contributes, fall into the background, in comparison to getting rid of subjective feelings of suffering, and the hallucinatory fulfillment of being a "whole subject" again on the economic, interpersonal, and bodily levels.

However, a core problem is that the sleep state and dream state the mass leader elicits in his followers simultaneously brings archaic regressions to an earlier form of psychology—the psychology of the primal horde, in which the Trump supporters easily turn into a violent mob against those that Trump designates as his enemies.

The Return of the Archaic

Trump, through various techniques, induces in his followers' regressions where they experience the leader as their threatening primal father to whose will they must submit. For example, we find in Trump's speeches what Adorno calls the most salient features in fascist agitators' speeches, "namely the absence of a positive programme and of anything they might 'give,' as well as the paradoxical prevalence of threat and denial . . . the leader can be loved only if [s/]he [her/]himself does not love."[58]

Instead of any positive program of the Trump administration, we encounter the paradoxical prevalence of denial, such as his "promise" to get rid of government-funded health care and other social services—programs many of his followers rely on. In Trump's speeches, we also find the paradoxical prevalence of *threat*. At several speeches, Trump said about protestors that "I'd like to punch him in the face" and "Knock the crap out of him, would you? . . . I promise you I will pay for the legal fees. I promise. I promise."[59]

At a rally near the White House on January 6, 2021, before his supporters stormed the Capitol, he announced to a cheering crowd: "And we fight. We fight like hell. And if you don't fight like hell, you're not going to have a country anymore." However, behind the call to engage in violent action there lies something else—the threat that if you do not follow the directives of the strong father, you will end up on the receiving end of that very destruction. Trump, throughout his speech, insinuates what will happen to those who do not follow his directives and are "strong" like him. As he points out, "Let, let the weak ones get out. This is a time for strength."[60]

Through the prevalence of threat, Trump promulgates the omnipotent threatening and *unbridled* primal father figure who does and gets anything he wants. Such a promulgation advances the followers' regression to the primal horde and awakens a part of their repressed archaic heritage, making them experience the leader as their dreaded primal father, to whom they must submit. It also generates the followers' passive-masochistic attitude, where they accept the leader's irrational aims, which contradict their rational economic and emotional self-interests.

In Trump's call for violence in his speeches, we see a parallel to the technique of the fascist agitator whose core aim is to promote an atmosphere of irrational emotional aggressiveness to transform the followers into "crowds bent on violent action without any sensible political aim and to create the atmosphere of the pogrom."[61] Before Trump had even finished his speech at the rally near the White House, about eight thousand people started moving toward the Capitol, yelling, "We're storming the Capitol!" In their attack on Capitol Hill, his followers willingly carried out the violence their leader had been calling for.

To understand why Trump's followers turned into a violent mob, we must also consider that he integrated his followers negatively. Since there are few positive contents locatable in Trump's goals, and because his followers have invested their positive libido in the leader figure, Trump's propaganda technique also utilizes negative content to integrate his followers, which assists in creating a violent mob. As outlined in the previous chapters, hatred, or the aggressive drive, can operate in the same unifying way as the love bond between the mass leader and his followers.[62]

Trump repeatedly uses the "sheep and bucks" (good and evil) propaganda device, where his followers appear as "good" and "pure" and marginalized groups and anybody who opposes him as "evil." The "evil others" (the bucks), which are mostly immigrants and migrants (particularly, but not only, from Mexico), help negatively integrate the Trump mass (the sheep), who are now bound together in love because they can direct their aggressive drives onto those evil others.

Furthermore, the identification of the Trump followers with one another via the same love object, Trump, allows the followers to suppress their primary hostility and jealousy toward one another (for loving the same love object). However, there remain traces of ambivalence toward the brothers and sisters of the Trump horde, which, as Adorno outlines, survive in fairy tales and daydreams, where brothers and sisters appear as vermin and other "low animals." Here the fascist agitator Trump exploits such ambivalence in his propaganda, comparing out-groups with vermin and "low animals."[63]

For example, Trump equated migrants and refugees with vermin who will "pour into and infest our country," and he repeatedly argued that minority Congress members in "rat-infested places."[64] Here he attaches adverse affects to vermin and other "low animals" and fuses them with out-group hatred. Those inside the Trump mass can suppress their hostility toward one another by projecting it upon the dehumanized out-group.

Löwenthal and Guterman outline how the fascist agitator blurs the identity of various groups as one "criminal group" that engages in a conspiracy against him to channel the followers' feelings of malaise, which results from precarity capitalism, into violent actions. "By portraying the enemy as a criminal, a degenerate, a low animal, a bug, the agitator stirs deep layers of hatred and frustration in his listeners; their itch to violence becomes unbearable, and their hatred of the unspeakable enemy overflows. He steps into the muddy pool of the malaise in order to channelize it into a stream of hate."[65]

In Trump's speech before his followers attacked the Capitol, he stirred up deep layers of hatred and frustration in his followers by blurring the identity of various groups that are part of the supposed conspiracy against him into one giant "criminal enterprise." To construct his "criminal enterprise," Trump repeatedly reinvokes the figure of the "noncitizen" together with the figure of the "felon." He also suggests that noncitizens engaged in crimes as they voted despite being excluded from the voting process and that they were thus responsible for his electoral defeat. Since he dehumanizes noncitizens as "criminals," there ought to be no objection to unleashing one's desire for cruel aggressiveness onto them.

However, to understand how Trump's followers turned into a violent mob and why the itch of violence became unbearable, we need to return to the core elements of the melancholia/mania complex. The reason for this easy move to violent action is threefold: first, in mania, where the ego and the ego ideal have fused, also the superego, which monitors the ego to keep it in line with the ideal and keeps a check on the followers' desire for cruel aggressiveness, is abolished. Once the superego's functions cease to exist, the mass followers can "freely" take out their desire for cruel aggressiveness onto those the mass leader determines as targets of hatred. Second, the manic state, which induces a hypnotic sleep and dream state, not only distracts the followers' attention away from the destructive goals of the leader but also generates their regression to the primal horde, where we encounter a shortcut from violent emotion to violent action. Third, in mania, we encounter an impoverishment of the ego "on the grand scale," which makes the followers submit themselves to the destructive aims of the leader. Followers have an impoverished ego because they transfer their narcissistic libido (or self-love) to the leader, thereby loving themselves again through the internalized leader.

However, once the leader possesses his followers' self-love, he consumes their egos.[66] Followers with consumed egos fail to be critical of anything the leader does or asks them to do. As Freud puts it: "In the blindness of love remorselessness is carried to the pitch of crime."[67] As we can see with the Trump followers' attack on Capitol Hill, in their blindness of love for their leader, they uncritically did what he asked them to do—and carried their remorselessness to the pitch of crime.

Trump: The "Great Little Man"

> Psychological ambivalence helps to work a social miracle. The leader image
> gratifies the follower's twofold wish to submit to authority and to be the
> authority himself.
> —THEODOR W. ADORNO, "FREUDIAN THEORY AND THE PATTERN
> OF FASCIST PROPAGANDA"

Trump also uses to advance ego ideal replacement in his followers the "great
little man" device, another standard technique of fascist agitators. In the
Trump rally in Louisiana, Trump starts his speech by describing his ascent
to power, depicting himself as the idealized "powerful man." Shortly there-
after, he switches to the "We": "We're on the rise . . . America will be
dominant, proud, rich. I am just the messenger."[68] The move from the "I"
to the "We" invites his followers to introject him into themselves and
replace their ego ideal with him.

However, at the same time as Trump promotes of himself the image of
a "powerful man," he points out that he is "just the messenger" of the
"greatness" that is to come in America. The idea that he is just the messenger contradicts the leader's depiction of himself as the "great man" who
alone is capable of bringing such greatness about. Here Trump uses (quite
literally) the "messenger" device, which is part of a larger structure of the
"great little man" device of fascist propaganda.

Hitler used this device at the beginning of his rise to power with his
insistence that "I am merely the drummer" of the "greatness" that was to
come in the Nazi regime. Trump, while insinuating the image of himself
as a "powerful man" to generate an idealization of himself and advance
the followers' transfer of their narcissistic libido to him, must also, for the
sake of those narcissistic elements the followers have not transferred to the
"powerful man" leader image but remain attached to their ego, still appear
like a "little man."[69]

In the Louisiana rally, Trump promulgated a picture of himself as the
"powerful man" to instigate processes of ego ideal replacement. At the same
time, for those elements of narcissistic libido his followers retained, he offered
a picture of himself as just the opposite, as being as weak as his listeners. As
Adorno points out, the contemporary agitator, akin to fascist agitators before

him, "presents himself not only as their superior, as the strong man, but simultaneously as just the opposite. He is as weak as they are."[70]

Here the agitator is like the followers, "a son subject to paternal authority, dependent on and at the service of something bigger than himself." This "greater entity" is no longer the father but a collectivity of all of the sons, who are gathered around a collectivity whose power is supposed to provide psychological compensation for the weakness of each component. Here the fascist leader gains power and his authority, much like the followers, from "giving himself up" to the collectivity.[71]

Adorno points out that while patriarchal elements are still present in Stalin and Mussolini, they are somewhat absent in Hitler, who "represents much more the rebellious, neurotically weak son who succeeds just by his neurotic weakness, which enables him to submerge completely with his equals in the movement."[72] Trump does not lack patriarchal elements to create the "superman" image, which is salient in his repeated promulgation of himself as a powerful man and his openly derogatory views and treatment of women. However, his use of the messenger trick shows that he did not do away with the son aspect of fascist propaganda.

Löwenthal and Guterman argue, similarly to Adorno, that fascism is "a revolt of the 'brothers' against parental authority." The fascist agitator, by encouraging his followers to engage in violent acts, does not "appear in the role of the restraining or moralizing father but rather as the elder brother who leads the small-fry gang in its juvenile escapades."[73] We can read the attack on the Capitol as an example where the elder brother Trump led his gang into a juvenile escapade, which contained the revolt of the community of brothers (and sisters) against parental figures.

Trump also used the "great little man device" to handle the COVID-19 pandemic. First, he reinforced his fantasy image as the "strong superman" by showing that he was not afraid of the virus, which he reinforced by not wearing facemasks, holding rallies during the pandemic, and calling those who wear masks weak. The underlying message is that he does not need any protection against the virus because, as a "superman," he has a "virile and strong" (male) body, which he further supports through sexist remarks. His potential followers, particularly white men, who are threatened with castration anxiety, can attenuate their anxiety through ego ideal replacement, allowing them to feel like a phallic superman.

It is thus of no surprise then that men were less likely to wear a mask.[74] Wearing a mask, much like wearing protection against a toxic environment in the Louisiana factories, signifies in far-right rhetoric that you are weak, which diminishes your manhood/masculinity. If you do not wear a mask (or take any precautionary measures in the factory), then you are, like your leader, a "superman" with a strong, virile, male body.[75]

When Trump got infected with the virus, it seemed that the image of the "superman" also got tainted. As such, Trump did everything to project that he remained the "superman." For example, he returned home early from the hospital, tweeting, "Don't be afraid. You're going to beat it," and pointing out that he is a "young and healthy" man, which is why he beat the virus so easily.[76] He even made plans to stage his departure from the hospital: he wanted to emerge from the hospital looking frail but then pull open his shirt to reveal a Superman T-shirt underneath. Trump later dropped the idea, most likely at his advisors' insistence. Trump still managed to make a carefully orchestrated show of strength, however. Upon release from the hospital and arrival at the White House South Lawn, he took off his mask and saluted from the South Portico balcony while his helicopter took off.[77] However, Trump need not have been so worried about appearing weak.

The "great little man" device outlines that while the leader must appear as strong, he must at the same time appear as weak. As Adorno puts it: "While appearing as a superman, the leader must at the same time work the miracle of appearing as an average person, just as Hitler posed as a composite of King Kong and the suburban barber."[78] In Trump's Superman T-shirt idea, the "great little man" device is taken to quite literal extremes. As such, given what I am arguing about fascist propaganda techniques, the stunt might actually have been an effective way to strengthen his base. Nevertheless, even without such theatrics, Trump's "King Kong" fearlessness in the face of the virus was complemented by his "suburban barber" aspect, implied by the fact that he did indeed get infected with the virus and is thus weak just like his followers.[79]

The "great little man" device strengthened the libidinal ties with his followers. For example, Neil Melton, a construction worker from Kansas, pointed out that he likes to see the president project strength, such as when Trump took off his mask on the balcony.[80] Melton is "in love" with Trump because he projects strength. At the same time, he approves of the president because his candor about his experience with the virus showed that

"Hey, I am just like you." Here, this Trump follower clearly expresses that the leader must project the contradictory image of himself as a phallic superman *and* as an average, weak man, to allow the follower, who has retained some parts of his narcissistic libido attached to his ego, still to experience the president as an enlargement of himself.

Here Trump's leader image gratified Melton's twofold wish to submit to authority and to be the authority himself. However, the problem with this gratification is that such propaganda techniques also engender regressions in the followers, where their unconscious attitude predominates, which makes them heed the call of the "strong" primal father to attack all those he designates as "weak" with the community of brothers.

Conclusion

Adorno points out that today's socialization of hypnosis in propaganda techniques has contributed to the rise of fascist movements in the twentieth century. As he puts it, "the leader's appropriation of mass psychology, the streamlining of their technique, has enabled them to collectivize the hypnotic spell." Nonetheless, Adorno agrees with Freud's assertion that some knowledge that the hypnotic spell and the renewal of archaic impulses are deceptive may remain, which he perceives in the "phoniness" of enthusiastic identification (or, more precisely, introjection) with the leader.[81]

He further points out that this increase in phoniness "may well terminate in sudden awareness of the untruth of the spell, and eventually in its collapse."[82] The phoniness of the enthusiastic introjection of the leader is also apparent in the interview with the Trump follower who, when he tells us that he salutes a cardboard standup of Trump every day at the same time, lets out a laugh. This laugh suggests a slight crack in the façade of his hypnotic state, where he is, after all, aware that the Trump festival is all a game and that the leader, whom he so enthusiastically supports, merely deceives him about his "great" qualities as a leader.

Furthermore, when the interviewer asked him what Trump had said on stage, he slightly hesitated before answering, "You're great." In this slight moment of hesitation, the phoniness of Trump and his assertion that "he is doing fantastic" might become apparent, and there precisely is where the hypnotic spell could break. Today we must do everything to dispel the hypnotic spell the far-right casts on the masses worldwide.

Of course, for this to happen, we must also address objective economic factors. Improving those, in the long run, might make people less vulnerable to the kinds of psychological techniques I have addressed in this chapter. We must also challenge economic, interpersonal, and bodily "success" standards, as they create the conditions for ego ideal replacement. But in the short run, we need to hasten the undoing of this spell the masses are under. I will further detail how this could happen in the conclusion.

CHAPTER V

The Culture Industry of Jokes

The Recruitment Tactics of the Alt-Right

Moreover, one repeatedly hears: "It is just a joke." *It is not.*
— KARL FALLEND, *UNBEWUSSTE ZEITGESCHICHTE*

While there certainly exists potential susceptibility for fascism among the masses, it is equally certain that the manipulation of the unconscious . . . is indispensable for the actualization of this potential.
— THEODOR W. ADORNO, "FREUDIAN THEORY AND THE PATTERN OF FASCIST PROPAGANDA"

The "alt-right" (short for alternative right) is a growing, internet-focused, neofascist, antisemitic, anti-Muslim, and antifeminist movement. As a power-seeking movement, is *not* about "edgy" rebellion and fun transgression. Instead its goal is to turn the United States into a "white homeland" via the genocide of racial minorities. The alt-right also aims to reach such a goal with the assistance of essential identities, traditional gender roles, human inequality, and an aggressive "troll culture" of internet dialogue.

The alt-right considers race, gender, and other markers of difference (sexual orientation, national origin, and body type) as natural and aims only to secure equality for those natures it ranks as better and above other natures (white, straight, nondisabled males). It "critiques" capitalism for not being unequal enough and aims to change U.S. society into a society where inequality is explicitly endorsed. The alt-right originates from internet forums dedicated to gaming, animation, and popular culture, including 4chan and Reddit. Alt-right trolls join discussions at other message boards that are not geared toward a right-wing audience, which allows them to reach an audience that does not necessarily hold far-right views.

The alt-right conceptualizes the world in conspiracies.[1] For example, it suggests that white people in the United States face a "white genocide" and a global conspiracy to wipe out "Caucasian genetic stock." It constructs Jews and Muslims as key actors in the "Death of the West" and caricatures Jews as the "masterminds" and Muslims as the "invaders" who come to destroy white hegemony. This idea is also an old fascist tactic where the aggressor appears as the victim; this is called "role reversal" in the psychological literature. Instead of being the aggressor who aims to eliminate its declared enemies, the aggressor depicts itself as the victim of the same groups it aims to destroy. Furthermore, the alt-right invented the notion of "cultural Marxism" as an antisemitic conspiracy theory, which suggests that "cultural Marxists" (implying Frankfurt School critical theorists) mass indoctrinated "the West" to abandon its Western Christian heritage, which they now aim to reclaim.[2]

The alt-right defines itself as "white nationalist" and rejects the term "white supremacist" or "neofascist" to suggest that the primary motivator for its focus on creating a "white homeland" is white sovereignty as opposed to racial hatred. Furthermore, this self-definition aims to distance itself from earlier iterations of (neo)fascist movements in the United States.[3] However, the alt-right is not a new phenomenon. Instead, the alt-right refers to a resurgent racist movement in the United States that rebrands past neofascist movements.

While earlier racist movements in the United States such as the Ku Klux Klan appealed predominantly to a rural, working-class audience, the alt-right, for example, through hip suits-and-ties conferences and speaking engagements on college campuses, aims to appeal to a young, middle-class, and college-educated audience. However, earlier neofascist movements in the 1980s and 1990s in the United States already started rebranding themselves away from the perception of being youth street gangs that attracted a rural working-class audience by encouraging young recruits to wear suits and ties and attend college.[4]

The alt-right also aims to rebrand itself as a "lighthearted and fun movement" to mainstream its neofascist ideology and to appeal to a bourgeois audience. In this chapter, I show that it seeks to achieve such an aim through its internet culture industry of what Freud termed "tendentious" (racist and sexist) jokes. Literature on the alt-right has hinted at the alt-right's self-presentation as a lighthearted and fun movement to appeal to millennials.[5] However, none of the authors answered the following question: How does the alt-right culture industry of tendentious jokes turn into an effective technique to recruit alienated, predominantly young, white men to its destructive political goals?

So far, no work in political theory explains how the alt-right's culture industry of jokes turns into a technique to acquire new followers. One reason is that most political theorists have not yet engaged in an in-depth study of the alt-right.[6] Another reason is that political theorists have so far focused primarily on the use of humor and jokes for democratic political ends.[7] Therefore, they have missed the role of jokes to advance regressive political ends.[8] Furthermore, few thinkers currently draw on the insights of psychoanalytic theory and early Frankfurt School Critical Theory to explain the alt-right.[9]

This chapter is innovative because it theorizes the role of tendentious jokes in mass psychology. While Freud hinted at such a role in his *Group Psychology and the Analysis of the Ego*, he did not further theorize it. In this chapter, I will embark on such a project by combining Freud's theorizing of tendentious jokes in his *Jokes and Their Relation to the Unconscious* with his theorizing of mass psychology in his *Group Psychology*. Such a project will assist me in explaining how the alt-right uses tendentious jokes as a propaganda technique to recruit predominantly alienated white millennial men.

Freud makes an essential distinction between humor and jokes. While he sees a democratic function in humor, he also explains how jokes can be used for destructive political ends because of the centrality of the unconscious in the joking process and the tendentious joke's ability to instigate regressive processes in the joke's consumer.

In masses with a central leader figure (such as the Trump mass), the followers can undo the tension between their ego and ego ideal by internalizing the idealized leader figure and replacing their ego ideal with the leader figure. Further developing Freud's critical theorizing of jokes, I will show that tendentious jokes have a similar function—the pleasure generated by tendentious jokes allows the followers to undo the tension between the ego and the ego ideal and feel satisfied with themselves, that is, as "whole" subjects again.

My foregrounding of how alt-right tendentious jokes undo the followers' tension between their ego and ego ideal underlines how the psychological and the economic are mediated.[10] In precarity capitalism, it has become more and more difficult, if not impossible, for (bourgeois) young white men to live up to their ego ideal—which is the result of classed, raced, and gendered economic, interpersonal, and bodily "success" standards and which generates their feelings of castration anxiety and failure.[11] Tendentious jokes are a successful recruitment tool for far-right hate groups such as the alt-right because they offer their followers relief from these feelings of anxiety and failure, making them feel "whole" as a (bourgeois, male, white) subject again—even while the economic conditions that generated their castration anxieties and feelings of failure remain intact.

However, we must also consider the racist and sexist joke's culture and history in the United States when analyzing how alt-right tendentious jokes could become a successful recruitment tool. As the sociologist Raul Pérez points out, there is a long history of racist (and, I would add, sexist) jokes in the United States.[12] For example, in the pre–Civil War period, blackface minstrel shows were a prominent source of "fun" entertainment for whites in the United States. Here white performers painted their faces black (using burnt corks or greasepaint) to dehumanize African Americans by "comically" juxtaposing them as inferior against supposedly racially superior whites. The core aim of such "fun" was to unite whites across class and ethnic backgrounds and to reassure them that Blacks were inferior and content with slavery while desensitizing white audiences from the horror and brutality of slavery.

Blackface performances also rechanneled class conflict by instilling in working-class whites the illusion that although capitalism brutally exploits them and they remain poor, at least they were superior to enslaved Africans. Pérez underlines that racist jokes continue to serve today as a mechanism for fostering social cohesion among whites and to reinforce the colonial idea that whites are "naturally" superior. While during and after the civil rights movement overt displays of racism in public were no longer easily tolerated, racist jokes continued to circulate in mass-market joke books, on the internet, and in the criminal justice system, even in an ostensibly colorblind society. The core function is to cover over the continuing racist attitudes by suggesting that it is all "just a joke."[13]

In this chapter, I show how the entire spectrum of the alt-right uses tendentious jokes to recruit. I show that alt-right racist and sexist jokes induce in the followers a regression to a hypnotic sleep and dream state that allows them to feel "whole" again. Here the tendentious joke's reinforcement of the colonial idea that white men are naturally superior to minorities (and women) contributes to generating white men's feeling of "wholeness." At the same time, such jokes lift the inhibition of the followers' aggressive drives and their repression of hatred toward racial and sexual minorities and women, which reduces barriers to committing violence against them and allows the alt-right to redirect their followers' desire for cruel aggressiveness toward its targets of hatred.

I analyze jokes from Andrew Anglin's neo-Nazi guide for how to use jokes when writing internet-friendly articles for the *Daily Stormer*, a neo-Nazi website.[14] I also analyze jokes from Milo Yiannopoulos, a former *Breitbart* contributor who aims to make the alt-right acceptable to a mainstream audience. Finally, I also outline how Trump's use of tendentious jokes that target women and minorities connects alt-right recruitment tactics to Trumpism.

The chapter comprises five sections, excluding the introduction and the conclusion. In the first section, "(Dis)connections Between Humor and Jokes," I outline Freud's theory of jokes and highlight the difference he identifies between humor and jokes. In the second section, "Bribing with Jokes," I outline how tendentious jokes can make the person who listens to the joke an ally of the teller of the joke. In the third section, "Hostile Alt-Right Jokes," I explain how hostile alt-right jokes become a successful recruitment tool. In the fourth section, "Sexually Aggressive Alt-Right Jokes," I explain how sexist jokes become a recruitment method for young men anxious about masculinity. Finally, in the fifth section, "The Joking Connection Between Trump and the Alt-Right," I outline how tendentious jokes connect Trump to the alt-right. In the conclusion, based on my analysis, I provide some suggestions what we must do to counter the growth of the alt-right.

(Dis)connections Between Humor and Jokes

There are three theories of humor: the superiority theory, the incongruity theory, and the relief theory. The superiority theory, which dominated the philosophical tradition until the eighteenth century (represented by thinkers such as Plato, Aristotle, and Hobbes), suggests that we laugh from feelings of superiority over other people. The incongruity theory can be traced to Francis Hutcheson's *Reflections Upon Laughter* from 1750 and is also present in the works of Kant, Schopenhauer, and Kierkegaard. It suggests that humor is produced by the experience of a felt incongruity between what we know or expect and what takes place in the joke or jest. The relief theory emerged in the nineteenth century with the work of Herbert Spencer, who explains that laughter is a release of pent-up energy. Freud's 1905 book *Jokes and Their Relation to the Unconscious* has further developed the relief theory. There Freud argues that laughter draws upon the energy we would use to repress our libidinal and aggressive drives, creating pleasure in us.[15]

In *Jokes*, Freud also started to outline some of the (dis)connections between humor and jokes, which he further described in his later text "Humour."[16] While Freud theorized that humor concerns the id (the unconscious), the ego, and the superego, he theorized that jokes mainly concern the id, which also underlines the centrality of unconscious processes to the joking process. In this chapter, I develop the relationship of jokes to the id, ego, superego, and ego ideal, which I then use as a theoretical foundation to explain the recruitment tactics of the alt-right.

What is humor? In general, humor, which for Freud is a "rare and precious gift" to which only some people have access, generates pleasure in us. It can arise in a person who adopts a humorous attitude (the humorist), while a second person, the listener, also derives pleasure from it. Alternatively, it can occur between two people, where the humorist makes a third person (who does not participate) the object of a humorous attitude. For Freud, the "yield of humorous pleasure arises from an economy in expenditure upon feeling."[17]

Freud gives the example of a person led to the gallows on a Monday who exclaims: "Well, the week is beginning nicely." The second person, the listener, expects the person led to the gallows to produce a sign of an affect such as anger, complaint, pain, or fear and is prepared to produce the same affect in herself. However, this emotional expectancy is disappointed because the person does not express an affect but instead makes a jest. Here, "the expenditure on feeling that is economized turns into humorous pleasure in the listener."[18]

What processes happen in the humorist? First, when a person adopts a humorous attitude, she withdraws psychical energy from her ego and transposes it onto her superego.[19] The new distribution of energy allows the humorist to treat herself like a child while simultaneously playing the part of the superior adult toward it. As Freud puts it, the humorist behaves toward herself "as an adult does towards a child when [s/]he recognizes and smiles at the triviality of interests and sufferings which seem so great to it."[20]

The now inflated superego considers the ego as tiny and all of its interests trivial, allowing it to suppress the ego's possibilities of reacting to suffering. Freud conceptualizes the superego in general as a severe and punishing master over the ego. However, in the text on humor, the superego, for the first time in his works, "speaks kindly words and aims to comfort the intimidated ego: Look! Here is the world, which seems so dangerous! It is nothing but a game for children—just worth making a joke about!"[21]

The humorous person's ego does not let itself be affected by the traumas of the external world, such as the trauma of being led to the gallows. Instead, it vows that such traumas are no more than occasions for it to gain pleasure by making a jest or joke. So humor is "not resigned; it is rebellious. It signifies not only the triumph of the ego but also of the pleasure principle, which is able to assert itself against the unkindness of the real circumstances."[22]

What are, then, some of the differences between humor and jokes? The joke, like humor, generates pleasure in us and has something liberating about it. However, according to Freud, humor also has grandeur, which is lacking in jokes. The grandeur in humor implies "the victorious assertion of the ego's invulnerability. The ego refuses to be distressed by the provocations of reality, to let itself be compelled to suffer."[23]

In contrast, jokes only serve to obtain a yield of pleasure or to place the yield of pleasure obtained in the service of aggression, which is why humor for Freud possesses more dignity than jokes. There is also a difference in how much pleasure humor and jokes produce. In humor, the superego grants the ego a "small yield of pleasure" through repudiating reality and providing an illusion.[24] However, humorous pleasure does not reach the intensity of the pleasure and vast amount of laughter generated by jokes, although we value this less intense pleasure generated by humor more than the pleasure generated by jokes and feel it to be especially liberating and elevating (without knowing why).

Why can jokes produce vast amounts of pleasure in us? To begin with, Freud distinguishes between "innocent" and "tendentious" jokes. Whereas innocent jokes serve no particular aim, tendentious jokes can be either hostile jokes, which serve the purpose of aggressiveness, or obscene jokes, which I call here sexually aggressive jokes, which serve the purpose of exposure.[25] As I will show in the following sections, the alt-right uses both hostile jokes directed against minorities and sexually aggressive jokes directed against women to recruit followers.

Whereas the pleasurable effect in innocent jokes is moderate, tendentious jokes can yield vast amounts of pleasure and are more successful in provoking laughter than innocent jokes because they produce pleasure not only via the joke itself but *also* via their ability to lift repressions. A tendentious joke generates vast amounts of pleasure in us because it "reduces the inhibiting forces, criticism among them, and makes accessible sources of pleasure which were under the weight of suppression."[26]

Freud distinguishes between jests and jokes but points out no consistent line. The jest is part of an early stage of the joke. It generally begins with an attempt to derive pleasure from the unrestricted use of words and thoughts. Suppose our reason terminates this form of play by concluding that what is taking place is senseless or nonsensical. In that case, the developing joke remains at its nascent jest state. Next, the joke (still nontendentious) strengthens the jest against the challenge of reason's critical judgment. Finally, the tendentious joke combats suppression to lift internal inhibitions. "Reason, critical judgment, suppression—these are the forces it [the tendentious joke] fights in succession; it holds fast to the original sources of verbal pleasure and, from the stage of the jest onwards, opens new sources of pleasure for itself by lifting inhibitions."[27]

Freud bases the distinction between two kinds of tendentious jokes on what kinds of inhibitions they can lift. Hostile jokes temporarily lift the repression of hostility, and sexually aggressive jokes lift the repression of what he calls "undisguised sexuality." When relating *Jokes* to *Civilization and Its Discontents*, it becomes clear that tendentious jokes produce pleasure in us because they allow us to temporarily receive our aggressive impulses (via hostile jokes) and direct libidinal impulses (via sexually aggressive jokes), which we have repressed into our unconscious, into our ego; this generates vast amounts of pleasure in us.

Freud points out that over the course of civilization, we have had to repress our "undisguised sexuality." Sexually aggressive jokes "provide a means of undoing the renunciation and retrieving what was lost." Here a man develops a "hostile trend against that second person," a woman, because he feels that she has rejected his sexual advances, which left his libidinal impulses inhibited.[28] The man makes a joke, which takes the woman as the object of sexual aggressiveness. As the joke exposes and shames the woman, it allows the man to retrieve lost sexual pleasure.[29]

Similarly, since our childhood and the "childhood of human civilization," we have had to repress direct hostile impulses toward other people (our aggressive drive). Because we had to renounce hostility by deeds, we have developed a new technique of verbal invective, in which the hostile joke plays a central part. By exploiting something ridiculous in the declared "enemy," the hostile joke allows us to direct aggression, which we are not allowed to express openly, toward the enemy, which generates pleasure in us.

In *Civilization and Its Discontents,* Freud also points out that it is difficult for us to give up our desire for cruel aggressiveness because, in allowing the ego to fulfill its old wishes for omnipotence, the satisfaction of the aggressive drive is accompanied by a high degree of narcissistic enjoyment.[30] In *Jokes,* he further outlines the connection between the aggressive instinct that emerges from the unconscious in the ego via the tendentious joke and the pleasure it generates. Insofar as far-right propaganda techniques affect the lifting of the inhibitions of aggressive impulses in their followers, which the far right then redirects toward its targets of hatred, we can now see more clearly that they attract followers because of the gratifications they offer, in the form of the vast amounts of pleasure generated by being allowed to express one's desire for cruel aggressiveness.

Like in humorous pleasure, also in jokes "the yield of pleasure corresponds to the psychical expenditure that is saved."[31] In jokes, we need "psychical expenditure" for erecting and maintaining an inhibition of hostility (our aggressive impulses) or undisguised sexuality (our direct libidinal impulses). By lifting the inhibition, the joke saves us such psychical expenditure, which we then release in laughter.[32] Freud provides the example of an urge to insult a specific person, which is, however, vehemently opposed by feelings of propriety or aesthetic culture. As a result, the insult cannot take place. However, if we can construct a joke out of the words and thoughts used for the insult, then with the assistance of the pleasure from the joke, the joke can gain sufficient strength to overcome the internal obstacle, and the insult can take place.[33] The yield of pleasure from the joke corresponds to the saved psychical expenditure needed to maintain the inhibition to make the insult, which we release in the form of laughter.

Bribing with Jokes

Another main difference between humor and tendentious jokes is that the maker of the joke can make the third person, who listens to the joke, an ally to the hostile and sexual aggression by bribing her with a yield of pleasure generated by the joke. As Freud puts it, the tendentious joke "will further bribe the hearer with its yield of pleasure into taking sides with us without any very close investigation. . . . This is brought out with perfect aptitude in the common phrase 'die Lacher auf seine Seite ziehen [to bring the laughers over to our side].'"[34]

While humor only demands one person (the humorist, who does not even need anyone else around to adopt a humorous attitude), jokes require *three* people: the person who makes the joke, the person who is the object of hostile or sexual aggressiveness, and the third person, an outside person, to whom the first person communicates the joke and who is necessary to complete the joke.[35]

Concerning the hostile joke, "By making our enemy small, inferior, despicable or comic, we achieve in a roundabout way the enjoyment of overcoming [her/]him—to which the third person, who has made no efforts, bears witness by [her/]his laughter." Moreover, the first person bribes the third person to become an ally of the first person because the joke produces pleasure in the listener without much effort besides listening to the joke.[36]

The pleasure derived from the hostile joke "diverts our interest . . . completely from the question of whether or not an injustice has been done" to the object of the hostile joke. Furthermore, the hostile joke "upsets our critical judgment" and so overcomes objections to hostility. As a result, the person who listens to the joke takes sides with the one who tells the joke *without* any very close investigation of the hostility contained in the joke. As a result, the hostile joke turns "the hearer, who was indifferent, to begin with, into a co-hater and co-despiser, and creates for the enemy a host of opponents where at first there was only one."[37]

Sexually aggressive (or obscene) jokes overcome the inhibitions of shame and respectability by utilizing their bonus pleasure. They bribe the listener (the third person) with an effortless satisfaction of his libido to side with the maker of the joke. Besides the man, who makes the joke, and the woman, who is the object of sexual aggressiveness, the sexually aggressive joke also needs an outside person, the third person, to whom the joke is communicated, for its completion. The joke exposes the woman "before the third, who, as a listener, has now been bribed by the effortless satisfaction of his own libido."[38]

The alt-right uses both hostile jokes directed against minorities and sexually aggressive jokes directed against women to draw those that come across such jokes on the internet onto their side. Furthermore, followers are pulled onto the side of the maker of the joke not only because they allow the followers to retrieve sources of lost (aggressive and sexual) pleasure but *also* because they allow them to undo the tension between their ego and their ego ideal, and both processes allow them to counter the feelings of failure and the castration anxieties around their subjectivities in precarity capitalism.

Freud repeatedly hints at the role of the joke in the mass in *Group Psychology*, but he does not further theorize the connection. For example, he points out that jokes allow us to circumvent the resistances and receive what is repressed into our ego, which increases our pleasure.[39] However, because Freud does not theorize jokes concerning the ego and the superego—he cannot further explain why jokes allow us to temporarily receive our repressed impulses into our ego, a necessary step in determining the role of jokes in mass psychology, which I aim to pursue in this chapter. Tendentious jokes can lift repressions because through them the functions of the superego are temporarily *abrogated*. As a result, the joke becomes a voice within us that "rebels against the demands of morality," that is, the superego's demands.[40]

Furthermore, because jokes temporarily abrogate the functions of the superego, which is the agency in us that monitors the ego to keep it in line with the ego ideal, we can both undo the tension between the ego and the ego ideal and temporarily receive repressed aggressive and libidinal impulses in our ego. Insofar as the superego is "the vehicle of the ego ideal by which the ego measures itself, which it emulates, and whose demand for ever greater perfection it strives to fulfill,"[41] the abrogation of the superego in tendentious jokes allows us to temporarily undo the split between the ego and the ego ideal, which generates a temporary relief from the demands of the ego ideal upon the ego, and this generates a cheerful mood in us because we are no longer plagued with the feelings of failure and castration anxiety generated by the objective conditions of suffering in precarity capitalism.

However, the superego is also the mental structure that keeps our libidinal and aggressive impulses, which lie dormant and are ready to be activated in the unconscious, in check. Because jokes temporarily abrogate the superego, *unconscious* processes predominate in the first (the teller) and third (the listener) person, which far-right forces manipulate for their destructive purposes. To underline the connection between (tendentious) jokes and the unconscious, Freud discusses jokes concerning topics where the unconscious becomes salient, including dreams and hypnotic states. Furthermore, a core difference between humor and jokes is that while Freud locates humor in the preconscious, he locates jokes in the *unconscious*.

Moreover, a joke is formed in the first person when she "drops a train of thought for a moment and that it then suddenly emerges from the unconscious as a joke." When the thought is plunged into the unconscious, a condensation of the thought takes place, which allows the maker of the joke to access childish sources of pleasure. While a joke is "the contribution made to the comic by the unconscious . . . humour would be the contribution made to the comic through the agency of the superego."[42] Jokes are the unconscious's contribution to the comic because jokes temporarily abrogate the superego, which allows us to temporarily receive aggressive and libidinal impulses in our ego and undo the tension between the ego and the ego ideal, which generates vast amounts of pleasure in us. In contrast, humor contributes to the comic via the agency of the superego because here the agency of the superego remains *intact* or perhaps alters slightly from its usual stern attitude to permit us small amounts of pleasure in the face of everyday suffering.

Furthermore, jokes engender regressive processes that put us into a hypnotic state, which underlines the centrality of jokes for far-right recruitment tactics. It is no coincidence that Freud returns to the theme of jokes in *Group Psychology* when he discusses the hypnotist's (the mass leader's) methods to manipulate his followers, which is based on his ability to distract the subject's (the potential follower's) attention away from the external world and the destructive aims of the leader, which contradicts the subject's rational economic and other self-interest, while entirely focusing her attention on the hypnotist. Such a method generates the follower's sleep and dream state, allowing the hypnotist (the leader) to manipulate the follower for his purposes.[43]

In *Group Psychology*, Freud points out that the method of making jokes is also based on distracting attention. As he put it, the "indirect methods of hypnotizing, like many of the technical procedures used in making jokes, have the effect of checking certain distributions of mental energies, which would interfere with the course of the events in the unconscious." In *Jokes and Their Relation to the Unconscious*, it becomes clear what Freud means here. Tendentious jokes must distract the hearer's attention (the third person, the potential far-right follower) away from the joking process so that the liberation and discharge of her repressed aggressive and libidinal impulses (which generate vast amounts of pleasure in her) can happen without interruption.[44]

To not awaken any attention in the third person, the tendentious joke must not arouse any conscious thought or intellectual interest, which can happen through several means. For example, the joke must be easy to understand and be kept as short as possible so "as to offer fewer points of attack to the attention." The joke can also put forward something in the joke's expression that catches the hearer or makes her fill the gaps in the joke to withdraw the joking process from the third person's attention.[45]

Once a hostile or sexually aggressive thought is wrapped in a joke, our attention is distracted away from the joking process, and we unconsciously entirely focus our attention on the joke thought. Because the yield of pleasure derived from the tendentious joke confuses our powers of criticism, we think it is the joke *thought* that gave us pleasure rather than the *form* of the joke, which, through the method of distracting attention, generates pleasure in us because it allows us to receive repressed aggressive and libidinal impulses in our ego. As a result, we misjudge that there is anything wrong with the content of the joke ("it is just a joke").[46]

As a result of distracting attention away from the joking process, we never exactly know what we are laughing about when we listen to a joke.[47] So jokes, akin to hypnoses, distract the third person's (the potential far-right follower's) attention away from the external world and conscious thinking (and with that, from the destructive aims of the movement that contradict her rational economic and other self-interests) and put her into a sleep and dream state in which her unconscious predominates. Alt-right recruitment tactics aim to generate such an unconscious state in its followers to manipulate them to support the movement's destructive aims.

Moreover, tendentious jokes establish a disposition unfavorable to criticism in the third person (the potential alt-right follower). Such a disposition, together with the fact that jokes engender regressive processes in us, ones in which our unconscious attitude predominates and the checks on our aggression are loosened (through the abrogation of the superego), creates a worrisome scenario where the third person, who listens to the joke, not only becomes an ally of the maker of the joke but can now easily be manipulated to take out their aggression onto alt-right targets of hatred.

Here it is important to note that Freud also places humor near regressive processes, which start with neurosis, culminate in madness, and include "intoxication, self-absorption, and ecstasy," because in humor the ego rejects the claims of reality through the triumph of the pleasure principle.[48] However, the humorist avoids crossing the boundary to regressive processes because in humor the superego functions remain intact or are only slightly altered.

In contrast, tendentious jokes make the third person *cross the boundary* to regressive processes because, here, the functions of her superego are temporarily abrogated. As a result, unconscious processes dominate in the hearer of the joke. Furthermore, tendentious jokes engender a hypnotic state in the hearer of the joke, which allows her to undo the sharp tension between her ego and her ego ideal, a tension generated by her inability to live up to the economic, interpersonal, and bodily "success" standards of precarity capitalism. As a result of such an undoing, the hearer of the joke finds herself in an ecstatic, self-absorbed (or fully narcissistic), and intoxicated state in which she experiences herself in a dreamlike hallucinatory manner as a "whole" subject again.

Wendy Brown draws on Marcuse's notion of "repressive desublimation" to explain the appeal of the alt-right, and her reading bears some parallels with Freud's critical theorizing of tendentious jokes. Repressive desublimation is the "nonliberatory release of instinctual energies in postwar capitalism."[49] Here the instinctual energies (the libidinal drives) no longer require repression and sublimation. Instead, they are now co-opted by and for capitalist production and marketing. Repressive desublimation offers a reprieve from the censorship of the superego and so gives rise to a "happy consciousness," which, however, easily aligns itself with the regime. Once pleasure and especially sexuality are everywhere incorporated into capitalist culture, pleasure becomes capital's tool to generate submission. Furthermore, when the subject is steeped in capitalist pleasure, her comprehension declines, and she becomes manipulable by the far right. In addition, a less strict superego makes one more relaxed regarding one's moral conduct, and social ills and wrongs are no longer registered as such.[50]

Tendentious alt-right jokes, insofar as they temporarily abrogate the demands of the superego, an abrogation that allows our libidinal and aggressive impulses to surface in our egos, contribute to repressive desublimation, which generates a "happy consciousness" in the followers, who no longer see anything wrong with the suffering caused by precarity capitalism. Furthermore, as such jokes circulate via the internet's culture industry, they are part of capitalist production and marketing that aims to generate subjects' submission.

However, Freud's critical theorizing of jokes shows that such "happy consciousness" is generated not only by releasing our libido, as Brown (via Marcuse) suggests, but also by releasing our desire for cruel aggressiveness. Furthermore, although Brown points out that repressive desublimation leads to new forms of violence by opening the spigot for the aggressive drive,[51] such violence is not only engendered by the lifting of inhibitions that makes the aggressive drive surface, as Brown suggests. Instead, the far right can engender such violence because the culture industry of jokes generates a hypnotic regression to a sleep and dream state, which reactivates archaic impulses in followers that can produce a shortcut from violent emotions to violent actions.

Hostile Alt-Right Jokes

The more profoundly society fails to deliver the reconciliation that the bourgeois spirit promised as the enlightenment of myth, the more irresistibly humor [or, more precisely, jokes] is pulled down into the netherworld, and laughter, once the image of humanness, becomes a regression to inhumanity.
—THEODOR W. ADORNO, "IS ART LIGHTHEARTED?"

The Southern Poverty Law Center counted over one hundred people killed or injured by perpetrators influenced by the alt-right in the period from 2014 to 2018.[52] As an example, after James Harris Jackson stabbed a Black homeless person with a sword in New York City, police found that he followed on his social media account people like Richard Spencer, the "father" of the alt-right, and the alt-right provocateur RamZPaul, who is best known for his joking YouTube videos and stand-up routines.[53] Are these actions all just jokes?

In this section, I outline how hostile alt-right jokes against minorities can turn into an effective recruitment method and instigate potential followers to take out their aggressive impulses onto objects of alt-right hatred. As an example, the alt-right stages frequent hostile jokes about the Holocaust. Whereas earlier white supremacist movements in the United States argued that the Holocaust never happened, the current alt-right treats it as a joke. For example, in response to an online article about a university contest for Holocaust art, alt-right trolls immediately posted absurd comments about their supposed family's experiences in concentration camps in the article's comment section, which treated the experiences of Holocaust survivors as a joke. One such joke reads: "All six of my grandmothers were survivors. They avoided being gassed by playing alto saxophone and electric piano solos for the guards while hiding in a pile of rubble."[54] The young white men who come across this hostile joke on the internet (often by accident) might initially harbor no *conscious* hostility toward Jews. However, the hostile joke bribes them with a yield of pleasure from this nonsensical joke and the lifting of inhibitions of hostility against Jews, which they have repressed in their unconscious, to take sides with the alt-right against the object of hostile aggression.

Since the pleasure derived from the hostile joke diverts their "interest so completely from the question of whether or not an injustice has been done" to the object of the joke,[55] the potential followers are bribed to take sides with the alt-right against the object of the hostile joke (Holocaust victims and survivors) *without* any particularly close investigation of the antisemitic content of the joke itself and the aggression it contains toward Jews. Furthermore, once it has made the potential followers laugh, a disposition most unfavorable for criticism will have been established in them.

As a result, the hostile alt-right joke creates "for the enemy a host of opponents where at first there was only one," which is particularly relevant for alt-right jokes that can reach large audiences through social media. How can hostile alt-right jokes instigate the followers to carry out acts of violence against targets of alt-right hatred? Tendentious jokes are "governed by two endeavors: to avoid criticism and to find a substitute for the mood."[56] Hostile alt-right jokes can make supporters and "co-haters" out of young white men because they allow them to recover the cheerful mood of childhood, where they are not plagued by the ego ideal's demands of adult male, white, bourgeois life.

Such a cheerful mood is the result of both the hostile joke's lifting of the inhibition of aggression and its undoing of the sharp tension between their ego and their ego ideal. The undoing of that tension allows them in a dreamlike fashion to feel like "whole" subjects (economically, interpersonally, and physically "successful") again, which allows them to get rid of the nagging feelings of failure and inferiority caused by their inability to live up to the standards of "success" in capitalism. While tendentious jokes instigate in the followers regressive processes, which allow them to feel "whole" on a subjective level and satisfied with themselves again, the same processes also open a space in which the followers can take out their aggression onto alt-right objects of hatred.

Tendentious alt-right jokes can instigate in the followers' acts of violence because they affect a regression to an "older form of psychology," the psychology of the primal horde, which is characterized by a shortcut from violent emotions to violent actions.[57] Alt-right jokes achieve such a regression in their followers by distracting attention away from the external world and the conscious joke thought, which puts the followers into a hypnotic sleep and dream state, where they can be better manipulated to carry out the alt-right's destructive political aims.

For example, in an alt-right internet meme, a Black man is depicted as a sad-looking "Pepe the frog," the alt-right's adopted mascot, stating, "You will always be a [n-word]."[58] This meme both expresses an open hostility toward Black men while also downplaying this hostility by wrapping it in a joke. This meme is kept short and is easy to understand. There are no subtleties to arouse any intellectual interest and distract attention away from the conscious joke thought, which uses racist language and images to perpetuate stereotypes about and hatred toward Black men.

Those white young men who harbor feelings of failure and inferiority because of their inability to live up to economic, interpersonal, and bodily "success" standards of precarity capitalism and who come across this hostile joke on the internet initially might not harbor any *conscious* hatred toward Black men. However, such hatred, together with racial schemes in which whites appear as "naturally" superior to Blacks (which white Europeans introduced in the United States to justify the colonial violence and exploitation toward enslaved Africans and the indigenous population), has been repressed but continues to slumber in their unconscious. The hostile joke bribes them to take sides with the maker of the joke (the alt-right). It turns them into co-haters of Black men by lifting the inhibition of aggressive impulses toward Black men, which permits them to temporarily receive such impulses in their egos, which generates vast amounts of pleasure in them.

Furthermore, the hostile joke, because it temporarily abrogates their superego (which lifts the inhibition of aggressive impulses toward Black men, which they have harbored in their unconscious), also allows them to undo the split between their ego and their ego ideal, which allows them to feel satisfied with themselves again and get rid of feelings of failure and frustration. Once their ego ideal coincides with their egos again, they can experience themselves in a dreamlike manner as "whole subjects."

The hostile joke thought assists such feelings of "wholeness" through creating an opposition between the sad Black man, who will never "make it" (who will always be nonwhole) and the happy white men (alt-right supporters), who now feel economically, interpersonally, and physically "successful." Here the hostile joke also brings back to consciousness racial schemes of the supposed natural superiority of whites and the inferiority of Blacks, which the followers have suppressed in their unconscious.

However, the abrogation of the superego in hostile jokes also creates a scenario where the followers' checks on their aggression are weakened, leaving them dominated by unconscious, archaic impulses. As a result, they are more likely to carry out open acts of violence against the alt-right's targets of hatred, such as the example of James Harris Jackson. After consuming the alt-right's culture industry of hostile jokes that target minorities, he stabbed a Black homeless person with a sword in New York City. The alt-right culture industry is, then, not at all innocent.

Another example of the alt-right's "fun" culture industry is Anglin's writing guide for the neo-Nazi website *Daily Stormer*. He demands from his contributors that "the tone of the site should be light" because a "light tone" helps attract new members to the alt-right.[59] More specifically, he points out that

> it should always be considered that the target audience is people who are just becoming aware of this type of thinking. The goal is to continually repeat the same points, over and over and over and over again. The reader is at first drawn in by curiosity or the naughty humor, and is slowly awakened to reality by repeatedly reading the same

points. We are able to keep these points fresh by applying them to current events.[60]

Anglin draws here on the main ingredient of fascist propaganda techniques—the incessant reiteration of a scarcity of ideas.[61] He adds to this technique by using tendentious hostile and sexually aggressive jokes, which he calls here "naughty humor." However, it is not so much the use of humor, as he claims, that allows him to recruit frustrated young white men to the alt-right. Instead, his use of tendentious jokes targets minorities and women, which allows him to pull such men, who come across his jokes on the internet (often by accident), to the alt-right's regressive political ideas. He confuses such jokes with humor.

Furthermore, Anglin's technique does not "awaken the readers to reality," as he claims. Instead, his propaganda techniques do the *exact opposite*—they distract the potential followers' attention *away from* reality, away from conscious reflection, and away from the fact that the alt-right's irrational goals contradict their rational interest. Anglin's advice to his contributors to monotonously repeat "the same [few] points, over and over and over and over again" is a method that puts them into a hypnotic state where the readers cease to see anything wrong with the alt-right's destructive political goals and are more likely to carry them out.

In addition, Anglin advises his contributors to use hostile jokes, which indirectly distract attention away from reality. Such jokes make allies out of those who consume his jokes by bribing them with a yield of pleasure and undoing the split between their ego and ego ideal. To promote this "naughty humor," Anglin provides his contributors with a list of "racial slurs" to use and adds that "while racial slurs are allowed/recommended, not every reference to non-white should not [*sic*] be a slur, and their use should be based on the tone of the article. Generally, when using racial slurs, it should come across as half-joking—like a racist joke that everyone laughs at because it's true. This follows the generally light tone of the site."[62]

The laughter the hostile alt-right jokes produce in the listener (Freud's "third person") is not so much because the hostile joke directed toward minorities has any truth content, as Anglin suggests. As Adorno points out, the "facts" presented by the culture industry must never be true. Instead, the culture industry's facts "tend towards deceit and . . . are merely an explosion of the untruth which already lies within the blindness of the facts themselves."[63] The hostile alt-right joke that targets minorities betrays any truth content and mainly serves to deceive the reading audience of the true state of affairs—that they are functioning as bribes of a yield of pleasure to lure the readers to become alt-right co-haters themselves.

Freud pointed out that a person's mental activity, particularly her imaginative or intellectual work, creates unfavorable conditions for gaining pleasure from tendentious jokes and allows us to counter their adverse effects.[64] Mental activity—or perhaps we could call it critical thinking—helps us become aware of the mechanisms of the joke, thereby interrupting the process that lifts the repressions of aggressive and libidinal impulses and generates pleasure in the maker of and listener to the joke.

Although Anglin is unaware of this psychological effect, he also discourages his potential followers' imaginative or intellectual work. "We are writing for the common man, so the language should be very simple, using a standard 8th grade vocabulary."[65] Here Anglin expresses not only the alt-right's contemptuous view of the "common man" he aims to recruit but also discourages in his potential followers engaging in any intellectual work themselves, which could create unfavorable conditions for the gaining of pleasure from alt-right hostile jokes. However, as products of the culture industry, he and his supporters are afflicted by the same infantile qualities he ascribes to his audience—his "writing guide" is full of grammatical and spelling errors.

Here is another hostile alt-right joke Anglin offers as an example to the contributors to his site. He tells his writers to "refer to Jewish journalists as 'ratlike Christ-killing terrorists.' And refer to teenagers who get arrested for racist Twitter posts as 'eternally noble warriors bravely fighting for divine war to protect the blood heritage of our sacred ancestors.' Flowery, cliched [sic], goofy prose is also highly encouraged." This hostile joke dehumanizes Jews by equating them with vermin and terrorists.[66] At the same time, it downplays such dehumanization by wrapping the hostile thought in "goofy prose."

The pleasure generated through the hostile joke allows the potential followers to feel better about themselves. The prose assists this process by generating an absolute opposition between Jews as bad and inferior and alt-right supporters as good and superior. At the same time, by abrogating the superego, the hostile joke allows the followers to temporarily receive their repressed aggressive impulses in their egos, which further enhances their pleasure. Furthermore, the hostile joke provides them with a target (Jews) upon whom to unleash their aggression, which the joke further assists through the dehumanization of Jews.

Although the alt-right portrays itself as atheist, the absolute good/evil opposition, as well as other terminology in this hostile joke, including "divine war," "blood heritage" (that is, the blood of the Christ), and "sacred ancestors" invoke Christian themes. As Adorno points out, today

> the highly rational, merciless, cynical, planning fascist, has little belief in Christ as in anything else, except power. But it is no less true that the anti-Semitic ideas which form the spearhead of fascism every-where could not possibly exercise such a strong appeal unless they had their strong sources, not only apart from, but also actually within Christian civilization.[67]

Fascism's source within Christianity expresses itself via the imagery of the Christ killers, the Pharisees, the moneychangers in the temple, and the Jew who forfeited salvation by not accepting baptism. Anglin's reference to the antisemitic stereotype as "Christ killers" in his depiction of Jewish journalists in this hostile joke "may reveal the specific, though partly unconscious historical memories which an anti-Semitic agitator calls back to life."[68] Anglin can bring such historical memories back to life because the antisemitic stereotype is wrapped in a hostile joke, which allows the followers to temporarily receive unconscious aggressive and libidinal impulses, including repressed Christian memories, in their egos.

The important point here is that the alt-right's culture industry of internet jokes, while claiming not "touch on anything serious," never-theless tends "to set patterns for the members of the audience without their being aware of it."[69] The alt-right's culture industry of hostile jokes sets up *patterns of violence* in its audience without them being aware of it. They engender regressive processes that allow them to see themselves as "whole white men" again. However, the same processes that allow them to feel better about themselves also allow them to receive aggressive impulses in their egos along with repressed racial schemes in which whites appear as "naturally" superior to minorities. Together with their regression to the psychology of the primal horde, such a scenario makes them more likely to take out their aggression onto the alt-right's targets of hatred.

Anglin actively encourages the taking out of violence onto targets of hatred through promoting guidelines on aggressive "troll methods," which involve a scenario where he encourages alt-right online trolls to "isolating and mass-assaulting" the alt-right's declared enemies. Furthermore, Anglin advises, "there should be a conscious agenda to *dehumanize* the enemy, to the point where people *are ready to laugh at their deaths.*"[70] So Anglin, by promoting "Lulz," which means *laughter at the expense of another,* aims to create an atmosphere of violent aggressiveness, which generates followers that are ready to murder alt-right enemies and laugh at their deaths. This, precisely, is the atmosphere of the pogrom.

As Anglin puts it, "It's illegal to promote violence on the internet. At the same time, it's totally important to normalize the acceptance of violence as an eventuality/inevitability . . . whenever someone does something violent, it should be made light of, laughed at."[71] Hostile and sexually aggressive alt-right jokes contribute to normalize the violent behavior the alt-right seeks to generate in its followers. The laughter that resounds in response to such jokes is nothing other than a regression to inhumanity.

Recently, observers of the alt-right have used the term "irony poisoning" to explain how alt-right humor desensitizes those that come across it on the internet. Irony poisoning implies that once a person has been exposed to or has shared enough ironic content online, the ironic joke becomes a belief. It also implies that online ironic memes have offline consequences, including that the person consuming ironic content, once desensitized, will then engage in violent acts toward alt-right targets of hatred.[72]

However, here Freud's distinction between irony and tendentious jokes helps us understand that "irony poisoning" is perhaps not the best way to explain why alt-right followers turn violent offline. The essence of irony, which is a subspecies of the comic, lies in saying the opposite of what one intends to convey to the other person but making the other person understand (such as by one's tone of voice or by some accompanying gesture) that one means the opposite of what one says.[73]

The core difference, as mentioned earlier, between irony and tendentious jokes is that while irony lies in the preconscious, tendentious (racist and sexist) jokes lie in the unconscious.[74] The (potential) violent behavior of alt-right followers results from *unconscious processes.* The tendentious joke temporarily lifts the inhibition of aggressive (and libidinal) impulses that lie dormant in the unconscious. Therefore, the follower, when consuming an alt-right joke, can receive such impulses temporarily in her conscious, which the alt-right can then redirect against its targets of hatred. Furthermore, tendentious jokes engender the follower's regression to a hypnotic state (and their wanting to remain in such a state, as it allows them to feel "whole" again), which can make them more prone to violence when offline, because in such a state their unconscious attitude predominates.

Also, alt-right jokes do not create racist and sexist beliefs, as the term "irony poisoning" suggests. Instead, such beliefs are already present in the potential follower's unconscious. Such beliefs date back to racist and sexist beliefs introduced by white Europeans, in which whites and men "naturally" appear superior to justify colonial exploitation and enslavement. Since whites have not worked through their violent past in the United States, such beliefs have been carried from generation to generation, and they remain in white people's unconscious until today. The tendentious joke's function is to lift a barrier to such beliefs, which allows them to surface from the unconscious to the conscious. Tendentious jokes also desensitize the maker and the consumer of jokes (after all, it is "just a joke"). Such desensitizing and moral disengagement in acting on existing beliefs happen gradually. While enjoying (or just smiling) at an alt-right joke might seem harmless, it paves the way for more hateful actions.

Sexually Aggressive Alt-Right Jokes

Patriarchal thinking and misogyny are central to the alt-right's brand of white supremacy. The alt-right is antifeminist, homophobic, and, particularly, transphobic. It portrays women as irrational, vindictive creatures who need men to rule over them and whom it aims to strip of any political role. The alt-right also declares that feminists threaten "white Western civilization," which shows how it includes feminists and women in its conspiracy framework. Here the alt-right projects its urges to destroy feminists and women onto its prospective victim so that the alt-right itself appears as the victim of the group it aims to destroy.

However, the alt-right also uses more subtle ways to recruit new followers. This section explains how sexually aggressive alt-right jokes that target women allow the alt-right to recruit white young men, who feel anxious about their masculinity, to its regressive political ideas and goals. Such anxieties refer also to economic but especially to interpersonal and bodily "success" standards, which demand from such men virility and sexual success with women, and which create castration anxieties on an interpersonal and bodily level.[75] These men's ego ideal is composed of such standards. Since they face challenges to live up to them, they feel a sharp tension between their ego and their ego ideal, with accompanying feelings of castration anxiety and failure. White male castration anxiety is salient in the alt-right's veneration of masculinity and its preoccupation with the idea of a thwarted or failed white Western masculinity.

Sexually aggressive alt-right jokes are a successful recruitment method because they provide these men with an easy yield of pleasure and allow them to satisfy their inhibited libidinal impulses. Furthermore, sexually aggressive jokes, much like hostile jokes, allow them to undo the sharp tension between their ego and their ego ideal, allowing them to feel in a dreamlike, hallucinatory manner, like "whole men" again and get rid of feelings of castration anxiety and failure around their white masculinity. At the same time, such jokes generate regressive processes in the men, making them express their sexual aggression on women through more direct violent means.

That misogyny is central to the alt-right's brand of white supremacy is also salient in Anglin's writing guide for the *Daily Stormer*. He provides his contributors not only with a series of misogynist terms to call women but also demands from them that "women should be attacked."[76] The alt-right attacks women through an aggressive online trolling of feminist writers and reporters, often using threats of sexual violence. As a result, many feminist blog writers and presenters have stopped writing altogether. It also attacks women by employing sexually aggressive jokes.

How can sexually aggressive jokes turn into a recruitment tool? Freud points out that the first person, a man, initially directs sexually exciting speech toward a woman to arouse a corresponding excitement via speech. If she reacts defensively, the man finds his "libidinal impulses inhibited by the woman." As a result, he develops hostility toward her. At this point, the sexually exciting speech becomes an aim in itself to shame and embarrass the woman in the shape of a sexually aggressive joke, and, as Freud points out, the "aggressiveness becomes positively hostile and cruel."[77]

In the alt-right, we find self-identified "beta males," who are ranked below "alpha males" because they lack the stereotypical heteronormative male qualities of self-assuredness and outgoingness. They develop a hostile trend toward women because they feel sexually rejected by them and, hiding in the anonymity of internet subcultures, blame women collectively for their lot.[78] To make them feel better about themselves and cope with their anxieties about their masculinities, they produce sexually aggressive jokes, which turn women into the object of their hostile and sexual aggressiveness.

At the same time, the sexually aggressive joke of the alt-right needs the third person, the listener, "in whom the joke's aim of producing pleasure is fulfilled," to complete the joke.[79] The third person is those young white men who come across sexually aggressive alt-right jokes on the internet (often by accident) and who feel anxious about their masculinity. Sexually aggressive jokes bribe them to become alt-right supporters by providing them with an easy yield of pleasure.

Let us, for example, take the sexually aggressive jokes of Milo Yiannopoulos, who made the alt-right attractive to a mainstream audience. His jokes, which go after women, feminists, the overweight, and transgender people, have earned him a fan audience and rave reviews from college students on his speaking tours across British and U.S. university campuses. Here is one of them:

> Radical feminism of course started in academia. Some would assume it is a type of brain cancer. But I've seen enough of universities to know we can conclusively say feminism is a bowel cancer. American college campuses have gone to shit. Smoking can take decades to give smokers lung cancer. But college can give women the cancer of feminism as early as their first semester.[80]

The use of terminology such as "bowel" and "shit" in this sexually aggressive joke supports Freud's argument that the content of sexually aggressive jokes is "what is excremental" and dates back to sexuality in childhood, where the sexual and the excremental are almost merged into a cloaca and barely distinguished.[81] The joke also contains the alt-right's belief that feminism threatens "white Western civilization." Here the alt-right's aggressive attack on feminists is reversed by depicting feminists as destroyers of college education and of young women. This hostile and cruel joke also exposes and shames the second person, who is the object of the sexual aggressiveness, the (feminist) woman, through associating her with bowel cancer and feces. The sexually aggressive joke, like all tendentious jokes, needs a third person, the listener, for its completion and to generate pleasure in both the teller and receiver of the joke.

Those young men on college campuses who listen to Yiannopoulos and feel rejected by women and anxious about their masculinity become that third person who completes the sexually aggressive joke through their laughter. To bribe them into becoming alt-right co-haters, Yiannopoulos employs the joke technique of an allusion, which implies replacement by something remotely connected (feminists and bowel cancer), which generates pleasure in the hearer because "the hearer reconstructs [the allusion] in his imagination into a complete and straightforward obscenity."[82]

However, for the joke technique to be effective and for it to generate laughter in the audience, the sexually aggressive joke must not arouse any intellectual interest or mental activity, which would interrupt the lifting of the inhibition of libidinal and aggressive impulses in the unconscious and its discharge into the followers' ego, which happens through the methods of distracting attention away from the joking process. Yiannopoulos also creates sexually aggressive jokes that distract attention from the joking process by being kept short and easy to understand. For example, he developed a "quiz" on Twitter that asked his followers if they would prefer (a) feminism or (b) cancer. He also created the slogan "Feminism Is Cancer," which became available as a line of T-shirts.

The sexually aggressive joke pulls the laughing young white men to the side of the alt-right because it temporarily undoes their superegos, which keeps a check on their repressed libidinal and aggressive impulses. This generates a scenario where their repressions are temporarily lifted and they can temporarily receive libidinal and aggressive impulses in their egos, which allows them to retrieve lost sexual pleasure. As Freud puts it: "Through the first person's smutty speech the woman is exposed before the third, who, as a listener, has now been bribed by the effortless satisfaction of his own libido."[83]

The joke also bribes young white men into becoming alt-right co-haters by allowing them to bring (via the abrogation of the superego) their repressed hatred toward women and sexist gender schemes, in which women appear as naturally inferior to men, into consciousness and to temporarily undo the tension between their ego and their ego ideal.

The problem with the sexually aggressive joke, like with the hostile joke, is, however, that the potential followers are no longer inclined to find anything wrong with the joke that has given them an easy yield of pleasure and allows them to feel satisfied with themselves. However, it also instigates regressive processes that open a space for them to take out their (sexual) aggression on women beyond the joke.[84]

Another sexually aggressive joke is the alt-right's "Cuckservative" meme. This sexist and racist meme refers to white conservative men whose wives supposedly seek out stronger Black men for sex. Richard Spencer, the alt-right's founder and the head of the white supremacist think tank known as the National Policy Institute (NPI), which lobbies for the alt-right and other white supremacist organizations and hosts regular meetings, explains that the alt-right uses the meme to call out traditional white conservative men for working against their white interests by not openly taking a stance against mass immigration.

The *Daily Shoah* invented the "Cuckservative" meme, which helped develop the alt-right's joking style. This alt-right online platform worked an antisemitic joke right into its name, and it mixes audio skits, parody songs, and interviews with fast-paced, jokey conversations laden with racial slurs, antifeminism, and antisemitism. Most importantly, its popularity, which has overtaken the NPI as the main "gathering" forum for the alt-right, has led to dozens of similar podcasts and "has defined some of the largest growth for the alt-right."[85] So, what are the deeper mechanisms that provoke sexually aggressive alt-right jokes to expand the alt-right's base?

For example, in the literal translation of "Cuckservative," which implies that conservative men's wives seek out stronger Black men for sex, the joke does not generate any laughter. Instead, the sexually aggressive joke uses the technique of "condensation accompanied by the formation of a substitute."[86] It abbreviates "cuckold" (a man whose wife cheats on him) and "conservative," then fuses them through an element in both terms that are alike—"cuck" (which also refers to a weak man) and "con." Here the formation of the substitute is the making of a composite word.

This play on words is part of the process used in sexually aggressive jokes. Just as in tendentious jokes, where condensation is a core joking technique to distract attention away from the joking process, in dream-work, dream thoughts are transformed into the manifest dream through condensation, which allows the sleep to remain uninterrupted. Furthermore, akin to dream-work, Freud also outlines the idea of "joke-work," which implies a choice of verbal materials and conceptual situations in the joke that allow "the old play with words and thoughts to withstand the scrutiny of criticism," so that the liberation and discharge of libidinal and aggressive impulses remain uninterrupted.[87]

The alt-right employs the joke's technique of condensation and the formation of a substitute in the "Cuckservative" meme to withstand the scrutiny of criticism to allow young white males who feel sexually rejected by women and are anxious about their masculinity to satisfy their inhibited libido and prop up their masculinity by denigrating and sexualizing women and Black men. At the same time, by ridiculing "sexually weak" white men, the joke exacerbates anxieties about heteronormative white masculinity and effectively contributes to disciplining young men into such masculinity.[88]

However, the abrogation of the superego in the sexually aggressive joke not only allows the potential followers to temporarily receive their libidinal and aggressive impulses in their egos, which generates their pleasure and allows them to undo the tension between their egos and ego ideals, but also creates a scenario where the followers' checks on their (sexual) aggression are weakened and where unconscious, archaic impulses can become dominant. Furthermore, the same regressive processes, which allow them to feel like "whole" men again, also create a regression to the psychology of the primal horde, where the "brother horde" willingly takes out its aggressive impulses on the targets of alt-right hatred: women.

For example, Elliot Rodger, a self-identified "beta male" and frequent contributor to the misogynist Manosphere (which has crossovers with the alt-right), drove to a University of California–Santa Barbara sorority house, planning to massacre the women whom he felt had sexually rejected him. He shot random people outside when he could not get in, killing six and wounding a dozen others before committing suicide.[89] He left us with a 137-page manifesto, "Elliot Rodger's Retribution," which he uploaded on YouTube minutes before the shooting: "You girls have never been attracted to me. I don't know why you girls are not attracted to me, but I will punish you all for it. . . . On the day of retribution, I am going to enter the hottest sorority house at UCSB and I will slaughter every single spoiled, stuck-up, blond [s.] I see inside there."[90]

Members of the Manosphere and alt-right defended the act, which underlines that they are not "lone wolf" acts but occur in the context of the far right. In such acts of terror, the alt-right's "fun" culture industry of sexually aggressive jokes plays a core role; these jokes allow them to recruit new followers and instigate their followers to carry out violent actions against targets of hatred. Given that these jokes can lead to such events in real life, it becomes apparent that we need to understand how sexually aggressive and hostile jokes affect the psyche and the acting out of alienated young white men.

The Joking Connection Between Trump and the Alt-Right

What are the connections between Trump and the alt-right? Hawley argues that Trump, his followers, and mainstream Republicans ought not to be confused with the alt-right and that Trump is not a neo-Nazi.[91] Although I grant that Trump fully aligns neither with the alt-right nor with fascism, these arguments should not obscure that his coming to power presented this movement with a window to make the alt-right acceptable to a mainstream audience.[92] As Shane Burley points out: "In the political sense, populism is the force by which hard fascist ideologues gain traction to move their political voice onto the national stage."[93] Furthermore, John Abromeit points out (via Adorno) that Trump has converted "genuine conservatives" into "pseudo-conservatives" in the United States, which are subjects who, in the name of upholding traditional U.S. values and institutions (such as the division of powers, the rule of law, civil rights, and equality of opportunity) aim at their conscious or unconscious *abolition*.[94]

In addition, the 2016 Trump electoral campaign energized the alt-right. The alt-right actively supported Trump during both presidential campaigns by aggressively trolling and attacking those who openly voiced any criticism of Trump, especially if their critics were female, Black, Jewish, or conservative. Trump never distanced himself from the alt-right during his first presidential campaign and instead interacted with the alt-right online. After his election, he failed to condemn hate crimes committed by this movement and appointed figures associated with the alt-right to the White House, including the White House chief strategist Stephen Bannon, who edited *Breitbart* and was influential in the Tea Party.[95] In July 2019, he invited controversial trolls and meme makers, some of them aligned with the alt-right, to the White House to assure himself of their continuing support during his second presidential campaign (which he received).[96]

I argue that the sharp tension between the ego and the ego ideal and ways to undo it remain a unifying force behind Trump's and the alt-right's propaganda techniques. However, there is a difference in how leaders and movements undo this split. As outlined in the previous chapter, the core means by which Trump followers achieve a "Trump festival," where they can undo the split between the ego ideal and the ego and move from the state of melancholia into a manic state to feel "great again," is through replacing their ego ideal with an identifiable leader—Trump. Although there are leading figures in the alt-right, they are several and more dispersed. Because of a lack of one central figure, ego ideal replacement is not the core psychological mechanism behind the alt-rights' propaganda tools.

Instead of replacing their ego ideal with an idealized leader figure, hostile and sexually aggressive alt-right jokes turn frustrated young white men into followers because they allow them (temporarily at least) to undo the split between their ego and ego ideals, which allows them to get rid of feelings of failure and frustration. Furthermore, such jokes provide them with a yield of pleasure and a temporary relief from the demands of adult life, which allows them to get rid of their feelings of failure and inferiority for not living up to precarity capitalism's economic, interpersonal, and bodily success standards.

Despite such differences in their core recruitment tactics, there is an uncanny connection among conservatives, Trumpism, and the alt-right in the United States. As Freud points out, "The presence of numerous inhibited drives, whose suppression has retained a certain degree of instability, will provide the most favorable disposition for the production of tendentious jokes."[97] Trump's propaganda created instability in suppressing libidinal and aggressive impulses, creating the context in which the alt-right's tendentious jokes could thrive.

Trump, in his public appearances, regularly makes hostile and sexually aggressive jokes. Elizabeth Levy Paluck and Michael Suk-Young Chwe point out that Trump, by using racist and sexist jokes, created an environment where hate crimes against minorities and women became socially sanctioned. In their view, it is not because subjects who commit hate crimes learn from Trump such hate crimes, but rather that "potential perpetrators are encouraged to act by the fact that Trump garnered votes and now holds the highest office. They infer from this that they have a better chance of escaping social and legal sanction than before his election."[98]

Although the authors make an important point here, we cannot explain the growing presence of misogynistic mass shooters and neofascist violence solely with the argument that those who perpetrate such violence think they will escape social and legal sanctions. There is something deeper going on, and to understand this, we need to draw on psychoanalytic theory. Trump's hostile and sexually aggressive jokes have lifted an inhibition of hostility and sexual aggression against minorities and women, further destabilizing the repression of direct libidinal and aggressive impulses in people.

His tendentious jokes have also provided people with targets of hatred (minorities and women) upon whom they can take out their hostile and sexually aggressive impulses. Trump has created a fertile context for the alt-right to find traction and enter the mainstream. Moreover, akin to the alt-right, Trump has incited violence against his targets of hatred (another connection between Trump and the alt-right). For example, immediately after Trump won the election, there was an increase in violent misogyny targeting women, with reports of men confronting women on the streets and threatening to "grab them by their pussy," a phrase Trump used during an off-camera moment that was recorded and subsequently gained much media attention.[99]

Furthermore, in the age of Trump, hate crimes against minorities, particularly immigrants and Muslims, have gone up significantly.[100] Moreover, since Trump blamed the COVID-19 pandemic on Asians, violence against people with Asian backgrounds (no matter what Asian background) has risen significantly in the United States. Finally, we can see an explicit connection between the alt-right and Trump when alt-right and other far-right followers, together with mainstream Trump supporters, stormed the U.S. Capitol on January 6, 2021.

Conclusion

Given the growing popularity of the alt-right, the question remains: What can we do to counter tendentious jokes and their derisive effects? One starting point for finding solutions is to understand better tendentious jokes and how they allow the growth of (neo)fascist movements. My chapter provides theorists' and practitioners' resources to criticize tendentious jokes and counter the "it is just a joke" defense.

Angela Nagle, who has problematic alliances with the far right, has made the argument that the left's excesses of liberal identity politics and "call-out culture" on the website Tumblr are partly responsible for the growing attraction of the alt-right, a countercultural, hipster, right-wing movement that celebrates transgression and rebellion. While in the 1960s the culture of transgression and rebellion was the domain of the left, today, it is the domain of the alt-right, which helps explain its rise.[101]

Similar to Nagle, Samir Gandesha suggests that the "moral puritanism" of the left, particularly in the form of intersectional identity politics, has provoked fascist segments of society. The reason for this is that while the increasingly uptight left polices "unacceptable" forms of speech and action, the alt-right adopts "a 20th-century avant-garde style" of sarcasm and other forms of dissidence that were formerly associated with the left.[102]

Such arguments are problematic because they blame the victim's supposed "uptightness" for far-right violence unleashed upon them. When the victims of racist and sexist alt-right violence draw much-needed boundaries to point out and protect themselves from that violence, they become responsible for the violence itself. Also, Nagle and Gandesha uncritically accept the alt-right's self-explanation for its growing popularity.

For example, in a coauthored article for *Breitbart* under Stephen Bannon, the alt-right agitator Yiannopoulos argues that people are drawn to the alt-right for the same reason Baby Boomers were drawn to the New Left: it "promises fun, transgression, and a challenge to social norms."[103] In response to this "article" in Anglin's antisemitic *Daily Stormer*, Phillip Wright, another alt-right agitator, reiterates the alt-right's narrative of itself as transgressive in the same way the New Left was in the sixties.[104]

Joan Braune points out that the supposed "pathologies on the left" do not have the explanatory power to grasp the neo-Nazi renaissance or misogynistic mass shooters as Nagle (and Gandesha) ascribes to them. As she puts it:

When the fascists provide their own genealogical narrative for rhetorical purposes, claiming that they are simply cultural transgressors reacting against liberal censorship, she takes them too much at their word. Over-the-top sensitivity on the left is better seen not as a major causal factor in the rise of the far-right, but more as a tool *used* by the far-right to advertise its supposed relevance and to mock and distract the left.[105]

Also, Nagle and Gandesha implicitly suggest that the left should develop its lighthearted culture industry of jokes and become more "fun" and less uptight to attract alienated young white men who would otherwise flock to the more "fun" alt-right. I reject the idea of a "fun left" for two core reasons. First, as Freud shows us, jokes, even originally nontendentious ones, are secondarily brought into relation for other purposes, such as exposure and "hostile, cynical and sceptical purposes."[106] Therefore, even while appearing as "harmless," left jokes can engender similar regressive processes and inhibition of critical thinking in consumers of such jokes. Also, left jokes would circulate through the culture industry of the internet.

However, as Adorno shows us, the culture industry of jokes (nontendentious and tendentious) does not create a capacity for critical thinking and imagination but inhibits both.[107] Insofar as Freud sees intellectual activity and an intact imagination as the precondition for undermining the production and positive reception of hostile and sexually aggressive jokes, left jokes contribute to their continuing circulation and derisive effects. Furthermore, more joking by the left will not address what causes predominantly young white men to become attracted to alt-right ideology. Jokes are *a tool to recruit*. It is not clear how merely using jokes in response will address the more significant causes, such as the adverse effects of precarity capitalism, standards of white heteronormative masculinity, and a general culture of racism and sexism.

In contrast to a joking left, I propose a left that risks being called a *Spielverderber* (a party-pooper or spoilsport) by critically analyzing the harmful effects of tendentious jokes. Such a left does not shy away from using the strategy of what Michael Billig called "unlaughter,"[108] which is the refusal to laugh when one encounters hostile and sexually aggressive jokes. To this end, political theorists must examine jokes not only for their use for democratic ends but also for how they can advance regressive political ends. At the same time, we must also challenge the more significant reasons why predominantly white men become attracted to the joking alt-right.

As my discussion of tendentious jokes shows, it is the internalized standards of economic, interpersonal, and bodily "success" that capitalist, patriarchal, and white society produces, and the fact that most young men cannot live up to such standards, that creates feelings of failure and frustration and makes young men attracted to tendentious alt-right jokes. Here we must openly challenge the standard of economic "success" and precarity capitalism, which has proven unable to enable most young men and women to support themselves economically. Furthermore, we must challenge the standards of heteronormative masculinity and the larger culture of racism and sexism in which the racist and sexist alt-right jokes culture thrives.

Only when people in the United States work through their racist past and confront difficult feelings of guilt and loss around such past will they be able to not laugh at racist jokes and counter a general jokes culture that has led to new forms of far-right violence against vulnerable groups. Furthermore, to undermine a sexist culture in the United States, we must also work through the history of violence toward women and address and redress the ongoing subtle and not-so-subtle forms of violence women face daily. In the concluding chapter, I will outline how we might envision such "working-through" from a psychoanalytic and critical theory perspective.

CHAPTER VI

Austria's Far Right

A Failed Working-Through of the Past

The past will have been worked-through only when the causes of what happened then have been eliminated. Only because the causes continue to exist does the captivating spell of the past remain to this day unbroken.

—THEODOR W. ADORNO, *GUILT AND DEFENSE*

Adorno composed *Was bedeutet: Aufarbeitung der Vergangenheit* (The meaning of working through the past) in 1959. Eight years later, at the invitation of the Socialist Students of Austria, Adorno gave the public talk *Aspekte des neuen Rechtsradikalismus* in 1967 at the University of Vienna, Austria.[1] However, as Volker Weiß has pointed out, we need to understand Adorno's Vienna talk as a continuation of *Aufarbeitung*, because many aspects of the new right extremism outlined in "Rechtsradikalismus" are already (and in more depth) formulated in *Aufarbeitung*.[2]

Adorno's core argument in *Aufarbeitung* is that the social conditions for manipulative mass psychology and the potential for totalitarian allegiance persisted in Germany after Hitler lost the war because Germans, instead of "working-through the past" (*Aufarbeitung der Vergangenheit*), opted for a "mastering of the past" (*Vergangenheitsbewältigung*). Whereas mastering the past implies closing the book on the past and removing it from memory, working-through the past implies an understanding of what has happened "that must work against forgetfulness," which entails working-through repressed feelings of guilt.[3] Instead of working-through the past, Germans deployed defense mechanisms that allowed them to remove the past from memory, contributing to the resurgence of new extremist right forces in Germany in the 1960s.

Although the core topic of *Rechtsradikalismus* is the resurgence of new right extremism in Germany, Adorno makes repeated references to the continuing threat of far-right extremism in Austria, as well. Today, about sixty years after Adorno's talk at the University of Vienna, this threat has become ever more salient with the continuing electoral successes of Austria's far-right Freiheitliche Partei Österreichs (FPÖ; Freedom Party of Austria, in short: Freedom Party), as well as the more recent growth of the far-right youth identitarian movement Austria (IBÖ), which takes inspiration from the FPÖ.

In my *The Politics of Repressed Guilt*, I explain that a successful working-through of the past entails that individuals and nations must make unconscious guilt feelings about a nation's violent past conscious.[4] I show how postwar and contemporary Austrians failed to work-through their violent Nazi past but instead utilized various defense mechanisms to keep guilt feelings repressed in the unconscious. As a result, the conditions for the resurgence of the far right remain intact today. In my "Mourning Denied: The Tabooed Subject,"[5] I expand my earlier book's analyses and show that a successful working-through of the past entails confronting oneself with unconscious guilt feelings *and* engaging in the painful work of mourning for the losses of the violent past. I explain that the taboos erected around the National Socialist genocide of Austrian Roma and Sinti (whom the Nazis persecuted as "gypsies") did not allow Austrians to mourn the loss of this part of the population. As a result, we encounter in Austria a failed working-through of their violent past, which leaves the conditions for a resurgence of the Nazi disaster intact.

In this chapter, I come back to some of the theoretical insights of *The Politics of Repressed Guilt* and "Mourning Denied" and use them to help us understand today's resurgence of the far right. I show that the taboo around Austria's National Socialist past is a barrier to an effective working-through of the past because it does not allow people to countenance their complicated feelings of guilt and engage in the work of mourning. Furthermore, Austrians transmit this taboo from one generation to the next. The far right's psychologically oriented propaganda techniques transform repressed feelings of guilt and loss into its electoral gains.

Even though, when compared to other European countries, Austria still has a well-functioning welfare system, and although the Austrian economy has performed better than many other European economies, including Germany, the 2008 economic crisis hurt employment standards and security, and precarious forms of employment emerged, together with a rise in unemployment.[6] While the Austrian Freedom Party also draws on themes of precarity capitalism to appeal to voters, it also exploits subjects' unresolved guilt and a failure to mourn Austria's violent National Socialist past to attract followers. However, those propaganda tactics that draw on Austria's failed working-through of the past are not disconnected from the economy insofar as such tactics are more successful in acquiring followers under conditions of precarity capitalism.[7]

In this chapter, I show that taboos erected around Austria's Nazi past, carried from one generation to the next, prevent Austrians from making unconscious guilt feelings conscious and hinder the work of mourning. Both result in people's failure to work-through the past. Psychologically oriented far-right propaganda techniques are effective in attracting Austrians whose rational economic and other self-interests contradict the policies of the FPÖ because they allow them to continue to master the past instead of working-through it. These techniques also function in the larger sociopolitical context in Austria, where mastering the past instead of working-through the past prevails.

The chapter comprises six sections, excluding the introduction and the conclusion. After establishing my theoretical framework, I explain how the taboo on Austria's violent Nazi past, which is carried from one generation to the next, generates a vast pool of contemporary Austrians that aim to master the past, which makes them susceptible to far-right propaganda techniques and prone to repeat the horrors of the past in the present.

Here I analyze the documentary *Und in der Mitte, da sind wir* (And in the middle we are), by Sebastian Brameshuber.[8] The documentary follows the lives of three teenagers (Ramona, Michi, and Andi) in the aftermath of the 2009 neo-Nazi attack, carried out by local youth, on survivors of the former concentration camp Ebensee during their participation in an annual memorial event. In the final two sections, I outline the devices the FPÖ uses to tap into the vast pool of Austrians who aim to keep feelings of loss and guilt repressed in their unconscious.

In "A Tabooed Past," I draw on Adorno's *Guilt and Defense*, the works of the core psychoanalytic thinkers of the early Frankfurt School Alexander and Margarete Mitscherlich,[9] and Freud's *Totem and Taboo* to explain how taboos become a barrier to a successful working-through of the past over several generations. In "Not Wanting to Touch the Tabooed Past Over Several Generations," I explain the effects of Ramona's mother's and grandmother's failure to work-through the past upon their (grand)daughter. In "A Denied Past and Patriarchal Family Structures," I explain that

Michi's parents' failure to work-through the past *and* patriarchal family structures make their son susceptible to far-right propaganda devices. I draw on Else Frenkel-Brunswik to explain the impact of family structures on children's susceptibility to fascism.[10]

In "Closing the Books on the Past and Democratic Family Structures," I outline how Andi's parents' failure to work-through the past makes their son susceptible to far-right propaganda devices, which democratic family structures can interrupt. In "The Emergence of the FPÖ," I outline the historical roots of the Freedom Party and discuss how its attempts to master the past assisted its early rise. Finally, in "The House of History Revisited," I outline the Austrian Freedom Party's techniques to acquire new followers.

A Tabooed Past

Adorno briefly mentions how taboos hinder working-through the past.[11] Alexander and Margarete Mitscherlich also mention that the taboos postwar elites erected stand in the service of forgetting the millions of murders of the National Socialist era.[12] However, Adorno and the Mitscherlichs did not establish a link between taboos and the failure to work-through the past in more depth, which I will pursue in this section by drawing on Freud's *Totem and Taboo*.

For Adorno, when people *work-through* the past, they work-through difficult feelings of guilt and make such feelings conscious. In contrast, when people *master* the past, they keep such feelings repressed in the unconscious. Furthermore, the deployment of defense mechanisms corresponds to the extent of unconscious guilt feelings people aim to keep repressed in the unconscious. In *Guilt and Defense*, Adorno outlines the various defense mechanisms postwar Germans used, such as the readiness to deny or minimize what had happened and insisting that instead of dwelling on the past they needed to "get on with things."[13]

While Adorno outlined that individuals and nations must work through their guilt, the Mitscherlichs explain that a successful working-through of the past *also* entails the work of mourning. Like Adorno, they point out that "the murder of millions of people cannot be mastered" but must be "worked-through." Such working-through not only implies living up to repressed guilt, as Adorno argues, but also implies "working-through the losses."[14]

The Mitscherlichs point out that Germans needed to mourn both the loss of the millions of victims of the Nazi regime *and* the loss of their leader (Hitler) both as a real person and as their narcissistic love object and representation of their collective ego ideal. "Hitler's death and his devaluation by the victors also implied the loss of a narcissistic object, and accordingly, an ego- or self-impoverishment and devaluation." Confronting unconscious guilt and the work of mourning are related tasks, since "without a working-through of guilt, however belated, there could be no work of mourning." However, instead of living up to guilt and mourning their losses, Germans resorted to defense mechanisms, such as derealizing the Nazi period and breaking off all affective bridges to the immediate past.[15]

However, Adorno and the Mitscherlichs did not, in more detail, discuss the barriers to successfully working-through the past. Freud outlined four themes in *Totem and Taboo* that allow me to show how taboos become an effective barrier to working-through guilt and loss. Taboos lead to a failure to make unconscious guilt feelings conscious and hinder the work of mourning, which result in people's failure to work-through the past.

In general, Freud points out that when someone or something is taboo, one is prohibited from approaching the tabooed subject or object, including discussing why it is taboo, which implies that the taboo is "expressed in prohibitions and restrictions." Taboo restrictions differ from moral restrictions because the former do not provide a system that explains in general terms why certain restrictions must be observed. Taboo prohibitions "have no grounds and are of unknown origin," and they impose themselves on us on their own account.[16]

Also, taboos are not only effective at one historical moment. Instead, they can travel from one generation to the next. Taboos "often survive with unbroken strength through long periods of history." Furthermore, taboos are connected to the unconscious. Most people are unaware of the effects taboos have upon them. Relatedly, the desire to *violate* the taboo also dwells in the unconscious. As such, "the basis of taboo is a prohibited action, for performing which a strong inclination exists in the unconscious."[17]

The first connection between taboos and a failure to work-through the past is that taboos lead to "a loss of memory—an amnesia—the motives for the prohibition [which is conscious] remain unknown."[18] For example, people can only work-through the past if there is a memory of past crimes. If there is a forgetting of such crimes, then members of the collectivity cannot work-through guilt and engage in the work of mourning, and an effective working-through of the past remains absent. Insofar as the taboo generates amnesia about aspects of the past, historical topics that have become taboo are likely to fade from people's memory.

Second, the taboo, besides the objective prohibition of "thou shalt not touch" (or discuss the taboo topic), also implies an "inhibition of thought." Insofar as the taboo inhibits our thinking, one of its side effects is to keep people's "state of knowledge at a low level." Here we find another barrier to a successful working-through of the past. We can only work-through guilt if we have knowledge of past crimes. Similarly, the work of mourning can be accomplished only "when one knows what one has to sever oneself from."[19] Therefore, even if there is a general knowledge about past crimes, if people have no memories regarding specific details because a taboo inhibits gaining such knowledge, they cannot successfully work-through the past.

However, even if a subject does have a memory of and knowledge about past crimes, this does not mean that they necessarily will work through the past. Here I have arrived at the third connection between the taboo and working-through the past. To effectively work-through guilt and engage in the work of mourning, a subject needs to have *empathy* for the lives that were lost, which requires not just knowledge of the murderous deeds the collectivity engaged in and the losses they engendered but also a feeling of care or concern for those lost lives.[20]

Taboos forestall any empathy for the victims of violent crimes because the principal prohibition of the taboo is the taboo against touching. The prohibition applies to immediate physical contact and extends to anything that directs one's thoughts to the forbidden object. The reason for the prohibition to touch or "come in contact with" the taboo is that "anyone who violates a taboo by coming into contact with something that is taboo becomes taboo [her/]himself and that then no one may come into contact with [her/]him."[21]

Here the taboo, which threatens that one can become tabooed and with that a shunned subject, is an effective barrier to working-through guilt and the work of mourning. People can only work-through guilt if they have empathy and thus some emotional attachment to the victims of crimes. However, the taboo of touching does not allow them to develop an emotional attachment with the victims of crimes, as developing such attachment involves directing their thoughts to the forbidden object (a nation's violent crimes). Also, people can only engage in the work of mourning, which is a process of gradual emotional detachment from the loved object, if they empathize with those who died. However, having empathy requires there to have been some emotional attachment in the first place, which the taboo forestalls.

As the Mitscherlichs point out, "That the same lack of empathy still appears today in relation to the wounded feelings of those whom Germany oppressed, supports the thesis that in history horrors can indeed be repeated."[22] The horrors of the past can be repeated because the lack of empathy with the victims of crimes can lead to renewed violence toward the victims, mainly because their presence touches on the tabooed subject and threatens a return of repressed feelings of guilt and loss.

I have arrived at the fourth and last aspect of the connection between the taboo and working-through guilt and loss. The taboo has a "paralyzing effect on the more highly organized capacities of the psyche, namely on the ability critically to work through reality."[23] For example, suppose an individual or collectivity observes a taboo regarding past crimes. In that case, it cannot make unconscious guilt feelings conscious, because such a task entails the ability to work-through reality critically. Furthermore, since the work of mourning entails a slow process that is accomplished over a long period, in which one learns, bit by bit, to accept the reality of the loss, the taboo, which paralyzes our ability to work-through reality, interrupts the work of mourning. As a result, we cannot work-through the past.

More specifically, Austrian postwar politicians created a taboo around conceiving Austria as a perpetrator nation; this taboo has extended over the generations and is still in effect in Austria today. They defined Austria, instead, as "the first victim of Nazism." The main aim of the taboo was to unify a fragmented nation after the war.[24] A taboo shared by a nation has a unifying effect because it prescribes a fixed verdict for an area of conflict.[25] The fixed verdict the taboo prescribed was an insistence on Austria's victim status and the conviction that Nazism was something largely alien to Austrian culture.[26]

The taboo declared an area of memory as untouchable (Austria as a perpetrator nation and its enthusiastic support of the Hitler regime), which told (or commanded) people that they must not touch the tabooed memory or ask any further questions. However, there was and continues to be collusion with the taboo. The broader population readily accepted the proscription offered by Austrian elites because the taboo spreads "a subjective sense of security against the consequences of the past."[27] Furthermore, it gave Austrians (over generations) the feeling that there is a part of Austria's history they do not need to feel guilty for.

As a result of the taboo, as Neuhäuser points out, there exists "still significant resistance to 'coming to terms with,' let alone 'working through' Austria's Nazi past."[28] Furthermore, Austria, in the recent publication of the annual status report of the "Worldwide Investigation and Prosecution of Nazi War Criminals," received, together with Lithuania and Ukraine, an F (fail) for its approach to International Holocaust Remembrance Day.[29] It is this F, which critiques a pool of Austrians who aim to keep guilt and loss repressed in their unconscious, that the Austrian Freedom Party's propaganda taps into.

In addition to the taboo on Austria's recent violent Nazi past, there also exists a taboo on its recent violent colonial past. As an example, Samudzi shows us that there are historical continuities between the genocide of Jews, Roma, and Sinti during the Nazi regime and Germany's early-twentieth-century genocide of the Ovaherero and Nama people in what was then German South-West Africa (present-day Namibia).[30]

One such continuity is the overall colonial racist classification of Germans (and Austrians as part of Hitler's regime) as the "master race" and all other races as "inferior." Other continuities are the concepts of *Rassenschande* (racial defilement) as a justification for racial separation, the criminalization of "mixed-race" marriages in German colonies and the metropole, and the Nazi Nuremberg laws, which prohibited relationships between white Germans and those they classified as "inferior."[31]

Austrians were implicated in the Ovaherero and Nama genocide. For example, the personal collection of the Austrian anthropologist and ethnologist Felix von Luschan, who supported colonialism, German nationalism, and eugenics, was composed of thousands of skulls of different Indigenous peoples from around the world and included Ovaherero and Nama skulls from genocide-era concentration camps.[32]

Since Austrians have not yet started to work-through their violent colonial past, such racist attitudes are passed on from one generation to the next. They continue to circulate in Austrians' unconscious view of "other races" as inferior today. The fascists utilized such unconscious racist attitudes in their propaganda techniques during the Nazi era, and the far right continues to use them in their techniques today.

Not Wanting to Touch the Tabooed Past Over
Several Generations

In the following sections, I analyze the documentary film *Und in der Mitte, da sind wir* (And in the middle we are). I show how the taboo of discussing Austria's involvement in the horrors of Hitler's regime has traveled down the generations and hindered Austrians from working-through the past effectively. The documentary follows, for over a year, the daily lives of three teenagers (Ramona, Michi, and Andi) who grew up and lived in Ebensee, Upper Austria, which was, between 1943 and 1945, the site of one of the most brutal satellite concentration camps of the extensive Mauthausen concentration camp system in Austria.

The Nazis built the camp to provide slave labor to construct enormous underground tunnels in which armament works for Hitler's war machinery were to be housed. Nine thousand Jews, Roma and Sinti, Eastern Europeans, and prisoners of war died of torture, malnutrition, disease, and exhaustion in the camp.[33]

Today, one can visit the former concentration camp grounds, which includes two mass graves, which serve as a memorial, and a big tunnel in the mountainside dug by camp slave labor during the Nazi regime. There is also a small museum in the center of town devoted to twentieth-century history, and it hosts an annual memorial event. The documentary traces the interactions of the three teenagers with their parents and grandparents, peers, teachers, and bosses in the aftermath of the 2009 violent neo-Nazi attack carried out by five local white male teenagers on concentration camp survivors during the memorial event.

A neo-Nazi group composed of five local Ebensee teenage boys aged between fourteen and seventeen, carrying machine guns and dressed in black blousons, military trousers, combat boots, and black hoods over their faces, emerged from two side tunnels. They attacked a group of frightened Ebensee concentration camp survivors during their visit to the mountainside tunnel during the anniversary ceremony. The young men shouted "Heil Hitler" and other Nazi slogans and shot pellets at the terrified group, injuring several. They also intimidated audience members and other attendees, walking up and down in front of them and shouting Nazi slogans.

The Freedom Party of Austria (FPÖ), in its quest to appeal to voters who aim to keep difficult feelings of guilt and loss at bay, downplayed this and the other attacks that repeatedly occur at Holocaust-era sites in Austria. For example, the then leader of the FPÖ, Heinz-Christian Strache, minimized the Ebensee attack by stating that it was nothing but a *Lausbubenstreich*—a boy's prank.[34] Furthermore, the FPÖ repeatedly challenged the *Verbotsgesetz*,[35] which forbids *Wiederbetätigung*—the reengagement in Nazi-related activities in Austria. For example, its recent leader, Norbert Hofer, argued that the *Verbotsgesetz* contradicts the "freedom of speech," which was dismissed at the European level.[36]

Such interventions by the Austrian Freedom Party and the general culture in Austria, which aims to close the book on the past, affect how Austrians deal with neo-Nazi activities. For example, attacks on Holocaust-era visitors have repeatedly occurred during the Ebensee yearly ceremonies without any consequences (and they continue to take place despite tightened security). And although the teenagers of the 2009 Ebensee attack were, for the first time, arrested and put on a trial under the *Verbotsgesetz*. However, one was acquitted, and only two of the other four teenagers received five-to-six-month prison sentences during the three-year probation period, although the *Verbotsgesetz* stipulates prison sentences between ten and twenty years. [37]

My analysis shows that the (grand)parents' failure to work-through Austria's past results from the general taboo of discussing this subject in Austria. The (grand)parents' failure to work through the past does not allow them to assist their (grand)children in coming to terms with difficult feelings of guilt and loss. All of the three teenagers' (grand)parents, instead of working-through the past, engaged in mastering the past.[38]

The documentary maker touches on the tabooed past by asking the teenagers' (grand)parents questions about Austria's and Ebensee's violent National Socialist past and about their reactions to the neo-Nazi attacks on the Ebensee memorial event. That the documentary maker is touching on a taboo topic is salient on two levels. First, the (grand)parents struggle even to discuss that topic, which underlines that they do not know how to deal with it. Also, none of them had visited any of the Holocaust-era sites even though they live within walking distance of them. Second, we encounter the (grand)parents' strong defensive reactions, which underlines that any violation of the taboo threatens to bring back repressed feelings of guilt and loss. The (grand)parents use the defensive reaction to keep feelings of guilt and loss repressed in the unconscious.

The (grand)parents aim to shield themselves from the memory of Austria's violent past and the return of repressed feelings of guilt and loss by not visiting any of the Holocaust-era sites. However, this task is particularly challenging, given that their homes are located in the vicinities of, or even *on*, the sites. For example, Ramona lives in the settlement established in the 1950s on the site where concentration camp inmates lived during the National Socialist era. The buses with camp survivors that visit the yearly memorial event drive directly past by Ramona's house. One can even hear the ceremony's proceedings from her house.

Furthermore, repressed feelings of guilt and loss threaten to return when the many buses with camp survivors arrive in their town every summer. The arrival of the buses in town threatens to touch the taboo and bring back difficult feelings of guilt and loss into consciousness—after all, the camp survivors come to Ebensee to *mourn* lost loved ones at the mass graves. Therefore, there is a conflict between what the visitors to the town are here specifically to do (mourn lost loved ones) and precisely what the Austrians in the town are trying to avoid doing.

The teenagers come from both working-class and middle-class backgrounds. However, what "working class" means in an Austrian context is somewhat different from what it means in the U.S. context, where the gap between the bourgeois and working class is more salient. Two teenagers also aim to enter traditional working-class jobs: Ramona trains to become a hairdresser (although her mother would like her to continue studying), and Michi trains to become a waiter in a local restaurant. Only Andi attends a high school with *Matura* (a high school degree that allows him to attend university). However, all teenagers live in rather nice and comfortable homes, which would signify that they are from the bourgeois class in the U.S. context.

At one point, Ramona sits on a park bench with a teenage female friend during the wintertime. Here we learn that the teenagers do not like "the buses with all the tourists arriving in town" during the summer. That the teenagers address the camp survivors as "tourists" and that they do not explicitly state why they come to town suggest that they are talking about a taboo topic. We also learn why they do not like the buses—their parents *forbid* their daughters to leave their homes when the buses with the camp survivors arrive, which underlines that the taboo around Austria's violent National Socialist past is expressed in prohibitions and restrictions.[39]

Furthermore, the teenagers do not receive any explanation from their (grand)parents as to *why* they are not allowed to leave their homes when the buses arrive, which underlines that the taboo does not provide a system that explains in general terms why certain restrictions must be observed.[40] Ramona's only explanation from her mother is because "someone could snatch you."

The Mitscherlichs point out that one of the dangerous aspects of taboos is that they create hostility and resentment because those who must obey taboos are "left in the infantile position of children forbidden to ask questions." They then project the hostility and resentment that the taboo has created within themselves upon groups that are different from them.[41] For example, it seems that Ramona's mother was not allowed to ask her parents any questions about Austria's violent Nazi past. Her mother (Ramona's grandmother) displays strong defense mechanisms when confronted with the tabooed topic, which suggests that her daughter (Ramona's mother) was also not allowed to touch the taboo.

As a result, the mother projected her hostility and resentment about being left in the infantile position onto the visiting camp survivors, who "could snatch up her daughter." Furthermore, in the construction of survivors of Austria's violent crimes as potentially dangerous, we see how colonial- and Nazi-era racist constructions in which Austrian (German) whites appear as racially superior and good and those they brutally exploited and murdered in the concentration camps as racially inferior and bad survive.

The taboo around Austria's violent Nazi past also generates resentment in the teenagers. For example, the mother's not allowing Ramona to leave the house when the camp survivors arrive in town generates hostility and resentment in the daughter. Furthermore, she is not allowed to ask why she must remain home, which adds to her resentment as she is now, like her mother before, left in an infantile position.

Also, not allowing the teenagers to leave their homes when the buses arrive contributes to a scenario where the teenagers see the camp survivors as threatening figures (why else forbid them from going out?). Furthermore, together with the fact that their parents provide them with colonial- and Nazi-era racist constructions of Holocaust victims as threatening figures who could "snatch them up" makes it more likely that the teenagers project their resentment and hostility about being kept in the infantile position onto the surviving victims of crimes, which makes it more likely for them to act out their resentment on them—by, for example, attacking them when they arrive in town to commemorate the crimes committed against them.

As Freud points out, there remains a strong desire to violate the taboo in the unconscious.[42] The reasons for the taboo aren't explained, which probably fuels some of the desire to violate the taboo. Ramona, for example, tells us that when the buses arrived last summer, she and her friend (who is also forbidden to leave her home during the ceremony) snuck out, which suggests that they wanted to violate the taboo. Nonetheless, Ramona also points out that the visitors "looked at us strangely," which underlines that, like her mother, the daughter also projects her hostility and resentment onto the victims of crimes and their descendants and that colonial- and Nazi-era racist classifications continue to circulate in present-day Austria.

The core problem with the taboo is that it generates a scenario where those subject to it fail to empathize with the victims of crimes, which connects back to the casting of victims as threatening figures.[43] Such a lack of empathy is salient concerning most teenagers that appeared in the documentary. We see Ramona and another teenage girlfriend, as an example, remaining emotionally detached when they have to visit the memorial event with their local high school class, where a speaker tells the visitors that 8,400 people were murdered in the Ebensee camp. Also, when she walks back to her house (which is just around the corner) after the event, she tells the interviewer that "it sucks" that she has to go to the memorial every year with school, which she repeats several times. Such a lack of empathy for the victims of crimes helps explain Austrian teenage neo-Nazi attacks on camp survivors.

In another scene with Ramona, her mother, and grandmother at their house, the documentary maker confronts the family with the taboo by asking questions about Ebensee's violent National Socialist past and about their reactions to the neo-Nazi attacks on camp survivors. Both the mother and the grandmother display strong defensive reactions (although they are qualitatively stronger on the grandmother's side), which underlines how the taboo travels from one generation to the next and sets up barriers for an effective working-through of the past.

In response to the question about Ebensee's violent past, Ramona's mother points out that "the youth are not like that anymore, but the old folks have given Ebensee a bad reputation; I don't know what they all did to make Ebensee so unpopular." Although she admits that "old folks" gave the town a bad reputation, she does not know "what they all did." Her statement is somewhat surprising given that their house is located in a former concentration camp, that buses of Holocaust survivors drive past their house every summer, and that one can hear the commemoration event from their house.

One explanation why the mother does not know what people in Ebensee did that gave her hometown a bad reputation is that the taboo inhibits thinking and keeps people's state of knowledge about past violent crimes at a low level.[44] Another explanation is that she uses defense mechanisms to keep feelings of guilt and loss surrounding Austria's Nazi crimes repressed. For example, the mother uses the defenses of denial and of minimizing, where "one denies or minimizes this knowledge so that one does not lose the possibility of identifying with the collective."[45] Since she does not know anything about the crimes the "old folks" committed, the mother can continue to safely identify with the collectivity that committed such crimes.

The mother also uses another defense mechanism, vagueness, such as using broad categories such as "youth" and "old folks," which allow her to shift guilt and responsibility for the horrors committed by Austrians away from her and her daughter's generation. As Adorno puts it, "Youth, generation and similar vague categories often play a role where responsibility is to be shifted from certain social groups, be it that one blames a generation for something bad, mostly the older one, or that one wants to let off another, mostly one's own, from all evil."[46]

The mother glorifies the youth as having moved on from the recent Nazi past ("they are not like that anymore"), in contrast to the "old folks," to shift responsibility (and guilt) away from her and her daughter's generation to the older generation. Her defense implicitly also excuses the repeated neo-Nazi attacks on concentration camp survivors who visit Ebensee, which the youth of Ebensee carried out (which shows that the new generation has not moved on from their violent National Socialist past, as the mother suggests).

In a rather loud voice and an agitated tone, the grandmother intervenes: "I think it just has to do with the concentration camp cemetery; I have to say, though, this is not the people's fault. Do you think they asked anyone whether it is OK to build a concentration camp? Back then, it was: 'Shut up, or you are dead!' I talked to a few, and they gave the soldiers, the prisoners bread as they walked past. . . . Because they were so poor. So, you *just can't declare the people here guilty*, just because they live and laugh here. We moved here. We don't know this at all" (emphasis added). The grandmother's agitated tone underlines what Adorno calls a "neurotic relation to the past," which leads to "defensive postures where one is not attacked, intense affects where they are hardly warranted by the situation and the absence of affect in face of the gravest matter."[47] While the grandmother does not display any affect in connection to the gravest matter—that the mass graves in the camp are the result of mass murders and that her house is located on the former campsite where NS victims were murdered, she is worried that people in Ebensee might be found guilty of the crimes committed in the camp.

More so than the mother and with more vehemence, the grandmother exonerates the collectivity from guilt and responsibility with her assertion that the mass murders committed in the concentration camp are "not the people's fault," and that one "can't declare the people here guilty." One reason is that she is a generation closer to such a past than her daughter. Furthermore, the vague category of "old folks" that the mother uses to exonerate herself and her daughter remains unclear and could implicate the grandmother's generation and the grandmother herself.

The grandmother uses here two defense mechanisms to exonerate herself and the collective from any guilt and responsibility for the crimes committed in the concentration camp. First, she uses terror as a defense strategy, suggesting that people were powerless to resist the Nazi terror.[48] She conveniently leaves out the question whether resistance would have been possible and whether Austrians who lived in the vicinity of concentration camps knew what was happening in them and either passively went along or were actively involved in their crimes. Second, to repress the picture of the collective and of herself being implicated in the crimes (which her daughter's reference to "old folks" brought up), she constructs a picture of the collective as composed of "good and altruistic people" who helped the "poor prisoners" by giving them bread. This defense mechanism of the "good Austrians" goes hand in hand with constructions of the victims imprisoned in camps as "bad" and that the victims deserved their punishment, which is a core defense strategy Austrian NS perpetrators used during the postwar trials to exonerate themselves from guilt and responsibility. Something of this also survives in the mother's idea that the camp survivors will "snatch up her daughter."

However, the grandmother's attempt to exonerate the collectivity (and herself) becomes interrupted by a slip of the tongue. Initially, she states that it was the soldiers whom the people helped. She then corrects herself that it was the prisoners they helped. Adorno found numerous such slips of the tongue in his analyses of postwar Germans' attempts to close the book on the past. He points out that such slips are "caused by the unconscious feeling of guilt, which disrupts the speaker's pattern of apology."[49] In the grandmother's slip of the tongue also something of the idea of the "bad" camp inmates survives (since she thinks that one ought to help the soldiers and not the inmates), which serves to exonerate the crimes of the "good Austrians."

We find another contradiction in the grandmother's statement. At first, she seemed defensive of the townspeople, but then she claims her family moved here only recently and that they did not know anything. This contradiction points to the moment of doubt in her defense—perhaps the people in Ebensee were guilty after all? This moment of doubt is also a moment where repressed guilt could return in the conscious, which she pushed back into the unconscious by distancing herself from the collectivity and adding that her family (and herself) could not know anything about the town's past, as they had only more recently moved there. Here the grandmother also invokes the defense of a "denial of the knowledge of the crime,"[50] denying that Nazi crimes happened all over Austria and not just in Ebensee. Again, the taboo's effects of keeping knowledge about past crimes low are salient here.

Here the granddaughter, Ramona, intervenes and points out that "it started when they did what they did in the tunnel . . . where did they report it? Abroad, everywhere." That Ramona does not directly address the neo-Nazi incident in their own community underlines that not only the recent Nazi past but also the neo-Nazi present is a taboo topic in the family (and in Austria in general). The grandmother agrees with Ramona and points out that "things got terrible" with the incident but adds right away that "they made a mountain out of a molehill. The boys just pulled a prank, and they used a toy gun. They just shot around for a bit. Sure it was not very pleasant for those who came here . . . but for me, it was really a boy's prank, and one needed to scold the boys [she laughs] . . . and if I had seen the boy running, I would not have stopped him. I would have told him: 'Run, be quick! Get lost!' Because by and large nothing really happened." Here the grandmother aims to further exonerate the collective of Ebensee (here the local teenage boys) by downplaying and minimizing the crime[51] and calling it nothing other than a humorous "boy's prank" that one should not have punished, because "nothing really happened." She also uses the defensive strategy of "exaggeration" by arguing that those that point to the severity of the neo-Nazi crimes are merely exaggerating (here that the international press made "a mountain out of a molehill").

Although the mother intervenes and points out that the teenagers involved in the attack did shout Nazi slogans, she also exonerates them by pointing out that the punishment was too severe, which contributes to minimizing the crime. Furthermore, she adds that the mother of one of the teenagers involved in the attack put all the blame on her child, which was, according to her, not fair; she should have asked herself instead, "What did I contribute that he did this?" Here, instead of acknowledging her responsibility for her daughter's failure to work through the past, the mother displaces her failed responsibility onto another mother.

Here the past and the present are connected on several levels. First, the grandmother's passionate attempts to exonerate the collectivity from the crimes in the Nazi past equal her passionate attempts to exonerate the collectivity from the crimes it commits in the present. The less severe defense mechanisms the mother displays in exonerating the crimes of the recent Nazi past also equal her less severe attempts to downplay the neo-Nazi attacks in the present, which suggests that perhaps the grandmother has more guilt and loss to repress than her daughter. The grandmother's closeness to the recent Nazi past might account for this difference.

Second, the (grand)parents' defensive attitude toward the recent Nazi past is connected to the neo-Nazi present in Ebensee. The defensive attitudes of the mother and grandmother allow them to keep difficult feelings of guilt and loss repressed in the unconscious. However, they also create a scenario where their children do not learn how to deal with difficult feelings of guilt and loss surrounding Austria's violent Nazi past that has been carried on from one generation to the next.

Therefore, the general taboo around Austria's Nazi past leads to the (grand)parents' failure to work-through the past. Such a failure affects their children and creates a scenario where they might repeat the past horrors in the present. Furthermore, the (grand)parents' defensive attitudes hinder educators' work, who aim to address the tabooed topic and initiate a process of working-through the past in the teenagers.

A Denied Past and Patriarchal Family Structures

In a scene in a high school class, the teacher makes the students read a script where a grandfather witnesses teenage boys who were attacking visitors to the Holocaust memorial. When the grandfather is about to make a phone call to inform the police about the attack, he notices that his grandson is missing and might be one of the attackers. The teacher asks the students to identify with the grandfather and discuss whether they would call the police to report the incident. Michi argues that he would not report the incident because his grandson would get a *Vorstrafe*, and his life would be ruined.

Furthermore, Michi points out that he knows one of the attackers and that he has changed a lot. This attacker seems to be the young man, a former neo-Nazi who knew about the yearly attacks on the memorial event attendees, who trains Michi to become a waiter in a local restaurant and becomes Michi's best friend over the course of the documentary. Here the teacher intervenes and draws a connection between the teenagers in the attack getting put on trial and how that might have been the reason they could change later on, attempting to make his students aware that only by bringing the attacks to light can people change.

Although the teacher does not reach Michi and most of the other students, one student does seem to be learning the teacher's lessons. For example, a young female classmate of Michi challenges him about whether these neo-Nazi attitudes would persist and whether they would just repeat their attacks if everyone stayed quiet about them. The students who are not learning these lessons seem to be the ones with parents who display defensive attitudes when confronted with the Nazi past and (neo-)Nazi present, such as Michi's.

When the interviewer asks Michi's parents (in the presence of Michi) if they have ever visited the Holocaust memorial in their town, both parents answer in a rather loud and emotional tone: "No! (and this is the only time the mother says something), which underlines that the interviewer has touched upon the taboo. Moreover, the father adds, "I don't know why I have never been there, but one must leave this topic behind. I do not want to have anything to do with that!" Here we can again see how the taboo affects thinking—the father does not know or ever has thought through why he is avoiding going to the Holocaust-era sites in his town. Furthermore, the taboo is also salient in the father's use of the defense strategy of "drawing a line under it" ("one needs to leave this topic behind") to keep feelings of guilt and loss, which touching the taboo threatens to make conscious, repressed in the unconscious.

Adorno points out that the defense strategy of wanting to "draw a line under it" represents a "symptom of an extremely dangerous social-psychological and political potential" because a person cannot experience any spontaneous feeling of guilt while they, at the same time, desperately defend against any such feeling becoming conscious.[52] Such a symptom has a dangerous social-psychological and political potential because the parents' inability to deal with feelings of guilt and loss prevents their children from dealing with such feelings. As a result, the parents (unconsciously) contribute to a scenario where their children might repeat the horrors of the past in the present and future.

Michi's father displays the same defensive attitude when the documentary maker touches on the taboo of the 2009 (neo-)Nazi attack on camp survivors: "I don't think they knew what they were doing and what consequences they would have to face. But of course, it is horrible. I have thought: What if this is my boy? . . . I don't think you can influence that in any way." Although the father acknowledges that the boys engaged in reprehensible acts, he exonerates them with the defense that they did not know what they were doing or what consequences their actions would have.

At the same time, the father aims to exonerate himself from any responsibility for such acts because, as a parent, according to him, one "cannot influence that in any way," meaning that he has no influence on whether his son becomes a (neo-)Nazi. The father does not grasp that his generation can and does influence the thoughts and actions of his children's generation. If the parents are unable to deal with the Nazi past, this is passed on to the next generation, and their children will not be able to deal with it either, and as a result, their children become susceptible to neofascist ideology.

Michi's neofascist leanings are evident at the beginning of the documentary, where we see him and a group of young boys (composed of children and teenagers) hanging out under a bridge to take a break from their yearly "Bratschen" walk.[53] Here Michi makes a joke about the horrors in the Ebensee camp. He points at graffiti that says "Fuck Nazis" and says,

"This shit must go. It should be forever Nazis." The other (younger) boys repeat after him, "Yes, it should be forever Nazis!"[54]

As Freud points out, the desire to violate the taboo remains in the unconscious,[55] and telling a Nazi joke is a way to safely violate the taboo, which they are not allowed to touch in their familial contexts. Furthermore, since parents have forbidden discussions of their Nazi past, they would be coming into conflict with the parents if they openly discussed it. Michi's telling of the Holocaust-era joke trivializes the taboo topic and allows him to avoid conflict with the parental figures. Also, Michi's attempt to eradicate the slogan "Fuck Nazis" and replace it with "Forever Nazis" (which the other teenagers enthusiastically support) can be a way of protecting murderous (grand)parental figures from harm (such as when their crimes might come to light).

Furthermore, the father does not seem to appreciate how his dominant role as the family patriarch renders his son susceptible to fascist ideology. In her contributions to the *Authoritarian Personality* study, Else Frenkel-Brunswick shows that children who grew up in families where the father was a dominating figure with whom the child and wife were not allowed to come into conflict and where a clear demarcation of stereotypical male and female sex roles existed are more susceptible to fascist ideology than those who grew up in families where sex roles are less rigid and where there is parity between the parents.[56] It also seems that in families with patriarchal structures the parents and children are more willing to obey taboos.

In Michi's family, *only* the father talks, and the mother is silent during interviews, or if she tries to say something, he talks right over her. The only time when the mother says something is in response to the question whether they have visited the memorial (a determined "No!"). Furthermore, neither his wife nor Michi ever contradict or challenge any of the father's statements. He is the definite *paterfamilias*; he has the say in the home.

Furthermore, according to Frenkel-Brunswick, men who grew up with dominating fathers tend to compensate for underlying weaknesses and show their independence "by implicit or explicit assertion of his superiority over women."[57] Michi asserts his superiority over women in a scene where his female teenage friends complain that they are excluded from the yearly "Bratschen" walks and the income they generate. While another male teenager is sympathetic to the women's complaint, Michi defends the exclusion of the women, stating, "That is OK, this is tradition."

Also, Frenkel-Brunswick points out that the son of a family with rigid gender roles and a dominating father figure can "never quite establish his personal and masculine identity; he thus has to look for it in the collective system where there is opportunity both for the submission to the powerful and retaliation upon the powerless."[58] Children who grew up and lived under conditions where the stronger father rules over the weaker (the wife and children) may find that they cannot live by any other rule.

We encounter Michi's difficulties with his male identity in a scene where, after his public breakdance performance in a local pub (which was attended by his mother but not his father), he confides his worries to his female friends that his performance makes him appear as "less of a man" or as gay. Furthermore, as the documentary proceeds, Michi entirely subordinates himself to his older male friend, the former neo-Nazi (possibly directly involved in the attacks) who trains Michi to become like him, a waiter and a "punk." Michi starts dressing, thinking, and acting like him. In one scene at Michi's house with his parents and his friend, his father expresses his concerns that his son might, through his older friend, become a neo-Nazi, since the boundaries of dress codes between neo-Nazis and punks seem to be fluid. Although the friend tries to assure the father that his son is "safe with him," the father asserts that he wants to have a few more years of control over his son and that "he has the say in the house."

The problem is that the father does not realize that his authoritarian role in the family has already contributed to a scenario where the son seeks out powerful male figures to whom he can subordinate himself. Furthermore, although Michi seemed, over the course of the documentary, to change, under the "training" of his older friend, the former neo-Nazi–turned-punk who now "hates Nazis," the point is that Michi *has completely subordinated himself* to him. Suppose the friend were still a neo-Nazi. In that case, one can assume that Michi would have followed him without any reservations in attacking the camp survivors at the annual memorial.

Closing the Books on the Past and Democratic Family Structures

Andi's parents, like all the other interviewed or mentioned parents, opt to close the book on Austria's violent Nazi past—neither parent has visited the Ebensee camp. As the father puts it: "I have never been there as a teenager, and the whole thing did not interest me as an adult. One knows, and it is sad enough, what happened, but . . . I think one should put it to rest and not bring it up repeatedly. It is tragic. It has happened, and one should make sure that that does not happen again, and look into the future."

Here the father assures us that he knows what has happened, although he does not directly say what specifically happened that is sad and tragic, which underlines that the recent Nazi past in Austria is also a taboo topic in this family. The father also uses the defense strategy of "drawing a line under it," which he expresses as wanting "to put it to rest" and not bring it up "over and over again."[59] Another defense strategy the father uses to fend off guilt and loss is to "look into the future." The father prefers to focus his gaze on the future to avoid looking at his community's violent Nazi past, which would bring up difficult feelings of guilt and loss. However, the problem with an orientation toward a "bright future" is that if one fails to work through and resolve the past, the past will continue to haunt the present and the future.

The father also uses displacement as a defense strategy: "Enough shady things are happening that are not right, there are so many corrupt people in the higher spheres where they steal, and that is not right either, that are our problems now, but that is also a crime." Here he claims political expertise, but his statement remains vague. It mainly serves to exonerate the collective (and himself) by displacing its past crimes onto supposedly "criminal elites" in the present.

Although the father asserts that "one should make sure that that does not happen again," his defensive attitude contributes to maintaining aspects of the taboo, such that the younger generation also can not come completely to terms with the past, which underlines the transgenerational effects of the parent's failure to work through the past. In a scene with Andi and his male teenage friend, we learn that Andi has never visited the Holocaust-era sites, except with the gun club (to which his father also belongs) to shoot guns in the tunnel built by imprisoned Holocaust victims.

Andi's friend has visited the former concentration camp twice with his school (a high school that offers a specialization in weapons technology) but assures us that "it is nothing, it is just a hole in the mountain, and one does not see more!" When the interviewer asks him if he learned what had happened there, the teenager answers: "I don't remember. I only remember the interesting part, not the stuff that bored me." He tells us that it was just a school trip, and the paucity of his memories underlines that we are again being confronted with a communal amnesia.

Here the teenager uses the same defensive strategy that the parental generation uses—to deny and minimize the crime ("it is nothing, just a hole in the wall").[60] His faulty memory is connected to his parents' generation, who aim to forget and close the book on the past, to "put it to rest," as Andi's father puts it. Furthermore, it is a result of the taboo, which leads to a loss of memory and amnesia[61] and seems to affect this teenager's memory in a very specific sense—he cannot remember anything connected to the repeated visits to the Holocaust-era sites. Furthermore, the teenager's experience when visiting the memorial resonates with his parents' not being interested in visiting the memorial—as Andi's father puts it: "The whole thing did not interest me as an adult."

In another scene, we learn that Andi and his friend are fascinated with military culture; they tell us that they know everything about World War I and II and watch documentaries about it. However, when the interviewer asks them what they know about what happened during World War II and the Nazi regime in Ebensee, Andi is silent and appears ignorant, and his friend says he has forgotten what he knew, which contradicts their earlier boast that they both "know everything" about World War II.

Here we can see how the taboo affects the younger generation in that it inhibits their capacity for critical thought.[62] That the teenagers do not know or cannot remember anything, even if they visited the Holocaust-era sites several times and had repeatedly listened to explanations about what had happened, underlines how the taboo is carried over from one generation to the next and underscores the transgenerational effects of a failed working-through of the past. They view history through the eyes of the perpetrators, who saw the victims as "nothing." Therefore, history itself becomes "nothing." There is no reason to remember.

Furthermore, the father's fascination with guns has been carried over from father to son and plays a crucial role in Andi's fascination with everything connected to the military. However, as Adorno points out, the youth needs to be warned about the fetish of everything connected to the military, as such a fetish generates people who obey orders uncritically.[63] Andi received his military fetish from his father. His father introduced him to shooting with guns at the age of seven, and in a later scene, we see Andi and his father together at a shooting range, where the father comments on his son's shooting ability.

The military fetish also assists Andi in constructing his male identity. In a scene with his friend, Andi holds a toy machine gun and explains that it is an Austrian assault rifle used by the Austrian military. He tells us that he got the gun two years ago and that they now use the guns to frighten people (which reminds us of the attacks on camp survivors, who used the same guns and makes us wonder if Andi was involved in the attacks). However, now he likes to shoot with real guns.

Andi points out, somewhat agitatedly, that "those that are against weapons should be beaten on their buds because they are just hippies, who are afraid." For him, "real men" like guns. "Hippies" seem to stand here for those who are afraid (feminized men), whereas those who are "real men" (like himself) are not afraid of weapons and like to shoot them.

Andi's ideal masculinity is also the result of his identification with his father, a "real man" who shoots real guns. Guns formed and confirmed Andi's masculinity already at a young age. He tells us that although he was afraid to shoot with real guns at the age of seven, he did it, and he liked it so much that he wanted to do it again. In another scene, we see him with his male friends at an outdoor war game, where the teenage boys shoot pellets at one another and excitedly discuss their strategies (which makes us wonder again if Andi participated in the attacks).

Both the parents' attempts to close the book on the past and the father's transfer of the military fetish to his son can make Andi susceptible to fascist ideology. However, an intervening factor is his father's and his mother's equality. As Frenkel-Brunswick points out, men who grew up in families that are not father dominated but mother oriented (rather than mother dominated) are less susceptible to fascist ideology.

Unlike in Michi's family, where the father was a dominating figure, this seems less the case in Andi's. His mother is rather vocal without being dominating. For example, when Andi's grades in the HAK (a business high school) worsen and he wants to leave school to become a gunsmith, we witness a scene where he has a discussion with his parents about what he is going to do with his life. We encounter a more relaxed atmosphere with Andi and his parents (unlike in the scenes with Michi and his parents, where one could sense much tension between the parents and between the son and his father). When the father mentions that Andi wants to join the military or the police force, the mother has no problem contradicting the father. She states that she has many reservations about her son going into the military or becoming a cop (although less so than joining the military). She points out that she would prefer him to finish his Matura (which allows him to attend university) and study music (which was an option before his grades worsened).

Unlike Michi's father, Andi's father does not feel the need to interrupt his wife when she speaks. Also, the mother does not force any profession onto her son. She says that he can do anything he likes (and she had the last word here), which underlines that she is not a dominating mother figure either, which Frenkel-Brunswick found in some cases of prejudiced men.[64] This scene underlines that the generational transmission of patriarchal structures has been to some extent interrupted and that Andi's family is not father dominated but mother oriented, which might contribute to Andi's being less likely to join neo-Nazi groups.

Frenkel-Brunswick points out that nonprejudiced men show what she calls a "principled independence," which includes coming into conflict with and displaying mild aggression to their parents, which is not detrimental but can have a positive effect on the basic good relationships with the parents. In contrast, prejudiced men do not dare contradict or show aggression toward parental figures. On the contrary, they submit themselves to parental authority out of fear, which is closely related to submission to authority in general.[65]

Unlike Michi, who never challenged his father or displayed any aggression toward him, Andi has no difficulty challenging his father. In a scene where he helps his father with woodworking, he disagrees with his father's argument that he should find work to pay his gym membership himself. He even gets mildly angry at his father—to which his father responds in a rather genuine manner. This scene also shows that Andi's father is not a threatening figure and that patriarchal structures are not monolithic in this father-child relationship.

Andi finds himself in a familial context that aims to close the book on Austria's violent Nazi past, and he is immersed in the military fetish, which are both elements that can contribute to teenagers becoming susceptible to (neo)fascist ideology. However, because patriarchal family structures are not completely rigid in his familial context, Andi, in the end, decided not to join the military or the police force or become a gunsmith. Instead, he took a step back from his gun-related activities to focus on improving his grades and continue practicing guitar, as his mother suggested he do—and which did not threaten his "masculine" identity.

To conclude, the culture of silence around Austria's Nazi past and patriarchal family structures are transferred from one generation to the next.

Both play a role that the past can be repeated in the present. The (grand) parents' closing the book on the past and patriarchal family structures make them responsible for their (grand)son's susceptibility to (neo)fascist ideology. However, it is not only the parents but the culture of Austria in general, where a silence around the Nazi past and patriarchal structures remain intact at all layers of society, that one must challenge to make sure the past is not repeated in the present. Joining the far right is a matter of both the psyche of the individual and the sociocultural aspects within which that psyche is embedded.

The Emergence of the FPÖ

The Freedom Party of Austria grew out of the Federation of Independents (VdU: Verband der Unabhängigen), a collection of former members of the NSDAP (Nationalsozialistische Deutsche Arbeiterpartei, National Socialist German Workers' Party, in short: the Nazi Party). After the end of Hitler's National Socialist (NS) regime, they were initially excluded from the political process. However, when former Nazis were allowed to organize politically in 1949, the VdU immediately (and alarmingly) received more than 11.7 percent of the votes and since then have been represented in the Austrian parliament with sixteen deputies.

After internal power struggles in the VdU, the nationalist wing of the party won and reorganized itself in 1955–1956 as the Freedom Party of Austria (FPÖ). Many former National Socialists who remained loyal to Nazi ideology after 1945, called the Ehemaligen (the formers), organized themselves politically in the VdU and then in the FPÖ. Their (self-)identification as "formers" suggests that their adherence to NS ideology lies in the past. However, their unbroken adherence to NS ideology continued after the war.

Initially, the Ehemaligen did not accept the narrative offered by the Austrian government that "Austria was Hitler's first victim." Instead, as the Austrian historian Margit Reiter puts it, "They mourned their lost power positions and NS ideals. Their self-victimization only occurred at the end of the war, which they experienced as a 'collapse' and where they saw themselves as victims of the winning powers."[66] The mourning of the Ehemaligen was, however, not an attempt to work-through the past, in which one mourned for the losses of the victims of the NS regime and the loss of their internalized ego ideal (the leader figure).

Instead, they engaged in what the Mitscherlichs call *narcissistic mourning*, which entails mourning one's losses of positions of power and ego ideals.[67] Their self-pity about their narcissistic losses after 1945 went hand in hand with an aggressive demarcation and devaluation of those they declared responsible for the defeat—the victorious allies and the Jews. As Reiter points out, "Anti-Semitism was besides anti-communism, anti-Americanism, and German nationalism a core of NS ideology and belonged to a core NS ideology-continuity after the end of the war *not only* but especially in the Ehemaligen milieu."[68] The VdU and then the FPÖ provided the Ehemaligen with a context where they could *openly* defend and confirm one another in such convictions.

The inaugural leader of the FPÖ was a former high-ranking National Socialist, Anton Reinthaller, who also spared the party's supporters from mourning the loss of their leader figure (Hitler). Reinthaller was a former member of the NSDAP Upper Austria, NS minister of agriculture, and SS brigade leader who received many SS badges of honor during Hitler's regime. Reinthaller expressed in his private letters unbroken Nazi convictions. His successor was Friedrich Peter, a member of the infamous first SS infantry brigade.[69]

The persistence of NS ideology after the war existed not only in the Ehemaligen milieu; it also existed, in a more hidden form, in the larger postwar Austrian population because the postwar Austrian establishment (the center-left SPÖ and conservative ÖVP) did not initiate a political process of working-through the past. Instead, akin to the FPÖ, it integrated former Nazis into its ranks despite an initial agreement about a process of denazification. It also provided Austrians with the official narrative that "Austria was the first victim of Hitler," which Austrians welcomed as it allowed them to close the book on the past.

While the VdU and then the FPÖ remained on the sidelines of Austrian politics for several years, the FPÖ made it into the mainstream of Austrian politics when Jörg Haider became the party's new leader in 1986. Haider grew up and was politically socialized in the Ehemaligen milieu (his father was a former Nazi stormtrooper). He learned fencing in a German nationalist fraternity; his fencing dummy was nicknamed "Wiesenthal,"[70] which underlines the transgenerational transmission of NS values and its political instrumentalization in the FPÖ.

Haider brought FPÖ into the mainstream of Austrian politics because he became the public apologist for the war generation and their children, which allowed Austrians to continue to keep the book on their past closed, underlining how the Freedom Party successfully tapped into the large pool of Austrians that aimed to master the past. Furthermore, Haider and the FPÖ have repeatedly issued ambiguous public statements and actions that deny and minimize Austria's involvement in the NS horrors. Under the leadership of Haider, the Freedom Party moved so far to the right that it was classified as an extreme-right party in 1993.[71] The Freedom Party's extensive use of media (press, TV, and newer media such as comics, homepages, websites, Facebook, Twitter, and so forth) assisted its rise. Haider repeatedly appeared in weekly magazines, adding to his visibility in the public sphere.[72]

In late 2017, the Freedom Party joined forces with the conservative ÖVP and formed a coalition government. While many thought this might "tame" the FPÖ, it did not. After yet another antisemitic incident in early 2018, the FPÖ, then the governing party, saw itself under substantial political pressure to review its historical roots and continuities with the Nazis. However, established historians critiqued the final report published by the FPÖ on December 23, 2019, and concluded that the central research goal of examining the FPÖ's antisemitism and its affinities to the far right had not been met.[73]

Today the FPÖ is firmly anchored in the European far right, which, while not united, takes up common positions on race and gender, including "ethnic nationalism," which implies the aim to create a "white homeland," if necessary with violence, and entails open forms of Islamophobia and antifeminism and veiled forms of "secondary antisemitism." As Lars Rensmann explains, secondary antisemitism is a "new form of Jew-hatred originat[ing] in the political and psychological desire to split off, repress, and downplay the memory of the Holocaust because such memory, with which Jews are often identified, evokes unwelcome guilt feelings."[74] Secondary antisemitism is a means to fend off unwelcome feelings of guilt and loss concerning the violent deeds of the past. Although the antisemitism "ban," which occurred first in Germany and with delay also in Austria, contributed to a taboo to openly expressing antisemitism in Austria, antisemitic sentiments did not disappear. On the contrary, they continued not only in the Ehemaligen milieu but also in the larger Austrian population in the form of a secondary antisemitism.

As Karin Stögner further points out, secondary antisemitism is a symptom to be found primarily in Germany and Austria, where antisemitism, because of the taboo on overt antisemitism, has not disappeared. Instead, it appears coded and becomes adaptable to areas that have nothing directly to do with the National Socialist past.[75] Secondary antisemitism during the postwar years was in Austria directed particularly toward "displaced persons" (DPs), who were Jews that had survived the Holocaust.

They reminded the Austrian population of their guilt (and loss), much as the camp survivors who come to Holocaust-era sites threaten to unearth difficult feelings of guilt and loss today. There are also parallels between how the Ehemaligen and the Austrian population today aim to fend off their feelings of guilt and loss pertaining to Austria's violent Nazi past. For example, the Ehemaligen attacked camp survivors in FPÖ periodicals as "criminals," which reappears in (grand)parents' constructions of camp survivors as threatening figures.[76]

To justify its goal of creating a "white homeland," the European far right and the Freedom Party of Austria adhere to the conspiracy theory of the "Great Replacement," which suggests that white Europeans (the "indigenous population") face the "threat" of being "replaced" or wiped out by "nonwhite" immigrants, especially Muslims.[77] The conspiracy theory of the "Great Replacement" combines racism, antisemitism, and antifeminism.

In this conspiracy, the veiled Muslim woman is constructed as a "threat" to Austrian national identity because her supposed fertility produces many children from "inferior" races and so drives the Great Replacement. To fight it, white Austrian women must give birth to as many white children as possible (akin to Nazi-era eugenic policies) to counter the threat of the Great Replacement. It blames feminism for distracting white women from their "natural" role as child producers and taking away the "natural" strength of men, both of which are needed in the struggle against the (imagined) foe.

Stögner further shows us how the FPÖ uses antifeminism to transmit antisemitic messages.[78] The FPÖ conceptualizes the Austrian national identity as threatened not only by the immigration of members of "foreign" cultures but also by those who do not fit neatly into the "natural" category of "man" or "woman." The antisemitic imaginary, where Jewish men appear "feminized" and Jewish women "masculinized," reappears in a coded form in the FPÖ's portrayal of the masculinized Austrian woman with autonomous sexuality who withdraws herself from the "natural" dictum to reproduce children in the fight against the Great Replacement.

The FPÖ portrays such acts as *Geburtenverweigerung* (birth-giving refusal) and portrays such women as "whores" who threaten Austrian "national identity" because they refuse to contribute to the birthrate of the white Austrian race and undermine the struggle against the Great Replacement. We find a disguised form of antisemitism also in the FPÖ's attempts to hinder the establishment of a House of History in Vienna.

The House of History Revisited

While Austrians were successful in deriding several attempts to establish a Haus der Geschichte Österreichs, (HGÖ; House of History Austria), in which Austria's involvement in the Nazi regime would be, for the first time in Austrian history, on display in some form in a public museum since the 1960s, this time they failed, and in November 2018, an HGÖ finally opened in Vienna's Neue Burg, a part of the Hofburg, "only" thirty years after a much larger version of a House of History opened in Germany.

Given Austria's resistance to work-through its Nazi past, an HGÖ, which promises that such a process, which allows Austrians to mourn their losses and confront themselves with guilt, could be finally started, ought to be cause for celebration (and hope). However, in the actual museum, as Neuhäuser points out, Austria's problematic role during Hitler's regime is "only documented in the restricted part of the already physically small current exhibition; it is thus somewhat hidden in the chronological flow of the exhibition and can be easily bypassed or missed."[79]

The FPÖ played a core role in ensuring that Austria's House of History, rather than allowing Austrians to work-through their violent Nazi past, would be a small museum with a collection in which such a past can be easily bypassed or missed. The main aim of this party's interventions around the museum was and continues to be a propaganda tactic to appeal to the large pool of Austrians who, rather than confronting themselves with difficult feelings of political guilt and loss, opt for closing the book on such a past.

In its original conception by Oliver Rathkolb (of the SPÖ, Social Democratic Party of Austria), a professor of recent history at the University of Vienna and his international team, the space devoted to the museum was already relatively small compared to similar museums—only three thousand square meters.[80] The FPÖ's aggressive interventions against the museum, while they aimed at (but did not succeed) in hindering the establishment of an HGÖ, succeeded in further downsizing the museum to a mere 1,800 square meters.

The unwillingness of Austrians to devote physical space to a House of History stands for their unwillingness to create a psychological space in which they could initiate a process that allows them to work-through Austria's Nazi past. The FPÖ's interventions around the museum helped them recruit new followers because it promised the derailment of the establishment of a house of history, so Austrians could avoid confrontation with difficult feelings of guilt and loss.

Specifically, the FPÖ attempted to hinder the partial relocation of a collection of old musical instruments to a higher floor in the Neue Burg, which was needed to make space for the museum. The FPÖ's efforts to stop the establishment of a House of History Austria were supported by far-right blogs and publications, who vehemently protested against the relocation. For example, Ursula Stenzel, the then FPÖ minister for Vienna's city government, demanded that moving the collection to another floor must be immediately stopped because with such a move, the "*most important* collection of musical instruments in the world" and "*a collection of great excellence and potential for visitors from all over the world*," would be "*verdrängt*" (repressed) and destroyed.[81] That a collection of old musical instruments that few have heard about and that was rather neglected all of a sudden turned into the "most important collection of musical instruments in the world" tells us that something else was at stake than just the collection's partial move from one floor to another.

One can read the movement of the musical instruments to another floor as the movement of repressed feelings of guilt and loss from the unconscious to consciousness. The FPÖ aimed to appeal to followers by derailing or destroying the establishment of a museum, which would expose Austria's shameful past and threaten them with a return of the repressed. At the same time, it projects such an attempt onto those who aim to create a space for Austrians to work-through their past. In Stenzel's statement, she argues that those who aim to create a House of History aim to *destroy* and *repress* the collection of old musical instruments, which exposes Austria's "great cultural heritage." Such a statement covers over the fact that it is the FPÖ who aimed to destroy (or derail) the establishment of a House of History.

The FPÖ offers potential followers an opportunity to bring the past into agreement with their narcissistic desires by promising them that it will keep the horrors of the past buried through derailing the creation of a space (the House of History) that could foreground such a past. The Austrian Freedom Party offers its (potential) followers an opportunity to close the book on the past. It also utilizes potential followers' narcissistic desires to belong to a "great collectivity" and thereby to feel significant rather than grapple with difficult feelings of guilt and loss.

The FPÖ provided them with a positive narrative of Austria through the exaggerated portrayal of an old collection of musical instruments. Here the FPÖ invites the followers to identify with the "excellent and great" collection of musical instruments, which stands for the "great collective Austria," to feel "great" themselves. The (potential) followers, rather than confronting themselves with feelings of guilt and loss, can feel "great and excellent" through the identification with Austria as a nation of "great cultural heritage."

The FPÖ also repeatedly stated that the collection of musical instruments could not be moved because we are dealing here with "highly sensitive art objects."[82] For example, the FPÖ's spokesman on cultural affairs, Walter Rosenkranz, demanded that the collection be left where it is because any movement of the "sensitive art objects" is not only too costly but could also lead to "lasting damages of the *hochkarätigen* [top-class] objects."[83]

Here, Austrians' sensitivity to their Nazi past is displaced onto the musical instruments. The collection appears to be sensitive to any movement (of guilt and loss from the unconscious to the conscious). Here the FPÖ aims to hinder the creation of a space where Austrians have to (or are invited to) address a topic that is highly sensitive for them (Austria's Nazi past) to hinder the movement of difficult feelings of guilt and loss from the unconscious to consciousness and to stifle a working-through of the past.

Rosenkranz also offers the followers an opportunity to bring the past in line with their narcissistic desires. He foregrounds that the FPÖ supports a view of Austria as a "great collective," first through deriding the establishment of the House of History Austria, which could make room for exposing another view, and second by foregrounding that Austria is not so much a collectivity with a shameful past but with a *hochkarätige* one. Again, the followers are invited to identify with such a "great nation" to feel "top-class" themselves.

Also, Rosenkranz's argument that the moving of the collection will incur too high a cost insinuates that the movement of one's repressed feelings of guilt and loss from the unconscious to the consciousness might be too "costly" for Austrians. Instead, they can feel *hochkarätig* by belonging to a nation that harbors *hochkarätige* musical instruments.

Although the FPÖ's interventions against the museum did not completely prevent its establishment, it successfully contributed to its downsizing. As Rosenkranz points out: "The [musical instrument collection] will stay at its current location and will not have to give way to the House of History. This is a success for the FPÖ, which, since the announcement of the project, has persistently campaigned for the [collection's] current location."[84]

Here the FPÖ's "success" in preventing the movement of the collection to another floor stands for its success in hindering the movement of Austrians' repressed feelings of guilt and loss from the unconscious to consciousness, which is the core appeal of this party for the large pool of Austrians who aim to close the book on the past instead of working-through it.

Conclusion

What can we do to engender a process that allows Austrians of all generations to work-through the past instead of mastering it? What can we do to break the transgenerational effects of the taboo to touch a nation's violent past? One thing that comes to mind here is that the teacher's effort in the documentary did reach one student; the only one that seemed willing to break with the taboo was the female teenager who challenged Michi's wanting to keep silent about the neo-Nazi attack on concentration camp survivors.

I assume that this teenager had parents who were less resistant to working-through the past and to confronting themselves with difficult feelings of guilt and loss. Here it seems that local educational programs should be geared toward the (grand)parents' generations, which aim to close the book on the past and thereby hinder efforts of educators to engender a process in teenagers to work-through the past. Such (grand)parents would need the education the teachers try to give to their children, so the (grand)parents can be more helpful and support their children in their efforts to work-through guilt and loss.

Such educational programs need to touch on the taboo to counter the defensive attitudes of the (grand)parental generation to regain memory and knowledge about Austria as a perpetrator nation. Only if they know what happened to the camp survivors and how the crimes of Austrians affected them and their descendants can they start to defy the taboos, start to work-through guilt feelings, and begin the work of mourning.

Only a working-through of the past can bring back what the taboo aims to do away with—the physical and emotional association with victims of Nazi crimes, who have been and continue to be part of Austrian communities. As the Mitscherlichs put it: "Discovering a capacity to feel compassion for people never before apprehended behind our distorting projections would give us back our ability to mourn."[85] Austrians must do everything to eliminate their distorting projections onto victims of crimes and rediscover their capacity to feel compassion for these victims.

Only if Austrians and other European nations (as Austria is not the only country that has this problem) openly defy the taboo and touch their shameful past can they rediscover their capacity to feel compassion for camp survivors and their descendants and engage in the difficult work of working-through guilt and mourning the loss of all those people that were murdered during the Nazi and colonial era, as well as their own losses. However, it is not only the parents but the culture of Austria in general, where a silence around the Nazi past and patriarchal structures remain intact in all layers of society, that one must challenge to make sure the past is not repeated in the present and the future. This underlines that the far right is a matter of both the psyche of the individual and the social-cultural aspects.

CHAPTER VII

Gratifications of Terror

The Austrian Identitarian Movement

The pan-European identitarian movement (IM) is a neofascist youth movement that is openly anti-Muslim, covertly antisemitic, and antifeminist. Akin to the alt-right in the United States, the IM is not engaged in "fun transgressions." Instead, it is a power-seeking movement with backing from those in power. It aims, akin to its National Socialist predecessors, to oppress the weak in society and create a "white homeland" in Europe, which it seeks to achieve through the genocide of racial minorities (immigrants and migrants). The identitäre Bewegung Österreich (IBÖ) was inspired by the French Bloc identitaire and is a branch of Europe's identitarian movement. It was founded in 2012 by the Austrians Martin Sellner, Patrick Lenart, and Alexander Markovics.[1]

The IM received significant media and public attention because of its regular, attention-grabbing actions, such as its deceptive "charity" action of distributing pork soup in Muslim neighborhoods (which practitioners of the Muslim faith cannot eat) in 2006 and its attacks on migrants in the Mediterranean Sea in 2017. Also, the IBÖ has received media and public attention (which it uses to attract followers) because of its destructive actions, including its attack on refugees protesting their living and working conditions in the refugee camps in Austria in 2013 and its 2016 violent attack on refugee actors performing a play exposing the tightened asylum rights and discrimination of refugees in Austria.

A core leader of the IBÖ is Martin Sellner, a philosophy and former law student at the University of Vienna. He frequents today the Neue Institutsgebäude at the University of Vienna, Austria, in which Adorno gave his talk *Aspekte des neuen Rechtsradikalismus*, on April 6, 1967. With the growth of the Austrian Freedom Party and the IBÖ, Adorno's repeated references to the dangers of a resurgent far right in Austria have become reality.[2]

In this chapter, I expose the psychologically oriented techniques Sellner uses in his book *Identitär: Geschichte eines Aufbruchs* to recruit predominantly young, male, white followers to support the IBÖ's violent aims.[3] While there are some analyses of the identitarian movement in Europe, this literature is mainly from an activist or journalist perspective.[4] Furthermore, there is little in-depth theoretical analysis on the IM and IBÖ in general and limited analysis that focuses on Sellner's writings and the Austrian context in particular. Furthermore, while there is some research on the IM in the European context, that research does not describe the psychologically oriented devices the IM uses to catch followers.[5] Furthermore, no work (that I know of) currently analyzes the IM from a psychoanalytic and an early Frankfurt School Critical Theory perspective.[6]

It is important to note that Adorno, in *The Psychological Technique of Martin Luther Thomas' Radio Addresses*, provides a more in-depth analysis of fascist propaganda techniques than he does in *Aspekte des neuen Rechtsradikalismus* and *Freudian Theory*. In this work, Adorno analyzed the U.S. Christian fascist agitator 1930s Thomas's radio addresses during his exile and his work with Paul Lazarsfeld on the social significance of radio. The core argument Adorno makes is that propaganda techniques function akin to the advertising strategies used by the culture industry. To deepen Adorno's analysis and to understand why people submit themselves to irrational goals that contradict their rational economic and other self-interests, I also draw on Adorno's *Freudian Theory* and on my theoretical framework, which outlines how far-right propaganda techniques produce in subjects a hypnotic sleep and dream state, allowing the neofascist movement to recruit them to their destructive aims. I will also draw on Adorno's contributions to the *Authoritarian Personality* (AP) study to further detail some of the devices Sellner is using.

However, to understand how Sellner can attract followers to his destructive "movement," we must also consider the objective conditions of suffering in capitalism, such as alienation, isolation, and exploitation. As the work of Hofmann and colleagues shows us, unemployment, especially for younger populations, is rising all over Europe, which has helped far-right parties and movements gain control in Europe. So notably, the younger generations experience subjective suffering caused by precarity capitalism. Young white men believe, given unconscious racist and sexist attitudes that date back to the European colonial and fascist eras, that they ought to have "success" on the economic, interpersonal, and bodily levels. Since they face growing challenges in living up to the fetish of "success" in precarity capitalism, they experience a sharp tension between their ego and their ego ideal, with connected feelings of castration anxiety, failure, and frustration.

The psychologically oriented devices of the far right offer their followers the opportunity to undo the tension between their ego and their ego ideal by inducing processes of ego ideal replacement with the idealized leader figure. The propaganda techniques of elements of the far right such as the alt-right and the IBÖ, where there is no identifiable leader or where there are numerous leaders, are different, and ego ideal replacement with the ideal leader figure is less central. In this chapter, I outline the psychologically oriented techniques the IBÖ uses that allow its followers to undo the split between their ego and their ego ideal. Furthermore, I show that these mechanisms also generate the followers' artificial regressions into sleep and dream states, stimulating them to express their desires for cruel aggressiveness onto the IBÖ's chosen foes.[7]

I group the devices in sections that show how they reinforce one another to capture followers and stimulate violent behavior in them. This chapter comprises four sections, excluding the introduction and the conclusion. "The Euphoria of Ongoing Action," explains how the "movement trick" and the "indefatigability device" work in tandem to catch followers. The Terror Strategy," discusses a series of recruitment techniques Sellner uses that generate and utilize fear while promising the followers gratification. "The Terrorized Unity," outlines how Sellner uses the "unity trick" to capture followers and how the "black hand device" exposes the falseness of any solidarity and unity within the IBÖ. "The Persecuted Innocents Who Attack Imagined Foes," discusses how Sellner uses the "persecuted innocence device," paranoid stereopathy, and the "democratic cloak device" to stimulate and rationalize violence in the followers. Finally, based on my analyses, in my concluding remarks I provide some hints of what we can do to counter the growth of the IM in Europe in general and the IBÖ in Austria in particular.

The Euphoria of Ongoing Action

This section outlines how Sellner uses the "movement trick" and the "indefatigability device" to catch followers. I also show how these devices induce in his potential followers artificial regressions that are akin to hypnosis, which make the followers surrender to and carry out the destructive goals of the IBÖ.

Since the fascist agitator does not want his followers to know that his main aims are violence, oppression of the weak, and the exhibition of power, he uses the "movement trick." Here he remains vague on what policies he is for and instead focuses on what he is *against*. He makes a fetish of the term *Bewegung* (movement) itself, without explaining where the movement is going. Thus, we find "the glorification of action, of something going on, [which] both obliterates and replaces the purpose of movement."[8]

That the IBÖ makes a fetish out of the movement is already salient in its name—it calls itself the identitarian *movement*. However, it is unclear what its aims are. Instead, Sellner remains vague on this point, and we learn mainly what the IBÖ is against, namely, anybody it classifies as "foreign," primarily immigrants and refugees from non-European nations, particularly (but not exclusively) those from Middle Eastern countries. The IM's main aim is to violently get rid of such "foreigners" in Europe through genocide.

For the IBÖ the movement itself becomes the aim, which is salient in the main focus of Sellner's book—a detailed description of the different forms of "actions" the movement engages in, which stretches over several of his chapters. Sellner also aims to distract the followers from his destructive aims, which will destroy the followers themselves (who have to sacrifice their lives for the movement) by repeatedly foregrounding the pleasure the movement will yield. As Adorno points out, "Since the goal is finally the enslavement of one's followers, they should be distracted from such a goal, and their ambition should be centered around the *pleasure* which the movement itself may yield, not around the ideas which it might possibly materialize."[9] The intent is to prolong the pleasure and override any thoughts of what destructive action is being carried out.

As an example, Sellner tells us about the IBÖ's first "great action," when a group of white male students aggressively disturbed a Caritas sit-in of refugees at the Votivkirche in Vienna in February 2013, which aimed to make the public aware of the tightening asylum-rights measures in Austria. Sellner tells us that the "activists" were before the action tense, but once they entered the church, they found themselves in "action mode": "This feeling is hard to describe in words. All the *tension* leaves and gives way to *focused clarity and spontaneity*. It is always a *drug*: just wonderful, and the effect remains throughout the entire action."[10]

Here the tension the followers feel also refers to the tension between their ego and the ego ideal, which is the result of their difficulties in living up to the economic, interpersonal, and bodily "success" standards of precarity capitalism and generates anxieties around their subjectivities and feelings of failure. The "drug" of action promises them, for a while at least, a pleasure that allows them to undo that tension between the ego and the ego ideal, which enables them to, in the dreamlike, hallucinated fulfillment of their ego ideal, feel "successful." Although they might not have success in real life, they can now feel "successful" via the action drug.

The pleasure of action is further prolonged by what happens after the action takes place, where the movement celebrates its "success" with beer and electro-punk music. Sellner expresses it this way: "Until today, I remember the *amazing unbound atmosphere* after the first great action, which justifies every excitement, effort, and blood-sweat. . . . Also, this feeling of success is hard to describe, and one can only experience it firsthand. Rightly: One needs to earn it in the fire of action."[11]

However, instead of generating "clarity," as Sellner suggests, the movement trick engenders in the followers the exact opposite. It engenders in them a sleep and dream state, where any clarity and consciousness about the actual state of affairs—the destructive goals of the movement that contradict their rational economic and other self-interests and the castrating conditions of precarity capitalism disappear, and their unconscious attitude appears.

Furthermore, with artificial regression into the sleep and dream state, any spontaneity, as Sellner proclaims, disappears. Instead, such an archaic regression generates a passive-masochistic attitude that makes the followers experience the movement as a threatening force to which they must fully submit and whose destructive goals they must carry out, even if such submission ultimately leads to their destruction.

In addition, undoing the tension between the ego and the ego ideal also eliminates (temporarily) the followers' superego, which keeps their egos in line with the ideal and their repressed aggressive impulses in check (Sellner hints at that with the idea that there is an "unbound atmosphere" in the IBÖ). Once the checks on their aggression are loosened and their unconscious attitude predominates, the followers are more likely to direct such aggression toward the movement's outside targets of hatred.

Here the movement as fetish, where the action turns a means into an end (that is, where the "means" are crucial but the "ends" matter less), gives the following message to the follower: "Who cares what you're doing because you'll enjoy doing it so much. If what you're doing creates such a euphoria, whatever outcome it produces is justified." Such a message allows the followers who engage in a destructive action to say to themselves: "If it felt this good to do it, it can't be wrong." As a result, the follower can silence any doubts about engaging in the destructive action.

The movement fetish, whose focus is on action, corresponds to the lack of theory provided by the fascist agitator. But, as Adorno points out, one should not underestimate these movements because of their lack of any theoretical underpinning: "The characteristic of these movements is the perfection of the propaganda means, combined with a blindness, yes, absurdity of their aims that should be reached with their means."[12] The National Socialist regime leaders, for example, were propagandists who put all their phantasy and productivity into propaganda techniques.

Propaganda also becomes the substance of the IBÖ, which further substitutes ends with means. Sellner explains that he dispenses with theory because "actions must deliver little text for many." Instead, to reach the masses, he explains, the IBÖ uses provocative pictures with slogans that are "in one second readable and understandable." The result is, according to him, a "mental rollercoaster" that "invites the receiver of our messages to be elevated to a higher level of understanding without having to exert [her/]himself too much."[13]

While Sellner expresses here his contempt for the intellectual capacities of his audience (which we also find in the alt-right), he also promises his followers that engaging in action will allow them to be "elevated" to the realm of ideas without having to engage in any exertion, which any theoretical analysis must contend with to yield results. However, creating a "mental rollercoaster" aims not to generate a "higher level of understanding," as he promises potential followers. Instead, Sellner aims to achieve with the "mental rollercoaster" the exact opposite: to *inhibit* any understanding of the destructive goals of the identitarian movement, so the followers blindly carry them out.

Similar to the "movement trick," the "indefatigability device" promises the followers a "drug" to feel better about themselves again.[14] At the same time, it creates hypnotic conditions that make it easier for the IBÖ to make people follow their destructive aims, which, again, contradict the rational economic and other self-interests of the followers. The "indefatigability device" implies a scenario where the fascist agitator emphasizes his being indefatigable himself, through which he sets an example for his followers: He sacrifices his entire life for the movement, and his followers must do the same.[15]

Sellner repeatedly points out his sacrifices: "One gets older and sees how former school colleagues walk past oneself in their studies and professional lives. It is impossible to do justice to everything. Activism is an unthinkable and unpaid 'job' which ruins every résumé."[16] Since he has sacrificed his career and life for the movement, he sets an example for his followers to do the same—they must sacrifice their professional and personal lives so they can constantly work, without any rest, for the movement.

Committed followers of the IBÖ must be indefatigable—they must sacrifice their time, career, and relationships to the movement. As he puts it, the movement "has the highest priority over family, university, profession, and leisure. . . . The whole movement is only here for the action, for which, like the fire brigade, it has to be always ready." Sellner does prescribe "rest days" for new followers, but mostly so the contrast between their new lives where they have to work for the movement constantly and their prior lives is not too stark. These rest days only are offered until they become committed followers—then they can never rest but have to be "always ready."[17]

As Adorno points out, the agitator wants the followers to be ready for the movement's actions, "but only under a kind of spell. . . . It is the activity of the hypnotized which is expected by fascist propaganda rather than that of responsible and conscious individuals. Thus, the insistence upon indefatigability works as a kind of *Narkotikum* [dope]."[18] The indefatigability device casts a hypnotic spell on the followers—the neofascist leader's call for constant work and sacrifice for the movement does not aim to generate a conscious or awake attitude in the followers. Instead, it generates a sleep state in them, in which the followers turn their attention away from the external world (the destructive aims of the movement and the objective conditions of suffering in precarity capitalism). Furthermore, it provides them with a narcotic (which Adorno does not further explain) because the sleep state also engenders in the followers a dream state, which allows them to replace the "Oh, if I were successful" with an "I am successful" and where the "I am" is given a hallucinatory representation,[19] which generates a state of euphoria in them.

Also, for the neofascist agitator, the dream state in his followers is central because it allows him to get rid of any external stimuli (such as people outside the movement that could make the followers aware of the absurdity of his aims) or internal stimuli (remnants of consciousness in the followers that might alert them of the wrongness of the movement's actions), which might interfere with the sleep state in his followers. As long as they are in a euphoric dream state, the followers are less likely to wake up, and their unconscious attitude prevails, allowing the leader to manipulate them for his destructive goals better.

Adorno further explains how this device uses the ambivalent relationship between sleeping and indefatigability to hypnotize the followers. The followers are repeatedly told that they are fully awake and must not sleep, which draws attention away from the fact that they are, in reality, being *asked to fall asleep and act while they are sleeping.* As Adorno points out, the followers, who are in reality asleep while they are repeatedly being told that they have to be or that they are indefatigable, offer less resistance to the will of the leader (or here, the movement) than they otherwise would.[20]

Sellner shrewdly plays on the ambivalent relationship between sleeping and indefatigability. For example, he tells his followers that they are the only ones awake; those who have not yet joined the movement are asleep. The IBÖ activists are the avant-garde "who understand precisely what it is all about," which Sellner also illustrates by referencing the film *The Matrix*. He asserts that activists are the ones who have "already woken up" and who float "between the sleeping batteries of the *Eingelullten* [the lulled ones]." The main task of the followers is to wake up "the ones who do not want to wake up."[21]

Here Sellner suggests that the movement's followers are awake and see things clearly, while those who have not yet joined are asleep and have no insight into reality. Here we have another connection to the "movement trick," which insinuates that the drug-like high of action gives way to "focused clarity" and provides the follower with insights they did not have before. However, the reality is the other way around: the followers are the ones that are "lulled" in by the drugs of indefatigability and action, which make them follow the destructive will of the leader and eradicate any insight into the destructiveness of the action itself.

However, Adorno does not mention that the movement trick also induces a hypnotic state in which the followers' unconscious predominates. The predominance of the unconscious results from the undoing of the tension between the ego and the ego ideal, which also implies (a temporary) abrogation of the superego. Such an abrogation allows the doped followers to temporarily receive their libidinal and aggressive impulses in their egos, which the IBÖ then redirects for its purposes.

It is not a coincidence that Sellner characterizes the movement as a *"jealous female lover"*[22] who is "reluctant to tolerate a career or rigorous studies and especially no real, time-consuming relationship. Every free moment, every free thought, every financial and bodily resource is spent on activism, if done seriously."[23] While the far-right leader accomplishes the integration of the fascist mass through promoting an idealization of himself, in contexts in which there are numerous movement leaders or no identifiable leaders, the same is accomplished via a process where the followers transfer their narcissistic libido to the *movement itself* (the "jealous female lover"). The movement fetish and the indefatigability device are central to such an enterprise. The followers must focus their mental and physical energy entirely on the movement, as any independence of thought could make them wake up to the reality of the movement's destructiveness.

That Sellner aims to have the followers transfer their narcissistic libido to the movement is also salient in his assertion that there is an initial "euphoric phase" (of being in love) with the movement. Furthermore, he sees the "strength of leadership," besides keeping a structure of discipline and order,[24] "keeping a spirit of community and excitement alive, which carries the newlings after the *finishing of the first euphoria further.*"[25]

Here we can see that the neofascist leadership's core aim is to keep the followers in a euphoric and uninterrupted dream state, keeping their unconscious attitude predominant. In other words, to make sure that the followers do not wake up and become aware that the leader's destructive aims contradict their economic and other self-interests, he has to repeatedly feed them with "drugs" (since drugs wear off after some time) to allow them, for prolonged periods, to remain in an unconscious state.

Sellner never gets tired of foregrounding that what one finds in the IBÖ is not boredom but excitement and euphoria, such as the promise of a house party the followers will be able to join and that will spill over to the streets, the campus, and the entire town. Indeed, this is also the euphoria and excitement that Sellner himself seeks in the movement. As he puts it, the initial phase of euphoria (being in love with the movement) always ends, but "for some (and the author of these lines and for sure many readers count themselves among this group) it never ends."[26]

It seems that Sellner too needs the euphoria the various psychologically oriented techniques offer his followers to help him feel better about sacrificing his life and career for the movement and to remain unaware of the violence and absurdity of his destructive aims. Here we can see how neofascism necessitates in the last resort a self-hypnosis, which Sellner has to effect onto himself over and over again and which allows him not to acknowledge the conflict between his particular interests and that of the movement.[27]

Throughout the book, to quell his followers' interpersonal and bodily castration anxieties, Sellner also suggests that young men who join the movement will be "successful" with young women. He provides the reader, on several occasions, with descriptions of how IBÖ men will meet attractive women in the "movement." But, as Bruns and colleagues point out, women mainly serve to prop up insecure masculine identities in the IM.[28] Therefore, instead of feeling "unmanly" by not having "success" with women, one joins the IBÖ, where such "success" is guaranteed.

However, although from the beginning the representation of women within the IM in the German-speaking context has been low and all leading functions continue to be carried out by men, women have played important roles as propagandists, despite how the movement devalues women. As Judith Goetz shows us, the IM attempted to promote women's "activism" by creating Edelweiß (Maidens Group Edelweiss) in 2015 and later Identitäre Mädels und Frauen (Identitarian Girls and Women).[29] However, these women's groups did not pursue their political agendas but supported the campaigns of their respective national or regional groups. Therefore, they adhered to and promoted the IM's antifeminist gender ideology, which considers femininity and masculinity as natural essences in hierarchical oppositions where women occupy a place below men.

Frenkel-Brunswick's theoretical framework provides a core explanation for why women support the antifeminist far right. She suggests that children who grow up in families where the father (or mother) is a threatening figure and where a clear distinction between stereotypical male and female sex roles exist generate a rigid character structure in the child. The child develops such a structure because her parents did not help her integrate her libidinal and aggressive drives, and, because of the threatening parental figures, she does not have an internalized but instead an externalized superego.

As a result, she needs a rigid character structure to keep her free-floating aggression (as well as her free-floating libido), which can break out at any time, repressed in the unconscious. Thus, women who grew up in such family constellations are drawn to the rigid gender and sexual roles that the far right offers them, even when it disadvantages them. Also, they feel threatened by anyone who challenges that structure, such as the LGBT+ community. Here the open hatred of the far right against sexual minorities further adds to the attraction of hate groups for such women.[30]

The Terror Strategy

Adorno groups together a series of psychologically oriented devices in the "terror strategy." The terror strategy generates and utilizes fear and ambivalence by pointing at the threat of an impending catastrophe. It is composed of quasi-rational surface stimuli with which it sets in motion irrational psychological mechanisms. While the emotions this strategy calls forth are distinctly negative, it *at the same time* promises "certain unconscious *gratifications* as supplementary effects of the negative statements."[31]

In this section, I discuss how Sellner uses three devices of the terror strategy: the "if you only knew trick," the "shiver down the spine device," and the "last hour device." These techniques draw on both fear *and* the promise of gratifications to catch new followers.

The first device of the terror strategy is the "if you only knew trick," which implies "the suggestion of mysterious dangers only known to the speaker."[32] The fascist agitator points to the future, when he will clarify what he merely hints at now. Such a hint at the future arouses curiosity in the listeners to join the organization or at least read his publications in the hope of being let in on his knowledge at a future date. The mere interest in what one will hear later creates an emotional tie between speaker and listener.

Adorno points out that the lure of innuendo grows with its vagueness because it allows for an unchecked play of the imagination and invites all sorts of speculation, which is enhanced in the masses through anonymous processes "above their heads" that they cannot control and that they aim to explain in personalistic, conspiracy-theory terms.[33] People today, perhaps even more so than in Adorno's time, feel themselves objects of anonymous social processes in precarity capitalism and are thus anxious to learn "what goes on behind the scenes," which helps explain the effectiveness of this device in today's far-right movements.

Sellner repeatedly points out that "the task of identitarian action is akin to a visual message in a bottle from the future, which makes much worse scenes visible here and now. The effect must be a healing shock that changes the whole consciousness."[34] Throughout the book, he uses grand-sounding terms such as the "Great Replacement" and "Islamization" to insinuate these "worse scenes from the future," but he does not explain their meaning. Such undefined terms arouse our curiosity, and we are inclined to continue reading until we find out what the "message in a bottle from the future" implies. When he finally reveals what the message suggests, he invites his readers to "explain" anonymous social processes via conspiracies where foreign populations (mostly immigrants and migrants from Muslim nations) "wipe out" what the IM calls indigenous (white) Europeans (or Austrians) in a "white genocide."[35]

The most dangerous aspect of this device is that it advances an irrational increase in the agitator's prestige and authority. The agitator knows what the others do not know, and he points at this difference by never saying *what* he knows or how much he knows. Adorno clearly understands this: "He always reserves for himself a surplus of knowledge which inspires awe and at the same time makes the public wish to participate in it."[36] This aspect of Sellner's "if you only knew" trick is salient in his assertion that "our downfall is a not yet comprehended *secret*. We do not yet know what happens with us . . . in the knowledge of the 'not-knowing,' there is hope. As singular and new as this crazy self-destruction that came over us is, it could also be the possibilities of a spontaneous regeneration and a turn."[37]

Since he is the only one who knows about the secret of impending (self-)destruction, he is the only one who knows what to do to keep such impending catastrophe at bay, which increases his authority in the reader's view. In awe of Sellner, the reader wishes to be let into the IM's secret and contribute to a "spontaneous regeneration and a turn" in Europe. Furthermore, it promises the reader spontaneity, which precarity capitalism has largely eradicated.

One of the central stimuli of the "if you only knew" trick is the deeper wish to belong and become part of a closed group, which, I suggest, results from the growing isolation people experience in precarity capitalist societies. Adorno points out: "Innuendo is a psychological means of making people feel that they already are members of that closed group that strives to catch them. The assumption that one understands something which is not plainly said, presupposes a kind of esoteric 'intelligence,' which tends to make accomplices of speaker and listener."[38] Furthermore, the device implies a threat to all those who do not know "what I mean." Such a threat tells the potential follower that joining the movement is safer than remaining outside of it.

In *Aspekte des neuen Rechtsradikalismus*, Adorno further details how the "if you only knew" trick draws on guilt feelings around the Holocaust in new far-right movements in Germany. The taboo established around the Holocaust through official laws turned into a means of antisemitic agitation by saying, with a wink: "We are not allowed to say anything, but we understand ourselves amongst us. We all know, what we mean."[39] As outlined in chapter 6, Austrians have largely failed to work-through their recent National Socialist past. As a result, Sellner has ample opportunity to utilize repressed feelings of guilt for his technique of innuendo.

Like the Austrian Freedom Party, the IBÖ is overtly anti-Muslim. It is *at the same* time deeply antisemitic.[40] However, Sellner never directly mentions the Holocaust or Jews, because of the taboo established around the Holocaust in Austria. However, he shrewdly uses the taboo around overt antisemitism in his innuendo technique. For example, he asserts that guilt feelings push the "indigenous youth"[41] into a "neurotic identity crisis" and that the radical left sees in immigrants a new revolutionary potential with whom they aim to replace the German *perpetrator Volk*.[42]

His references to guilt and the perpetrator—but speaking about the Holocaust and Jews not directly but only in a coded form—give the follower the feeling that she knows what he is talking about and that she is already part of the movement that tries to catch her. Furthermore, he aims to exonerate Austrians and demonize those that seek to foster a "working-through the past" (as they create a "neurotic identity crises of indigenous youth" and become part of the conspiracy that aims to wipe out the "German perpetrator *Volk*"). Also, by referring to guilt as "German guilt" and to the perpetrator as German, the followers are made to believe there is "no need to feel guilty" as an Austrian.

Sellner also uses the "*Schauder*," or "shiver down the spine device," the second terror strategy Adorno outlines. Here the fascist agitator "terrorizes his audience by constantly pointing out all sorts of threats to them. He does not rely so much on their desire for happiness as on their fear that things may become even worse, while ceaselessly stressing that they are desperate even now." Such constant terror makes people give up thinking and reacting in the "*Rette-sich wer kann*" (those who can save themselves, do so) pattern, which is an attitude favorable to obedience to a leader who promises to think and act for them if only they join the movement.[43] Also, this device uses a future threat to justify preemptive "self-defense," which implies a justification of destructive acts.

If they are going to wipe us out in the future, then we're justified in wiping them out now to prevent that in the name of self-defense. While the surface effect is for people to organize themselves to combat the danger by joining the movement, Adorno points to a more unconscious result, namely, that "they *enjoy* the description of atrocities because they themselves want to commit them some day."[44] Here we can see how the device plays on both—fear and the promise of pleasure—to be allowed one day to unleash one's repressed desire for cruel aggression onto the IBÖ's chosen foes.

Sellner repeatedly uses the "shiver down the spine device" by pointing out that "things will get worse in the future." The adverse effects of the "Great Replacement" can be already felt, but they "will become much worse" in the future.[45] However, the enjoyment of the description of the atrocities and the promise that one day *they* will be able to commit them, which generates even vaster amounts of pleasure in the followers, assists the *Schauder* device, as such pleasure allows them to undo the tension between their ego and their ego ideal. Such undoing generates a euphoric state that makes them feel better about the castrating conditions of precarity capitalism and (through the abrogation of their superego) allows the followers to receive their aggressive impulses in their egos, which the leader redirects to his chosen foes outside the movement (which I will come back to below).

Sellner also employs antifeminist and racist gender ideology in his "shiver down the spine device." Behind the image of white women as mothers, whose duty is to raise the birthrate of white Austrians (akin to Nazi race policies), and the pretty woman as a sexualized object, which the IBÖ uses to make insecure men feel "successful" on the interpersonal and bodily levels, we find (like in the rhetoric of the Austrian Freedom Party) the racist and sexist image of the "fertile veiled Muslim woman" as a "threat," as she supposedly bears many children and thereby becomes responsible for demographically marginalizing and ultimately wiping out the white race.

Langman and Schatz outline that white "extinction anxiety" also exists in the United States, which describes the fear of certain white people over changing demographics, namely, higher birth rates and immigration of people of color. The fear is that whites will become a minority in America, losing power and privilege and losing the nation to people of color, Jews, and Muslims.[46] Also, in Europe, through heightened immigration and migrations of people of color, such "extinction anxiety" exists among white Europeans, who remain a majority and have all the power in European societies. The IM plays on and further heightens such anxiety through the invention of a "white genocide," in which the demonized figure of the "veiled Muslim woman" is central.

Another terror strategy Sellner uses is the "last hour device," which "consists of the direct or indirect assertion that a catastrophe is imminent, that the situation is desperate and has reached a peak of crisis, that some change must be made immediately."[47] Here the audience is *ermahnt* (admonished) to act fast and join the movement immediately. As he puts it: "Unending problems are piling up in front of us, and my generation has already grown up in the shadow of the coming *catastrophes.* . . . Islamization and the Great Replacement. We live, so it seems, in the contractions of a great downfall."[48] Sellner alerts his audience that the situation is desperate and has reached a peak of crisis because "indigenous (white) Europeans" are already being "wiped out" by a growing immigrant population from Islamic countries in the *große Austausch*, the "Great Replacement," through which also an "Islamization" takes place, which eradicates European "civilized culture."

Sellner suggests that only if one joins the IBÖ now and acts *immediately* and without any delay do we "have a realistic chance to get this heavy crisis behind us to maintain our heritage, the European civilization, and the people of Europe." However, he makes clear that "we are the *last* generation" of youth that can stop this disaster because "the descendants of the indigenous Europeans are already so marginalized" that they will lack in the numbers and strength to do so.[49]

However, it is not just that followers join the IBÖ because of, as Adorno puts it, the simple consideration, which is also salient in advertising, that people tend to forget what they do not carry out right now. As he puts it, "terroristic propaganda works only 'on the spot.' "[50] Instead, the propaganda techniques Sellner employs aim to put his followers into a hypnotic sleep and dream state in which they get to save European "civilization" and European (white) people if they join the movement and act now.

European white colonizers (and then the Nazis) already sold the same dream in their quest to wipe out those they deemed as "uncivilized" to justify their exploitation of natural resources and brutal enslavement of Africans and indigenous populations in "their" colonies. Here we can also see how neofascist "movements" such as the IBÖ draw on colonial (and fascist) racial classifications, such as the hierarchical opposition of European culture as "civilized," "modern," and hence superior, in opposition to the "premodern" culture of "uncivilized" races. The German (and Austrian) *Herrenmenschen* have employed such a binary to brutally exploit, subjugate, and exterminate those they considered as naturally inferior them.

We cannot underestimate the lure of this fantasy of being the "last hope" to save the world. It allows the potential followers to feel heroic and significant rather than feel how they do currently, that is, crushed and unimportant. Such a hallucinatory dream state, in which the followers heroically save European "civilization," enables them to continue sleeping instead of being woken up to face their unheroic reality and the destructive aims of the IBÖ.

Furthermore, with European civilization and European white people at stake, no action is too extreme for such a worthy cause and at such a desperate hour. As Adorno points out, "there is an easy transition from warning of the danger of catastrophe to advertising it. If the situation is desperate, desperate means are necessary: The answer to the 'imminent danger of Communism' is the eradication of Communists, radicals, and 'those evil forces,' that is, the pogrom."[51]

However, the tactics employed by neofascist agitators go beyond the simple advertising techniques described by Adorno. Instead, it is the regression to a sleep and dream state that allows (through undoing the tension between their ego and their ego ideal) the IBÖ followers to feel heroic. This regression also makes also their unconscious attitude prevail and temporarily abrogates their superego, which keeps their desire for cruel aggression in check.

Totalitarian measures are also salient in Sellner's hope for the near future. He describes a scenario where the IBÖ has succeeded in "getting past the heavy crises" and, as a result, has managed to establish itself together with far-right parties across Europe. In this fantasy future, the IM's idea of "remigration" (another term coined by the IM) has been adopted and turned into laws by far-right parties who are now ruling European countries. Sellner imagines that these laws will lead to a "European *Hidschra*," "a state-promoted mass emigration" of minority Europeans advanced by "ministries of remigration." The IBÖ brings these masses of emigrants to *Aufnahmezentren* (reception centers) *outside* Europe, where they can apply for asylum, but 98 percent of their asylum applications are denied.[52] It does not take too much imagination to read Sellner's future as a new pogrom, akin to the Nazi regime's, where special laws and ministries forcibly removed and then mercilessly exterminated Jews, Roma and Sinti, and other vulnerable groups in concentration camps.

Sellner includes an illustration of this toward the end of his book: a drawing depicts a mass of people, denoted as "foreigners," in backpacks, lined up in front of the Euro sign, waiting to leave Europe.[53] This drawing is eerily reminiscent of pictures of Jews and other groups lined up before being delivered to their deaths in the camps. It exposes that what Sellner "psychologically promises by his total approach is, in the last analysis, the pogrom rather than the achievement of any aim apart from such an outbreak."[54]

The Terrorized Unity

In this section, I will outline how Sellner uses the "unity trick" and the "black hand device" to catch followers. The "unity" trick entices people into joining the movement because of the solidarity it promises. But once someone has joined the movement, the "black hand device" fosters distrust to keep people ever vigilant, even toward fellow movement members. Both of these devices continue the themes of the previous two sections—they promise the potential follower pleasure through unity but at the same time aim to keep the "unity" integrated through fear and distrust.

Adorno points out that the concept of unity, as fascist agitators use it in the "unity trick," is void of any specific content. Instead, "unity as such is exalted as an idea. The formalism of this ideal makes it possible to put it surreptitiously into the service of the most sinister purpose."[55] For example, the US American Christian fascist agitator Martin Luther Thomas pleads for unity, but always in a manner that makes certain primary forms of disunity, particularly the prevailing class differences and differences in social status, appear justified.

Furthermore, certain groups, including communists, radicals, skeptics, and Jews, must remain outside Thomas's unity because they, according to him, endanger it. "Thus, the unity that he advocates is nothing but the ideal of a comprehensive organization of those who participate in his repressive interests, the 'right people.' "[56] However, the "unity trick" only serves to integrate the followers negatively. The followers can only experience unity with other followers and identify themselves with one another (which happens via their shared love for the movement) if they are allowed to redirect their hostile feelings toward those that must remain outside the unity.

Also Sellner uses the "unity trick" to attract followers. He argues that the IBÖ is an inclusive community, since his "higher vision" allows him to unify contradicting aims and ideas so that "unity can emerge in multiplicity."[57] However, when considering who is allowed in the IBÖ's supposed "unity in multiplicity," its formalistic aspect becomes salient. For Sellner, it is only "indigenous [white] Europeans" who are allowed to be part of his unity, and all immigrants and migrants, particularly those with Muslim backgrounds (but not only those), Jews, people on the left, and those who disagree with his ideas must remain outside his unity. So the unity he promotes is the unity of those "right people" who participate in the IBÖ's repressive interests. Furthermore, those that must remain outside the unity serve as a negatively integrating force, as those inside the unity can only suppress their hostility toward one another and their jealousy and to be "in love with the same female lover" (the movement) by redirecting such hostility toward the "evil outsiders."

Furthermore, Adorno points out that the fascist agitator remains vague about his education, political *Werdegang*, and what knowledge or characteristics he has that could justify him as a political leader capable of creating "unity." The vagueness about his personal and political aims serves to "herd together most different types of listeners who are willing to follow him the more blindly, the less exactly they know who he is and what he stands for. A certain abstractness, interspersed with petty concrete references to daily life, is characteristic of the patterns of the fascist agitator."[58] Besides remaining vague about the political goals of the IBÖ, Sellner remains unclear about his own political *Werdegang* and his qualifications as a political leader. The "emptier" his portrayal of himself, the more his followers can make up fantasies about him in the space of his image that he leaves blank for them.

In *Aspekte des neuen Rechtsradikalismus*, Adorno refers to the "unity trick" in connection with the "unity complex" in Germany. When compared to the histories of England and France, Germany developed its national identity quite late, which is why insecurities about national identity are higher in Germany than in other Western European countries. Such insecurities contribute to an overestimation of national identity and explain the panic Germans experience when confronted with the idea of the nation splitting up. Here Adorno also points out that the "unity complex" can be applied to Austria,[59] but he does not further elaborate on *how* we can apply this complex to the Austrian case.

Other tricks exploit vulnerabilities regarding various standards of being "successful," but the "unity trick" feeds on fears about Austria's national identity. For example, during the Austrian-Hungarian Empire, Austrians considered themselves Germans. After 1918, when Austria became its own country, Austrians across the political spectrum continued to feel like Germans and favored unification with Germany, which the Allies prohibited in the treaties signed after World War I.

Austria's Anschluss (1938) during Hitler's regime allowed Austrians to become German again, which is one reason why Austrian society enthusiastically welcomed Hitler. After World War II, most Austrians, except some right-wing groups, began to create an Austrian national identity and consider themselves different from Germans. However, such an identity is also connected to their wanting to master the past instead of working-through it, which they aimed to achieve by distancing themselves from the Hitler regime—as Austrians, they are not Germans, and therefore, they are not guilty of the crimes committed by Hitler's regime.

However, the insecurity of "who we are as Austrians" remains a salient feature because Austrians aimed to close the book on the past. The return of repressed guilt and loss also threatens their insecure Austrian identity, accompanied by anxiety. Sellner's "unity trick" feeds upon that anxiety. To begin with, he promises that Austrians, once they join the IBÖ, can consider themselves "real Germans" again, which he underlines with statements like "the German-Germans" also have the right to identity.[60]

Here he draws on and further intensifies the fear of splitting up, which connects to Austrians' anxiety about their national identity. He asserts that allowing immigrants into Austria creates a "splitting up" of the "indigenous population" and that "against this fear of scattering, we build a 'unity of the patriots,' which goes beyond the boundaries of a movement and party."[61] Here he promises potential followers that once they join the unity of the IBÖ, they will be part of a unity that also will provide them with a secure (or whole) national identity.

Adorno further points out that the "unity trick" "feeds upon the existing feeling that no true solidarity exists in modern society, and channels these feelings for very specific interests, the interest of his racket, which is antagonistic to solidarity."[62] Sellner repeatedly points out that if one joins the "unity of the patriots," one is bestowed with a "good functioning community," as well as mutual trust, solidarity, and courage.[63] He underlines his promise that one can find in the IBÖ a *real* community, where "people box together, read together and just hang out. A *WG* [flat sharing] feeling of life," which, he adds, "makes activism something one *must* do, to something one *wants* to do." Furthermore, he asserts that joining the IBÖ allows the followers to be part of a "strong community of dashing types, which can defend one in an emergency."[64] Last but not least, he asserts that the followers can earn respect from such "dashing types" by participating in the movement's actions.

Sellner's promise of a "well-functioning community" must sound enticing for young people in a modern capitalist society, where they feel isolated and atomized.[65] Furthermore, since they mostly feel weak and like failures, it must also sound enticing to be protected by "a strong community of dashing types" whose respect one can earn through participating in "IBÖ activism." However, behind his promises of a "true solidarity" lurks the reality that his racket contradicts any true solidarity.

Sellner argues that the "unity of patriots" is composed of three parts: first, the "avant-garde" of the IBÖ, where the development of a "real strategy" happens; second, a patriot party (the Austrian Freedom Party); and third, the now activated "silent majority," all sticking together in a "patriot solidarity." As he puts it, these three parts of the "patriot unity" "*must* stand together in solidarity. The motto is: to march separately and to *schlagen* [hit] in unity" to stop the "Great Replacement."[66]

In his motto, that the parts of the "unity" *must hit* in solidarity, the price for feeling oneself strong and protected in the IBÖ racket surfaces: The substitute for isolation is not solidarity but obedience to the movement's aim to carry out violence against those vulnerable people who must remain outside his racket and who are in most need of solidarity. That the IBÖ racket, in the last instance, is *antagonistic* to any solidarity within the "patriot unity" itself is salient in Sellner's use of the "black hand device."

This device is part of the terror strategy. Here, the fascist agitator applies terror not only to his opponents but also toward his followers. Under National Socialism, this technique played a prominent role. For Adorno, this technique foreshadowed the complete atomization of the whole population as it occurs in totalitarian states. Moreover, it complements the "unity trick" and integrates the divergent elements of the organization by keeping the members in a permanent state of *mutual distrust*.[67]

Besides integrating the unity, this technique also has a psychological effect. As Adorno points out: "Whoever enters the organization is made to understand that there is no way out, and the character of irrevocability thus bestowed upon his decision works only as an emotional tie to the racket. The effect is by no means fear. *People tend to love that which they cannot quit*—to identify themselves with even their prison walls. It is this particular disposition on which the fascist emphasis upon *Feme* ['the black hand device'] persistently feeds."[68] The agitator establishes the organization's irrevocability by making clear to the followers that once one joins, "*there is no way back*. The sacrifice of the individual to the collectivity . . . means that one has to surrender totally, with soul and body, without qualification and reservation. . . . The wish to 'get out' of a compulsory community is the primary gesture by which the longing for freedom expresses itself. Nothing is more hideous to the fascist than this desire," and the fascists severely punish any desire for freedom.[69]

Similarly, Sellner tells his followers that there is no way back once one joins the IBÖ, which is salient in his demand that they have to sacrifice themselves *completely* to the collectivity, with soul and body and without qualification and reservation. To cite him again: the IBÖ is akin to a "jealous female lover," and "every free moment, every free thought, every financial and bodily resource is spent on activism, if it is done seriously."[70]

Furthermore, suppose anybody dares to long for freedom from the compulsory IBÖ community. In that case, he warns her that "*never* is one allowed to use the public opinion created by the enemies as the basis of an opportunistic distancing and *to distance oneself* as a party from all of the activist forces."[71] Once one joins the identitarian movement, *there is no way out*; one is forever bound to the IBÖ. To illustrate a scenario where the followers start to love what they cannot quit, he constructs the movement into a "jealous female lover."

Toward the end of the book, Sellner puts it aptly: "History is only made" through *"sacrifice ready*, convinced, mostly young followers."[72] Such a complete sacrifice might not seem too enticing for the young followers he aims to attract. However, Sellner must also point out that the result of such a sacrifice will be that they can "make history" and save white European "civilization," which allows them to feel better about not living up to the economic, interpersonal, and bodily "success" standards of precarity capitalism.

However, the fascist agitator has something else in store to secure the followers' complete surrender to the movement: *discipline*. As Adorno further explains: "Terror, directed against the insiders, strengthens the authority which appears absolute only if no infringement whatsoever is tolerated, if the strictest *discipline* is enforced. This can be achieved only if even the slightest deviation is branded as treachery, and ruthlessly persecuted."[73]

Such terror surfaces in the fascist agitator's warnings that their followers need to be alert about the "dangerous forces" that are working from inside to destroy the movement.[74] As Adorno further points out, the "fascist racket is the very parody of that '*Volksgemeinschaft*,' the people's community, that it boasts of being. Fellow members of fascist organizations are more jealous, more suspicious, more ready to 'liquidate' each other than even the most hard-boiled competitors."[75]

Sellner terrorizes his (potential) followers with the "black hand device" and aims to keep them in line with the assistance of discipline. He repeatedly comes back to the topic of discipline, for example, in his argument that the "strength of leadership," besides keeping the followers "in love" with the movement and in a euphoric state, is "the ability to keep a structure of discipline and order." He again and again emphasizes discipline, such as in his assertion that activists are "nothing without discipline."[76]

Under the headline of his chapter titled "Discipline in Vienna," he furthermore points out that "against the onslaught from outside and the *creeping dissolution from inside* . . . only *discipline* helps." Sellner's warning about the "creeping dissolution from inside" terrorizes his followers by telling them that the IBÖ will persecute the slightest deviation and keeps them in a permanent state of mistrust. The terror of the "black hand device" starkly contradicts Sellner's picture of the IBÖ as a "well-functioning community" where one can find mutual trust and solidarity.[77]

Adorno, on the other hand, realized the need to question the use of discipline. In his talk in Vienna, Adorno pointed out that today's youth "needs to be warned from the drill in any shape, from the suppression of their private sphere and their style of life. And one needs to warn them from the culture of the so-called order, which is not supported by reason, especially from the term 'discipline,' which is presented as a *Selbstzweck* [an end in itself] without asking the question 'discipline for what?'" For Adorno, here belongs the fetish of everything connected to the military.[78]

Sellner, however, avoids questioning. He repeatedly refers to the military as a model for the discipline he aims to enforce in the IBÖ, such as when he asserts with satisfaction that the IBÖ has managed to create space for itself in the public sphere from a "military standpoint." He also points out that in the Austrian military, one learns the kind of discipline that allows the IBÖ to avoid any failure in their actions. As he puts it, "In action planning, training is the most important element. We go through every task, every scenario, and every requested reaction from changing plans until termination."[79]

In other words: the IBÖ punishes any departure from its military discipline, which could cause a failure of its destructive actions. The IBÖ plans and orchestrates every movement and reaction according to military discipline. Therefore, Sellner's repeated promise that the followers gain "spontaneity" once they join the IBÖ is nothing but a recruitment tactic. Furthermore, Sellner threatens that "there is *little solidarity for failure* in our camps."[80]

So, those who become followers of the IBÖ in the hopes of getting rid of feelings of anxiety and failure through an ecstatic mass movement are, in the end, kept in a state of permanent terror of making any failures, as such failures might lead to a scenario where the solidarity they have been promised shows its true face—that they face the same violence inside the "patriotic unity" that they are authorized to unleash at those outside the unity.

The Persecuted Innocents Who Attack Imagined Foes

While the devices I discussed in the previous three sections draw primarily (albeit not exclusively) on repressed libidinal drives and the followers' gratifications from surrendering to the IBÖ movement, this section outlines how the IBÖ stimulates and then utilizes their aggressive drives. In particular, I will discuss the "persecuted innocence device," paranoid stereopathy, and the "democratic cloak device" and show how they work together to stimulate and rationalize the followers' violence.

One can encounter the "persecuted innocence device" in the fascist agitator's dwelling upon his innocence. The question as to whether he is an aggressor or victim is raised as "he is not merely an irreproachable and unselfish character, and it is just because of his higher moral qualities that he is subject to permanent persecution—to threats and conspiracies of his enemies."[81]

Here, the aggressive, sadistic tendencies this device appeals to do not differentiate between the aggressor and the victim. On the contrary, both notions remain to a certain extent, interchangeable psychologically because they date from a development phase where subject and object, ego and outer world, are not yet clearly established. The interchangeability of aggressor and victim "makes it possible to blame the prospective victim for the very same crime one wants to commit oneself. By 'projection' one unconsciously makes events appear real which exist only in one's imagination."[82]

In other words, the fascists projected their desire to take out their aggression onto their prospective victims, so in the end, the fascists appeared as the ones who are innocent and persecuted and their prospective victims as the aggressors. So, the real aim of this device was to *stimulate* violence against a helpless population in their followers and rationalize such violence under the guise of self-defense.[83] It is no coincidence that the fascists developed the "persecuted innocence device" in naming their highly aggressive elite guard the SS (Schutzstaffel, "protective corps").

Also, Sellner uses the "persecuted innocence device" to stimulate and rationalize violence in his followers. For example, on April 16, 2016, members of the IBÖ violently attacked the performance of *Die Schuzbefohlenen* (The wards) by the Austrian Nobel Prize laureate Elfriede Jelinek, which exposes Europe's inhumane treatment of asylum seekers and was performed by asylum seekers from Syria, Iraq, and Afghanistan. Shortly after the play started, between thirty and forty young white men ran onto the stage, in front of the seven hundred audience members, bearing flyers with the slogan "Multiculturalism Kills" and throwing fake blood into the audience. The IBÖ followers also physically attacked the performers and several audience members and beat, pushed, and physically injured them. The police arrested several of them for assault.[84]

Sellner repeatedly returns to this violent attack and portrays it in distorted fashion. To "prove his innocence," he paints the picture of the IBÖ as a "peaceful and nonviolent" movement. To support such an illusion, he argues that IBÖ activism relies on Gandhi's idea of using nonviolent action to obtain "a peaceful regime change" (rather than violent attacks on innocent people). He also calls the attack an "aesthetic intervention," which is the preferred form of "identitarian activism" and which, he assures us, is "free of violence, unmasked and not awkward or inhuman . . . it is ideally creative and beautiful!"[85]

Sellner's description of the IBÖ's violent attack on vulnerable refugees as an example of where the creative and the beautiful converge points at what Adorno determined to be the fascist agitator's dream: "the unification of the horrible and the wonderful, the drunkenness of an annihilation that pretends to be salvation."[86] The drunkenness of Sellner's dream, in which the IBÖ, through "beautiful aesthetic interventions," saves "white Europeans" from annihilation by asylum seekers, distracts from the fact that it is the IBÖ that aims to annihilate the most vulnerable people and not the other way around.

To further support the illusions that the IBÖ is "innocent," Sellner invokes Martin Luther King Jr., who bases his theory and practice of nonviolent protest on Gandhi, in the context of the U.S. civil rights movement. Sellner argues that he and his followers trained "akin to the American civil law movement not to react when confronted with blows, kicks, and burns" to prepare for what was a peaceful and nonviolent protest.[87] Here we see the projective mechanisms at play: those whom the IBÖ violently attacks (innocent refugees) turn into the aggressive ones the IBÖ has to protect itself from, which serves to stimulate and rationalize aggression against refugees under the guise of self-defense.

Sellner repeatedly constructs a scenario where the "innocent IBÖ" is persecuted, particularly by the media and what he terms the "violent left." He also repeats the far-right (and often left) discourse that classifies the antifascist movement as a "terror organization" whose "violent crimes" against the IBÖ are not "effectively and appropriately prosecuted" by the Austrian justice system, while the IBÖ is constantly and unjustly persecuted. For Sellner, only when the hegemony of the left has fallen and "we are living in a normal constitutional state" will the IBÖ not be persecuted any longer.[88]

In his deployment of the "persecuted innocence device," Sellner also constructs those he violently attacks as aggressive. For example, he states that Jelinek, the playwright, has "agonizing and bare hatred" against Austria.[89]

Here the IBÖ projects its own agonizing and bare hatred upon the playwright. The main aim of such projection is to simulate and rationalize the IBÖ's violent attack on vulnerable refugees.

The "persecuted innocence device" is also salient in the banners the IBÖ unfurled during their violent attacks. For example, during their attack on the play, they used the banner stating "Multiculturalism Kills," which they emphasized by throwing fake blood at the audience. According to Sellner, these symbols "exposed for every rational observer the bloody and humiliating reality of open borders."[90] Again, Sellner is projecting onto the prospective victims the crime he wants to commit himself—which is the pogrom that removes refugees and other "foreigners" from Austria.

The IBÖ has repeatedly also used the slogans "Immigration Kills Europe, and Emigration Kills Africa."[91] In these slogans, the IBÖ uses "association transitions," a technique that connects different ideas in illogical ways. Instead, a common element, in this case, the word "kills," creates a false connection or equivalence between isolated, logically unconnected statements. Here the genocides committed by Europeans (and Austrians) on the African continent (for which Europeans still have not or only marginally taken responsibility), as well as the irrational goal of the IBÖ to commit genocide on people of African descent in Austria, are projected onto the prospective victims. African migrants and immigrants turn here into those who supposedly "kill Europeans," which also has the convenient side effect of exonerating Europeans for their colonial violence and the violence the neo-Nazis aim to unleash on people of African descent.

The main aim of this technique is "*the complete breakdown of a logical sense* within the listeners. . . . They are to give up the element of resistance that is implied in any act of responsible thinking as such. They are to follow the leader first intellectually, and finally in person through thick and thin."[92] Sellner aims at his followers' complete breakdown of thinking, so that they follow the movement's destructive aims through "thick and thin."

To contribute to such a breakdown of thinking (and feeling for the prospective victim), Sellner also uses the technique of "paranoid stereopathy." Here the agitator fights against windmills and builds up a paranoid system he later attacks. Adorno notes that this mechanism is of particular importance since it shows the deep-rooted tendency in fascism to attack images rather than the reality supposedly represented by those images.[93] He points out that there are two reasons why the foes of fascism (Jews and communists) are largely fictitious—because in reality there are too few actual objects of hatred and his followers' paranoia. The fascist agitator "consciously or unconsciously reckons with a 'paranoiac' attitude among his listeners, *a kind of persecution mania* which craves the confirmation of its bogies. Knowing that he can get hold of his followers only by satisfying this craving, he cuts his imagery to fit their psychological desires."[94]

So paranoid stereopathy, which plays on the followers' persecution mania, works with the "persecuted innocence device," where the fascist agitator stylizes himself and the movement as persecuted. To fit the psychological desires of the followers, the agitator attributes excessive power to the chosen foe. Here "the disproportion between the relative social weakness of the object and its supposed sinister omnipotence is by itself evidence that the projective mechanism is at work." Adorno points out that in antisemitism the idea of omnipresence *replaces* the notion of omnipotence "because no actual 'Jewish rule' [omnipotence] can be pretended to exist, so that the image-ridden subject has to seek a different outlet [omnipresence] for his power fantasy in ideas of dangerous, mysterious ubiquity."[95]

Throughout his book, Sellner builds up a paranoid system in which immigrants in general and Muslim immigrants in particular appear as an omnipotent threat to "white Europeans." In such a paranoid system of windmills, the IBÖ appears as a necessary force that must strengthen itself to protect Europe "against the onslaught of the faceless *superior strength*" of immigrants.[96] The disproportion between Sellner's constructed image of immigrants' "superior strength" that threatens Europe with an "onslaught" and immigrants' actual status of being the socially and economically most vulnerable part of the population exposes that projection is at work here. To hide this disproportion, Sellner must also replace the idea of omnipotence with omnipresence because he can't pretend that Muslim immigrant or refugee rule exists in today's Western capitalist societies. In the U.S. context, such paranoid system manifests as the growing anxiety over the impending imposition of "Sharia law."[97]

This device also helps explain the focus on Muslim women as a "threat" (which is otherwise hard to understand given their vulnerability and disempowerment in society). Sellner does so with repeated references to demography and the "growing strength in numbers" of Muslim immigrants. As he puts it, to defend one's "ethnocultural identity," "one has to put up a fight always and at any time against the *numerical superiority* of the invaders." In Sellner's paranoid system, the veiled Muslim woman as a "threat' reappears. For example, Sellner aims to underline the "threat of the omnipresence" with the image of a young, veiled woman with a stroller and four children, which suggests that the supposed fertility of the Muslim woman generates the "numerical strength of the invaders" that leads to the "Great Replacement" of the white Austrians. At the same time, the white Austrian women are enjoined to produce more white babies to secure the survival of the "superior" white European race.[98]

In addition, behind the racist and sexist image of the veiled Muslim woman who bears many children (and therefore must engage in much sexual activity with Muslim men), repressed sexual urges lurk. Here the IBÖ members project their repressed sexual urges (which they must sacrifice for their female lover, the movement) upon the veiled Muslim woman. Adorno explains how the Nazis constructed a sexualized image of Jews: "The Jews are supposed to be unencumbered by the standards of Puritan morality, and the more strictly one adheres oneself to these standards, the more eagerly are the supposed sex habits of the Jews depicted as *schmutzig* [sordid]."[99]

However, in Sellner's paranoid stereopathy we find also supposedly positive constructions of his enemies. As he puts it: "We are perhaps already too few. One finds dynamism, strength, dominance, and the will to conquer mainly with youths with migration backgrounds. They grow up in families with many brothers and mostly in tight quarters. This demographic overpressure, the feeling of community of the family, and in the end an unencumbered national identity make them superior."[100] Sellner's argument that Muslim youth have a "feeling of community and family" relates to the antisemitic idea of "Jewish togetherness," which implies "a warm, family-like, archaic, and very 'in-group-like' texture of the out-group," which seems to be denied to the members of the in-group, who grew up in a thoroughly technological society.[101]

Also, he further cements the paranoid system of Muslims' threatening omnipresence with the fantasy of "demographic overpressure," where minority youths grow up with many brothers in tight quarters. However, also a supposedly positive image appears here—the illusion that the awful living conditions of immigrants and migrants in Austria supposedly generate dynamism, strength, and dominance in their male children, which suggests that they have both masculine strength and strength in numbers. So, if their living conditions are not so awful (as they generate all these desirable traits in the youth with migrant background), he can avoid any portrayal of them as victims rather than "threats." Here the male minority youth also serves as a projection screen for what Sellner promises his followers will obtain by joining the identitarian movement of Austria to become "whole" men. The supposedly positive construction confirms the paranoid system of windmills against which the IBÖ needs to fight.

Adorno also points out that this scheme of a quasi-natural incorrigibility is for the antisemite more critical than the content of any standard reproaches themselves. "By constructing the nature of the Jew as unalterably bad, as innately corrupt, any possibility of change and reconciliation seems to be excluded. The more invariant the negative qualities of the Jew appear to be, the more they tend to leave open only one way of 'solution': the eradication of those who cannot improve."[102] One can see this in Sellner's constructions, where the (Muslim) immigrants are unalterably bad, with no possibility of reconciliation. In Sellner's ideal future vision, when the far right has won all over Europe, the IBÖ will greet those on the left who are also white Austrians) who change their thinking (and join the neofascists) with open arms because we "must stand above all conflicts, we are one Volk, one Culture, and one Civilization."[103] However, nowhere does he mention the possibility of reconciliation with immigrants and migrants and the case of their inclusion into his contrived unity.

Instead, he reiterates at several points that Muslim immigrants cannot be integrated into European society, which he underlines in his depiction of what happens by the year 2040 if the IBÖ does not intervene: Muslims rule in Europe, and he adds that *"one cannot think about assimilation and integration. On the contrary: Europeans, who have become the minority in their countries, must adapt themselves."*[104] Given their unalterable "bad nature," he has only one "solution" for them: their violent expulsion and extermination.

For this to happen, Sellner also uses the "democratic cloak device," which suggests that the violence the IBÖ aims to unleash on its chosen foes occurs within the bounds of democracy. Adorno points out that fascist agitators have to reckon with strong democratic values in societies, such as the United States, which is why they transform such values for their purposes. As he puts it: "The American attack on democracy usually takes place in the name of democracy."[105]

Sellner has to reckon with democratic values in Austria. Therefore, his attack on democracy has to take place in the name *of* democracy. He repeatedly asserts that the IBÖ "adheres to the constitutional state and democracy." To support his claim, he calls the ultimate (and only) IBÖ goal, the violent expulsion of minorities of non-European descent from European countries, a "*democratic* overturning of left *multi-kulti* [a degrading German term for 'multicultural'] ideology."[106]

While Sellner, akin to the authoritarian personalities described in *The Authoritarian Personality*, aims to (semiconsciously) get rid of democracy and establish the rule of the strong, he at the same time calls antidemocratic those whose only hope lies in the maintenance of democratic rights—those who defend a multicultural society. He insists that the (left) idea of multiculturalism is nothing but an "undemocratic experiment" and asserts that anybody who aims to challenge far-right politicians such as Trump, Putin, Orban, and Le Pen—his role models who themselves aim to get rid of democracy under the cover of democracy—as "undemocratic."[107]

In Sellner's writings, one also finds a striking *Verzerrung*, a distortion, of democratic ideas. As an example, he asserts that insofar as the state "opens the borders and does not deport illegals, it is an ideology state, which withdraws completely from democracy."[108] Again, he uses the vague stereotype of an all-comprising democracy as an instrument against any specific democratic content, here the protection of minority rights.

Sellner, furthermore, also utilizes *the complex of autonomy*, which is supposed to be guaranteed in democracy but remains not fully realized in the ruling capitalist system. Adorno points out that fascists used slogans such as "Now One Can Vote Again," which was very effective, "as it gave people the feeling that one would get into the possession of the freedom, the free decision making, the spontaneity, *with exactly the movement, which aims to abolish freedom*."[109] Sellner promises that once one joins the IBÖ, one can realize freedom by pointing out that once the IBÖ is in power, "real political debates" can finally take place in public. He also uses the complex of autonomy in his assertion that the IBÖ is, in its essence, an "escape hatch" from the "lifelong mental prison of *multi-kulti* ideology," in which, according to him, "the entire population of Western democracies finds itself."[110]

He further underlines the essence of the IBÖ as an "escape hatch" with the image of a "small forest of freedom of the right." He asserts that "in its clearings the strangest encounters occur and under its roof leaves the strangest flowers bloom." Unfortunately, however, this small forest finds itself in front of the walls of a high-security prison. Behind the walls, imprisoned white people, "who all have had enough of foreigners, observe their freedom and wait for an opportunity to flee and join them in the small forest."[111]

However, as outlined in the previous section with the IBÖ's use of terror against those inside the IBÖ, the IBÖ promises its followers freedom with the same gesture that aims to establish prison cells for its followers. So, the drunken image of the "small forest of IBÖ freedom" is nothing but a psychologically oriented device that makes the potential follower believe that she will become free and enjoy free decision making and spontaneity with precisely that movement which aims to *abolish* freedom.

Sellner also insinuates in this drunken image the (sexual) pleasure the movement holds in store for those who join it ("the strangest encounters take place"), which again shows us how the promise of pleasure is central to why people join such (self-)destructive movements. Furthermore, he argues that if one joins the identitarian movement, one can assist in the "great prison breakout."[112] Here he suggests again that once one joins the movement, one can engage in heroic deeds, such as liberating an "imprisoned" population.

However, that the IBÖ aims to abolish freedom not only for those inside the IBÖ (which he sells as "freedom") but more generally is also salient in Sellner's assertion that anybody who might object to what he calls "the now dominant right-extremist views in media" will be subject to "waves of termination."[113] Insofar as anybody who might want to leave the inner circles of the IBÖ is subject to terror, it does not take much imagination to see that anybody who objects to the IBÖ's ideas and terms, once it has established itself as the most powerful force in Europe, will be subject to "waves of termination."

Conclusion

How can we undermine the rise of the identitarian movement? I suggest that looking carefully at the writings of far-right leaders, as I did in this chapter, and carefully describing the tricks they are using is important to establish a counterpropaganda, which explains to potential followers why the IBÖ wants to attract them and how it is attracting them.

Counterpropaganda needs to make explicit the many ways the identitarian movement offers a "drug" to potential followers, be it through the movement fetish, the indefatigability device, or the various terror strategies that provide irrational gratifications for the potential followers. Although the devices generate pleasure in the followers and allow them to feel better about themselves by undoing the split between their egos and their ego ideals, they also set the stage for the hypnotic sleep and dream state where the unconscious predominates. Furthermore, since now their superego is temporarily abrogated, they can receive their repressed aggressive urges in their egos, which the IBÖ can now redirect for its destructive aims. Successful counterpropaganda also needs to emphasize the irrational and fetishistic characteristics of all the "sacrifices" demanded by far-right leaders.

Furthermore, counterpropaganda needs to carefully point at how the IBÖ aims to stimulate and rationalize violence by constructing its foes as violent and itself as "persecuted and innocent." It must also carefully describe the paranoid stereopathy in created images of far-right enemies and point out that such images contradict the reality of those it aims to describe, to effectively dissolve them.[114] Furthermore, counterpropaganda needs to point at this ultimate twisting of terror toward the "in-group" in far-right rackets, which exposes the farce of solidarity and community it promises its followers. Finally, it must also question everything connected to the military fetish and the IBÖ's focus on drill and discipline.

Counterpropaganda must be as transparent as possible to expose each case where the IBÖ distorts democratic ideas in the name of democracy.[115] However, ultimately counterpropaganda can only be successful if it also dismantles the values implied in capitalism, such as economic, interpersonal, and bodily "success," and provides an alternative economic system, which allows the youth to thrive, so they do not need to seek escapes from their suffering in far-right movements. Here, it must expose how such an economic system generates a certain coldness and does away with solidarity, which the far right can use in its propaganda tactics. Furthermore, counterpropaganda must show how standards in capitalism reinforce patriarchal standards of masculinity and "whiteness," which generate young white men's castration anxieties around their subjectivities and which neofascist forces use to catch them for their sinister purposes.

Suggestions for Undermining
the Far Right Today

T he shocks generated in our childhood, by precarity capitalism, and through living in nations with violent histories become scars on our bodies and minds. Far-right propaganda techniques prey upon such scars, and they are effective because they allow us, by generating an "ecstatic high" in a sleep and dream state, to (temporarily, at least) forget about and not feel such scars. However, the sleep and dream state also makes our unconscious attitude dominant in us, which the far right can then redirect for its destructive aims. Insofar as we want to remain in such a state (as it allows us to avoid countenancing our painful scars), we keep returning to and supporting the far right to get "high" again.

While throughout this book I have used the term "followers," I am using "we" here deliberately, as we all have a system of scars that are difficult for us to touch and that we want to forget. Therefore, we are not protected from getting caught by the far-right propaganda techniques that I have outlined in this book. We all must touch our scars and work-through the past to become less vulnerable to such methods. In this concluding chapter, I will provide some theoretical concepts and practical ideas for accomplishing such a difficult task. I will also outline why we remain morally and legally responsible for committing atrocities under the "spell of hypnosis." Finally, I outline that we must reintroduce the notion of the revolutionary proletariat to create a better society where people do not need illusions of wholeness.

The Scars of Precarity Capitalism

In *Aspekte des neuen Rechtsradikalismus*, Adorno suggests that to dissuade people from being seduced by new right-wing propagandists, we need to make the techniques they use to catch followers "real, give them a drastic name, describe them in detail, describe their implications, because ultimately nobody wants to be the stupid one or, as one would say in Vienna, to be the '*Wurzen*' [root]. And that the whole is based on a gigantic psychological root technique, a gigantic psychological rip-off, that is definitely to be shown."[1]

This book explained the "psychological root technique" used by far-right leaders, parties, and movements in the United States and Europe. I exposed and described in detail the psychologically oriented propaganda tricks the far right (Trump and the alt-right in the United States, and the Freedom Party and identitarian movement of Austria in Europe). I also described their implications in detail. However, I argue that just naming these tricks, as Adorno seems to suggest, is *not* enough to make people not fall for them (or make a *Wurzen* out of them).

My disagreement is twofold: first, psychologically oriented propaganda tricks function in the context of precarity capitalism, which generates "scars" on people's bodies and minds, and second, they operate on an *unconscious* level. Regarding the first point, people fall for far-right propaganda tricks not so much because they are stupid—or that their fear of looking foolish prevents them from falling for them—as Adorno suggests. Also, insofar as the hope is to get people who are already supporting the far right to stop, labeling them stupid is not going to help convince them to do otherwise and will likely make them more resistant, instead.

People fall for such tricks because of the objective conditions of suffering, what I called the castrating conditions of precarity capitalism—the threat of declassing, the impossibility of "up-classing," exploitation, alienation, and isolation. The castrating conditions, which subjects experience as daily shocks, generate subjective forms of suffering, which people experience as feelings of "nonwholeness" around their subjectivities. These experiences turn into *Narben* (scars) on their bodies and minds, which far-right propaganda techniques prey on.

In *Aspekte des neuen Rechtsradikalismus*, Adorno also uses the notion of "scars" to argue that the presence of fascist movements in the United States and elsewhere today is the expression of the fact that the socioeconomic content of democracy has not been realized but only remained an ideal: "One could understand the fascist movements as wound marks, the scars of a democracy that has not lived up to its name until today." Above all it is the possibility of *Verelendung* (impoverishment, or the threat of declassing) in capitalism for all, despite promises of a "good life" under democracy, that generates such wounds and that manifest themselves in fascist movements today.[2]

However, it is not only the threat of declassing, as Adorno suggests, that generates the scars of democracy. As I have shown in this book, it is also the impossibility to "up-class" and the exploitation, alienation, and isolation of precarity capitalism that mutilate (or castrate) subjects and imprint themselves as wounds on people's bodies and minds. Such wounds also turn into scars because of the unchallenged fetish of "success" on the economic, interpersonal, and bodily levels that prevails in capitalist societies.

Such a fetish generates classed, gendered, and raced castration anxieties and feelings of nonwholeness, given the impossibility of achieving such "success" for most people under the conditions of precarity capitalism. The ongoing COVID-19 pandemic meant for many people the threat or the actual loss of jobs and income, loved ones, and bodily vitality and has added another layer to our "system of scars."

As Apostolidis points out, in precarity capitalism "'shock' is now a 'normal' part of 'working life.'" While migrant day workers in the United States (and also in Europe), being singled out for particularly harsh treatment in precarity capitalism, experience such shocks acutely, "workers throughout the economy know and feel" them. However, workers on all levels turn to the far right *not* because it resonates with their daily shocks in precarity capitalism, as Apostolidis argues.[3]

Instead, they get captured because such daily shocks generate wounds that turn into scars on the bodies and minds of capitalist subjects on all levels of the work hierarchy (albeit to different degrees). The far right exploits these scars for their destructive aims because its propaganda techniques allow subjects to forget and *not* to feel the scars on their bodies on minds. Furthermore, the far right not only preys on the scars generated by the daily shocks workers experience because of the objective conditions of suffering in precarity capitalism, as Apostolidis suggests; they are also the result of subjects' inability to live up to the fetish of "success" not only on an economic but also the interpersonal and bodily level. In addition, the far right preys on the scars generated through our experiences in child-hood and those layers of scars generated by the violent history of the nations we live in.

Far-right propaganda techniques are successful because they allow workers, in a dreamlike, hallucinatory fashion, to experience themselves without any scars on their bodies and minds and feel themselves "whole" again. The far right offers the possibility of becoming numb to the objective conditions of suffering and the daily shocks experienced in precarity capitalism. However, to understand the psychological processes involved here, we need to draw from Freudian psychoanalytic terminology, as I employ in this book, and not reject such explanations, as Apostolidis and other critical theorists today do.[4]

Here I have arrived at the second point why it is not enough to merely describe the propaganda techniques to counter neofascism today—they operate on an *unconscious* level. People feel like "nonwhole" subjects with accompanying castration anxieties because they cannot live up to the economic, interpersonal, and bodily "success" standards prevalent in capitalism, which imprints itself as a system of scars on their bodies and minds. This creates, using psychoanalytic terminology, a sharp tension between their ego and their ego ideal.

In psychoanalytic language, far-right techniques are effective because they allow followers to undo the split between their ego and their ego ideal, which engenders in them an artificial regression to a hypnotic sleep and dream state. In the far-right mass with a clearly identifiable leader figure, such an undoing is the result of the followers' replacement of their ego ideal with the idealized leader figure (the hypnotist who steps into the ego ideal of each follower).

In chapter 4, I show that U.S. followers introject their idealized leader (Trump) and replace their ego ideal with him, which allows them to undo the tension between their ego and their ego ideal and move out of a state of melancholia, where they are plagued with feelings of nonwholeness and inferiority, and into a euphoric state of mania, where they can feel "whole," or without any scars, again.

Similar processes occur in the far-right mass with no central leader figure. In chapter 5, I show that the alt-right uses tendentious jokes that target minorities and women to attract predominantly young white men. Such jokes turn into a recruitment tool because they allow the followers to undo the tension between their ego and their ego ideal; such an undoing puts them into a sleep state and generates in them an "ecstatic high" akin to the mania the Trump mass experiences and that allows them in a dreamlike, hallucinatory fashion to feel "whole" and without scars again.

This sleep and dream state, however, is not innocent. It creates a dangerous scenario in which the followers can easily take out their aggression in violent acts toward the far right's chosen foes. The following elements assist this circumstance: First, in the sleep and dream state, the follower's unconscious attitude predominates, which generates a scenario, to come back to a metaphor Freud uses, where the rider (the follower) can no longer guide her powerful horse (the unconscious), and the unconscious now guides the rider, which the far right utilizes for its destructive ends.[5]

Second, undoing the split between the ego and the ego ideal also temporarily abrogates the superego (which keeps the aggressive and libidinal drives in check), which allows the followers to receive repressed aggressive and libidinal drives in their egos. Receiving their repressed drives in their egos generates vast amount of pleasure in them, which allows them to feel better about themselves. Furthermore, relaxing the restrictions of the superego allows their repressed racist and sexist schemes to become conscious.

Third, the hypnotic sleep and dream state also engenders a regression to an older form of psychology, the psychology of the "primal horde," which makes the followers experience the leader as the threatening primal father and the movement as the terrifying "primal brother horde." This generates a passive-masochistic attitude that makes them subordinate themselves to the will of the leader or movement, who can now redirect the followers' desire for cruel aggressiveness as well as their hatred toward minorities and women, which is no longer held in check by the superego, toward its chosen foes.

Furthermore, the system of scars is also generated in our childhood.[6] It is no coincidence that Adorno returns to the topic of scars in *Die revidierte Psychoanalyse* when he challenges the attempts of revisionist accounts of psychoanalysis (such as ego psychologists) to do away with experiences one has had in childhood. We must pay attention to such experiences because they generate our "character," which is how society imprints itself on our bodies and minds and generates, according to Adorno, "a system of shocks and *Narben* [scars], which are never completely integrated."[7]

As Frenkel-Brunswick shows us, children who grow up in families where the father was a threatening figure who dominated his wife and children and where a clear distinction between stereotypical male and female sex roles existed (which are salient in both the U.S. and Austrian contexts) are more susceptible to fascist ideology than those who grew up in families where the sex roles are less rigid and there is parity between the parents. However, Frenkel-Brunswick sees family structures as determined by socioeconomic conditions.[8]

In families with patriarchal family structures, the child does not get any assistance in integrating her libidinal and aggressive drives. Furthermore, because of the threatening parental figure, the child does not internalize her superego, which means that external (rather than internal) figures and standards guide her moral conduct. To keep her "free-floating aggression," which can break out at any time, in check, she develops a rigid character structure, which underlines how experiences in our childhood imprint themselves on our bodies and minds as a system of scars, which the far right exploits.

Since such a subject, as an adult, continues to be guided by external authority figures and not by an internalized superego, she is prone to submit herself to authority figures (such as far-right leaders and movements) who provide her with venues to release her constant efforts to keep her aggressive (and libidinal) drives in check. Furthermore, the far right utilizes such a rigid character structure by, for example, offering the followers rigid and hierarchical gender roles, which makes it easier for them to keep their aggressive (and libidinal) drives in check.

Furthermore, the far right utilizes such a rigid character structure to catch followers because its propaganda technique (through relaxing the superego) allows the followers to no longer make efforts to suppress their libidinal and aggressive drives. Such a theoretical framework also helps explain why women (with a rigid character structure) support the antifeminist and antiqueer far right and why the far right's profound hatred toward transgender subjects (who challenge rigid gender roles) attract followers. The followers want such a rigid structure, even when it disadvantages them, and feel threatened by anyone (such as transgender subjects) that challenges that structure.

To undermine the cycle where the followers keep being made miserable by the castrating conditions of precarity capitalism but find hallucinated satisfaction in the far right's promises of feeling whole and without scars, it is not enough to merely describe the "gigantic psychological rip-off" they are under (although that is necessary too). Instead, we must counter the conditions that generate scars on our bodies and minds, which far-right propaganda tools use to mobilize unconscious processes in us.

Adorno realizes that when he points out that while there exists a susceptibility for fascism among the masses, it is the manipulation of the unconscious that is indispensable for the actualization of this potential.[9] Therefore, what we must do is to address these conditions and make the unconscious conscious. However, far-right propaganda techniques prevent this and further push the (pre)conscious in followers into the unconscious. Here the crucial question remains: What can we do to counter fascist propaganda devices?

A Repressed Past

In his "Remembering, Repeating, and Working-Through," Freud explains why Adorno's naming or describing of fascist propaganda tactics is insufficient to break the hypnotic spell that the far-right masses are under today. He states that "giving the resistance a name could not result in its immediate cessation. One must allow the patient time to become more conversant with the resistance that is unknown to [her/]him, to work through it," to curb her compulsion to repeat and act out her repressed memories.[10]

In Freudian theory, "resistance" is closely connected to the concept of repression and the unconscious. The ego establishes the resistance against the strength of libidinal and aggressive impulses that lie in wait in the unconscious to unleash themselves and direct the ego. The resistances allow only portions of the repressed material, often disguised, to enter our consciousness, such as in dreams. When we go to sleep, we intentionally turn away from the external world, which allows us to lower the resistances that aim to keep our libidinal and aggressive drives repressed in the unconscious. This makes dream formation possible. When awake, we use artifices (such as tendentious jokes) to allow what is repressed to circumvent the ego's resistance so that we can receive it temporarily into our ego, which we experience as pleasurable.[11]

Far-right propaganda techniques artificially generate a prolonged hypnotic sleep state in the followers (through undoing the split between their ego and their ego ideal) to circumvent the resistances that keep aggressive and libidinal drives in check. Such a scenario makes the followers artificially turn away from the external world and reality and away from the conflict between their economic and other interests and the destructive interests of the leaders or movements they support.

The core reason followers want to stay in a sleep state that makes them continue to support far-right leaders and movements that are bad for them is the dream state, which becomes possible given the lowering of the resistance in the sleep state. The dream state not only generates vast amounts of pleasure in the followers but also allows them, in a hallucinatory fashion, to feel whole again and forget the scars on their bodies and minds generated by the socioeconomic conditions of precarity capitalism.

However, the difference between a dream we have in regular sleep and the hypnotic sleep engendered artificially in far-right masses is that when we wake up, we resume our relations with the external world and reality and realize that our dream was merely a hallucination. In contrast, in far-right masses, where the leader or movement artificially induces a prolonged sleep and dream state (to which the followers contribute through self-hypnosis), the followers do not resume their relations with the external world or realize that their "wholeness" or being without scars is just a dream, which shows that sleep and dream formation in the fascist masses is a form of psychosis.[12]

So, what does it then mean that "one must allow the patient time to become more conversant with the resistance that is unknown to him[/her], to work through it"? For Freud, the compulsion to repeat, which takes place under the conditions of resistance, is a way of remembering the "shocks and abrupt pushes" through which we experience society and which imprint themselves on our bodies and minds as a "system of scars." Here we can understand resistance as the resistance to our touching our scars and our keeping them repressed in our unconscious instead of confronting ourselves with the painful memories that generated our scars, which leads to our compulsion to repeat and act out our repressed memories.

For example, as outlined in chapter 4, the structural amnesia imposed by industry (capitalism) and its supporters does not allow subjects in Louisiana (and in the United States more generally) to work through and mourn the actual and ideal losses in precarity capitalism that generated their wounds. Instead of mourning the actual losses (the loss of their jobs, health, community, and a clean environment) generated by precarity capitalism and the failure to achieve the ideals (the fetish of economic, interpersonal, and bodily "success"), they incorporated these objects and ideals into themselves, which process generated the structure of melancholia.

In addition, in the United States, the structure of melancholia is also generated through repressed memories of the nation's violent past. White subjects in particular repress disturbing memories about their white ancestors being capable of genocide on the indigenous population and their brutal enslavement of African Americans. As a result of such failed working-through the past, most whites in the United States cannot mourn the loss of this population and the continuing adverse effects of their violent history on the (remaining) indigenous and African American population in present-day U.S. society.

Instead of working-through the painful memories that generated their scars (which is assisted through the fetish of "success" and the United States' failure as a nation to work through its colonial past), they repeat and act out repressed memories by, for example, supporting a leader (Trump) whose policies further entrench the objective conditions of suffering in capitalism, which adds fresh layers of scars onto their bodies and minds. The failure to work-through the past also generates a scenario where subjects repeat and act out the violence of the past in far-right movements.

In melancholia, subjects turn the negative feelings they harbor toward the lost objects against their egos, and they experience a sharp tension between their ego and their ego ideal, accompanied by intense feelings of inferiority and self-deprecation. Trump's propaganda techniques allowed him to attract followers because they enabled Americans to move from melancholia into a manic state by replacing their ego ideal with the idealized "whole" leader figure. In the manic state, the followers' egos can again coincide with the ego ideal. Here, like a mirage, the scars on their bodies and minds disappear, and, in a dreamlike, hallucinatory fashion, they can feel "great again."

In addition, undoing the split between the ego and the ego ideal also lowers their resistance, which allows the followers not only to receive their repressed aggressive and libidinal drives in their egos but also their repressed racist and sexist schemes, which are the legacy of colonial classifications that have been suppressed in subjects' unconscious and carried on from one generation to the next—the supposed natural "superiority" of whites and of men and the supposed "inferiority" of all other races and women, which white European colonialists introduced to justify their violence against and the exploitation of the indigenous population and enslaved Africans. The far right can now redirect white male anger and frustration at "falling from the top of the racial and sexual hierarchy" (which shows that they still adhere to colonial classifications) toward racial and sexual minorities and women. Such redirecting has the convenient side effect that capitalism as a system remains untouched, and it also divides the raced and gendered proletariat.

We can also see the violence committed against racial and sexual minorities (particularly transgender subjects) and women by the alt-right in the United States today, which I have outlined in chapter 5, as a way of remembering the "shocks" through which the millennial followers' experiences of precarity capitalism as well as repressed memories of the nation's violent past, which imprinted themselves on their bodies and minds as a system of scars. By joining the alt-right, they can now project their ancestors' murderous deeds on the descendants of the victims, who now appear as a "threat" because they supposedly want to unleash a "white genocide," which underlines a continuation of the past, taken up by those who cannot accept that past as wrongful. With that they can also displace the "threat of castration" by the vampire Capital and their actual castration in precarity capitalism onto vulnerable populations.

In the context of the United States, working through one's resistances means touching the scars generated by the actual and ideal losses engendered by precarity capitalism. Furthermore, it entails working-through its violent past, including slavery and the genocide of the indigenous population and its ongoing legacies. As Alyosha Goldstein puts it, native liberation is indispensable in the collective struggle against (neo)fascist forces in the United States because of "the specific ways in which variations on fascism and white supremacy continue to shape settler colonial nations and imperial nation-states."[13] It also means working-through the disturbances that patriarchal family contexts generate in their children.

In chapter 6, I argued that the taboo around Austria's violent National Socialist past, which is carried from one generation to the next, is a barrier to effectively working-through the past because it does not allow people to work-through difficult feelings of guilt around Austria's involvement in the Nazi crimes, which is a precondition for them to engage in the work of mourning the loss of the Austrian population murdered by the NS regime and the loss of Hitler as their ego ideal.

The repeated attacks of neo-Nazi youth groups on concentration camp survivors at Holocaust memorials all over Austria, which I also described in chapter 6, is a way of repeating (rather than working-through) the shocks of the past—their (grand)parents as potential murderers of a vulnerable population. Here I have also explained how patriarchal family structures with threatening father (or mother) figures generate scars in their children, which contribute to creating rigid character structures that render them more susceptible to fascism.

I have also shown that the Austrian Freedom Party attracts followers because it allows them to master the past instead of working-through it, so they do not have to touch their scars—such as in its efforts to prevent the establishment of a House of History museum, which threatened to be a significant contributor to the much-needed working-through process.

My analysis of the Austrian identitarian movement in chapter 7 also out-lined how the Nazi classification of Austrians (as Germans) as the superior *Herrenmenschen* and those groups the Nazis victimized as "inferior" has been passed from one generation to the next (and which the Nazis had them-selves taken from the European colonial era) and continue to circulate in the unconscious of the population in present-day Austria. Such a construc-tion allows white Austrians to displace their system of scars generated by the castrating conditions of precarity capitalism and Austria's violent past onto their prospective victims, who now appear, in the paranoid construc-tion of the "Great Replacement," where immigrants and migrants aim to wipe out "European whites," as a "threat" to them—and through which (as the colonialists and the Nazis before them) they can justify their geno-cide of vulnerable populations.

In Austria, working-through one's past would mean not only touching the scars generated by precarity capitalism but also those produced by Aus-tria's violent Nazi past and its contributions to European colonial vio-lence.[14] Working-through one's past would also mean touching the scars generated in childhood in one's family contexts. Here the question remains: How can we become more conversant with our resistances and work to overcome them?

Working-Through the Past

To not fall for the "psychological rip-off" of far-right propaganda, we must work-through the shocks we have been exposed to since our childhood and in precarity capitalism. Touching our "system of scars" and remembering their origins is a long and painful process, but it is worth it because ultimately it promises (to a certain degree, at least) that we can counter the disturbances in our personalities upon which far-right propaganda tricks prey. In this section, I engage with David McIvor's account of working-through the past in his *Mourning in America: Race and the Politics of Loss*, followed by my account of "embodied reflective spaces," to generate some ideas about what we must do (and not do) to successfully work-through the past.[15]

McIvor analyzes the Greensboro Truth and Reconciliation Commission (GTRC) that operated in Greensboro, North Carolina, from 2004 to 2006 to show us that the GTRC can be used as a model of a "democratic theory of mourning," one that can be applied to other cases of working-through the United States' violent past. The GTRC addressed the Greensboro Massacre of November 3, 1979, where thirty-five Ku Klux Klansmen violently interrupted a scheduled rally planned by the Communist Workers Party (CWP) in a Black public-housing neighborhood, shooting five CWP members and activists dead and wounding ten others. An all-white jury acquitted all of the KKK members.[16]

The commission heard public testimony from surviving members of the CWP, the KKK, and others associated with the event to investigate the causes and consequences of the Greensboro Massacre. McIvor argues against an agonistic politics of mourning, where the victimized use, for example, the friend/enemy distinction to protest their victimizers; this mode of mourning keeps the victims stuck in what the object-relations theorist Melanie Klein named the "paranoid-schizoid position"—where they engage in splitting, idealizing one side as "all good" (the friends) and demonizing the other side, toward whom the resistance is directed, as "all bad" (the enemies).[17]

McIvor argues that for a "democratic politics of mourning" to happen, the victimized must transition out of the paranoid-schizoid position into what Klein termed the "depressive position." Such a transition is enabled when the victimizer and the victimized enter *together* into a "potential space." For McIvor, a truth and reconciliation commission can serve as the Kleinian idealized "whole object," which would offer a "holding space" that allows the participants to recognize the wholeness and ambivalence of self and other and disrupts both parties' defenses of idealization, splitting, or denial.[18]

While I appreciate McIvor's celebration of the TRC model as a means to work-through the United States' violent racist past, there are some problems with his theoretical framework. To begin with, he draws on Kleinian psychoanalytic thought to theorize how we might effectively work-through the past, which leads him to theorize a "democratic politics of mourning" that focuses on "wholeness." The use of such language is problematic because, first, it implies an outcome of working-through the past that leads, as he puts it, to a "depressive awareness of whole object relations and the ambivalence within self, other, and world," and, second, it is enabled by idealized "whole others."[19]

Regarding the first problematic, as I have shown in this book, one of the core reasons why far-right propaganda tactics work to attract followers is because they offer subjects who feel "nonwhole" an illusory "wholeness." The Kleinian "depressive position" offers a similar illusion, namely, that one can achieve wholeness through "whole object relations" within oneself, others, and the world. However, I have characterized such a position as the *manic* position, in which followers have the illusion of being "whole" and feeling "great" again, which allows the followers to move out of their melancholic position, where they feel like failures.

As I will further discuss in the next section, a successful working-through the past or mourning must *do away* with the illusion that we can achieve wholeness and instead be based on a subject that accepts her holes (which I call a subject-in-outline). As for my second point, McIvor argues that the TRC must function as the Kleinian "whole object," which, while idealized, "also licenses a process of deidealization by which the ongoing conflicts and fissures of democratic societies can be clarified and made subject to social action."[20] However, as I have also shown, propaganda tactics work to create the illusion of "wholeness" in followers through processes of idealization involving the transfer of the followers' (disappointed) narcissistic libido onto the idealized "whole" figure of the far-right leader or movement, to cover over the conflict between their destructive aims and the self-interests of their followers. Such a process makes the followers "fall in love" with the leader or the movement, which strengthens the libidinal bonds between the followers and the leader and among the followers (via their shared love for the leader or movement).

Such love bonds in two directions (toward the leader or the movement and toward the other followers) make the followers blind (just as "love is blind") toward the destructive goals of the leader or movement and the contradiction between their rational interests and the interests of the far right. However, insofar as such psychological processes also generate a hypnotic sleep and dream state in the followers, it generates the preconditions for the followers' violence. Insofar as the participants in the TRC achieve "wholeness" via the idealized "whole object," McIvor's theoretical account, instead of clarifying ongoing conflicts, further leads to covering over and intensifying such conflicts.

Working-through the past must allow the followers to leave the narcissistic state of "wholeness," which they experience in the sleep and dream state, and with that "fall out of love" with the idealized leader figure and the movement. For this to happen, a working-through of the past must do away with any form of idealization and striving for wholeness. This means that, at the end, the followers must confront the anxiety-ridden reality of the hole in their subjectivities and the bitter truth that they can never achieve any wholeness through an idealized object.

Furthermore, we also encounter in McIvor's work a problematic idealization of what the TRC can do. Here fascists (the KKK), once they enter into a "potential space" with those who survived their murderous attack (Black subjects and left organizers) via the "whole object" of the TRC, will magically engage in an "inclusive dialogue and deliberation" across differences, generate "collaboration across lines of social division," and through social contact even eradicate stereotypes.[21] As the work of Joan Braune shows us, such an idealization of the potential of the TRC misunderstands the growing threat for vulnerable groups that (neo)fascists pose in the United States (and elsewhere). Also, contrary to McIvor's worries about victimized groups using the friend/enemy distinction when organizing resistance to (neo)fascists, as this makes them supposedly stuck in the "paranoid-schizoid position," Braune points out that we *must* use such language, to make clear that members of (neo)fascist hate groups are *not* our friends, because they "participate in a growing social movement that seeks political power to further its genocidal aims, and which has support and backing in high places."[22]

Furthermore, McIvor's idealized outcome of the TRC suggests the possibility of collaborating with (neo)fascists. His suggestion is problematic because during the process of collaboration we might forget that they are our enemies (which is further assisted through giving up the friend/enemy distinction) but instead identify with them and believe that they are our "friends." This may go so far that we start excusing and even assisting their violent acts and forget to critique them.[23]

In addition, McIvor's insistence that the victimized must enter with neo-fascists into a "potential space" to generate "inclusive dialogue and deliberation" can further assist the growth of hate groups instead of undermining them. Braune points out that to undermine the growth of the far right, it is essential that we not offer a platform to the enemy in the hopes of having a "dialogue," such as interviewing them in media outlets or inviting them to speak or debate at university campuses. As she puts it, such platforming "usually simply provides a larger audience to propagandists, whose cause benefits from the publicity and attention and who rarely enter into dialogue or debates as honest actors."[24]

Furthermore, platforming the far right can also play into victim-blaming and does not allow the persecuted to set much-needed boundaries. However, clear boundaries with white supremacists (such as the message that they are not welcome at our concerts) are often the only way to deal with a threatening situation and keep targeted people safe, especially in cases where law enforcement turns a blind eye to neofascist attacks.[25]

Furthermore, McIvor's argument that the emerging fissure during the GTRC, where white participants aimed at "reconciliation" and Black participants aimed at "truth," opened up a "dialogic space" between them that did not exist before is another idealization. Instead, the whites' insistence on "reconciliation" is nothing but the general pressure whites in the United States put on victimized groups, particularly Black people, to forgive racist acts immediately and in a nonthreatening manner. In addition, the focus on "reconciliation" can do harm to the victimized, who already have high levels of responsibility to protect their communities from white supremacist hate groups and now are pressured to take on additional emotional labor to engage with them on TRCs.[26]

And although McIvor aims to theorize "the middle space" between agonistic (in which mourning leads to the mobilization of the victimized communities against the aggressor) and consensualist acts of mourning (which aim to deny that there are any racial conflicts), he ends up on the side of the latter. In the process of doing so, he also engages in splitting. For example, he argues that organizing protest movements against victimization can generate a "killing rage" of the victimized against their victimizers, which continues the cycle of violence. Such a portrayal of hate groups as being threatened by those they persecute, if they protest against them, resurfaces in his characterization of the Black Lives Matter movement as engaging in "militant resistance" and is also reminiscent of how the far right portrays anybody that opposes them as a "threat."[27] By the end of McIvor's argument, the "democratic arts of mourning" have turned into the "all good" and organized protest into the "all bad"; this is the very kind of splitting McIvor aimed to counter with his theoretical framework.

Such a view delegitimizes and even demonizes organized resistance movements of victims of racial hatred, setting them as equal to or worse than the actions of the fascists against whom they protest. As Braune points out, the organized protest on the left, including protests of the Antifa movement, which is maligned by both the media and some sectors of the left, against the growing threat that (neo)fascists pose to vulnerable communities today is essential because the far right today is not just some fun and edgy cult phenomenon but a growing, power-seeking movement with backing from powerful people. In addition, given how the identitarian movement constructs a "violent left," particularly a "violent antifascist movement," using the "persecuted innocence" device, which makes the perpetrators appear as victims to rationalize its aggression against helpless victims under the guise of self-defense, the left needs to rethink its construal of the antifascist movement as "violent" instead of reinforcing such a construct.[28]

Finally, McIvor's argument that social contact between the fascists and those they victimize will "erode stereotypes and the affective-cognitive schemas that hold those stereotypes in place" is simply wrong.[29] In the *Authoritarian Personality* study (as well as in other texts on fascism), Adorno repeatedly dismisses any optimism, as we find in McIvor's account of a "democratic politics of mourning," that stereotypes will disappear through personal contact with the stereotyped object. In capitalism experience itself is predetermined by stereotypy, and the prejudiced person is incapable of a new experience. As Adorno puts it: "There is no simple gap between experience and stereotypy. Stereotypy is a device for looking at things comfortably; since, however it feeds on deep-lying unconscious sources, the distortions which occur are not to be corrected by taking a *real* look. Rather, experience itself is predetermined by stereotypy." In all situations where the prejudiced subjects of the AP study were introduced to racial minorities who were very different from the stereotyped view they held about them, they would interpret whatever the minorities were, said, or did through the lens of the stereotype and hold it against them.[30]

How can we conceptualize spaces that allow us to work through the past? Previously I have outlined the concept of "embodied reflective spaces," in which working through the past can take place to counter the guilt/ defense complex.[31] Nations that struggle with a difficult past and its legacies in the present need to create spaces where people can confront and engage with their feelings of guilt and loss, to counter a scenario where such feelings can be used in far-right propaganda tactics and continue the cycle of violence today.

As Rensmann points out, even if the public process of working-through Germany's Nazi atrocities has been "slow and arduous," it has been "crucial for the evolution of postwar Germany's political culture and cultural democratization."[32] However, what Rensman does not mention is that such an "evolution" not only entails a working-through a nation's recent violent Nazi past but *also* entails a working-through of its recent violent colonial past, which Germany (like Austria) has not yet accomplished.[33]

Embodied reflective spaces can help the new generation understand that they have unpleasant feelings about something they are not responsible for in an immediate sense and why this is so. Because of the problems I have outlined earlier in this conclusion, I suggest that such spaces not be geared toward a direct engagement between hate groups and those they victimize. Instead, the most important spaces in which to begin the process of working-through resistance are educational spaces, where children, youths, young adults, and adults can learn about the effects of precarity capitalism on their daily lives and about the violent past of the nations they live in.

Here it is essential that such reflective spaces be embodied, which means that the students deal with the emotions around the past rather than learning mere "facts." Embodied reflective spaces are important, especially since much of the propaganda tactics the far right uses are about meretriciously converting how people feel—failure, guilt, and loss—into a temporarily more pleasant feeling. Here educational spaces must address how the students' (white) (grand)parents and ancestors were involved in such atrocities, how they were connected to capitalism, and how the students continue to benefit from the atrocities today. Teachers and professors should receive some training in psychoanalytic thought to do this effectively. If these difficult emotions are not addressed, they can be exploited by far-right forces for their destructive aims.

An example of such an embodied reflective space was in the documentary I analyzed in chapter 6, where a high school teacher makes the teenagers aware that only by bringing the neo-Nazi teenage attack on Austrian concentration camp survivors to light and putting the perpetrators on trial instead of remaining silent about them, and only by outlining the connection between the past (Austria's involvement in Nazi crimes and its silence around it) and the present (repeated teenage neo-Nazi attacks on concentration camp survivors that remind them of such a past), can people change.

I also noted that the students not learning these lessons have parents who display defensive attitudes when confronted with the Nazi past and (neo-) Nazi present. The problem with the (grand) parents' attempts to master the past instead of working-through it is that it hinders the work of educators who aim to encourage their children to work-through their resistance and touch their scars so that they do not repeat the horrors of the past in the present, by, for example, joining the alt-right or the identitarian movement. Also, akin to Austria, in the context of the United States, one must work with the (grand)parental generation to foster a working-through the past because here too defenses are most salient. Currently, (grand)parents in the United States aim to master their violent past by making moves to ban specific categories of books, particularly those in "critical race theory" and Black history, which could foster students' working-through the past. Such actions in the United States tie in with the attempts of (grand) parents in Austria to master the past instead of working-through the past.

Here educational programs also need to reach the (grand)parent's generation to better support their children in dealing with the complex feelings of failure, guilt, and loss, which, when not addressed, are transmitted from one generation to the next and contribute to their (grand)children's repeating the atrocities of the past in the present.

The Subject-in-Outline Revisited

In this section, I return to two theoretical concepts, "the moment of the limit" and the "subject-in-outline,"[34] to rethink, first, how the hypnotized followers can wake up from their dream of "wholeness" and, second, how we must conceptualize subjectivity to counter propaganda techniques that are successful because they allow subjects to feel "whole." Both are important theoretical concepts to engender a working-through instead of a repeating of a violent past.

Regarding the first question, the moment of the limit (to which Adorno's nonidentical and the Lacanian Real alludes) refers to those moments where far-right propaganda tools cannot completely put their followers into a hypnotic state.[35] Instead, in this brief moment, the followers can interrupt the dream of economic, interpersonal, and bodily "wholeness," see the reality of their continuing objective and subjective forms of suffering in precarity capitalism, and feel the scars on their bodies and minds such suffering has created.

Furthermore, the moment of the limit connects to the bodily moment of suffering. Far-right propaganda tools attract followers by allowing them in the sleep state to turn their attention away from reality and their suffering in precarity capitalism (and their childhood) and instead, in the dream state, feel "whole" or "great" again. However, the harsh reality is that the followers continue to suffer in precarity capitalism, despite the illusory promises that the leader or movement will secure a "better life" and realize democracy for them (by getting rid of democracy).

Here the scars of precarity capitalism (such as workers' mutilated bodies through exploitation) remain as wounds that remind them of the ongoing suffering in precarity capitalism they aimed to get rid of in their minds through "ecstatic highs" offered by the far right. Furthermore, scars continue to hurt. It is in this moment of feeling such pain that we encounter the moment of the limit, which is the moment that allows the followers to realize that their "wholeness" is just an illusion. They can wake up from the hypnotic spell, fall out of love with their leader or movement, and start thinking and acting for themselves again.

Furthermore, at the moment of the limit, the followers can also begin a process of touching their system of scars through processes of working-through their past instead of repeatedly consuming the "drugs" offered to them by far-right propaganda techniques that make them forget their scars. Once they touch their scars through working-through the past, they will then be able to understand the origins of their scars, the shocks they have been exposed to since their childhood, and the daily shocks they continue to be exposed to in their day-to-day working lives in precarity capitalism.

The moment of feeling their scars will allow them to partially (though not fully) integrate such shocks and make it possible for them to live with their scars. At this moment, they will have less need to turn to the far right and the illusions of "wholeness" offered, and propaganda techniques that utilize subjects' scars to catch followers will become less effective or ineffective. Once the far-right followers wake up from their hallucinatory sleep and dream state, they can also realize that the vampire Capital, rather than allowing them to become "whole" on the economic, interpersonal, and bodily levels, eats holes into their bodies and minds and generates their scars.

However, living with one's scars does not mean having to accept the castrating conditions that the vampire Capital has created. Instead, once one can live with the scars, one does not need to repeat them or act them out anymore. Instead, one can now understand the origins of one's scars and can start to organize with other workers to overthrow capitalism, instead of supporting leaders and movements that aim to keep capitalism intact.[36]

My concept of the subject-in-outline is also central to contest the far right. This concept implies acknowledging the moment of the limit (or the hole) in one's subjectivity.[37] It moves within the tension of a certain coherence (the subject) while acknowledging that it remains a nonwhole subject and that one can never achieve any wholeness (the outline). The concept of the subject-in-outline can counter far-right propaganda on several levels.

First, as outlined in this book, subjects' classed, raced, and gendered castration anxieties and feelings of "nonwholeness" around their subjectivities are heightened in precarity capitalism because of their inability to live up to the fetish of "success" on the economic, interpersonal, and bodily levels. The core reason subjects fall for far-right propaganda tactics is that they can cover over their scars and feel, in a dreamlike, hallucinatory fashion, as if they are "whole" again.

Once people acknowledge and even embrace the idea that they are fundamentally "nonwhole" and that reaching any wholeness is impossible, they can better curb the compulsion to achieve "wholeness." At that moment, psychologically oriented propaganda techniques that promise them "wholeness" will become less effective or ineffective. Once subjects are accepting of their nonwholeness, they will no longer pursue the unattainable desire for wholeness and will become less vulnerable to far-right propaganda tactics.

For example, once potential followers accept that they cannot become whole, the alt-right technique of consuming tendentious racist and sexist jokes (as outlined in chapter 5) that promise "wholeness" becomes less convincing. Instead of seeking an "emotional high" via the alt-right, the predominantly white and male followers will understand that under conditions of precarity capitalism it is difficult, if not impossible, to live up to economic, interpersonal, and bodily "success" standards. Here it is also crucial that we challenge standards of masculinity, which are impossible to live up to and make young men feel like failures.

As another example, once subjects acknowledge that they remain subjects-with-holes, the recruitment tactics of the Austrian identitarian movement (as outlined in chapter 7), which allow their followers to undo the tension between their ego and their ego ideals and generate in them an "ecstatic high" (such as the "movement trick"), making the followers feel "whole," have less attraction. Furthermore, since such subjects will be better positioned to work-through Austria's violent past, the followers will no longer act out their repressed memories against vulnerable populations. Instead of building up a paranoid system in which immigrants appear as an omnipotent threat to white Europeans against which they must fight in the act of "self-defense," they can help immigrants have a better life in Austria.

Second, the "subject-in-outline" can assist in starting a process of working-through our resistances and touching our system of scars. Subjects who strive for wholeness aim to forget what has generated their system of scars, which makes them susceptible to far-right propaganda that offers them such forgetting. In contrast, subjects-in-outline, who embrace the holes in their subjectivity, remain open to working-through and becoming conversant with their resistances and their unconscious. As a result, they are less susceptible to far-right propaganda techniques.

Third, the concept of a subject-in-outline can assist in curbing subjects' compulsion to act out of their repressed memories of a nation's violent past. A subject that remains an outline is better positioned to work-through the past than one that aims at wholeness. Subjects-in-outline are better positioned to work-through the past because they move within the tension of a certain level of identification with the collective (the subject) without wholly identifying with it (the outline), enabling them to confront complicated feelings of guilt and loss.

Too weak an attachment allows one to evade responsibility for what the collective did in the past—such as if I would claim to be European instead of Austrian, thereby avoiding the guilt of Austria's violent crimes committed on defenseless populations during (and after) the NS regime. Still, a certain level of identification with the collective allows one to feel guilt for the crimes perpetrated by the collective and acknowledge the loss of the population that such crimes engendered (which, as I outlined in chapter 6, Austrians continue to avoid concerning its crimes committed during the NS regime and colonialism).

However, the subject-in-outline implies I am not too firmly identified with the collective. Such a firm identification seems to be a particular hindrance for most white Americans to work-through their violent past. Since they are often wholly identified with their nation and want to view their national identity exclusively in positive terms, any acknowledgment of the murderous crimes of the (white) collective becomes a threat to their subjectivity. Here the concept of the subject-in-outline is also helpful to overcoming resistance and fostering a working-through.

Here one has some identification with the collective (which is necessary to feel guilt and loss). Still, one is not overidentified with it, as overidentification generates a "whole" subject who cannot work-through the past but merely engages in defensive attitudes. Therefore, it only threatens me if my subjectivity is wholly wrapped in the collective. However, if I remain a subject-in-outline, I am less likely to use defensive mechanisms to fend off feelings of guilt and loss, and will be in a better position to work-through the past.

Fourth, subjects' remaining subjects-in-outline can assist a process where they can engage in the complex process of working-through their losses (the work of mourning). As a result, they can acknowledge their actual losses in precarity capitalism (such as the actual loss of their jobs, limbs, community, and a clean environment) as well as the losses engendered by a nation's violent past and unattainable ideals of economic, interpersonal, and bodily "success." Instead of loving what is no longer possible or has never been possible, the followers can now integrate negative feelings toward the lost objects and ideals instead of attacking themselves in the structure of melancholia (which I have discussed in chapter 4).

Here the followers also realize that it is not their personal "fault" that they cannot reach these ideals but that reaching them is impossible because of the structural conditions of precarity capitalism. At this point, the tension between people's ego and their ego ideal is lessened in severity, and the far right has fewer opportunities to use its propaganda. Instead, it becomes apparent to the followers that the far right is not providing solutions to the real problems but merely drawing their attention away from them. Since the followers no longer need to repress the memories of the actual and ideal losses, they also have no more need to displace the negative feelings that they have turned against their egos onto external objects of hatred.

Fifth, the concept of the subject-in-outline is also helpful in touching those scars generated in our family contexts. Patriarchal family structures in which we encounter a threatening father (or mother) figure and rigid gender roles develop a rigid character in their children. If subjects were raised with a less rigid character, something more like a subject-in-outline, then the far right would have fewer opportunities to catch them. Furthermore, such upbringing would also make it easier for them to work-through their past and present scars.

Sixth, the subject-in outline accepts that we cannot tell whole stories about our past and present that generated our system of scars but that we can accept the hole in them. It is in such a hole where we can also feel and connect with the story, which is central to dealing with the feelings of failure, guilt, and loss that are exploited by propaganda tactics. Such feelings are suppressed with attempts to narrate a whole story. The outcome of such open-ended storytelling is a subject-in-outline, who is in a position to work through the past and resolve such difficult feelings because his or her identity is not rigidly attached to the story of the nation.

On the Responsibility of Hypnotized Masses

In this section, I would like to outline the relationship between agency and hypnosis to argue that far-right leaders and movements and their followers are morally and legally responsible for their hateful acts and violence toward vulnerable groups, even if such violence happened under the spell of hypnosis.

Such a clarification will assist in countering the attempts to dismiss psychoanalysis by critical theorists such as Martin Jay, who (supported by a chorus of other thinkers who dismiss the insight of Freudian psychoanalysis to explain the rise of the far right) recently argued that drawing on psychoanalysis stigmatizes the followers as "pathological," which serves to excuse their reprehensible acts and distances them from their actual moral responsibility.[38]

To begin with, I do not argue that (potential) followers of hate groups, or society as a whole, must undergo "group therapy" to undermine propaganda tactics that prey on subjective forms of suffering generated by the objective conditions of precarity capitalism. As Adorno outlines in *The Authoritarian Personality*, such a "cure" of prejudiced subjects in the United States (as well as Austria) is "problematic, because of their large number as well as because they are by no means 'ill,' in the usual sense, and, as we have seen, at least on the surface level are often better 'adjusted' than the non-prejudiced ones."[39]

Similarly, Erich Fromm, in "Politics and Psychoanalysis," points out that the idea of "mass analysis" is problematic, as it ignores how the psychological conditions that make subjects susceptible to fascist propaganda are affected by economic conditions. While psychoanalysis cannot replace politics, Fromm also pointed out that psychoanalysis has a core role to play in politics because it helps us explain the social genesis of illusions people harbor, and that such a function is also why it is rejected by the official institutions of society, particularly its scientific officials.[40]

In this book I have exposed how subjects become prey to the illusion of "wholeness" the far right offers them because the real objective conditions of suffering in precarity capitalism make it impossible for them to live up to the bourgeois fetish of "success." I have also outlined that the same psychological processes that create the illusion of "wholeness" engender a regression to a hypnotic sleep and dream state. Far-right leaders and movements engender such a hypnotic state in their followers to better manipulate them for their destructive goals. Here my theoretical account, which suggests that the far right and its followers engage in reprehensible acts under the spell of hypnosis, raises some important questions.[41]

1. To what degree does someone still make their own choices while under hypnosis?
2. Does one make an ongoing choice to stay hypnotized?
3. Can one refuse to be hypnotized by a leader, movement, or ideology?
4. Are there degrees of hypnosis? Are some people more hypnotized than others?
5. Does waking up from hypnosis immediately return one to one's prior mental state before the hypnosis?

1. To what degree does someone still make their own choices while under hypnosis? The followers become hypnotized in the process of undoing the split between their ego and their ego ideal, either through putting the

mass leader (the hypnotist) in place of their ego ideal (when there is an identifiable leader) or through other techniques, including tendentious jokes and the "movement trick" (when there is no identifiable leader). However, the hypnotized retain moments of agency, which are salient in their *willingness* to become hypnotized.

Far-right leaders and movements are not hypnotizing followers against their will. Instead, the followers are playing a willing part in this, because they feel like they are getting something out of it. So the followers are contributing to their state of wanting to be less aware and critical of their and the leader's or movement's actions. Furthermore, once under the hypnotic spell, the followers still retain agency because they willingly contribute to *remaining* in the hypnotic state through repeated acts of self-hypnosis, by choosing, for example, to repeatedly consume neofascist literature and to associate with other neofascists who confirm the validity of their hatred toward their chosen foes.

2. Does one make an ongoing choice to stay hypnotized? Yes, because the followers actively participate in remaining in the sleep and dream state through repeated acts of self-hypnosis in order not to "fall out of love" with the leader and the movement, which generates gratifications for them. As Adorno points out, hypnosis in fascism implies repeated acts of self-hypnosis on the side of the hypnotized followers, which allows them to remain willingly ignorant, so they do not have to acknowledge the conflict between their rational economic and other interests and the irrationality of the aims of the leader or movement. Furthermore, the irrationality of the hidden final goals of the movement produces a *bad conscience* within each fascist, which self-hypnosis allows one to overcome. Adorno states:

> Here the hypnotic element comes into play. It helps to overcome the bad conscience. The fascist stops thinking, not because [s/]he is stupid and does not see [her/]his own interest, but he does not want to acknowledge the conflict between [her/]his particular interest and that of the whole. . . . [S/he] has to switch it on [her/]himself, again and again, in order not to lose [her/]his spurious faith. Fascist hypnotism may be characterized as being essentially self-hypnotism.[42]

The followers are *not* stupid and *know* that there is a conflict between their particular rational interests and the irrational interests of the leader and the movement, but *they do not want to acknowledge* such conflict.

Psychologically oriented propaganda techniques can capture followers because they allow them to deny the conflict and remain in the hypnotic sleep and dream state. Furthermore, they allow them to overcome their bad conscience of contributing to hateful actions and allow them to deny that they are doing anything wrong.

Therefore, the techniques work in part because they are enabling people who are already tempted by the less effortful path of denial. One of the core reasons why followers want to remain in the sleep state is that such a state also engenders a euphoric "dream state," which allows them in a hallucinatory manner to feel "whole again" and without any scars, quelling their castration anxieties and feelings of failure generated by the objective conditions of suffering in precarity capitalism (without such conditions changing).

3. Can one refuse to be hypnotized by a leader, movement, or ideology? Since there is willingness and a choice on the side of followers to become and remain hypnotized (through repeated acts of self-hypnosis), they can also refuse to become hypnotized. It is this moment of agency that makes them *responsible* for any reprehensible acts they have carried out while under the hypnotic spell. Of course it is also leaders and the movement that are responsible for inciting them to carry out such acts. In this moment, the possibility of resisting the hypnotic spell also enters. As Freud puts it: "As we know from other reactions, individuals preserved a variable degree of personal aptitude for reviving old situations of this kind. Some knowledge that in spite of everything hypnosis is only a game, a deceptive renewal of these old impressions, may however remain behind and take care that there is a resistance against any too serious consequences of the suspension of the will in hypnoses."[43]

Freud suggests here that the hypnotized retain a moment of awareness that the archaic regression and their euphoric feelings of "wholeness," which far-right propaganda techniques engender in them, are deceptive and that (self-)hypnosis is only a game. In such a moment of awareness, there is the possibility that they can *resist* the suspension of their will, wake up from their dream and sleep state, and refuse their subordination to the destructive will of the leader or the movement.

4. Are there degrees of hypnosis? Do some people get more hypnotized than others? Freud explains in the passage just cited that "we know from other reactions [that] individuals preserved a variable degree of

personal aptitude for reviving old situations of this kind."[44] In *Group Psychology and the Analysis of the Ego*, Freud outlines that the varying degrees of the distance between subjects' ego and their ego ideal engenders different aptitudes to artificially regress to the old psychology of the "primal horde," which far-right propaganda techniques engender.

Those followers whose separation between the ego and the ego ideal is not far advanced have a greater aptitude to artificially regress into the hypnotic sleep state and dream state, by investing the leader figure (or movement) with the perfections they seek to obtain through idealizing him.[45] Other followers, whose separation between the ego and the ego ideal is more advanced, are less prone to invest the leader figure with such perfections and thus have less aptitude to regress to an older form of psychology. However, via identification with those who have already regressed, they too can get "carried away" into the sleep and dream state.[46]

Psychologically oriented propaganda techniques that aim at inducing artificial regressions in them to catch them have a more difficult task with those followers whose separation between the ego and the ego ideal is further advanced, as they are less likely to transfer their narcissistic libido to an idealized leader figure, which also makes it more likely for them to resist the hypnotic spell. It is, then, no coincidence that Freud mentions these varying degrees of aptitude to get hypnotized in the same citation where he points at the possibility of *resisting* the hypnotic spell, because the followers, in spite of finding themselves in a dream and sleep state, retain the knowledge that it is just a dream.

However, followers that have a high aptitude to artificially regress to the sleep and dream state remain responsible for the destructive deeds they carry out "under the spell" because they *choose* to transfer their (upset) narcissistic libido to a leader figure or movement to feel "whole" again and *consciously contribute* to remaining in their euphoria through repeated acts of self-hypnosis. Also, those followers that do not as easily regress into the hypnotic state remain responsible for their destructive acts because of their willingness to get "carried away" by identifying with the already hypnotized followers.

5. Does waking up from hypnosis immediately return one to one's prior mental state? No. For example, Freud outlines that tendentious jokes, which engender a hypnotic state in the consumer of the joke, create a *disposition* in them that is unfavorable to critical and conscious thinking,[47] which

would break the hypnotic spell and allow the followers to wake up from their sleep and dream state.

Such a disposition builds up over time (for example, through repeatedly consuming tendentious alt-right jokes to gain vast amounts of pleasure in acts of self-hypnosis), so changes in those who exit neofascist groups might not be sudden and is also a matter of degree, which is also dependent on one's aptitude to get hypnotized. As such, the analogy of hypnoses still holds because the gradual creation of a disposition to avoid critical thinking explains why former neofascists need to spend years unlearning the ideology they consumed to uphold their hypnotic state.

The Overthrow of Capitalism

> The call to abandon their illusions about the condition is a call to abandon a condition which requires illusions.
> —KARL MARX, "CONTRIBUTION TO THE CRITIQUE OF HEGEL'S *PHILOSOPHY OF RIGHT*"

In this book, I exposed how subjects become prey to the illusion of "wholeness" the far right offers them because the real objective conditions in precarity capitalism make it impossible for them to live up to the bourgeois fetish of "success" in its classed, raced, and gendered guises. While such an illusion of "wholeness" quells their castration anxieties, it does not entice them to generate any change in society. So, the objective conditions that caused their suffering on a subjective level remain intact.

To counter their wanting to join the far right, which provides them with the illusion of "wholeness" on a subjective level, we must, as Marx points out, first of all, abandon a condition that requires illusions—in other words, we must abandon or overthrow capitalism (which also affects family structures) to make people less vulnerable to the kinds of psychological techniques I have addressed in this book. For this to happen, we must reintroduce the Marxian notion of a revolutionary proletariat.

Marx argued that the formation of the revolutionary proletariat was central in England because, at his time, it was the center of capital. A proletarian revolution in England would immediately inspire other nations and generate a world proletarian revolution. Likewise, as Andrew Kliman points out, in today's neoliberal (or precarity) capitalist societies, forming a revolutionary proletariat is central in the United States because it is the center of capital today.[48] A proletarian revolution in the United States could inspire proletarian revolutions in neighboring nations and, from here, turn into a world proletarian revolution that liberates all oppressed peoples, from all countries, from their chains. However, for this to happen, the proletarians of the world and people from other classes who sympathize with the proletariat need to unite.

However, the far right aims to undermine such a unification with their various propaganda tricks, which generate in subjects the illusion of "wholeness" by, for example, arguing that white, male workers are "superior" to minority workers or female workers, which pits these groups of workers against one another and divides the revolutionary proletariat. Apostolidis suggests that to create *solidarity* between different groups of workers, we must introduce worker centers. For workers hit hardest by precarity capitalism (migrant workers), the shared care for a common place encourages trust in others and nourishes day laborers' and collaborators' capacities for collective action.[49]

He argues that worker centers can also enable a "migrantizing of the citizen," which implies a process whereby (U.S.) citizens as workers on all levels of the work hierarchy learn to grasp that they are subject to the same economic hardships (albeit to a different degree) as migrant workers, which would "create practical opportunities for different groups of workers to 'recognize in their own precarity' the precarity of others and discover dynamics of precaritization that envelop all," which would also foster solidarity among different groups of workers.[50]

While I find Apostolidis's idea of expanded workers' centers to create solidarity among different groups of workers to counter the rise of the far right compelling, one needs to develop it on several levels. First, while the concept of "migrantizing citizens" aims to challenge the citizen/migrant opposition, it does leave out those at all levels of the work hierarchy in the United States and elsewhere who are not citizens (such as permanent residents), whose rights have been curtailed. Trump also used the figure of the "noncitizen" as a core figure to redirect his followers rage (such as in his speech before his violent mob stormed the Capitol). So we must rethink such terminology.

Second, although Apostolidis suggests that workers' centers can create solidarity for the sake of collective workers' action, he does not think such action should lead to overthrowing the capitalist system. Instead, he suggests that such action should only lead to reforms within capitalism.[51] However, while reforms within capitalism, as Marx has already shown us in "The Critique of the Gotha Program," are essential, if they are enacted alone and without the idea of a revolutionary proletariat that overthrows capitalism, then they will not amount to any changes but are merely a Band-Aid to deal with the worst effects of capitalism.[52]

Since reforms alone within capitalism merely better the objective conditions of suffering on a surface level (which generates subjective forms of suffering on a subjective level, upon which propaganda preys) but do not do away with capitalism itself, reforms will not, in the long run, undermine the appeal of the far right, as Apostolidis suggests. To undermine the appeal, we must not only enact reforms within capitalism (which are also often merely enacted in the interests of the bourgeois class—to exploit the workers more insidiously) but also envision the overthrow of capitalism through the "revolutionary proletariat."

To counter an idealization of the revolutionary proletariat we must also envision it in the context of the subject-in-outline. So instead of envisioning it as a "whole" revolutionary force, it moves within the tension of a certain wholeness (the subject), which is necessary for its agency, but accepts its nonwholeness (or its holes), which is necessary for those often excluded in the "whole" of the classic Marxian notion of revolutionary proletariat (such as minority, female, and transgender workers) to enter (or exit) the proletariat-in-outline and so contribute to strengthen it as a revolutionary force.

Second, since Apostolidis dismisses a psychoanalytic framework, he underestimates the importance of illusions of "wholeness" for (white) workers to make them subjectively feel better about themselves (although in reality nothing has changed), which are partly the result of the far right's denigration of migrants and other racialized workers. So his argument that making (white) workers on all levels of the work hierarchy aware that they experience similar precarity and daily shocks in their work lives as migrants and other racialized workers could generate solidarity among different groups of workers is not very convincing.

In addition, Apostolidis underestimates how not only the daily shocks to which workers are exposed to in their daily work lives but also experiences in our childhood and living in a nations with a violent past, which have not been worked-through, all contribute to our "system of scars," which can hinder the reaching of solidarity between white workers and the raced and gendered proletariat. Workers on all levels of the work hierarchy, and here particularly white workers, must touch and work through their system of scars, which has been generated not only by precarity capitalism but by their childhoods and through their white ancestors' murderous deeds toward the indigenous population and enslaved Africans.

Nonetheless, such working-through the past could happen in workers' centers, which need to be expanded worldwide to create an international revolutionary proletariat-in-outline that overthrows capitalism. However, to counter the problems where the victimizers (white males) work through the past with those they victimize (as outlined in my discussion of McIvor's work), I suggest that such worker centers create spaces for white men alone to work through their and their nation's violent past and their open or veiled violence toward women and minorities, so they do not overburden racial and sexual minorities and women with the additional emotional labor required to enter into a dialogue with them. Furthermore, such working-through by white males could also help undermine patriarchal family structures.

Such worker centers could also target potential and actual far-right followers, who, through working through their resistances (among themselves), could "wake up from the dream" and realize that far-right propaganda effectively keeps exploited workers on all levels from uniting to overthrow capitalism. Furthermore, as their engagement in workers' centers is based on the idea of the subject-in-outline, they no longer search for wholeness but embrace their nonwholeness and so realize that the far right brands minority and female workers as inferior to make them feel "whole" again.

In addition, since having a greater distance between the ego and the ego ideal helps people resist the appeal of far-right propaganda techniques, we must assist subjects in such a process. Insofar as the *Authoritarian Personality* study found out that subjects who grew up in families with democratic family structures have more distance between their ego and their ego ideal and have less need to claim that they are living up to their ideal, undermining patriarchal family structures will assist in helping subjects have more distance between their ego and their ego ideal and be less vulnerable to far-right propaganda techniques.

Here it is necessary to get rid of the fetish of "success," in its gendered, raced, and classed guises, as it is such a fetish, together with the immense suffering caused by precarity capitalism, that leads to subjects' hunger for wholeness and the success of the far right today. Here, suppose subjects have less or no pressure to live up to unattainable standards of "success." In that case, they can more readily admit that they cannot live up to their ego ideal without feeling threatened by their subjectivities.

Furthermore, their embrace of the idea of remaining subjects-with-holes also allows them to generate less rigid subjectivities that have less need of a stern superego to keep unconscious impulses repressed, which, as I have shown, plays into the hands of propagandists. A less stern superego might in general counter subjects' willingness to join the far right, which allows them to undo the superego and obtain pleasure through obtaining their libidinal and aggressive drives in their ego.

However, when I argue for a less stern superego, I do not argue that we must dissolve the superego to counter the far right today, as Samir Gandesha has suggested.[53] We need a functioning *and* internalized superego to keep our libidinal and aggressive drives in check. As I have shown in this book, far-right propaganda tools are so effective in catching followers because they also temporarily abrogate their superego, which allows the followers to receive their aggressive drives and their repressed hostility toward minorities and women into their consciousness.

However, a less stern superego might allow them to obtain small amounts of pleasure (such as in humor), which might help with their suffering but avoid a scenario where they turn to the "drugs" offered by the far right to feel better about themselves. The hope and goal is that white workers on all levels of the work hierarchy, instead of blindly submitting themselves to the far right's destructive goals, join the gendered and raced proletariat and undertake the core task of today—to overthrow capitalism and recreate a society where people do not need any illusions.

Notes

Introduction

The epigraph to this introduction is from Theodor W. Adorno, *Guilt and Defense: On the Legacies of National Socialism in Postwar Germany*, trans. J. Olick and A. Perrin (Cambridge, MA: Harvard University Press, 2010), 225. This standalone essay was published in 1955 as part of a larger work, *Gruppenexperiment* (Group Experiment), a study conducted mostly in 1950–1951 by the members of the Frankfurt School after their return from U.S. exile, about the legacies of National Socialist ideology in postwar West Germany, which has only recently become available to an English-speaking audience.

1. Keeping the dialectics between the socioeconomic and psychological is also a challenging enterprise, and it required my constant awareness to not reduce the one to the other.
2. Theodor W. Adorno, *Negative Dialectics*, trans. E. B. Ashton (1966; London: Continuum, 1973), 5.
3. See, for example, Albena Azmanova, *Capitalism on Edge: How Fighting Precarity Can Achieve Radical Change Without Crisis or Utopia* (New York: Columbia University Press, 2020); and Paul Apostolidis, "Desperate Responsibility: Precarity and Right-Wing Populism," *Political Theory* 50, no. 1 (2021). While Apostolidis dismisses psychoanalysis, Azmanova seems more open to psychoanalytic approaches to study the far right (although she does not employ them in her work).

4. See, for example, John Abromeit, "The Concept of Pseudo-Conservatism as a Link Between the Authoritarian Personality and Early Critical Theory," *Polity* 54, no. 1 (January 2022): 29–57; and Gregory J. Menillo, "'Variation Within a Single Paradigm': The Latent Authoritarian Dynamics of the Culture Industry," in *How to Critique Authoritarian Populism: Methodologies of the Frankfurt School*, ed. J. Morelock (Leiden: Brill, 2021), 239–66.

5. See, for example, Peter E. Gordon, "The Authoritarian Personality Revisited," in *Authoritarianism: Three Inquiries in Critical Theory*, ed. W. Brown, P. E. Gordon, and M. Pensky (Chicago: University of Chicago Press, 2018), 45–84; and Martin Jay, "The Authoritarian Personality and the Problematic Pathologization of Politics," *Polity* 54, no. 1 (2022): 1124–45. I will further elaborate on and challenge such a chorus in chapter 3 of this book.

6. I do not aim to establish a rational/irrational binary in the book. For example, while the far right serves the rational self-interest of white capitalists, it does *not* serve the rational interests of white workers, who have been increasingly subjected to extreme economic and social precarity under contemporary capitalist conditions. Instead, it is a pathological "choice" for white workers because the far right circumscribes their choices and does not make them believe in liberation through revolutionary agency as a possibility.

7. Theodor W. Adorno, "Freudian Theory and the Pattern of Fascist Propaganda" (1951), in *The Culture Industry: Selected Essays on Mass Culture*, ed. J. Bernstein (London: Routledge, 2002), 149, emphasis added.

8. I agree with Adorno that the new far right uses the same or similar standardized psychologically oriented tricks as fascist agitators in the previous century and that "little new has been added to the old repertoire." Theodor W. Adorno, *Aspekte des neuen Rechtsradikalismus* (1967, Berlin: Suhrkamp Verlag, 2019), 37.

9. Max Pensky has mentioned the importance of subjectivity in studying the far right, but he needed to develop such an argument in more detail. Max Pensky, "Radical Critique and Late Epistemology," in *Authoritarianism: Three Inquiries in Critical Theory*, ed. W. Brown, P. E. Gordon, and M. Pensky (Chicago: University of Chicago Press, 2018), 85–124.

10. Castration anxiety refers to subjects' fears about being nonwhole subjects.

11. For example, on the political theory side Christopher C. Brittain argues that what motivates evangelical supporters of Donald Trump (despite the various other reasons they mentioned) is a fear over the potential loss of their current social status. Christopher C. Brittain, "Donald Trump and the Stigmata of Democracy: Adorno and the Consolidation of a Religious Racket," in *How to Critique Authoritarian Populism: Methodologies of the Frankfurt School*, ed. J. Morelock (Leiden: Brill, 2021), 384. On the political science side, Diana C. Mutz points out that Trump appealed to those who felt economically "left

behind" *and* those who felt that the economy threatened their privileged class status. Diana C. Mutz, "Status Threat, Not Economic Hardship, Explains the 2016 Presidential Vote," *PNAS* 19, no. 115 (2018): E4330–39.

12. For example, on the political theory side, Andrew Kliman suggests that economic distress is not the source of Trump's strong support from working-class whites. Instead, Trumpism is, for him, a manifestation of long-standing ideas (dating back to slavery) of whites being at the top of the racial ladder and the privileges associated with such a position, which U.S. politicians (including Trump) used to win the support of whites of all classes and that allowed them to divide the working-classes. Andrew Kliman, "Combatting White Nationalism: Lessons from Marx," *Critique of Political Economy* (2017). Similarly, Lilliana Mason and colleagues, on the political science side, do not mention economic distress but foreground racial attitudes to explain that in the United States there exists across the political spectrum a wellspring of social animosity toward marginalized minority groups (such as nonwhite immigrants). Rather than generating such animosity, they argue, Trump acted like a "lightning rod" and attracted those already harboring such animosity. Lilliana Mason, Julie Wronski, and John V. Kane, "Activating Animus: The Uniquely Social Roots of Trump Support," *American Political Science Review* 115, no. 4 (2021): 1508–16.

13. Currently white men have better and higher-paying jobs, and racial minorities, particularly minority women, find themselves in the most dangerous, low-paid, and degrading jobs.

14. The superego is the result of both internalized external authority (of one's parents and later authority figures in our lives) and the aggressive internal drives.

15. Amy Allen, "Psychoanalysis, Critique, and Praxis," *Critique and Praxis* 13 (2019), https://blogs.law.columbia.edu/praxis1313/amy-allen-psychoanalysis-critique-and-praxis/.

16. In chapter 6, I draw on the Austrian psychoanalytic thinker Else Frenkel-Brunswik to explain how patriarchal family structures generate children susceptible to fascist propaganda. See Else Frenkel-Brunswik, "Personality as Revealed Through Clinical Interviews," in *The Authoritarian Personality*, by T. W. Adorno, E. Frenkel-Brunswik, D. J. Levinson, and R. N. Sanford (London: Verso, 2019), 291–489.

17. Adorno, "Freudian Theory," 147.

18. I am not capitalizing the "alt-right" or the "identitarian movement" to counter the idea that these are somehow respectable movements.

19. Herbert Marcuse, foreword to the second edition of *Prophets of Deceit: A Study of the Techniques of the American Agitator*, 2nd ed., ed. L. Löwenthal and N. Guterman (London: Verso, 2021), xlii. Insofar as this book illuminates the

psychological mechanisms that established politicians and parties—Trump and the Austrian Freedom Party—use to recruit people, I am not merely studying "the fringe." Furthermore, in the chapter on the alt-right, I analyze the *Daily Stormer* (an openly antisemitic source) and alt-right sources that aim to make neofascist ideas acceptable to a mainstream audience and are thus less "extreme" only in appearance but *not* in substance.

20. For example, Abromeit points out that fascism is an extreme form of right-wing populism. See John Abromeit, "Critical Theory and the Persistence of Right-Wing Populism," *Logos* 15 (2016): 2–3. In a more recent article, he furthermore states that the debate among scholars over whether Trump is more authoritarian or populist "overlooks the fact that right-wing populism and authoritarianism very often go hand in hand as the experience of European fascism in the 1920s and the 1930s made clear." See John Abromeit, "Frankfurt School Critical Theory and the Persistence of Authoritarian Populism in the United States," in *Critical Theory and Authoritarian Populism*, ed. J. Morelock (London: University of Westminster Press, 2018), 18. Similarly, Shane Burley explains that it is through populist forces that neofascist movements (such as the alt-right) find traction in the mainstream. See Shane Burley, *Fascism Today: What It Is and How to End It* (Chico, CA: AK Press, 2017), 51.

21. George Hawley, *Making Sense of the Alt-Right* (New York: Columbia University Press, 2017).

22. Such as those strong reactions by Austrians that I encountered in response to my book *The Politics of Repressed Guilt: The Tragedy of Austrian Silence* (Edinburgh: Edinburgh University Press, 2018). See Claudia Leeb, "Austria's Repressed Guilt in Theory and Practice: Personal Encounters," in *Remembering the Holocaust in Germany, Austria, Italy, and Israel: "Vergangenheitsbewältigung" (Mastering the Past) as a Historical Quest*, ed. V. Pinto (Leiden: Brill, 2021), 25–38.

23. For example, in a recent article, I show that Marx had a keen understanding that any attempt of subjects to aim at a whole subjectivity leads us into the realm of the fetish. It is fetishes in various forms that the far and extremist right offer their followers to create an illusory world where they can feel like "whole subjects" again. Claudia Leeb, "Mystified Consciousness: Rethinking the Rise of the Far Right with Marx and Lacan," *Open Cultural Studies* 2, no. 1 (2018): 236–48.

24. Theodor W. Adorno, Else Frenkel-Brunswik, Daniel Levinson, and Nevitt Sanford, *The Authoritarian Personality* (London: Verso, 2019). See, for example, the special issue on *The Authoritarian Personality* in *Polity* 54, no. 1 (January 2022); and *The South Atlantic Quarterly* 117, no. 4 (2018). I will discuss

and engage with some of the authors that contributed to these volumes in this book.

25. Such a project would require more broadly engaging with all the early Frankfurt School thinkers.

26. For example, I engage with Löwenthal and Guterman in chapters 1 and 4. See Leo Löwenthal and Norbert Guterman, *Prophets of Deceit: A Study of the Techniques of the American Agitator* (London: Verso, 2021). I also engage with Alexander and Margarete Mitscherlich, who revived psychoanalytic thought at the Goethe University in Frankfurt after World War II, in chapter 6. See Alexander Mitscherlich and Margarete Mitscherlich, *The Inability to Mourn: Principles of Collective Behavior*, trans. B. R. Placzek (New York: Grove, 1975). I draw on Herbert Marcuse in the introduction. See Marcuse, foreword to the second edition. And I draw on Erich Fromm in the conclusion. See Erich Fromm, "Politics and Psychoanalysis," in *Critical Theory and Society*, ed. S. E. Bronner and D. M. Kellner (London: Routledge, 1989), 213–18.

27. Also, I introduce decolonial thinkers to foreground how far-right propaganda tactics prey on subjects' unconscious racist attitudes to catch followers. Furthermore, I introduce feminist scholarship and feminist thinkers to outline the gendered dimension of each of the far-right "cases" that I explain in the United States and Austria.

28. Sigmund Freud, *Civilization and Its Discontents* (1929), ed. J. Strachey and trans. P. Gay (New York: Norton, 1989); Sigmund Freud, *Group Psychology and the Analysis of the Ego* (1921), ed. J. Strachey, ed. and trans. P. Gay (New York: Norton, 1989).

29. Sigmund Freud, *Jokes and Their Relation to the Unconscious* (White Press, 2013).

30. Claudia Leeb, *Power and Feminist Agency in Capitalism: Toward a New Theory of the Political Subject* (Oxford: Oxford University Press, 2017).

1. Castration Anxiety and Capitalism

The epigraphs to this chapter are from Sigmund Freud, *New Introductory Lectures on Psycho-Analysis: The Standard Edition*, ed. and trans. J. Strachey (1933; New York: Norton, 1990), 108; and Theodor W. Adorno, "Die revidierte Psychoanalyse," in *Sociologica II. Reden und Vorträge*, ed. M. Horkheimer and T. W. Adorno (Berlin: Suhrkamp Verlag, 1962).

1. I put "race" into quotation marks to underline the social-constructedness of this category, which I will further detail in the second section.

2. Different levels of economic affluence and inequality, different colonial histories, different forms of government, different family structures, different ideologies, and different religious traditions play a role in the surge of the far right in creating an authoritarian character that is susceptible to fascist propaganda, and they need further study. The primary focus of my book is to outline the psychologically oriented tactics the far right uses to catch people susceptible to far-right propaganda.

3. I call these states sleep and dream states and will further elaborate on them in chapter 3.

4. Theodor W. Adorno, *Aspekte des neuen Rechtsradikalismus* (1967, Berlin: Suhrkamp Verlag, 2019), 6, 10.

5. Theodor W. Adorno, "Die revidierte Psychoanalyse," in *Sociologica II. Reden und Vorträge*, ed. M. Horkheimer and T. W. Adorno (Suhrkamp Verlag, 1962), 129.

6. Adorno, "Die revidierte Psychoanalyse," 123.

7. Adorno, *Aspekte*, 10.

8. In the United States, given the denigration of manual labor and the bourgeois ideology of "upward mobility," most people objectively part of the working classes identify with the bourgeois class or hope to "move up" to that class, which is why I make this distinction here.

9. Albena Azmanova, *Capitalism on Edge: How Fighting Precarity Can Achieve Radical Change Without Crisis or Utopia* (New York: Columbia University Press, 2020), 105–6. She defines the far right as "an expression of broadly shared and lasting *anxiety* triggered by perceptions of physical insecurity, political disorder, cultural estrangement, and employment insecurity" (2:69, emphasis added).

10. Since Azmanova does not employ a psychoanalytic theoretical framework, she cannot further elaborate on the details of these anxieties or how the far right utilizes those anxieties.

11. Langman and Schatz point out that the supposedly meritocratic individualism of capitalism leaves many people unconsciously ashamed when they seemingly fail or "Others" seem to step ahead, especially if such Others are stigmatized as "inferior." The rhetoric of far-right parties contributes to repress shame and to deflect shame-induced anger and hatred away from the self and instead toward various Others. Lauren Langman and Avery Schatz, "The Dialectic of Unreason: Authoritarianism and the Irrational," in *How to Critique Authoritarian Populism: Methodologies of the Frankfurt School*, ed. J. Morelock (Leiden: Brill, 2021), 167–99.

12. I am putting "higher" in quotation marks to make explicit the underlying capitalist ideology, which naturalizes the existing class hierarchies and considers those "higher" in the class hierarchy as more worthy subjects.

13. Louis Althusser, "Preface to Capital, Volume I," in *Lenin and Philosophy and Other Essays*, trans. B. Brewster (New York: Monthly Review Press, 2001), 57–70.
14. Taking out loans creates a precarious situation for U.S. working-class students, as they often have high college debts and reduced chances of securing a job that will allow them to pay back their debt. In contrast, in the Austrian context, tuition for schools and universities remains low, and the state provides generous funding for students from working-class origins (which they do not have to pay back), which contributes to generate a more equal society.
15. In chapter 2, I explain that process as ego ideal replacement.
16. Wendy Brown, *The Ruins of Neoliberalism: The Rise of Anti-Democratic Politics in the West* (New York: Columbia University Press, 2019), 8.
17. Johanna Fernández, "On the Historical Roots of US Fascism," in *For Antifascist Futures: Against the Violence of Imperial Crisis*, ed. A. Goldstein and S. V. Trujillo (Brooklyn, NY: Common Notions, 2022), 47.
18. Fernández, "On the Historical Roots of US Fascism," 47. Similarly, on the political science side, Green and McElwee suggest that Trump appealed to white working-class voters by linking economic issues to an investment in racial hierarchies. Jon Green and Sean McElwee, "The Differential Effects of Economic Conditions and Racial Attitudes in the Election of Donald Trump," *Perspectives on Politics* 18, no. 1 (2020): 360.
19. Anibal Quijano and Michael Ennis, "Coloniality of Power, Eurocentrism, and Latin America," *Nepantla: Views from South* 1, no. 3 (2000): 533–80.
20. Quijano and Ennis, "Coloniality of Power, Eurocentrism, and Latin America," 533.
21. Quijano and Ennis, "Coloniality of Power, Eurocentrism, and Latin America," 550.
22. María Lugones, "Heterosexualism and the Colonial/Modern Gender System," *Hypatia* 22, no. 1 (2007): 186–209.
23. George Padmore, *How Britain Rules Africa* (1936; New York: Negro Universities Press, 1969), 4.
24. Aimé Césaire, *Discourse on Colonialism,* trans. J. Pinkham (1950; New York: New York University Press, 2020), 36.
25. James Q. Whitman, *Hitler's American Model: The United States and the Making of Nazi Race Law* (Princeton, NJ: Princeton University Press, 2017).
26. Anne Spice, "Blood Memory: The Criminalization of Indigenous Land Defense," in *For Antifascist Futures: Against the Violence of Imperial Crisis*, ed. A. Goldstein and S. V. Trujillo (Brooklyn, NY: Common Notions, 2022), 41.
27. In later chapters, I will detail the psychological processes involved.

28. Adorno, *Aspekte*, 11–12.

29. Karl Marx, *Das Kapital: Kritik der politischen Ökonomie, Erster Band, Buch I: Der Produktionsprozeß des Kapitals*, in Karl Marx and Frederick Engels, *Werke*, Band 23 (Bonn: Dietz Verlag, 2001), 247. All translations from *Das Kapital* are mine. Marx calls the "means of production," which include all physical elements that go into producing goods, such as natural resources and machines, the fixed part of capital, or "dead work," which becomes "enlivened" through the blood of "living work," that is, the labor power, or the bodily and mental capacities of the worker.

30. Marx, *Das Kapital I*, 246–47.

31. Marx, *Das Kapital I*, 246–47.

32. Marx, *Das Kapital I*, 271.

33. Marx, *Das Kapital I*, 440.

34. Althusser, "Preface to Capital," 54.

35. Marx, *Das Kapital I*, 246–47.

36. Paul Apostolidis, "Desperate Responsibility: Precarity and Right-Wing Populism," *Political Theory* 50, no. 1 (2021): 3.

37. Apostolidis, "Desperate Responsibility," 8.

38. That specifically these Latina laborers find themselves in such jobs (and not whites) is also the legacy of colonial capitalism's raced division of labor, which Apostolidis does not mention.

39. Marx, *Das Kapital I*, 246–47.

40. Which I will further discuss when I elaborate the fourth form of alienation.

41. See my discussion of this technique in chapter 3.

42. Similarly, carrying cell phones with us means we are always available, 24/7, to work. It was never going to make lives "easier" for us. Rather, it only makes us work more, faster, without ever taking a break.

43. Jason Del Rey, "How Robots Are Transforming Amazon Warehouse Jobs—for Better and Worse," *Vox*, December 11, 2019, https://www.vox.com/recode/2019/12/11/20982652/robots-amazon-warehouse-jobs-automation.

44. Marx, *Das Kapital I*, 440.

45. While all classes in capitalist society experience alienation, there is a difference in how different classes experience such alienation. While the gendered and raced working class finds its mental and physical powers depleted as a result of alienated labor, the bourgeois class finds itself confirmed in its position of power.

46. Marx, "Economic and Philosophic Manuscripts," 72.

47. Marx, "Economic and Philosophic Manuscripts," 74.

48. Marx, "Economic and Philosophic Manuscripts," 74.

49. Marx, "Economic and Philosophic Manuscripts," 77.

50. Which I will further explain in chapter 2.

51. Adorno, "Die revidierte Psychoanalyse," 133.

52. Adorno, "Die revidierte Psychoanalyse," 131.

53. Theodor W. Adorno, *Guilt and Defense: On the Legacies of National Socialism in Postwar Germany*, trans. J. Olick and A. Perrin (Cambridge, MA: Harvard University Press, 2010), 219.

54. Theodor W. Adorno, E. Frenkel-Brunswik, D. J. Levinson, and R. N. Sanford, *The Authoritarian Personality* (London: Verso, 2019), 618.

55. What Adorno does not mention is that such stereotypes are the historical legacies of colonial classifications that the Nazis took over.

56. Adorno, *Aspekte*, 5:619.

57. Theodor W. Adorno, "Culture Industry Reconsidered," in *The Culture Industry: Selected Essays on Mass Culture*, ed. J. Bernstein (1951; London: Routledge, 2002), 98.

58. Weigel shows us how digital capitalism, where workers of all classes must use digital platforms for their jobs, generates a compulsion to constantly check that platform (such as email); such compulsion generates pleasures and anxieties, which the far right can exploit. Moira Weigel, "The Authoritarian Personality 2.0," *Polity* 54, no. 1 (2022): 169.

59. Max Horkheimer and Theodor W. Adorno, *Dialektik der Aufklärung* (1944; Frankfurt: Fischer Taschenbuch Verlag, 1998), 150, 146. The German term *verkümmern* refers to the term *Kummer* (sorrow) as well as to "castration" (the *kümmerliche* phallus). Moreover, the German terms *Verstummung* and *Verkümmerung* both refer to *Verstümmelung* (mutilation). *Verstümmelung* in German refers to the *Stummel*, which signifies a shrunk/cut-off/short phallus, in contrast to the *Stachel* (sting), which signifies a functioning/strong phallus.

60. Theodor W. Adorno, "How to Look at Television," in *The Culture Industry: Selected Essays on Mass Culture*, ed. J. Bernstein (1951; London: Routledge, 2002), 167.

61. L. Löwenthal and N. Guterman, eds., *Prophets of Deceit: A Study of the Techniques of the American Agitator* (London: Verso, 2021), 17.

62. Löwenthal and Guterman, *Prophets of Deceit*, 15, 18.

63. Löwenthal and Guterman, *Prophets of Deceit*, 18.

2. Psychoanalytic Concepts

The epigraph to this chapter is from Theodor W. Adorno, *Guilt and Defense: On the Legacies of National Socialism in Postwar Germany*, trans. J. Olick and A. Perrin (Cambridge, MA: Harvard University Press, 2010), 224.

1. While the English translation of that text uses the term "group," Freud used the more comprehensive term *Masse* (mass), which early Frankfurt School critical theorists used when drawing on this text to study fascist masses and which I also use in this chapter.

2. Adorno does briefly refer to the centrality of the aggressive drive in "Freudian Theory and the Pattern of Fascist Propaganda" (1951), in *The Culture Industry: Selected Essays on Mass Culture*, ed. J. Bernstein (London: Routledge, 2002).

3. The translators used the term "instinct" for Freud's concept of "Trieb," which means "drive." I used the word "drive" and corrected direct quotes from Freud and Adorno. I retained, however, the notion of "instinctual," such as in "instinctual wishes." While libido can be easily detected, the death drive is more challenging to detect and often escapes our grasp unless it is allied with Eros. Sigmund Freud, *Civilization and Its Discontents*, ed. J. Strachey and trans. P. Gay (1930; New York: Norton, 1989), 80.

4. Sigmund Freud, *Group Psychology and the Analysis of the Ego*, ed. J. Strachey, ed. and trans. P. Gay (1921; New York: Norton, 1989), 29.

5. Freud, *Civilization and Its Discontents*, 82. Insofar as the aggressive drive is the main representative of the death drive, I will use this term from here on.

6. Freud, *Civilization and Its Discontents*, 69–70.

7. Freud, *Civilization and Its Discontents*, 112.

8. Butler mentions the centrality of Freud's death drive to grasp the rise of Trump. However, she does not elaborate on that idea in more detail. Judith Butler, "Genius or Suicide," in *Trumpism and Its Discontents*, ed. Osagie K. Obasogie (Berkeley, CA: Public Policy Press, 2020), 232.

9. Freud, *Civilization and Its Discontents*, 81.

10. Freud, *Civilization and Its Discontents*, 81, emphasis added.

11. Freud, *Civilization and Its Discontents*, 82.

12. Freud, *Group Psychology*, 55, 90, emphasis added. In *Group Psychology*, Freud detailed the processes of regression, which allows mass leaders to direct their followers' sexual and aggressive impulses for their aims.

13. Freud, *Civilization and Its Discontents*, 60. Here it becomes clear that it is not just the aggressive drive that is dangerous and that civilization needs to suppress. It is the libidinal drive as well.

14. Freud, *Civilization and Its Discontents*, 60, 28.

15. Freud, *Civilization and Its Discontents*, 29.

16. Freud, *Civilization and Its Discontents*, 52.

17. Freud, *Civilization and Its Discontents*, 83.

18. Sigmund Freud, *New Introductory Lectures on Psycho-Analysis: The Standard Edition*, ed. and trans. J. Strachey (1933; New York: Norton, 1990), 73.

19. Freud, *Civilization and Its Discontents*, 84. The original severity of the super-ego does not merely represent the severity of how the external authority has treated the subject; it also (and perhaps more crucially) represents one's aggressiveness toward oneself. Freud, *Civilization and Its Discontents*, 92.
20. Freud, *Civilization and Its Discontents*, 84, 91.
21. Freud, *New Introductory Lectures*, 136.
22. Freud, *New Introductory Lectures*, 97.
23. Freud, *New Introductory Lectures*, 97.
24. Freud, *Civilization and Its Discontents*, 89, 97. Insofar as fascist forces have manipulated such *Unbehagen*, Freud had a point with his argument that this sense of guilt is one of the core problems civilization has to deal with.
25. Freud, *Civilization and Its Discontents*, 107.
26. Freud, *Civilization and Its Discontents*, 65, 68.
27. Freud, *Civilization and Its Discontents*, 69.
28. Freud, *Civilization and Its Discontents*, 109.
29. Freud, *Civilization and Its Discontents*, 108.
30. Freud, *Civilization and Its Discontents*, 69, emphasis added.
31. Freud, *New Introductory Lectures*, 91, 89.
32. Freud, *Group Psychology*, 80.
33. Freud, *Group Psychology*, 81.
34. Freud, *New Introductory Lectures*, 99, 87. However, the portions of the ego and superego that are unconscious do not possess the "irrational characteristics" of the unconscious. Freud, *New Introductory Lectures*, 93.
35. Freud, *New Introductory Lectures*, 88, 99, 95, 99.
36. Freud, *New Introductory Lectures*, 92. This notion of the unconscious as not knowing the passage of time is particularly relevant when considering how guilt impulses that pertain to past atrocities and have been repressed in the unconscious can be reactivated by far-right propaganda techniques in the present.
37. Freud, *New Introductory Lectures*, 95.
38. Freud, *New Introductory Lectures*, 94, 97.
39. Freud, *New Introductory Lectures*, 96. Freud wrote the lectures in 1932, and they were originally published in 1933.
40. Freud, *New Introductory Lectures*, 98, emphasis added. Freud shows the diagram on the same page.
41. Freud, *New Introductory Lectures*, 98.
42. In this text, Freud draws on and critically assesses the theories of mass psychology established by Gustave Le Bon in his *Psychologie des Foules/Psychology of Crowds* (1895; n.p., 2017) and other thinkers. While he dismisses the theoretical framework of other thinkers and is critical of Le Bon's lack of

theorizing the relationship between the leader and the mass followers, he draws on and retains Le Bon's foregrounding of the unconscious in a mass.

43. Freud, *Group Psychology*, 4. Freud examines two masses—the Catholic Church and the army. I am using the notion of "subject" instead of "individual" to outline that there is no "free and autonomous subject" but that the subject is always a result of power structures. However, she is never wholly subjected to power. I retain the notion of the "individual" in original citations of Freud.

44. Freud, *Group Psychology*, 12, 13.

45. Freud, *Group Psychology*, 9, 11, emphasis added.

46. Freud, *Group Psychology*, 13.

47. Freud, *Group Psychology*, 15, 13–14.

48. Freud, *Group Psychology*, 13–14.

49. Freud, *Group Psychology*, 13–14.

50. Freud, *Group Psychology*, 17.

51. Freud, *Group Psychology*, 17.

52. Freud, *Group Psychology*, 31.

53. Freud, *Group Psychology*, 59.

54. Freud, *Group Psychology*, 41, 35, 50. Here, the object of each mass member's sexual drive is the mass leader, which is the common element that allows the mass followers to identify with one another.

55. Freud, *Group Psychology*, 41.

56. Freud, *Group Psychology*, 72. His reference to a "small cultural group" must be understood in comparison to civilization in general, which is the main reference point in *Civilization and Its Discontents*. Fascist mass movements, although they are not small per se, refer to such a "small cultural group."

57. Freud, *Group Psychology*, 72.

58. Freud, *Group Psychology*, 43.

59. Freud, *Group Psychology*, 66.

60. Freud, *Group Psychology*, 66–67.

61. Freud, *Group Psychology*, 67.

62. Sigmund Freud, "On Narcissism: An Introduction" (1914), in *The Standard Edition of the Complete Psychological Works of Sigmund Freud*, vol. 14: *(1914–1916): On the History of the Psycho-Analytic Movement, Papers on Metapsychology and Other Works*, ed. J. Strachey and A. Freud (London: Hogarth, 1957), 101, 98.

63. Freud, "On Narcissism," 94.

64. Freud, "On Narcissism," 94.

65. In my reading, I follow Freud's earlier and later resurrected idea of the separation between the ego ideal and the superego.

66. Freud, "On Narcissism," 95. In this early text, Freud points out that the mental instance (which he later termed the superego) that makes sure that the ego ideal is in line with the ego derives from the authority of the subject's parents and those who trained and taught them. Freud, "On Narcissism," 96. In his later text *Civilization and Its Discontents*, we learn that the superego is set up to monitor the subject's aggressive drives. Here, he notes that it results from both (external authority and internal drives).

67. Freud, *New Introductory Lectures,* 81.

68. Freud, "On Narcissism," 95, 94.

69. Freud, *New Introductory Lectures,* 86.

70. Freud, *Group Psychology,* 81.

71. Sigmund Freud, *Totem and Taboo: The Standard Edition,* ed. J. Strachey and trans. P. Gay (1913; New York: Norton, 1990), 174.

72. Freud, *Group Psychology,* 61.

73. Freud, *Group Psychology,* 81.

74. Freud, *Group Psychology,* 48, 57.

75. Freud, *Group Psychology,* 81.

76. Freud, *Group Psychology,* 82.

77. Freud, *Group Psychology,* 82.

78. Freud, "On Narcissism," 101.

79. Freud, "On Narcissism," 101.

80. Freud, *Group Psychology,* 56.

81. Freud, *Group Psychology,* 56.

82. Freud, "On Narcissism," 94.

83. Freud, "On Narcissism," 91.

84. Freud, *Group Psychology,* 79.

85. Freud, *Group Psychology,* 79. I will come back to the need for a "strong chief" with greater libido in the sixth section.

86. Freud, *Group Psychology,* 79.

87. Freud, "On Narcissism," 89.

88. Freud, "On Narcissism," 88.

89. Freud, *Group Psychology,* 56–57, emphasis added.

90. Freud, *Group Psychology,* 52. Freud ascribes these functions in *Group Psychology* to the ego ideal. However, since he, in later texts, explains them to be the functions of the superego, I follow Freud's later elaboration.

91. Freud, *Group Psychology,* 57.

92. Freud, *Group Psychology,* 84.

93. Freud points out that while Le Bon outlines the connection between psychological masses and hypnosis, Le Bon does not elaborate on who replaces the hypnotist in the psychological mass.

94. Freud, *Group Psychology,* 58, 12.

95. Freud, *Group Psychology*, 96.

96. Freud, *Group Psychology*, 58, 96.

97. Freud, *Group Psychology*, 97.

98. Freud, *Group Psychology*, 11.

99. Freud, *Group Psychology*, 11, 73.

100. Freud, *Group Psychology*, 73, 69.

101. Freud, *Group Psychology*, 76, 70. Freud calls it a regression to a "primitive" mental activity, a term that is problematic because of its connotation to colonized peoples, whose cultures (as Freud understands them) Freud draws on to outline the notion of the primal horde *in Totem and Taboo*.

102. Freud, *Group Psychology*, 7, 69.

103. Freud, *Totem and Taboo*, 185. Here gods were created.

104. Freud, *Totem and Taboo*, 178–79, 180.

105. Freud, *Totem and Taboo*, 186, 185.

106. Freud, *Group Psychology*, 70, 71.

107. Freud, *Group Psychology*, 79.

108. Freud, *Civilization and Its Discontents*, 52, 109, emphasis added.

109. I will further detail this in chapter 3.

3. Sleeping and Dreaming While Awake: Adorno Revisited

The epigraph to this chapter is from Theodor W. Adorno, "Freudian Theory and the Pattern of Fascist Propaganda" (1951), in *The Culture Industry: Selected Essays on Mass Culture*, ed. J. Bernstein (London: Routledge, 2002).

1. Theodor W. Adorno, *Guilt and Defense: On the Legacies of National Socialism in Postwar Germany*, trans. J. Olick and A. Perrin (Cambridge, MA: Harvard University Press, 2010), 225.

2. Eli Zaretsky points to a more positive reception of Freud in the United States before the rise of neoliberal capitalism. Eli Zaretsky, "Liberalism and Mass Psychology: The American Experience," *Polity* 54, no. 1 (2022): 59–83.

3. Peter E. Gordon, "The Authoritarian Personality Revisited," in *Authoritarianism: Three Inquiries in Critical Theory*, ed. W. Brown, P. E. Gordon, and M. Pensky (Chicago: University of Chicago Press, 2018), 45–84, 75.

4. Gordon, "The Authoritarian Personality Revisited," 63.

5. Adorno, "Freudian Theory," 152.

6. Gordon, "The Authoritarian Personality Revisited," 56–57.

7. T. W. Adorno, E. Frenkel-Brunswik, D. J. Levinson, and R. N. Sanford, *The Authoritarian Personality* (London: Verso, 2019).

8. Gordon, "The Authoritarian Personality Revisited," 52.

9. Adorno et al., *The Authoritarian Personality*, xlvi, 5.

10. Adorno et al., *The Authoritarian Personality*, 5.

11. Adorno et al., *The Authoritarian Personality*, xiv, 10.

12. Robin Marasco, "There Is a Fascist in the Family: Critical Theory and Antiauthoritarianism," *South Atlantic Quarterly* 117, no. 4 (2018): 792.

13. Theodor W. Adorno, *Aspekte des neuen Rechtsradikalismus* (1967, Berlin: Suhrkamp Verlag, 2019), 41.

14. Adorno, *Aspekte*, 41, 43.

15. Federico Fichtelstein, "The Authoritarian Personality and the History of Fascism," *Polity* 54, no. 1 (2022): 100.

16. Paul Apostolidis, "Desperate Responsibility: Precarity and Right-Wing Populism," *Political Theory* 50, no. 1 (2021). He also argues that the "distinction between material and psychological sources of support for Trump" is "dubious" (16).

17. Martin Jay, "The Authoritarian Personality and the Problematic Pathologization of Politics," *Polity* 54, no. 1 (2022): 142. I will further challenge Jay in the book's conclusion.

18. Samir Gandesha, "'A Composite of King Kong and a Suburban Barber': Adorno's 'Freudian Theory and the Pattern of Fascist Propaganda,'" in *Spectres of Fascism: Historical, Theoretical, and International Perspectives*, ed. Samir Gandesha (London: Pluto, 2020), 128. He argues similarly in "Identifying with the Aggressor," 155.

19. Gandesha, however, rejects such a theoretical account, which is salient in his repeated dismissal of Adorno's insistence that in order to understand how fascist propaganda works we need to grasp how they engender followers' regressive processes.

20. Robin Marasco, "There Is a Fascist in the Family: Critical Theory and Antiauthoritarianism," *South Atlantic Quarterly* 117, no. 4 (2018): 793.

21. Adorno, "Freudian Theory," 132.

22. Adorno, "Freudian Theory," 134.

23. Sigmund Freud, *Civilization and Its Discontents*, ed. J. Strachey and trans. P. Gay (1930; New York: Norton, 1989), 52.

24. Adorno, "Freudian Theory," 149–150.

25. Adorno, "Freudian Theory," 136, emphasis added. Insofar as fascist demagogues, via their propaganda devices, artificially produce the libidinal bond between themselves and their followers, fascism is not an expression of spontaneous drives (and thus cannot be reduced entirely to the psychological).

26. Adorno, "Freudian Theory," 141.

27. Adorno, "Freudian Theory," 139.

28. However, to do justice to Adorno, he does point out that it is impossible to discuss the very subtle theoretical differentiation between identification and introjection, and that he contents himself with a few observations on the relevance of the doctrine of identification to fascist propaganda and fascist mentality. Adorno, "Freudian Theory," 139. Also, Margarete and Alexander Mitscherlich suggest that the bond between the leader and her followers is based on identification. Alexander Mitscherlich and Margarete Mitscherlich, *The Inability to Mourn: Principles of Collective Behavior*, trans. B. R. Placzek (New York: Grove, 1975), 22–23.

29. Sigmund Freud, *Group Psychology and the Analysis of the Ego*, ed. J. Strachey, ed. and trans. P. Gay (1921; New York: Norton, 1989), 57. See the fourth section of chapter 2 in this volume.

30. Adorno, "Freudian Theory," 140.

31. Adorno, "Freudian Theory," 145.

32. Adorno, "Freudian Theory," 144.

33. Theodor W. Adorno, *The Psychological Technique of Martin Luther Thomas' Radio Addresses* (1975; Redwood City, CA: Stanford University Press, 2000), 86.

34. Adorno, "Freudian Theory," 145.

35. Adorno, "Freudian Theory," 136.

36. Adorno, "Freudian Theory," 136. Adorno also underlines that Freud does away with the idea of primordial traits ascribed to masses, which we find in the idea of a specific mass or herd instinct (136). Zaretsky's argument that Freud theorized a herd instinct in *Group Psychology* is then not correct. Zaretsky, "Liberalism and Mass Psychology," 89.

37. Adorno, "Freudian Theory," 137.

38. Adorno, "Freudian Theory," 138–39.

39. Adorno, "Freudian Theory," 138.

40. Adorno, "Freudian Theory," 138, emphasis added.

41. Samir Gandesha's reading of Freudian theory, in which he aims to distance Adorno from this aspect of Freud's thought, is therefore not correct. Samir Gandesha, "How Do People Become a Mass?," *Polity* 54, no. 1 (2022): 84–106, esp. 96–97.

42. Adorno, "Freudian Theory," 141, 139.

43. Adorno, "Freudian Theory," 140.

44. Adorno, "Freudian Theory," 141.

45. Adorno, "Freudian Theory," 141.

46. Adorno, "Freudian Theory," 142.

47. Adorno, "Freudian Theory," 140–41.

48. Adorno, "Freudian Theory," 146.

49. Adorno, "Freudian Theory," 147.

50. Adorno, "Freudian Theory," 147.

51. Adorno, "Freudian Theory," 136.

52. Adorno, "Freudian Theory," 136–37.

53. See, for example, Michael J. Thompson, "Th. W. Adorno Defended Against His Critics, and Admirers: A Defense of the Critique of Jazz," *International Review of the Aesthetics and Sociology of Music* 41, no. 1 (2010): 37–49.

54. Adorno, "Freudian Theory," 144.

55. Zoé Samudzi, "Reparative Futurities: Postcolonial Materialities and the Ovaherero and Nama Genocide," in *For Antifascist Futures: Against the Violence of Imperial Crisis*, ed. A. Goldstein and S. V. Trujillo (Brooklyn, NY: Common Notions, 2022), 53–67.

56. Adorno, *Guilt and Defense*, 147.

57. Adorno, *Guilt and Defense*, 149, 150.

58. I have elaborated on the defense mechanisms of Austrians to deny their involvement in the atrocities of the Nazi regime and its consequences in Claudia Leeb, *The Politics of Repressed Guilt: The Tragedy of Austrian Silence* (Edinburgh: Edinburgh University Press, 2018).

59. Adorno, *Guilt and Defense*, 115.

60. Adorno, *Guilt and Defense*, 126.

61. Adorno et al., *The Authoritarian Personality*, 605.

62. Adorno et al., *The Authoritarian Personality*, 609.

63. Adorno et al., *The Authoritarian Personality*, 609, 611.

64. A core theoretical assumption of the AP study, which the psychoanalyst Else Frenkel-Brunswik developed and which Adorno endorsed, was that the potentially fascist character has "free-floating aggressiveness" because they grew up in authoritarian family structures that did not allow them to internalize their superego (which is the agency in us that monitors our desire for cruel aggressiveness). Instead, they have an externalized superego, which means that external authority figures rather than internalized morality standards direct and judge their actions and keep our desire for cruel aggressiveness in check. Furthermore, when such external authority figures, through propaganda techniques, weaken the mental barriers that keep subjects' aggression in check, subjects become encouraged to "canalize" their free-floating aggressiveness toward a chosen enemy. I will come back to this framework in chapter 6 and the conclusion.

65. Adorno et al., *The Authoritarian Personality*, 611.

66. Freud, *Group Psychology*, 76.

67. Freud, *Group Psychology*, 76.

68. Freud, *Group Psychology*, 74.

69. Freud, *Group Psychology*, 74.

70. Freud draws on Sandor Ferenczi, *First Contributions to Psychoanalysis* (1909; London: Routledge, 1994), to outline two forms of hypnosis here. One is

coaxing and soothing and derived from the mother, and another is threatening and derived from the father. However, Freud mainly discusses the role of the *threatening father* in mass hypnosis. Zaretzky's reading of the centrality of the mother in Freud's texts on mass psychology is then not correct. Zaretsky, "Liberalism and Mass Psychology," 76.

71. Freud, *Group Psychology*, 74, emphasis added.

72. Freud, *Group Psychology*, 75.

73. Adorno, *The Psychological Technique*, 13.

74. Adorno, *The Psychological Technique*, 14–15.

75. Adorno, *The Psychological Technique*, 13–14.

76. Adorno, *The Psychological Technique*, 14, 14n9.

77. Adorno, *The Psychological Technique*, 14.

78. Adorno, "Freudian Theory," 137.

79. Adorno, "Freudian Theory," 138.

80. Adorno, *The Psychological Technique*, 15n10.

81. Adorno, *The Psychological Technique*, 15n10. Joan Braune points out that alt-right followers must constantly assure themselves that their "white identity is very deep" and complex; otherwise, their identity is at constant risk of dissolution, which points to this element of self-hypnosis outlined by Adorno. Joan Braune, "Void and Idol: A Critical Theory Analysis of the Neo-Fascist Alt-Right," *Journal of Hate Studies* 15, no. 1 (2019): 11–37, 29.

82. The self-hypnosis element also hints at why fascists remain morally and legally responsible for their hateful actions performed while under the "spell of hypnosis," which I will further detail in the conclusion.

83. Menillo argues that we can best understand the relationship between Adorno's culture industry and his work on the social psychology of fascism with the conceptual schema of Freud's theory of dream interpretation. He understands the culture industry and fascism as "two different dreams of the same dreamer," in which standardization and pseudoindividualization are their underlying dynamics. However, he could further elaborate on this important insight. Gregory J. Menillo, "'Variation Within a Single Paradigm': The Latent Authoritarian Dynamics of the Culture Industry," in *How to Critique Authoritarian Populism: Methodologies of the Frankfurt School*, ed. J. Morelock (Leiden: Brill, 2021), 26.

84. Sigmund Freud, *Jokes and Their Relation to the Unconscious* (1905; White Press, 2013), 237; Freud, *Group Psychology*, 28.

85. Freud, *Group Psychology*, 23; Sigmund Freud, *New Introductory Lectures on Psycho-Analysis: The Standard Edition*, ed. and trans. J. Strachey (1933; New York: Norton, 1990), 24.

86. Freud, *New Introductory Lectures*, 20, 18.

87. Freud, *New Introductory Lectures*, 21.

88. Freud, *Jokes*, 238; Freud, *New Introductory Lectures*, 23.

89. Freud, *New Introductory Lectures*, 21.

90. Freud, *New Introductory Lectures*, 19.

91. Freud, *New Introductory Lectures*, 19–20.

92. Freud, *New Introductory Lectures*, 19–20.

93. Freud, *New Introductory Lectures*, 19–20.

94. Freud, *New Introductory Lectures*, 19–20.

95. Freud, *New Introductory Lectures*, 24, 20.

96. Freud, *New Introductory Lectures*, 25, 26.

97. Freud, *New Introductory Lectures*, 34.

98. Adorno, "Freudian Theory," 153.

99. Adorno, "Freudian Theory," 151.

100. Adorno, "Freudian Theory," 152.

101. Gordon, "The Authoritarian Personality Revisited," 66.

102. Adorno, "Freudian Theory," 153.

103. Adorno, "Freudian Theory," 153.

4. From Melancholia to Mania: The Rise of Trump

The epigraphs to this chapter are from Theodor W. Adorno, "Freudian Theory and the Pattern of Fascist Propaganda" (1951), in *The Culture Industry: Selected Essays on Mass Culture*, ed. J. Bernstein (London: Routledge, 2002), 136; and Arlie R. Hochschild, *Strangers in Their Own Land: Anger and Mourning on the American Right* (New York: New Press, 2016), 228.

1. I see the case study of Louisiana as representative of struggling Americans at large who followed Trump. If we understand why people in Louisiana supported Trump, we can also understand the appeal of Trump across the United States. I also analyze other interviews with his followers, a Trump rally in Louisiana, and Trump's handling of the COVID-19 pandemic.

2. Hochschild, *Strangers in Their Own Land*, 228.

3. For example, Lenz, who also conducted ethnographic work with Trump supporters in the "red states," pointed out how white evangelicals in the Midwest voted for Trump because of their anxiety about their insecure economic circumstances. Lyz Lenz, *God Land: A Story of Faith, Loss, and Renewal in Middle America* (Bloomington: Indiana University Press, 2019). Similarly, Denker's ethnographic work in Appalachia foregrounds the socioeconomic roots of Trump supporters. Angela Denker, *Red State Christians* (Minneapolis: Fortress, 2019).

4. As outlined in the introduction, the success of far-right propaganda techniques is also the result of the availability of people susceptible to such methods, which results from several factors (such as authoritarian family structures, colonial histories, party structures, etc.). As an example, Marasco draws on the work of the psychoanalytic thinker Frenkel-Brunswik's contribution to *The Authoritarian Personality* study (which I will discuss in more detail in chapter 6), which shows us how children who were raised in authoritarian family structures are more susceptible to fascist propaganda. According to Marasco, authoritarian family structures are "deeply embedded in the foundation of American life" and produce children susceptible to fascist propaganda in the United States. Robin Marasco, "There Is a Fascist in the Family: Critical Theory and Antiauthoritarianism," *South Atlantic Quarterly* 117, no. 4 (2018): 803. While Marasco focuses on the factors that generate susceptibility to fascism in the United States, I am foremost concerned with Trump's techniques to attract such people.

5. The plant is based in Lake Charles, which is among the 2 percent of U.S. counties with the highest toxic emissions per capita.

6. According to the American Cancer Society, Louisiana has the second-highest incidence of cancer for men and the fifth-highest male death rate from cancer in the nation. Hochschild, *Strangers in Their Own Land*, 26.

7. Hochschild, *Strangers in Their Own Land*, 31.

8. Hochschild, *Strangers in Their Own Land*, 4.

9. Hochschild, *Strangers in Their Own Land*, 104.

10. Hochschild, *Strangers in Their Own Land*, 196.

11. Hochschild, *Strangers in Their Own Land*, 196.

12. Karl Marx, "Contribution to the Critique of Hegel's Philosophy of Right: Introduction," in *The Marx-Engels Reader*, ed. R.C. Tucker (Princeton, NJ: Princeton University Press, 1978), 64.

13. Abromeit points out that while Trump has continued emphasizing key elements of the Tea Party ideology, for example, its antigovernment, antiunion, anti-immigrant, probusiness, propolice, and promilitary stance, he has adopted more authoritarian rhetoric. John Abromeit, "Frankfurt School Critical Theory and the Persistence of Authoritarian Populism in the United States," in *Critical Theory and Authoritarian Populism*, ed. J. Morelock (University of Westminster Press, 2018), 17–18.

14. Karl Marx, "Nationalökonomie und Philosophie," in *Die Frühschriften: Von 1837 bis zum 'Manifest der Kommunistischen Partei' 1848*, ed. S. Landshut (Stuttgart: Alfred Kröner Verlag, 1971), 298.

15. Hochschild, *Strangers in Their Own Land*, 143.

16. Hochschild, *Strangers in Their Own Land*, 86.

17. Hochschild, *Strangers in Their Own Land*, 90.

18. Hochschild, *Strangers in Their Own Land*, 196, 189.
19. Hochschild, *Strangers in Their Own Land*, 196.
20. Hochschild, *Strangers in Their Own Land*, 112.
21. In reality, most companies recruited international well-trained workers for the positions higher up in the economic hierarchy and Mexican and Filipino workers for the lower ranks. Today only 10 percent of jobs are in the plants. The plants suppressed other lines of work in Louisiana, such as tourism and the fishing industry, created pollution, and did nothing to resolve the many problems saddling the state.
22. In the 2016 election, Trump won 58.09 percent of the vote, and in 2020 he won 58.5 percent of the vote in Louisiana.
23. Hochschild, *Strangers in Their Own Land*, 226.
24. Sigmund Freud, "Mourning and Melancholia" (1917), in *Collected Papers*, ed. J. D. Sutherland (London: Hogarth, 1957), 155.
25. Hochschild, *Strangers in Their Own Land*, 52, 226.
26. Alyosha Goldstein, "The Anti-Imperialist Horizon," in *For Antifascist Futures: Against the Violence of Imperial Crisis*, ed. A. Goldstein and S. V. Trujillo (Brooklyn, NY: Common Notions, 2022), 292.
27. He calls such fascist trends a version of what Angela Y. Davis called "incipient fascism," which uses the law enforcement–judicial-penal apparatus to stifle the overt and latent revolutionary trends developing among nationally oppressed people. Alberto Toscano, "The Returns of Racial Fascism," in *For Antifascist Futures: Against the Violence of Imperial Crisis*, ed. A. Goldstein and S. V. Trujillo (Brooklyn, NY: Common Notions, 2022), 251–52.
28. As McIvor points out, the far right can mobilize in Americans defense mechanisms against the guilt (and loss) of a violent racist past that has not been worked through. These defense mechanisms in turn can perpetuate that cycle of violence. David McIvor, "Claudia Leeb's *The Politics of Repressed Guilt: The Tragedy of Austrian Silence* with David McIvor, Lars Rensmann, and Claudia Leeb," *Critical Horizons* 21, no. 1 (2020): 66.
29. Freud, "Mourning and Melancholia," 154.
30. Freud, "Mourning and Melancholia," 159.
31. Freud, "Mourning and Melancholia," 158.
32. Freud, "Mourning and Melancholia," 159, 155.
33. Which I have also briefly elaborated in the fourth section of chapter 2.
34. Sigmund Freud, *Group Psychology and the Analysis of the Ego*, ed. J. Strachey, ed. and trans. P. Gay (1921; New York: Norton, 1989), 82.
35. Freud, *Group Psychology*, 81.
36. Christina Tarnopolsky, "Melancholia and Mania on the Trump Campaign Trail," *Theory & Event* 20, no. 1 (2017): 114.
37. Tarnopolsky, "Melancholia and Mania on the Trump Campaign Trail," 112.

38. Freud, *Group Psychology*, 82.

39. Freud, "Mourning and Melancholia," 155.

40. Freud, *Group Psychology*, 57.

41. Adorno, "Freudian Theory," 152.

42. Freud, *Group Psychology*, 75.

43. Freud, *Group Psychology*, 11.

44. Adorno, "Freudian Theory," 148.

45. Adorno, "Freudian Theory," 133.

46. Sigmund Freud, *New Introductory Lectures on Psycho-Analysis: The Standard Edition*, ed. and trans. J. Strachey (1933; New York: Norton, 1990), 23–24.

47. Freud, "Mourning and Melancholia," 159.

48. See the "Narcissistic Mass Love" section of chapter 2.

49. Freud, *Group Psychology*, 56.

50. Sigmund Freud, "On Narcissism: An Introduction" (1914), in *The Standard Edition of the Complete Psychological Works of Sigmund Freud*, vol. 14: *(1914–1916): On the History of the Psycho-Analytic Movement, Papers on Metapsychology and Other Works*, ed. J. Strachey and A. Freud (London: Hogarth, 1957), 94.

51. See the "Narcissistic Mass Love" section of chapter 2.

52. Brian Naylor, "Read Trump's Jan. 6 Speech, a Key Part of Impeachment Trial," NPR, February 10, 2021, https://www.npr.org/2021/02/10/966396848/read-trumps-jan-6-speech-a-key-part-of-impeachment-trial.

53. Though his father gave him his first million and he comes from generations of white male bourgeois privilege.

54. "Trump Supporter: I Salute a Cardboard Trump," CNN, February 18, 2017, http://www.cnn.com/videos/politics/2017/02/18/donald-trump-supporter-gene-huber-intv-nr.cnn.

55. Freud, *New Introductory Lectures*, 23.

56. Alexander Mitscherlich and Margarete Mitscherlich, *The Inability to Mourn: Principles of Collective Behavior*, trans. B. R. Placzek (New York: Grove, 1975), 60.

57. Freud, *Group Psychology*, 17.

58. Adorno, "Freudian Theory," 141.

59. Hochschild, *Strangers in Their Own Land*, 224.

60. Naylor, "Read Trump's Jan. 6 Speech."

61. Adorno, "Freudian Theory," 132–33.

62. Freud, *Group Psychology*, 41.

63. Adorno, "Freudian Theory," 147. As Bazian points out, in Trump's earlier tweets in the 2020 elections he argued that the four democratic minority women of color representatives should "go back and help fix the totally broken and crime-infested places from which they came." Hatem Bazian,

"Islamophobia, Trump's Racism, and 2020 Elections," *Islamophobia Studies Journal* 5, no. 1 (2019): 8.

64. Ben Zimmer, "What Trump Talks About When He Talks About Infestations," *Politico*, July 29, 2019, https://www.politico.com/magazine/story /2019/07/29/trump-baltimore-infest-tweet-cummings-racist-227485/.

65. L. Löwenthal and N. Guterman, eds., *Prophets of Deceit: A Study of the Techniques of the American Agitator* (London: Verso, 2021), 52.

66. Freud, *Group Psychology*, 56–57.

67. Freud, *Group Psychology*, 57.

68. Hochschild, *Strangers in Their Own Land*, 223.

69. Ross and Rivers, who studied Trump's presence on Twitter, further point out that his language is simple and informal, allowing him to appear "closer to the people." He consolidates such closeness to the people through the nature of his tweeting, which regularly includes typos alongside spelling and grammatical errors and sometimes responds to what he has just watched on cable television. Andrew S. Ross and Damian J. Rivers, "Donald Trump, Legitimisation, and a New Political Rhetoric," *World Englishes* 39, no. 4 (2020): 623–37.

70. Theodor W. Adorno, *The Psychological Technique of Martin Luther Thomas' Radio Addresses* (1975; Redwood City, CA: Stanford University Press, 2000), 17.

71. Adorno, *The Psychological Technique*, 17. Here the fascist leader image is no longer a paternalistic one, which, according to Adorno, reflects the status of the father in the present phase of social development, where he is no longer psychologically a superior social agency, because he can no longer guarantee the survival of his family.

72. Adorno, *The Psychological Technique*, 141.

73. Löwenthal and Guterman, *Prophets of Deceit*, 49, 29.

74. Arwa Mahdawi, "Men Are Less Likely to Wear Masks—Another Sign That Toxic Masculinity Kills," *Guardian*, May 16, 2020, https://www.theguardian .com/commentisfree/2020/may/16/men-masks-coronavirus-protests -masculinity-kills.

75. It comes of no surprise that it is "hypermasculine" men (who are anxious about their masculinity) who voted again for Trump in the recent presidential elections.

76. Which turns the reality, that he is seventy-seven years old and clinically obese, into its opposite.

77. Tom Batchelor, "Trump Reportedly Planned to Rip Open Shirt to Reveal Superman Logo After Discharge from Hospital," October 11, 2020, https:// www.independent.co.uk/news/world/americas/us-politics/trump

-coronavirus-superman-tshirt-hospital-latest-white-house-covid-b958130
.html.

78. Adorno, "Freudian Theory," 141.

79. Not to mention that Trump has access to health care treatment and world-class medical facilities, which are denied to the gendered and raced proletariat in the United States.

80. "Trump Says Not to Fear COVID-19. Do Americans Agree?," *BBC News,* October 7, 2020, https://www.bbc.com/news/election-us-2020-54443147.

81. Adorno, "Freudian Theory," 153. Freud, *Group Psychology,* 76. In the conclusion of the book, I will come back to this argument of Freud.

82. Adorno, "Freudian Theory," 153.

5. The Culture Industry of Jokes:
The Recruitment Tactics of the Alt-Right

The epigraphs to this chapter are from Karl Fallend, *Unbewusste Zeitgeschichte* (Vienna: Erhard Löcker Verlag, 2016), 82, emphasis added; and Theodor W. Adorno, "Freudian Theory and the Pattern of Fascist Propaganda" (1951), in *The Culture Industry: Selected Essays on Mass Culture,* ed. J. Bernstein (London: Routledge, 2002), 150.

1. Adorno explains how the fascists' conception of the world's involving conspiracies appeals to the masses because they feel themselves to be objects of social processes that happen above their heads and out of their control. Therefore, they are "anxious to learn what is going on behind the scene. At the same time, they are prone psychologically to transform the anonymous processes to which they are subject into personalistic terms of conspiracies, plots by evil powers, secret international organizations, etc." Theodor W. Adorno, *The Psychological Technique of Martin Luther Thomas' Radio Addresses* (1975; Redwood City, CA: Stanford University Press, 2000), 54.

2. Braune shows us that these conspiracy theories apply antisemitic tropes to the Frankfurt School. The alt-right invented the label "cultural Marxism" to dismiss the insights of the Frankfurt School because it opposed fascism and antisemitism and provided crucial intellectual resources capable of challenging the alt-right's ideas. Furthermore, neofascists know that the Frankfurt School took on the Nazis through government institutions and NGOs. In addition, since it is embarrassing to admit why their opponents do not take them seriously, they must portray the Frankfurt School's followers as having been brainwashed. Joan Braune, "Who's Afraid of the Frankfurt School? 'Cultural Marxism' as an Antisemitic Conspiracy Theory," *Journal of Social Justice* 9 (2019): 20.

3. Since scholars who use the term "white nationalist" to define the alt-right contribute to masking the alt-right's continuity with earlier neo-Nazi movements (for example, George Hawley, *Making Sense of the Alt-Right* [New York: Columbia University Press, 2017], 1–16), I use the terms "neofascist" or "white supremacist" to underline its continuity. I have opted not to capitalize the term "alt-right" (as Hawley, for example, does), as this provides too much respect for a neofascist hate group.

4. Joan Braune, "Void and Idol: A Critical Theory Analysis of the Neo-Fascist 'Alt-Right,'" *Journal of Hate Studies* 15, no. 1 (2019): 30.

5. See, for example, Hawley, *Making Sense of the Alt-Right*, 3–20; Shane Burley, *Fascism Today: What It Is and How to End It* (Chico, CA: AK Press, 2017), 63; David Neiwert, "Is That an OK Sign? A White Power Symbol? Or Just a Right-Wing Troll?," Southern Poverty Law Center, September 19, 2018; and Alice Marwick and Rebecca Lewis, "Media Manipulation and Disinformation Online," *Data and Society Research Institute* (2017): 27.

6. Most of the literature on the alt-right is from a political science perspective (for example, Hawley, *Making Sense of the Alt-Right*) or a journalistic and/or activist perspective (for example, Burley, *Fascism Today*).

7. Including Simon Critchley, *On Humour* (New York: Routledge, 2002); John Lombardini, "Civic Laughter: Aristotle and the Political Virtue of Humor," *Political Theory* 41, no. 2 (2013): 203–30; and Lori Marso, "Feminist Cringe Comedy: Dear Dick, the Joke Is on You," *Politics and Gender* 15, no. 1 (2019): 107–29.

8. And while there is a recent, growing field of "critical humor studies" in the United States, which outlines the uses of jokes for regressive political ends, psychoanalytic theory finds in this field (not unlike the field of political theory) only marginal and mainly critical reception. See, for example, Michael Billig, *Laughter and Ridicule: Towards a Social Critique of Humour* (London: Sage, 2005); Leslie Picca and Joe R. Faegin, *Two-Faced Racism: Whites in the Backstage and Frontstage* (New York: Routledge, 2007); Mónica Romero-Sánchez, Mercedes Durán, Hugo Carretero-Dios, Jesús L. Megías, and Miguel Moya, "Exposure to Sexist Humor and Rape Proclivity: The Moderator Effect of Averseness Ratings," *Journal of Interpersonal Violence* 25, no. 12 (2009): 2339–50; Raúl Pérez and Viveca Greene, "Debating Rape Jokes vs. Rape Culture: Framing and Counterframing Misogynistic Comedy," *Social Semiotics* 26, no. 3 (2016): 265–82; Manuela Thomae and G. Tendayi Viki, "Why Did the Woman Cross the Road? The Effect of Sexist Humor on Men's Rape Proclivity," *Journal of Social, Evolutionary, and Cultural Psychology* 7, no. 3 (2013): 250–69.

9. An exception is the work of Joan Braune, who mainly draws on Erich Fromm's psychoanalytic theory to explain the alt-right. As I consider her one

of the most accurate observers of the alt-right from a philosophical perspective, I will cite her work throughout this chapter and return to her work in the conclusion.

10. Braune, "Void and Idol," 28, makes a similar argument when she points out that the alt-right is a result of economic (particularly the growing gap between what capitalism claims to offer and what it delivers) and psychological conditions (particularly a void of meaning). Similarly, Johnson points out that the dehumanization created by capitalism has created the psychological conditions that lead people to support strongman leaders and the growing alt-right movement. Laurie M. Johnson, *Ideological Possession and the Rise of the New Right: The Political Thought of Carl Jung* (New York: Routledge, 2019), 133.

11. Asking the question why well-educated people are drawn to the alt-right, Greg Johnson, an alt-right supporter, points out that the career prospects of college-educated whites have declined in the United States, so "a growing number of young whites are returning home to live with their parents, remaining unemployed or underemployed for a long time and their resentment grows." Cited in Hawley, *Making Sense of the Alt-Right*, 79. Here we can see how white far-right followers assume that whites ought to have good jobs, which is a result of how colonial racist classifications, which, when not worked through (which is the case in the United States), are carried on from one generation to the next.

12. Raúl Pérez, "Racism Without Hatred? Racist Humor and the Myth of 'Color-Blindness,'" *Sociological Perspectives* 60, no. 5 (2017): 956–74.

13. Pérez, "Racism Without Hatred?," 5, 15.

14. Ashley Feinberg, "This Is the *Daily Stormer*'s Playbook," *Huffington Post*, December 13, 2017, https://www.huffpost.com/entry/daily-stormer-nazi -style guide_n_5a2ece19e4b0ce3b344492f2; you can find the study guide at the end of the article.

15. Sigmund Freud, *Jokes and Their Relation to the Unconscious* (1905; White Press, 2013).

16. Sigmund Freud, "Humour," in *The Standard Edition of the Complete Psychological Works of Sigmund Freud*, vol. 21, *The Future of an Illusion, Civilization and Its Discontents, and Other Works*, ed. J. Strachey, A. Freud, A. Strachey, and A. Tyson (1927; London: Hogarth, 1961), 159–66.

17. Freud, "Humour," 166, 161.

18. Freud, "Humour," 162.

19. Freud points out that one can observe an extensive displacement of energy from one agency onto another (as we find it in humor) also in melancholia and mania where we see a "cruel suppression of the ego by the superego and a liberation of the ego after that pressure" (Freud, "Humour," 165), which

underlines how processes in humor and jokes are connected to processes in the psychological mass. For a discussion of the oscillation between melancholia and mania, see chapter 4.

20. Freud, "Humour," 163.
21. Freud, "Humour," 164, 166.
22. Freud, "Humour," 163.
23. Freud, "Humour," 162.
24. Freud, "Humour," 163, 166.
25. Freud, *Jokes*, 137. I base such a definition on Freud's assertion that a man laughing at an obscene joke, which is cruel toward the woman, "is laughing as though he were the spectator of an act of sexual aggression." Freud, *Jokes*, 139.
26. Freud, *Jokes*, 148, 183–84.
27. Freud, *Jokes*, 200.
28. Freud, *Jokes*, 145, 13. Freud's discussion of sexually aggressive jokes is itself at times problematic, especially his argument that "women's incapacity to tolerate undisguised sexuality" is responsible for turning men into sexual aggressors through jokes (Freud, *Jokes*, 144). I, therefore, include the notion that "he feels" he has been rejected.
29. Freud, *Jokes*, 142.
30. Freud, *Civilization and Its Discontents*, 81.
31. Freud, *Jokes*, 170.
32. There can be external and internal obstacles to making a tendentious joke. An external obstacle is, for example, when the joke is directed against people in powerful positions. An internal obstacle is generated in what Freud calls a highly developed aesthetic culture (which he related to bourgeois culture) that does not permit any expressions of undisguised sexuality and aggression in people. In contrast to the overcoming of external obstacles, the overcoming of internal obstacles can provoke more laughter because it takes more psychical expenditure to erect and maintain internal obstacles.
33. Freud, *Jokes*, 197–98.
34. Freud, *Jokes*, 148.
35. Freud, *Jokes*, 209.
36. Freud, *Jokes*, 147, 142.
37. Freud, *Jokes*, 148, 193.
38. Freud, *Jokes*, 143.
39. Sigmund Freud, *Group Psychology and the Analysis of the Ego*, ed. J. Strachey, ed. and trans. P. Gay (1921; New York: Norton, 1989), 81.
40. Freud, *Jokes*, 158.
41. Sigmund Freud, *New Introductory Lectures on Psycho-Analysis: The Standard Edition*, ed. and trans. J. Strachey (1933; New York: Norton, 1990), 81.
42. Freud, *Jokes*, 246, 250; Freud, "Humour," 165.

43. Freud, *Group Psychology*, 75.
44. Freud, *Group Psychology*, 75; Freud, *Jokes*, 223.
45. Freud, *Jokes*, 222–23.
46. "The thought sees to wrap itself in a joke because in that way it recommends itself to our attention and can seem more significant and more valuable, but above all this wrapping bribes our powers of criticism and confuses them. We are inclined to give the thought the benefit of what has pleased us in the form of the joke; and we are no longer inclined to find anything wrong that has given us enjoyment and so to spoil the source of a pleasure. If the joke has made us laugh, moreover, a disposition most unfavourable for criticism will have been established in us." Freud, *Jokes*, 191.
47. Freud, *Jokes*, 225.
48. Freud, "Humour," 163.
49. Wendy Brown, *The Ruins of Neoliberalism: The Rise of Anti-Democratic Politics in the West* (New York: Columbia University Press, 2019), 164.
50. Brown, *The Ruins of Neoliberalism*, 165–67.
51. Brown, *The Ruins of Neoliberalism*, 167.
52. Keegan Hankes and Alex Amend, "The Alt-Right Is Killing People," Southern Poverty Law Center, February 5, 2018.
53. Jan Ransom, "White Supremacist Who Killed Black Man to Incite Race War Sentenced to Life in Prison," *New York Times*, February 13, 2019, https://www.nytimes.com/2019/02/13/nyregion/james-harris-jackson -timothy-caughman.html.
54. Cited in Hawley, *Making Sense of the Alt-Right*, 25.
55. Freud, *Jokes*, 148–49.
56. Freud, *Jokes*, 193, 186.
57. See chapter 2 for a detailed explanation of Freud's idea of a regression to the primal horde.
58. The Anti-Defamation League provides information on Pepe the Frog: https://www.adl.org/education/references/hate-symbols/pepe-the-frog.
59. Andrew Anglin, "*Daily Stormer* Style Guide" (2017), cited in Feinberg, "This Is the *Daily Stormer*'s Playbook."
60. Anglin, "*Daily Stormer* Style Guide."
61. Adorno, "Freudian Theory," 133.
62. Anglin, "*Daily Stormer* Style Guide."
63. Adorno, *Culture Industry*, 86.
64. Freud, *Jokes*, 324–25.
65. Anglin, "*Daily Stormer* Style Guide."
66. Anglin, "*Daily Stormer* Style Guide." In chapter 4, I showed how Trump relates minorities to vermin to dehumanize them, which is another uncanny connection between Trump and the alt-right.

67. Adorno, *The Psychological Technique*, 77.

68. Adorno, *The Psychological Technique*, 77.

69. Adorno, "How to Look at Television," 167.

70. Anglin, "*Daily Stormer* Style Guide."

71. Anglin, "*Daily Stormer* Style Guide."

72. "On Being Diagnosed with Irony Poisoning," *Diggit*, https://www .diggitmagazine.com/column/being-diagnosed-irony-poisoning.

73. Freud, *Jokes*, 256.

74. Freud, *Jokes*, 258.

75. See chapter 1 for further elaboration.

76. Anglin, "*Daily Stormer* Style Guide."

77. Freud, *Jokes*, 141. Freud distinguishes between "smut" and a sexually aggressive joke; while smut happens, according to him, in working-class contexts when the woman appears, a sexually aggressive joke happens while in "higher social levels," without the woman present, and when men are alone with each other (142).

78. Burley, *Fascism Today*, 85.

79. Freud, *Jokes*, 142.

80. Milo Yiannopoulos, "Full Text: Milo on How Feminism Hurts Men and Women," *Breitbart*, October 7, 2016, https://www.breitbart.com/social -justice/2016/10/07/full-text-milo-feminism-auburn/.

81. Freud, *Jokes*, 139.

82. Freud, *Jokes*, 142.

83. Freud, *Jokes*, 143.

84. Kathryn Ryan and Jeanne Kanjorski outline a significant relationship between the enjoyment of sexist jokes in men "and their self-reported likelihood of forcing sex and use of psychological, physical, and sexual aggression against their partners." Kathryn M. Ryan and Jeanne Kanjorski, "The Enjoyment of Sexist Humor, Rape Attitudes, and Relationship Aggression in College Students," *Sex Roles* 38, nos. 9/10 (1998): 753–54. Also, more recent research shows that sexist jokes normalize and increase the acceptance of sexual violence against women (Romero-Sánchez et al., "Exposure to Sexist Humor and Rape Proclivity"; Pérez and Greene, "Debating Rape Jokes vs. Rape Culture") and found that sexist attitudes and self-reported rape proclivity are correlated with exposure and acceptance of sexist jokes (Thomae and Viki, "Why Did the Woman Cross the Road?").

85. Burley, *Fascism Today*, 63.

86. Freud, *Jokes*, 18.

87. Freud, *Jokes*, 33, 125, 188, 239.

88. As Abadenifard points out, jokes police "the heteronormative, patriarchal gender norms currently at work within the Anglo-American gender order."

Mostafa Abadenifard, "Ridicule, Gender Hegemony, and the Disciplinary Function of Mainstream Gender Humour," *Social Semiotics* 26, no. 3 (2016): 243.

89. Adam Nagourney, Michael Cieply, Alan Feuer and Ian Lovett, "Before Brief, Deadly Spree, Trouble Since Age 8," *New York Times*, June 1, 2014, https://www.nytimes.com/2014/06/02/us/elliot-rodger-killings-in -california-followed-years-of-withdrawal.html.

90. See Josh Glasstetter, "Elliot Rodger, Isla Vista Shooting Suspect, Posted Misogynistic Video Before Attack," Southern Poverty Law Center, May 24, 2014, https://www.splcenter.org/hatewatch/2014/05/24/elliot-rodger-isla -vista-shooting-suspect-posted-misogynistic-video-attack.

91. Hawley, *Making Sense of the Alt-Right*, 132.

92. Nguyen and Zahzah have also pointed out that while casting Trump as a fascist has delegitimized some of his illiberal policies, it also exceptionalized his administration and veiled how U.S. presidents before him, including liberal ones, have affirmed similar practices draped in a liberal veneer. Nicole Nguyen and Yazan Zahzah, "'Make Fascism Great Again!': Mapping the Conceptual Work of 'Fascism' in the War on Terror," in *For Antifascist Futures: Against the Violence of Imperial Crisis*, ed. A. Goldstein and S. V. Trujillo (Brooklyn, NY: Common Notions, 2022), 133.

93. Burley, *Fascism Today*, 51.

94. John Abromeit, "The Concept of Pseudo-Conservatism as a Link Between the Authoritarian Personality and Early Critical Theory," *Polity* 54, no. 1 (January 2022): 47.

95. Heidi Beirich and Susy Buchanan, "2017: The Year of Hate and Extremism," Southern Poverty Law Center, February 11, 2018.

96. Katie Rogers, "In Social Media Summit, Trump Praises Loyal Meme Makers," *New York Times*, July 12, 2019; Charlie Warzel, "Uncle Trump Wants You! (To Join His Troll Army)," *New York Times*, July 19, 2022.

97. Freud, *Jokes*, 207.

98. Elizabeth L. Paluck and Michael Suk-Young Chwe, "Confronting Hate Collectively," *PS: Political Science & Politics* 50, vol. 4 (2017): 990–992, 990.

99. Cassie Miller and Alexandra Werner-Winslow, "Ten Days After: Harassment and Intimidation in the Aftermath of the Election. (Anti-Woman Incidents)," *Southern Poverty Law Center*, November 29, 2016.

100. Daryl Johnson, "Report: Rise in Hate Violence Tied to 2016 Presidential Election," *Southern Poverty Law Center*, March 1, 2018.

101. Angela Nagle, *Kill All Normies: Online Culture Wars from 4Chan and Tumblr to Trump and the Alt-Right* (London: Zero Books, 2017).

102. Samir Gandesha, "The Authoritarian Personality' Reconsidered: the Phantom of "Left Fascism"," *The American Journal of Psychoanalysis* 79, vol. 4 (2019): 601–624, 617.

103. Milo Yiannopoulos, "An Establishment Conservatives Guide to the Alt Right," *Breitbart*, March 29, 2016, https://www.breitbart.com/tech/2016/03/29/an-establishment-conservatives-guide-to-the-alt-right/.

104. Philip Wright, "The Normies Guide to the Alt-Right," *Odyssey Online*, September 2, 2016, https://www.theodysseyonline.com/normies-guide-alt.

105. Joan Braune, "Kill All Normies and Against the Fascist Creep," *Marx and Philosophy Review of Books* (2017).

106. Freud, *Jokes*, 193.

107. Horkheimer and Adorno, *Dialektik der Aufklärung*, 146.

108. Michael Billig, *Laughter and Ridicule: Towards a Social Critique of Humour* (Thousand Oaks, CA: SAGE, 2005).

6. Austria's Far Right: A Failed Working-Through of the Past

The epigraph to this chapter is from Theodor W. Adorno, *Guilt and Defense: On the Legacies of National Socialism in Postwar Germany*, trans. J. Olick and A. Perrin (Cambridge, MA: Harvard University Press, 2010).

1. Adorno's talk had this title; the lecture was then published a book: Theodor W. Adorno, *Aspekte des neuen Rechtsradikalismus* (Berlin: Suhrkamp Verlag, 2019). All the citations from *Rechtsradikalismus* were translated from German into English by the author.

2. Volker Weiβ, "Nachwort," in Adorno, *Aspekte des neuen Rechtsradikalismus*, 59–88, 60.

3. Adorno, *Guilt and Defense*, 183, 223.

4. Claudia Leeb, *The Politics of Repressed Guilt: The Tragedy of Austrian Silence* (Edinburgh: Edinburgh University Press, 2018).

5. Claudia Leeb, "Mourning Denied: The Tabooed Subject," in *The Democratic Arts of Mourning: Political Theory and Loss*, ed. D. McIvor and A. Hirsch (Lanham, MD: Lexington, 2019), 65–82.

6. Christoph Hermann and Jörg Flecker, "The Austrian Model and the Financial and Economic Crisis," in *A Triumph of Failed Ideas: European Models of Capitalism in the Crisis*, ed. S. Lehndorff (European Trade Union Institute, 2012), 121–36.

7. As the work of Rathgeb shows us, the Austrian Freedom Party styles itself as the new "working-class party." However, it merely established an

opposition between what it calls the "makers" ("native" workers) and the "takers" (immigrants) and used such a classification to exclude immigrant workers from welfare benefits. Furthermore, while the FPÖ claims to support the "native workers" in its actual policies, it has undermined workers by shifting the balance of power from union delegates to employer representatives, tax cuts, and, more recently, welfare cuts for noncitizens. Philip Rathgeb, "Makers Against Takers: The Socio-Economic Ideology and Policy of the Austrian Freedom Party," *West European Politics* 44, no. 3 (2021): 635–60.

8. Sebastian Brameshuber, *Und in der Mitte, da Sind Wir*, documentary video (IMDbPro, 2014).

9. Alexander Mitscherlich and Margarete Mitscherlich, *The Inability to Mourn: Principles of Collective Behavior*, trans. B. R. Placzek (New York: Grove, 1975).

10. Else Frenkel-Brunswik, "Personality as Revealed Through Clinical Interviews," in *The Authoritarian Personality*, by T. W. Adorno, E. Frenkel-Brunswik, D. J. Levinson, and R. N. Sanford (London: Verso, 2019), 291–489.

11. Adorno, *Guilt and Defense.*

12. Mitscherlichs, *The Inability to Mourn*, 99.

13. Adorno, *Guilt and Defense*, 53.

14. Mitscherlichs, *The Inability to Mourn*, 1–5, xvi–xvii.

15. Mitscherlichs, *The Inability to Mourn*, 24, 50. They argue that such defense mechanisms are a means to ward off the experience of a mass melancholy, which would have made them experience their egos as severely impoverished and devalued.

16. Sigmund Freud, *Totem and Taboo: The Standard Edition*, ed. J. Strachey and trans. P. Gay (1913; New York: Norton, 1990), 24–25.

17. Mitscherlichs, *The Inability to Mourn*, 107; Freud, *Totem and Taboo*, 41.

18. Freud, *Totem and Taboo*, 39.

19. Mitscherlichs, *The Inability to Mourn*, 91, 66.

20. Mitscherlichs, *The Inability to Mourn*, 42.

21. Freud, *Totem and Taboo*, 29, 35–36.

22. Mitscherlichs, *The Inability to Mourn*, 104.

23. Mitscherlichs, *The Inability to Mourn*, 105.

24. Thomas U. Berger, *War, Guilt, and World Politics After World War II* (Cambridge: Cambridge University Press, 2012), 88.

25. Mitscherlichs, *The Inability to Mourn*, 100.

26. Peter Utgaard, *Remembering and Forgetting Nazism: Education, National Identity, and the Victim Myth in Postwar Austria* (New York: Berghahn, 2003), 27.

27. Mitscherlichs, *The Inability to Mourn*, 99.

28. Stephan Neuhäuser, "Coming to Terms with the Past: The Case of the 'House of Austrian History' (Haus der Geschichte Österreich) in the Wake of the Rise of Populist Nationalism in Austria," *Modern Languages Open* 1 (2020): 1–18, 4.

29. Efraim Zuroff, "Worldwide Investigation and Prosecution of Nazi War Criminals (April 1, 2018–December 31, 2019): An Annual Status Report," Simon Wiesenthal Center–Israel Office, Snider Social Action Institute, October 2020, https://swcjerusalem.org/wp-content/uploads/2020/12/SWCJ-Annual Report-2019.pdf.

30. The 1904–1908 Herero Wars led to the murder of 80 percent of the Ovaherero people and over half of the Nama.

31. Zoé Samudzi, "Reparative Futurities: Postcolonial Materialities and the Ovaherero and Nama Genocide," in *For Antifascist Futures: Against the Violence of Imperial Crisis*, ed. A. Goldstein and S. V. Trujillo (Brooklyn, NY: Common Notions, 2022), 54–55. Samudzi explains that Eurocentric knowledge production (such as through the eugenic "sciences") developed racial classifications through which Africans appeared as premodern and "less civilized" to Europeans, who were exclusively associated with modernity and "civilization." Such "knowledge" was used to justify European brutal colonial violence and exploitation of Africans.

32. He sold his collection to the museum at the beginning of the twentieth century to the American Museum of Natural History in New York City, which doubled the size of its physical anthropology collection and positioned them as leaders in the field. There are recent attempts to foreground the role of Austria-Hungary's Hapsburg Empire in European colonial violence. See Walter Sauer, "Habsburg Colonial: Austria-Hungary's Role in European Overseas Expansion Reconsidered," *Austrian Studies* 20 (2012): 5–23.

33. Jews made up 30 percent and later 40 percent of the prisoners.

34. "Die Nachwirkungen der Neonazi-Attacke in Österreich," *Deutschlandfunk*, July 25, 2023, https://www.deutschlandfunk.de/die-nachwirkungen -der-neonazi-attacke-in-oesterreich-100.html.

35. The *Verbotsgesetz* passed in the immediate aftermath of World War II, on May 8, 1945, and was intended to further the de-Nazification of Austria.

36. "SPÖ kritisiert Hofer wegen Aussagen zu Verbotsgesetz," *Die Presse*, January 28, 2016, https://www.diepresse.com/4914111/spoe-kritisiert-hofer-wegen -aussagen-zu-verbotsgesetz.

37. "Neonazi-Störaktion in Ebensee: Drei Schuldsprüche," *Die Presse*, https:// www.diepresse.com/615017/neonazi-stoeraktion-in-ebensee-drei -schuldsprueche.

38. However, the documentary does not clarify if the (grand)parents were far-right supporters. I suspect the adults in the documentary span the political spectrum.

39. Freud, *Totem and Taboo*, 24.

40. Freud, *Totem and Taboo*, 24.

41. Mitscherlichs, *The Inability to Mourn*, 92, 93.

42. Freud, *Totem and Taboo*, 41.

43. Mitscherlichs, *The Inability to Mourn*, 104.

44. Mitscherlichs, *The Inability to Mourn*, 91.

45. Adorno, *Guilt and Defense*, 53.

46. Adorno, *Guilt and Defense*, 79.

47. Adorno, *Guilt and Defense*, 214.

48. Adorno, *Guilt and Defense*, 101.

49. Adorno, *Guilt and Defense*, 71.

50. Adorno, *Guilt and Defense*, 53.

51. Adorno, *Guilt and Defense*, 53.

52. Adorno, *Guilt and Defense*, 138.

53. A yearly walk, with pagan and Christian undertones, carried out by young boys.

54. The Austrian psychoanalytic thinker Karl Fallend argues that teenagers make such jokes to find closeness to familial identification figures, including their threatening features, which remain hidden in the culture of silence around the Holocaust in Austria. As he puts it, "[Grand]parents as potential murderers become harmless when their (potential) acts become trivialized. Such trivialization finds broad acceptance. It is just a joke." Karl Fallend, *Unbewusste Zeitgeschichte* (Vienna: Erhard Löcker Verlag, 2016), 79.

55. Freud, *Totem and Taboo*, 41.

56. Frenkel-Brunswik, "Personality as Revealed."

57. Frenkel-Brunswik, "Personality as Revealed," 259.

58. Frenkel-Brunswik, "Personality as Revealed," 370.

59. Adorno, *Guilt and Defense*, 138.

60. Adorno, *Guilt and Defense*, 53.

61. Freud, *Totem and Taboo*, 39.

62. Mitscherlichs, *The Inability to Mourn*, 91.

63. Adorno, *Aspekte*, 29.

64. Frenkel-Brunswik, "Personality as Revealed," 371.

65. Frenkel-Brunswik, "Personality as Revealed," 351–352.

66. Margit Reiter, "Antisemitismus in der FPÖ und im 'Ehemaligen'-Milieu nach 1945 in Österreich," in *Jahrbuch für Antisemitismusforschung* (hg. von Stefanie Schüler-Springorum für das Zentrum für Antisemitismusforschung der Technischen Universität Berlin, 2018), 27:120.

67. Mitscherlichs, *The Inability to Mourn.*

68. Reiter, "Antisemitismus in der FPÖ," 120, emphasis added.

69. Margit Reiter, "Anton Reinthaller und die Anfänge der Freiheitlichen Partei Österreichs (FPÖ). Der politische Werdegang eines Nationalsozialisten und die 'Ehemaligen' in der Zweiten Republik," *Vierteljahreshefte für Zeitgeschichte* 66, no. 4 (2018).

70. The Jewish Austrian concentration camp survivor Simon Wiesenthal brought fugitive Austrian NS war criminals to trial.

71. Heribert Schiedel, "Antisemitismus und völkische Ideologie: Ist die FPÖ eine rechtsextreme Partei?," in *AfD & FPÖ: Antisemitismus, Völkischer Nationalismus und Geschlechterbilder*, ed. S. Grigat (Nomos Verlag, 2017), 103.

72. Ruth Wodak, "From Post-Truth to Post-Shame: Analyzing Far-right Populist Rhetoric," in *Approaches to Discourse Analysis*, ed. C. Gordon (Washington, DC: Georgetown University Press, 2021), 175–92, 32.

73. Neuhäuser, "Coming to Terms with the Past."

74. Lars Rensmann, "Guilt, Resentment, and Post-Holocaust Democracy: The Frankfurt School's Analysis of 'Secondary Antisemitism' in the Group Experiment and Beyond," *Antisemitism Studies* 1, no. 1 (2017): 4.

75. Karin Stögner, "Secondary Antisemitism, the Economic Crisis, and the Construction of National Identity in the Austrian Print Media," *Critical Sociology* 44, no. 4–5 (2018): 728. She shows us how antisemitism reappears in a coded manner in the continuing anti-Americanism and in debates about the financial crisis in Austria today.

76. While the Ehemaligen concealed their antisemitic sentiments in public behind secondary antisemitism, in private they voiced their unbroken NS convictions that they regretted that not all Jews had been exterminated. Reiter, "Antisemitismus in der FPÖ," 124–26.

77. In chapter 7, I will analyze how the identitarian movement in Austria uses this conspiracy theory as a propaganda tool.

78. Karin Stögner, "Angst vor dem neuen Menschen. Zur Verschränkung von Antisemitismus, Antifeminismus und Nationalismus in der FPÖ," in *Antisemitismus, völkischer Nationalismus und Geschlechterbilder. Interdisziplinäre Antisemitismusforschung*, Stephan Grigat (hg.), AfD & FPÖ (Baden-Baden: Nomos, 2017), 7:137–61. Therefore, Islamophobia has not replaced antisemitic discourse in Austria, as Hafez suggests. Farid Hafez, "From 'Jewification' to 'Islamization': Anti-Semitism and Islamophobia in Austrian Politics Then and Now," *ReOrient*, 2019.

79. Neuhäuser, "Coming to Terms with the Past," 11.

80. Oliver Rathkolb, "Der lange Schatten der 8er Jahre. Kritische Geschichtsbetrachtung und Demokratiebewusstsein," in *APuZ. Zeitschrift der Bundeszentrale für politische Bildung*, (Bonn, 2018), 34–35.

81. "Stenzl: 'Wir dürfen uns nicht selbst abschaffen,'" *diepresse.com*, September 24, 2015; OTS, "FPÖ-Waltern: 'Haus der Geschichte.'" Emphasis added.
82. OTS, "Kulturausschuss: Kritik am Standort für Haus der Geschichte bleibt," October 1, 2015.
83. "FPÖ-WalterRosenkranz: 'Haus der Geschichte' gefährdet Sammlung alter Musikinstrumente und Weltmuseum." FPÖ press release, OTS0054, September 9, 2015.
84. "FPÖ-Walter Rosenkranz: 'Haus der Geschichte' gefährdet Sammlung alter Musikinstrumente und Weltmuseum." FPÖ press release, OTS0054, September 9, 2015.
85. Mitscherlichs, *The Inability to Mourn*, 67.

7. Gratifications of Terror:
Identitarian Movement Austria

1. I am referring to the agitator with the male pronoun. Although female agitators are in the IM, the IM male leadership excludes them from leadership roles.
2. Similar to the alt-right in the United States, to attract a college-educated audience, the IBÖ aims to rebrand itself away from a violent neo-Nazi street gang by portraying itself as a "fun movement" where alienated white men can achieve pleasure, solidarity, and community.
3. Martin Sellner, *Identitär: Geschichte eines Aufbruchs* (Albersroda, Germany: Verlag Antaios, 2019). Antaios press publishes far-right books in the German-speaking context. All translations from German to English are mine. I only describe some of his techniques, as explaining all of them would go beyond the boundaries of this chapter.
4. See, for example, Julian Bruns, Kathrin Glösel, and Natascha Strobl, *Die Identitären: Handbuch zur Jugendbewegung der neuen Rechten in Europa* (Munster: Unrast Verlag, 2018).
5. While Sellner aims to win followers through his book, the IBÖ also uses, akin to the alt-right, online social networks and video channels to spread its right-extremist messages.
6. Azmanova and Dakwar examine the German IM mainly through Habermas. Albena Azmanova and Azar Dakwar, "The Inverted Postnational Constellation: Identitarian Populism in Context," *European Law Journal* 25, no. 5 (2019): 494–501.
7. Insofar as the transfer of narcissistic libido occurs toward the movement and not a central leader figure, I suggest that a regression to the "brother horde" occurs, which engenders in them a passive-masochistic attitude because it

signals to them that if they are not with the horde, they will suffer the same fate as the father the horde once killed.

8. Theodor W. Adorno, *The Psychological Technique of Martin Luther Thomas' Radio Addresses* (1975; Redwood City, CA: Stanford University Press, 2000), 31.

9. Adorno, *The Psychological Technique*, 32, emphasis added.

10. Sellner, *Identitär*, 45, emphasis added.

11. Sellner, *Identitär,* 45, emphasis added.

12. Theodor W. Adorno, *Aspekte des neuen Rechtsradikalismus* (1967, Berlin: Suhrkamp Verlag, 2019), 23.

13. Sellner, *Identitär*, 78.

14. I have also explained the "indefatigability device" in chapter 3.

15. Adorno, *The Psychological Technique*, 13–14.

16. Sellner, *Identitär*, 158.

17. Sellner, *Identitär*, 50, 158.

18. Adorno, *The Psychological Technique*, 14.

19. Sigmund Freud, *Jokes and Their Relation to the Unconscious* (White Press, 2013), 238.

20. Adorno, *The Psychological Technique*, 14–15.

21. Sellner, *Identitär*, 231, 248.

22. This is one of the few times women enter the text, usually, as here, in connection with negative stereotypes.

23. Sellner, *Identitär*, 157–58, emphasis added.

24. Which I will further discuss later in this chapter.

25. Sellner, *Identitär*, 159.

26. Sellner, *Identitär*, 165, 159, emphasis added.

27. Adorno, *The Psychological Technique*, 15n10.

28. Bruns, Glösel, and Strobl, *Die Identitären*, 221.

29. Judith Götz, " 'Patriotism Is Not Just a Man's Thing': Right-Wing Extremist Gender Policies Within the So-Called Identitarian Movement," *Journal of Modern European History* 20, no. 3 (2022).

30. The women's groups also assisted in popularizing the core IBÖ's "gender policy" with a racist spin, which is the image of the "vulnerable white woman" who requires protection from the supposed "mass rape" by immigrant or migrant men.

31. Adorno, *The Psychological Technique*, 54, emphasis added.

32. Adorno, *The Psychological Technique*, 54.

33. Adorno, *The Psychological Technique*, 54.

34. Sellner, *Identitär*, 48.

35. The IM aims to support this conspiracy by portraying foreigners as violent criminals (in general and specifically against women and children) and

abusers of welfare. See Reem Ahmed and Daniela Pisoiu, "Uniting the Far Right: How the Far-Right Extremist, New Right, and Populist Frames Overlap on Twitter—a German Case Study," *European Societies* 23, no. 2 (2021): 232–54.

36. Adorno, *The Psychological Technique*, 55.

37. Sellner, *Identität*, 276.

38. Adorno, *The Psychological Technique*, 55–56.

39. Adorno, *Aspekte*, 35.

40. Here I disagree with the analyses of Azmanova and Dakwar, who argue that the identitarian movement is "firmly anti-Muslim, occasionally anti-Semitic, and vehemently anti-immigrant." Azmanova and Dakwar, "The Inverted Postnational Constellation," 495.

41. He refers to white Austrians who do not have any immigrant or migrant background.

42. Sellner, *Identität*, 238, 186.

43. Adorno, *The Psychological Technique*, 62–64.

44. Adorno, *The Psychological Technique*, 61, emphasis added.

45. Sellner, *Identität*, 48.

46. Lauren Langman and Avery Schatz, "The Dialectic of Unreason: Authoritarianism and the Irrational," in *How to Critique Authoritarian Populism: Methodologies of the Frankfurt School*, ed. J. Morelock (Leiden: Brill, 2021), 182.

47. Adorno, *The Psychological Technique*, 64.

48. Sellner, *Identität*, 270, emphasis added.

49. Sellner, *Identität*, 239, 237, 242.

50. Adorno, *The Psychological Technique*, 65.

51. Adorno, *The Psychological Technique*, 66–67.

52. Sellner, *Identität*, 264.

53. Sellner, *Identität*, 245.

54. Adorno, *The Psychological Technique*, 32.

55. Adorno, *The Psychological Technique*, 47.

56. Adorno, *The Psychological Technique*, 50.

57. Sellner, *Identität*, 30.

58. Adorno, *The Psychological Technique*, 11.

59. Adorno *Aspekte*, 22, 21.

60. Sellner, *Identität*, 262.

61. Sellner, *Identität*, 226–7.

62. Adorno, *The Psychological Technique*, 48.

63. Sellner, *Identität*, 151.

64. Sellner, *Identität*, 164.

65. However, when I discuss the IBÖ's use of terror against its followers, it will become evident that the IBÖ is antagonistic to solidarity and mutual trust

and that Sellner merely uses the "unity trick" to channel such feelings for the interests of his racket.

66. Sellner, *Identitär*, 228, 232. The avant-garde, through creating a "vision of an alternative future" through the use of media, music, fashion, and language, provides all of these three parts with a "strong identity and a strong feeling of community." Sellner, *Identitär*, 229.

67. Adorno, *The Psychological Technique*, 69.

68. Adorno, *The Psychological Technique*, 69–70, emphasis added.

69. Adorno, *The Psychological Technique*, 69.

70. Sellner, *Identitär*, 157–58.

71. Sellner, *Identitär*, 233, emphasis added.

72. Sellner, *Identitär*, 272, emphasis added.

73. Adorno, *The Psychological Technique*, 68, emphasis added.

74. He has reasons for such warnings, as rackets attract racketeers and leave them to join other rackets from whom they expect more. Adorno, *The Psychological Technique*, 68.

75. Adorno points out that on the June 30, 1934, a large number of Nazis were shot. Many of whom may not have been conspirators at all and were killed only because of the propagandistic effect of such terror against one's own followers. Adorno, *The Psychological Technique*, 70.

76. Sellner, *Identitär*, 159, 157.

77. Sellner, *Identitär*, 245, 151, emphasis added.

78. Adorno, *Aspekte*, 29.

79. Sellner, *Identitär*, 250, 60.

80. Sellner, *Identitär*, 39, emphasis added.

81. Adorno, *The Psychological Technique*, 11.

82. Adorno, *The Psychological Technique*, 12.

83. Adorno, *The Psychological Technique*, 12.

84. Maria Sterkl, "Theaterstück gestürmt: Verfassungsschutz ermittelt gegen Identitäre," *Der Standard*, April 15, 2016. Here we can see a parallel to how Austrians staged protests to counter the performance of Thomas Bernhard's *Heldenplatz* in the 1980s, which exposed the continuing antisemitic attitudes and their deadly effects upon Austrian Jews who returned to Austria after Hitler lost the war. Claudia Leeb, *The Politics of Repressed Guilt: The Tragedy of Austrian Silence* (Edinburgh: Edinburgh University Press, 2018), chap. 4.

85. Sellner, *Identitär*, 122, 47.

86. Adorno, *The Psychological Technique*, 131.

87. Sellner, *Identitär*, 128.

88. Sellner, *Identitär*, 202.This device connects to the "democratic cloak device," which I will discuss in the fourth section of this chapter.

89. Sellner, *Identität*, 125.

90. Sellner, *Identität*, 126.

91. Sellner, *Identität*, 58–9.

92. Adorno, *The Psychological Technique*, 36, emphasis added.

93. Adorno, *The Psychological Technique*, 106.

94. Adorno, *The Psychological Technique*, 106, 456, emphasis added.

95. Adorno et al., *The Authoritarian Personality*, 613, 614.

96. Sellner, *Identität*, 166, emphasis added.

97. I am indebted to the press editor, Robert Fellman, for this addition.

98. Sellner, *Identität*, 167, 272, emphasis added.

99. Adorno et al., *The Authoritarian Personality*, 642.

100. Sellner, *Identität*, 239.

101. Adorno et al., *The Authoritarian Personality*, 643.

102. Adorno et al., *The Authoritarian Personality*, 637.

103. Sellner, *Identität*, 279.

104. Sellner, *Identität*, 240, 236, my emphasis.

105. Adorno, *The Psychological Technique*, 50.

106. Sellner, *Identität*, 201, 244, emphasis added.

107. Sellner, *Identität*, 614, 264, 134.

108. Sellner, *Identität*, 134.

109. Adorno *Aspekte*, 39, 40, emphasis added.

110. Sellner, *Identität*, 269, 142.

111. Sellner, *Identität*, 251.

112. Sellner, *Identität*, 151.

113. Sellner, *Identität*, 259.

114. Adorno, *The Psychological Technique*, 107.

115. Adorno, *The Psychological Technique*, 51.

Concluding Remarks: Suggestions for Undermining the Far Right Today

1. Theodor W. Adorno, *Aspekte des neuen Rechtsradikalismus* (1967, Berlin: Suhrkamp Verlag, 2019), 54.

2. Adorno, *Aspekte*, 18.

3. Paul Apostolidis, "Desperate Responsibility: Precarity and Right-Wing Populism," *Political Theory* 50, no. 1 (2021): 17–18.

4. See chapter 3 for further discussion of the dismissal of Freudian theory within critical theory circles today.

5. Sigmund Freud, *New Introductory Lectures on Psycho-Analysis: The Standard Edition*, ed. and trans. J. Strachey (1933; New York: Norton, 1990), 96. See also the second section of my chapter 2.

6. For a sustained discussion of this topic see Claudia Leeb, "Authoritarian Family Structures and the Resurgence of the Extremist Right: Overpowering Unconscious Forces," in *Authoritarianism and Neoliberalism*, ed. Arthur Bueno (London: Verso, forthcoming).

7. Theodor W. Adorno, "Die revidierte Psychoanalyse," in *Sociologica II. Reden und Vorträge*, ed. M. Horkheimer and T. W. Adorno (Berlin: Suhrkamp Verlag, 1962), 123.

8. Else Frenkel-Brunswik, "Personality as Revealed Through Clinical Interviews," in *The Authoritarian Personality*, by T. W. Adorno, E. Frenkel-Brunswik, D. J. Levinson, and R. N. Sanford (London: Verso, 2019). I discuss Frenkel-Brunswik's work in chapter 6.

9. Theodor W. Adorno, "Freudian Theory and the Pattern of Fascist Propaganda" (1951), in *The Culture Industry: Selected Essays on Mass Culture*, ed. J. Bernstein (London: Routledge, 2002), 150.

10. Sigmund Freud, "Remembering, Repeating, and Working-Through: Further Recommendations on the Technique of Psycho-analysis II" (1914), in *The Standard Edition of the Complete Psychological Works of Sigmund Freud*, vol. 12: *1911–1913: The Case of Schreber, Papers on Technique, and Other Works*, ed. J. Strachey (London: Hogarth, 1958), 55.

11. Freud, "Remembering," 81.

12. Freud, *New Introductory Lectures*, 19–20. Resistance is a conflict between the unconscious repressed, which seeks expression, and the conscious, which aims to prevent its expression. The manifest dream is a compromise between these two tendencies. The dream communicates what the unconscious wants to say, but only in a distorted and unrecognizable form. However, while in a regular dream repression leaves enough of the resistance intact, which leads to dream censorship (18–20), fascist propaganda tactics aim to circumvent any dream censorship, to keep the followers in the sleep and dream state.

13. Alyosha Goldstein, "The Anti-Imperialist Horizon," in *For Antifascist Futures: Against the Violence of Imperial Crisis*, ed. A. Goldstein and S. V. Trujillo (Brooklyn, NY: Common Notions, 2022), 290. Also Spice outlines the white society's continuing violence toward, surveillance of, and incarceration of the indigenous population who aim to defend their protected territory, in its quest to invade such territory. Anne Spice, "Blood Memory: The Criminalization of Indigenous Land Defense," in *For Antifascist Futures: Against the Violence of Imperial Crisis*, ed. A. Goldstein and S. V. Trujillo (Brooklyn, NY: Common Notions, 2022), 33–42.

14. While there are some signs (especially in the younger generations) that Austria is slowly confronting its violent Nazi past, the confrontation with its violent colonial past has largely remained absent.

15. David McIvor, *Mourning in America: Race and the Politics of Loss* (Ithaca, NY: Cornell University Press, 2016).

16. The Civil Rights Center and Museum in Greensboro did not mention the massacre, protests, or trials that followed. They claimed it had nothing to do with Greensboro, to not disturb the picture of Greensboro as the primary model for racial justice in the South.

17. McIvor, *Mourning in America*, 26.

18. McIvor, *Mourning in America*, 96.

19. McIvor, *Mourning in America*, 157, 74. Throughout the book, he also contributes to the dismissal of Freud so salient in critical theory contexts today.

20. McIvor, *Mourning in America*, 142.

21. McIvor, *Mourning in America*, 35, 101, 182.

22. Joan Braune, "A Partial Typology of Empathy for Enemies: Collaborationist to Strategic," in *No Pasarán!: Antifascist Dispatches from a World in Crisis*, ed. S. Burley, T. Lavin, and D. Renton (Chico, CA: AK Press, 2022), 393.

23. Braune, "A Partial Typology of Empathy for Enemies," 397.

24. Braune, "A Partial Typology of Empathy for Enemies," 396–97.

25. Braune, "A Partial Typology of Empathy for Enemies," 393, 396–97. It seems to me that McIvor engages in such victim blaming when he argues that the "CWP's rigid, polarized distinctions between the abject capitalist/Klan enemy and the idealized fallen members [who represented the 'invincible Communist spirit'] supported their refusal to cooperate with the state criminal trial, which, once again, helped to facilitate the KKK members' acquittal." McIvor, *Mourning in America*, 19.

26. McIvor, *Mourning in America*, 152; Braune, "A Partial Typology of Empathy for Enemies," 395–96.

27. McIvor, *Mourning in America*, 47, 110. To do justice to McIvor, in a more recent article he seems to be more critical of the concept of "reconciliation" and shows that such a focus can also counter the effective organization of protest movements. David McIvor, "The Mendacity of Reconciliation in an Age of Resentment," *American Journal of Economics and Sociology* 76, no. 5 (2017): 1133–55.

28. As Bruns et al. point out, the classification of the IM (right) and the antifascist movement (left) as a similar problem has made it easier for the IM to catch followers in university and school settings. Julian Bruns, Kathrin Glösel, and Natascha Strobl, *Die Identitären: Handbuch zur Jugendbewegung der neuen Rechten in Europa* (Munster: Unrast Verlag, 2018), 13.

29. McIvor, *Mourning in America*, 35.

30. Theodor W. Adorno, Else Frenkel-Brunswik, Daniel Levinson, and Nevitt Sanford, *The Authoritarian Personality* (London: Verso, 2019), 617.
31. Leeb, *The Politics of Repressed Guilt*, conclusion.
32. Lars Rensmann, *The Politics of Unreason* (Albany: State University of New York Press, 2018), 387.
33. Zoé Samudzi, "Reparative Futurities: Postcolonial Materialities and the Ovaherero and Nama Genocide," in *For Antifascist Futures: Against the Violence of Imperial Crisis*, ed. A. Goldstein and S. V. Trujillo (Brooklyn, NY: Common Notions, 2022), 67.
34. Claudia Leeb, *Power and Feminist Agency in Capitalism: Toward a New Theory of the Political Subject* (Oxford: Oxford University Press, 2017).
35. This underlines that the followers retain some agency and hence responsibility, which I further outline later in this conclusion.
36. I will further detail this in the last section.
37. There are also some overlaps with Braune's idea that to counter the growth of the far right we must "refuse to fill the void" and avoid idols (or idealizations, as we find it in McIvor's account of working-through), as it is idols in the far right that allow subjects to "escape the void." Joan Braune, "Void and Idol: A Critical Theory Analysis of the Neo-Fascist Alt-Right," *Journal of Hate Studies* 15, no. 1 (2019): 34.
38. Martin Jay, "The Authoritarian Personality and the Problematic Pathologization of Politics," *Polity* 54, no. 1 (2022): 144.
39. Adorno, *Aspekte*, 748.
40. Erich Fromm, "Politics and Psychoanalysis," in *Critical Theory and Society*, ed. S. E. Bronner and D. M. Kellner (London: Routledge, 1989), 218.
41. I am indebted to reviewer 1 for these crucial questions.
42. Theodor W. Adorno, *The Psychological Technique of Martin Luther Thomas' Radio Addresses* (1975; Redwood City, CA: Stanford University Press, 2000), 15n10.
43. Sigmund Freud, *Group Psychology and the Analysis of the Ego*, ed. J. Strachey, ed. and trans. P. Gay (1921; New York: Norton, 1989), 76.
44. Freud, *Group Psychology*, 76.
45. Freud, *Group Psychology*, 79. Adorno has further developed this insight of Freud in his "great little man" fascist propaganda device.
46. Freud, *Group Psychology*, 79.
47. Sigmund Freud, *Jokes and Their Relation to the Unconscious* (White Press, 2013), 191.
48. Andrew Kliman, "Combatting White Nationalism: Lessons from Marx," *Critique of Political Economy* (2017): 14.
49. Apostolidis, "Desperate Responsibility," 21.
50. Apostolidis, "Desperate Responsibility," 23–24.

51. Apostolidis, "Desperate Responsibility," 20.

52. Karl Marx, "Critique of the Gotha Program," in *The Marx-Engels Reader*, ed. R. C. Tucker (Princeton, NJ: Princeton University Press, 1978), 525–41.

53. Samir Gandesha, "The 'Authoritarian Personality' Reconsidered: the Phantom of 'Left Fascism,'" *American Journal of Psychoanalysis* 79, no. 4 (2019): 609–10.

Bibliography

Abadenifard, Mostafa. "Ridicule, Gender Hegemony, and the Disciplinary Function of Mainstream Gender Humour." *Social Semiotics* 26, no. 3 (2016): 234–49.

Abromeit, John. "The Concept of Pseudo-Conservatism as a Link Between the Authoritarian Personality and Early Critical Theory." *Polity* 54, no. 1 (January 2022): 29–57.

Abromeit, John. "Critical Theory and the Persistence of Right-Wing Populism." *Logos* 15 (2016): 2–3.

Abromeit, John. "Frankfurt School Critical Theory and the Persistence of Authoritarian Populism in the United States." In *Critical Theory and Authoritarian Populism*, ed. J. Morelock, 3–28. London: University of Westminster Press, 2018.

Adorno, Theodor W. *Aspekte des neuen Rechtsradikalismus.* 1967. Berlin: Suhrkamp Verlag, 2019.

——. "Die revidierte Psychoanalyse." In *Sociologica II. Reden und Vorträge*, ed. M. Horkheimer and T. W. Adorno, 119–38. Berlin: Suhrkamp Verlag, 1962.

——. "Culture Industry Reconsidered" (1951). In *The Culture Industry: Selected Essays on Mass Culture,* ed. J. Bernstein, 98–106. London: Routledge, 2002.

——. "Freudian Theory and the Pattern of Fascist Propaganda" (1951). In *The Culture Industry: Selected Essays on Mass Culture*, ed. J. Bernstein, 150–51. London: Routledge, 2002.

——. *Guilt and Defense: On the Legacies of National Socialism in Postwar Germany.* Trans. J. Olick and A. Perrin. Cambridge, MA: Harvard University Press, 2010.

———. "How to Look at Television" (1951). In *The Culture Industry: Selected Essays on Mass Culture,* ed. J. Bernstein, 158–77. London: Routledge, 2002.

———. "Is Art Lighthearted?" In *Notes on Literature*, ed. R. Tidermann, 2:247–53. New York: Columbia University Press, 1992.

———. *Negative Dialectics* (1966). Trans. E. B. Ashton. London: Continuum, 1973.

———. *The Psychological Technique of Martin Luther Thomas' Radio Addresses* (1975). Redwood City, CA: Stanford University Press, 2000.

Adorno, Theodor W., Else Frenkel-Brunswik, Daniel Levinson, and Nevitt Sanford. *The Authoritarian Personality.* London: Verso, 2019.

Ahmed, Reem, and Daniela Pisoiu. "Uniting the Far Right: How the Far-Right Extremist, New Right, and Populist Frames Overlap on Twitter—a German Case Study." *European Societies* 23, no. 2 (2021): 232–54.

Allen, Amy. "Psychoanalysis, Critique, and Praxis." *Critique and Praxis* 13 (2019). https://blogs.law.columbia.edu/praxis1313/amy-allen-psychoanalysis-critique-and-praxis/.

Althusser, Louis. "Preface to *Capital* Volume I." In *Lenin and Philosophy and Other Essays*, trans. B. Brewster, 57–70. New York: Monthly Review Press, 2001.

Apostolidis, Paul. "Desperate Responsibility: Precarity and Right-Wing Populism." *Political Theory* 50, no. 1 (2021).

Azmanova, Albena. *Capitalism on Edge: How Fighting Precarity Can Achieve Radical Change Without Crisis or Utopia.* New York: Columbia University Press, 2020.

Azmanova, Albena, and Azar Dakwar, "The Inverted Postnational Constellation: Identitarian Populism in Context." *European Law Journal* 25, no. 5 (2019): 494–501.

Bazian, Hatem. "Islamophobia, Trump's Racism, and 2020 Elections!" *Islamophobia Studies Journal* 5, no. 1 (2019): 8–10.

Beirich, Heidi, and Susy Buchanan. "2017: The Year of Hate and Extremism." Southern Poverty Law Center, February 11, 2018.

Berger, Thomas U. *War, Guilt, and World Politics After World War II.* Cambridge University Press, 2012.

Billig, Michael. *Laughter and Ridicule: Towards a Social Critique of Humour.* London: SAGE, 2005.

Brameshuber, Sebastian, dir. *Und in der Mitte, da sind wir.* Video. IMDbPro, 2014.

Braune, Joan. "Kill All Normies and Against the Fascist Creep." *Marx and Philosophy Review of Books*, 2017.

———. "A Partial Typology of Empathy for Enemies: Collaborationist to Strategic." In *No Pasarán! Antifascist Dispatches from a World in Crisis*, ed. S. Burley, T. Lavin, and D. Renton, 388–412. Chico, CA: AK Press, 2022.

———. "Void and Idol: A Critical Theory Analysis of the Neo-Fascist 'Alt-Right.'" *Journal of Hate Studies* 15, no. 1 (2019): 11–37.

———. "Who's Afraid of the Frankfurt School? 'Cultural Marxism' as an Antisemitic Conspiracy Theory." *Journal of Social Justice* 9 (2019a): 1–25.

Brittain, Christopher C. "Donald Trump and the Stigmata of Democracy: Adorno and the Consolidation of a Religious Racket." In *How to Critique Authoritarian Populism: Methodologies of the Frankfurt School*, ed. J. Morelock, 366–88. Leiden: Brill, 2021.

Brown, Wendy. *The Ruins of Neoliberalism: The Rise of Anti-Democratic Politics in the West.* New York: Columbia University Press, 2019.

Bruns, Julian, Kathrin Glösel, and Natascha Strobl. *Die Identitären: Handbuch zur Jugendbewegung der neuen Rechten in Europa.* Munster: Unrast Verlag, 2018.

Burley, Shane. *Fascism Today: What It Is and How to End It.* Chico, CA: AK Press, 2017.

Butler, Judith. "Genius or Suicide." In *Trumpism and Its Discontents*, ed. Osagie K. Obasogie, 231–35. Berkeley, CA: Public Policy Press, 2020.

Césaire, Aimé. *Discourse on Colonialism* (1950). Trans. J. Pinkham. New York: New York University Press, 2020.

Critchley, Simon. *On Humour.* London: Routledge, 2002.

Denker, Angela. *Red State Christians.* Minneapolis, MN: Fortress, 2019.

Fallend, Karl. *Unbewusste Zeitgeschichte.* Vienna: Erhard Löcker Verlag, 2016.

Fernández, Johanna. "On the Historical Roots of US Fascism." In *For Antifascist Futures: Against the Violence of Imperial Crisis*, ed. A. Goldstein and S. V. Trujillo, 43–52. Brooklyn, NY: Common Notions, 2022.

Fichtelstein, Federico. "The Authoritarian Personality and the History of Fascism." *Polity* 54, no. 1 (2022): 107–23.

Ferenczi, Sandor. *First Contributions to Psychoanalysis.* 1909; London: Routledge, 1994.

Frenkel-Brunswik, Else. "Personality as Revealed Through Clinical Interviews." In *The Authoritarian Personality*, by T. W. Adorno, E. Frenkel-Brunswik, D. J. Levinson, and R. N. Sanford, 291–489. London: Verso, 2019.

Freud, Sigmund. *Civilization and Its Discontents* (1929). Ed. J. Strachey, trans. P. Gay. New York: Norton, 1989.

———. *Group Psychology and the Analysis of the Ego* (1921). Ed. J. Strachey, ed. and trans. P. Gay. New York: Norton, 1989.

———. "Humour" (1927). In *The Standard Edition of the Complete Psychological Works of Sigmund Freud*, vol. 21: *The Future of an Illusion, Civilization and Its Discontents, and Other Works*, ed. J. Strachey, A. Freud, A. Strachey, and A. Tyson, 159–66. London: Hogarth, 1961.

———. *Jokes and Their Relation to the Unconscious* (1905). White Press, 2013.

———. "Mourning and Melancholia" (1917). In *Collected Papers*, ed. J. D. Sutherland, 4:152–70. London: Hogarth, 1957.

———. *New Introductory Lectures on Psycho-Analysis: The Standard Edition* (1933). Ed. and trans. J. Strachey. New York: Norton, 1990.

———. "On Narcissism" (1914). In *The Standard Edition of the Complete Psychological Works of Sigmund Freud*, vol. 14: *On the History of the Psycho-Analytic Movement, Papers on Metapsychology, and Other Works*, ed. J. Strachey and A. Freud, 67–102. London: Hogarth, 1957.

———. "Remembering, Repeating, and Working-Through: Further Recommendations on the Technique of Psycho-analysis II" (1914). In *The Standard Edition of the Complete Psychological Works of Sigmund Freud*, vol. 12: *The Case of Schreber, Papers on Technique, and Other Works*, ed. J. Strachey, 145–57. London: Hogarth, 1958.

———. *Totem and Taboo: The Standard Edition* (1913). Ed. J. Strachey and trans. P. Gay. New York: Norton, 1990.

Fromm, Erich. "Politics and Psychoanalysis." In *Critical Theory and Society*, ed. S. E. Bronner and D. M. Kellner, 213–18. London: Routledge, 1989.

Gandesha, Samir. "The 'Authoritarian Personality' Reconsidered: The Phantom of 'Left Fascism.'" *American Journal of Psychoanalysis* 79, no. 4 (2019): 601–24.

———. "'A Composite of King Kong and a Suburban Barber': Adorno's 'Freudian Theory and the Pattern of Fascist Propaganda.'" In *Spectres of Fascism: Historical, Theoretical, and International Perspectives*, ed. Samir Gandesha, 120–41. London: Pluto, 2020.

———. "How Do People Become a Mass?" *Polity* 54, no. 1 (2022): 84–106.

———. "Identifying with the Aggressor: From the Authoritarian to Neoliberal Personality." *Constellations* 25, no. 1 (2018): 147–64.

Goldstein, Alyosha. "The Anti-Imperialist Horizon." In *For Antifascist Futures: Against the Violence of Imperial Crisis*, ed. A. Goldstein and S. V. Trujillo, 287–304. Brooklyn, NY: Common Notions, 2022.

Gordon, Peter E. "The Authoritarian Personality Revisited." In *Authoritarianism: Three Inquiries in Critical Theory*, ed. W. Brown, P. E. Gordon, and M. Pensky, 45–84. Chicago: University of Chicago Press, 2018.

Götz, Judith. "'Patriotism Is Not Just a Man's Thing': Right-Wing Extremist Gender Policies Within the So-Called Identitarian Movement." *Journal of Modern European History* 20, no. 3 (2022).

Green, Jon, and Sean McElwee, "The Differential Effects of Economic Conditions and Racial Attitudes in the Election of Donald Trump." *Perspectives on Politics* 18, no. 1 (2020): 358–79.

Hafez, Farid. "From 'Jewification' to 'Islamization': Anti-Semitism and Islamophobia in Austrian Politics Then and Now." *ReOrient* (2019).

Hankes, Keegan, and Alex Amend. "The Alt-Right Is Killing People." Southern Poverty Law Center, February 5, 2018.

Hawley, George. *Making Sense of the Alt-Right*. New York: Columbia University Press, 2017.

Hermann, Christoph, and Jörg Flecker. "The Austrian Model and the Financial and Economic Crisis." In *A Triumph of Failed Ideas: European Models of Capitalism in the Crisis*, ed. S. Lehndorff, 121–36. European Trade Union Institute, 2012.

Hochschild, Arlie R. *Strangers in Their Own Land: Anger and Mourning on the American Right*. New York: New Press, 2016.

Hofmann, Julia, Carina Altreiter, Jörg Flecker, Saskja Schindler, and Ruth Simsa, "Symbolic Struggles Over Solidarity in Times of Crisis: Trade Unions, Civil Society Actors, and the Political Far Right in Austria." *European Societies* 21, no. 5 (2019): 649–71.

Horkheimer, Max, and Theodor W. Adorno. *Dialektik der Aufklärung* (1944). Fischer Taschenbuch Verlag, 1998.

Jay, Martin. "The Authoritarian Personality and the Problematic Pathologization of Politics." *Polity* 54, no. 1 (2022): 1124–45.

Johnson, Daryl. "Report: Rise in Hate Violence Tied to 2016 Presidential Election." Southern Poverty Law Center, March 1, 2018.

Johnson, Laurie M. *Ideological Possession and the Rise of the New Right: The Political Thought of Carl Jung*. London: Routledge, 2019.

Kliman, Andrew. "Combating White Nationalism: Lessons from Marx." *Critique of Political Economy* (2017).

Langman, Lauren, and Avery Schatz. "The Dialectic of Unreason: Authoritarianism and the Irrational." In *How to Critique Authoritarian Populism: Methodologies of the Frankfurt School*, ed. J. Morelock, 167–99. Leiden: Brill, 2021.

Le Bon, Gustave. *Psychologie des Foules/Psychology of Crowds*. Independently Published, 1895/2017.

Leeb, Claudia. "Austria's Repressed Guilt in Theory and Practice: Personal Encounters." In *Remembering the Holocaust in Germany, Austria, Italy, and Israel: "Vergangenheitsbewältigung" (Mastering the Past) as a Historical Quest*, ed. V. Pinto, 25–38. Leiden: Brill, 2021.

——. "Mourning Denied: The Tabooed Subject." In *The Democratic Arts of Mourning: Political Theory and Loss*, ed. D. McIvor and A. Hirsch, 65–82. Lanham, MD: Lexington, 2019.

——. "Mystified Consciousness: Rethinking the Rise of the Far Right with Marx and Lacan." *Open Cultural Studies* 2, no. 1 (2018): 236–48.

——. *The Politics of Repressed Guilt: The Tragedy of Austrian Silence*. Edinburgh: Edinburgh University Press, 2018.

——. *Power and Feminist Agency in Capitalism: Toward a New Theory of the Political Subject*. Oxford: Oxford University Press, 2017.

Lenz, Lyz. *God Land: A Story of Faith, Loss, and Renewal in Middle America*. Bloomington: Indiana University Press, 2019.

Lombardini, John. "Civic Laughter: Aristotle and the Political Virtue of Humor." *Political Theory* 41, no. 2 (2013): 203–30.

Löwenthal, Leo, and Norbert Guterman. *Prophets of Deceit: A Study of the Techniques of the American Agitator*. London: Verso, 2021.

Lugones, María. "Heterosexualism and the Colonial/Modern Gender System." *Hypatia* 22, no. 1 (2007): 186–209.

Marasco, Robin. "There Is a Fascist in the Family: Critical Theory and Antiauthoritarianism." *South Atlantic Quarterly* 117, no. 4 (2018): 791–813.

Marcuse, Herbert. Foreword to the second edition of *Prophets of Deceit: A Study of the Techniques of the American Agitator*, ed. L. Löwenthal and N. Guterman. London: Verso, 2021.

Marso, Lori. "Feminist Cringe Comedy: Dear Dick, The Joke Is on You." *Politics and Gender* 15, no. 1 (2019): 107–29.

Marwick, Alice, and Rebecca Lewis, "Media Manipulation and Disinformation Online." Data and Society Research Institute, 2017.

Marx, Karl. "Contribution to the Critique of Hegel's Philosophy of Right: Introduction." In *The Marx-Engels Reader*, ed. R. C. Tucker, 53–65. Princeton, NJ: Princeton University Press, 1978.

——. "Critique of the Gotha Program." In *The Marx-Engels Reader*, ed. R. C. Tucker, 525–41. Princeton, NJ: Princeton University Press, 1978.

——. "Economic and Philosophic Manuscripts of 1844." In *The Marx-Engels Reader*, ed. R. C. Tucker, 66–125. Princeton, NJ: Princeton University Press, 1978.

——. *Das Kapital: Kritik der politischen Ökonomie, Erster Band, Buch I: Der Produktionsprozeß des Kapitals*, in *Karl Marx Frederick Engels Werke*, bd. 23. Bonn: Dietz Verlag, 2001.

——. "Nationalökonomie und Philosophie." In *Die Frühschriften: Von 1837 bis zum 'Manifest der Kommunistischen Partei' 1848*, ed. S. Landshut, 225–316. Stuttgart: Alfred Kröner Verlag, 1971.

Mason, Lilliana, Julie Wronski, and John V. Kane, "Activating Animus: The Uniquely Social Roots of Trump Support." *American Political Science Review* 115, no. 4 (2021): 1508–16.

McIvor, David. "Claudia Leeb's *The Politics of Repressed Guilt*: The Tragedy of Austrian Silence, with David McIvor, Lars Rensmann, and Claudia Leeb." *Critical Horizons* 21, no. 1 (2020): 63–79.

——. "The Mendacity of Reconciliation in an Age of Resentment." *American Journal of Economics and Sociology* 76, no. 5 (2017): 1133–55.

——. *Mourning in America: Race and the Politics of Loss*. Ithaca, NY: Cornell University Press, 2016.

Menillo, Gregory J. "'Variation Within a Single Paradigm': The Latent Authoritarian Dynamics of the Culture Industry." In *How to Critique Authoritarian*

Populism: Methodologies of the Frankfurt School, ed. J. Morelock, 239–66. Leiden: Brill, 2021.

Miller, Cassie, and Alexandra Werner-Winslow. "Ten Days After: Harassment and Intimidation in the Aftermath of the Election (Anti-Woman Incidents)." Southern Poverty Law Center, November 29, 2016.

Mitscherlich, Alexander, and Margarete Mitscherlich. *The Inability to Mourn: Principles of Collective Behavior*, trans. B. R. Placzek. New York: Grove, 1975.

Mutz, Diana C. "Status Threat, Not Economic Hardship, Explains the 2016 Presidential Vote." *PNAS* 19, no. 115 (2018): E4330–39.

Nagle, Angela. *Kill All Normies: Online Culture Wars from 4Chan and Tumblr to Trump and the Alt-Right*. London: Zero, 2017.

Neiwert, David. "Is That an OK Sign? A White Power Symbol? Or Just a Right-Wing Troll?" Southern Poverty Law Center, September 19, 2018.

Neuhäuser, Stephan. "Coming to Terms with the Past: The Case of the 'House of Austrian History' (Haus der Geschichte Österreich) in the Wake of the Rise of Populist Nationalism in Austria." *Modern Languages Open* 1 (2020): 1–18.

Nguyen, Nicole, and Yazan Zahzah. "'Make Fascism Great Again!': Mapping the Conceptual Work of 'Fascism' in the War on Terror." In *For Antifascist Futures: Against the Violence of Imperial Crisis*, ed. A. Goldstein and S. V. Trujillo, 131–44. Brooklyn, NY: Common Notions, 2022.

Padmore, George. *How Britain Rules Africa* (1936). New York: Negro Universities Press, 1969.

Paluck, Elizabeth L., and Michael Suk-Young Chwe. "Confronting Hate Collectively." *PS: Political Science & Politics* 50, no. 4 (2017): 990–92.

Pensky, Max. "Radical Critique and Late Epistemology." In *Authoritarianism: Three Inquiries in Critical Theory*, ed. W. Brown, P. E. Gordon, and M. Pensky, 85–124. Chicago: University of Chicago Press, 2018.

Pérez, Raúl. "Racism Without Hatred? Racist Humor and the Myth of 'Color-Blindness.'" *Sociological Perspectives* 60, no. 5 (2017): 956–74.

Pérez, Raúl, and Viveca Greene. "Debating Rape Jokes vs. Rape Culture: Framing and Counterframing Misogynistic Comedy." *Social Semiotics* 26, no. 3 (2016): 265–82.

Picca, Leslie, and Joe R. Faegin. *Two-Faced Racism: Whites in the Backstage and Frontstage*. London: Routledge, 2007.

Quijano, Anibal, and Michael Ennis. "Coloniality of Power, Eurocentrism, and Latin America." *Nepantla: Views from South* 1, no. 3 (2000): 533–80.

Rathgeb, Philip. "Makers Against Takers: The Socio-Economic Ideology and Policy of the Austrian Freedom Party." *West European Politics* 44, no. 3 (2021): 635–60.

Rathkolb, Oliver. "Der lange Schatten der 8er Jahre. Kritische Geschichtsbetrachtung und Demokratiebewusstsein." In *APuZ. Zeitschrift der Bundeszentrale für politische Bildung*, 34–35. Bonn, 2018.

Reiter, Margit. "Antisemitismus in der FPÖ und im 'Ehemaligen'-Milieu nach 1945 in Österreich." In *Jahrbuch für Antisemitismusforschung*, 27:117–49. Hg. von Stefanie Schüler-Springorum für das Zentrum für Antisemitismusforschung der Technischen Universität Berlin, 2018.

——. "Anton Reinthaller und die Anfänge der Freiheitlichen Partei Österreichs (FPÖ). Der politische Werdegang eines Nationalsozialisten und die 'Ehemaligen' in der Zweiten Republik." *Vierteljahreshefte für Zeitgeschichte* 66, no. 4 (2018).

Rensmann, Lars. "Guilt, Resentment, and Post-Holocaust Democracy: The Frankfurt School's Analysis of 'Secondary Antisemitism' in the Group Experiment and Beyond." *Antisemitism Studies* 1, no. 1 (2017): 4–37.

——. *The Politics of Unreason*. Albany: State University of New York Press, 2018.

Romero-Sánchez, Mónica, Mercedes Durán, Hugo Carretero-Dios, Jesús L. Megías, and Miguel Moya. "Exposure to Sexist Humor and Rape Proclivity: The Moderator Effect of Averseness Ratings." *Journal of Interpersonal Violence* 25, no. 12 (2009): 2339–50.

Ross, Andrew S., and Damian J. Rivers. "Donald Trump, Legitimisation, and a New Political Rhetoric." *World Englishes* 39, no. 4 (2020): 623–37.

Ryan, Kathryn M., and Jeanne Kanjorski. "The Enjoyment of Sexist Humor, Rape Attitudes, and Relationship Aggression in College Students." *Sex Roles* 38, no. 9/10 (1998): 743–56.

Samudzi, Zoé. "Reparative Futurities: Postcolonial Materialities and the Ovaherero and Nama Genocide." In *For Antifascist Futures: Against the Violence of Imperial Crisis*, ed. A. Goldstein and S. V. Trujillo, 53–67. Brooklyn, NY: Common Notions, 2022.

Sauer, Walter. "Habsburg Colonial: Austria-Hungary's Role in European Overseas Expansion Reconsidered." *Austrian Studies* 20 (2012): 5–23.

Schiedel, Heribert. "Antisemitismus und völkische Ideologie: Ist die FPÖ eine rechtsextreme Partei?" In *AfD & FPÖ: Antisemitismus, Völkischer Nationalismus, und Geschlechterbilder*, ed. S. Grigat, 103–19. Baden-Baden: Nomos Verlag, 2017.

Sellner, Martin. *Identitär: Geschichte eines Aufbruchs*. Verlag Antaios, 2019.

Shulman, George. "Genres of Loss." In "Mourning Work: Death and Democracy During a Pandemic," by D. McIvor, J. Hooker, A. Atkins, A. Athanasiou, and G. Shulman, *Contemporary Political Theory* 20, vol. 1 (2020): 165–99.

Spice, Anne. "Blood Memory: The Criminalization of Indigenous Land Defense." in *For Antifascist Futures: Against the Violence of Imperial Crisis*, ed. A. Goldstein and S. V. Trujillo, 33–42. Brooklyn, NY: Common Notions, 2022.

Stögner, Karin. "Secondary Antisemitism, the Economic Crisis, and the Construction of National Identity in the Austrian Print Media." *Critical Sociology* 44, no. 4/5 (2018): 719–32.

Tarnopolsky, Christina. "Melancholia and Mania on the Trump Campaign Trail." *Theory & Event* 20, no. 1 (2017): 100–28.

Thomae, Manuela, and G. Tendayi Viki, "Why Did the Woman Cross the Road? The Effect of Sexist Humor on Men's Rape Proclivity." *Journal of Social, Evolutionary, and Cultural Psychology* 7, no. 3 (2013): 250–69.

Thompson, Michael J. "Th. W. Adorno Defended Against His Critics, and Admirers: A Defense of the Critique of Jazz." *International Review of the Aesthetics and Sociology of Music* 41, no. 1 (2010): 37–49.

Toscano, Alberto. "The Returns of Racial Fascism." In *For Antifascist Futures: Against the Violence of Imperial Crisis*, ed. A. Goldstein and S. V. Trujillo, 243–55. Brooklyn, NY: Common Notions, 2022.

Utgaard, Peter. *Remembering and Forgetting Nazism: Education, National Identity, and the Victim Myth in Postwar Austria*. Berghahn, 2003.

Warzel, Charlie. "Uncle Trump Wants You! (to Join His Troll Army)." *New York Times*, July 19, 2022.

Weigel, Moira. "The Authoritarian Personality 2.0." *Polity* 54, no. 1 (2022): 146–80.

Weiβ, Volker. "Nachwort." In *Aspekte des neuen Rechtsradikalismus*, by T. W. Adorno, 59–88. Suhrkamp Verlag, 2019.

Whitman, James Q. *Hitler's American Model: The United States and the Making of Nazi Race Law*. Princeton, NJ: Princeton University Press, 2017.

Wodak, Ruth. "From Post-Truth to Post-Shame: Analyzing Far-Right Populist Rhetoric." In *Approaches to Discourse Analysis*, ed. C. Gordon, 175–92. Washington, DC: Georgetown University Press, 2021.

Zaretsky, Eli. "Liberalism and Mass Psychology: The American Experience." *Polity* 54, no. 1 (2022): 59–83.

Index

Abadenifard, Mostafa, 281n88
Abromeit, John, 149, 256n20, 272n13
Adorno, Theodor W.: on alienation,
31–32, 33; on antisemitism, 216–17;
AP study and, 9, 67–70, 82, 190, 236;
Aspekte des neuen Rechtsradikalismus,
17, 24–25, 68, 155–56, 190, 207,
222–23; *The Authoritarian Personality*,
33, 218, 244; on castration, 15;
criticism of, 267n19; culture industry
and, 34–35, 74, 80, 190; "Culture
Industry Reconsidered," 34; *Dialektik
der Aufklärung*, 34–35; on far right, 65,
107, 112–13, 190, 194–96, 222; fascism
and, 2, 70–75, 80–83, 141, 190,
194–96, 227, 254n8, 267n25, 275n71,
276n1; with "great little man" device,
76–77; *Guilt and Defense*, 1, 32, 38, 66,
80–81, 155, 158, 253; hypnosis and,
245; with identification and
introjection, 268n28; "identity
thinking" and, 34; on impoverished
egos, 107; "indefatigability" device

and, 85–86; influence of, 8–10; "Is
Art Lighthearted?," 135; jokes and,
135, 153; on leaders and followers,
116–17; on masses and primordial
traits, 94, 268n36; movement trick
and, 197; narcissistic regressions and,
75–80; on Nazis, 291n75; on new
right extremism in 1960s Germany,
24–25; nonidentity and, 1, 34;
"persecuted innocence device" and,
214–15, 218; phoniness and, 92–93,
119; psychoanalytic theory and, 12,
65, 66–70; *The Psychological Technique
of Martin Luther Thomas' Radio
Addresses*, 74, 85, 87, 190, 275n71,
291nn74–75; "Die Revidierte
Psychoanalyse," 15, 17, 31–32, 225;
self-hypnosis and, 87, 270n81; "sheep
and bucks" propaganda device and,
73–74; stereotypy and, 236; terror
strategy and, 199–205; on
unconscious, 38, 68–69, 121, 173;
"unity trick" and, 205–11;

persecution mania and, 82–83; secondary, 182–83, 287n76; stereotypes, 33–34, 216–17, 261n55

anxieties: with digital capitalism, 261n58; extinction, 203; far right with, 258nn9–10. *See also* castration anxiety

Apostolidis, Paul, 28, 69, 223–24, 249–51, 253n3, 260n38, 267n16

AP study. *See Authoritarian Personality* study

archaic inheritance, 76, 87

archaic regressions, 11, 66, 86–88, 107–8, 112, 193, 246

Asians, 151

Aspekte des neuen Rechtsradikalismus (Aspects of new right radicalism) (Adorno), 17, 24–25, 68, 155–56, 190, 207, 222–23

atrophy (*Verkümmerung*) of imagination, 35, 36, 261n59

Aufarbeitung der Vergangenheit ("working-through the past"), 155–56, 158–61, 164–65, 169–71, 187–88, 201, 231–38

Aussaugung (sucking out), of labor power, 26, 29

Austria: antisemitism in, 291n84; economy, 156; Germany and, 207; House of History museum, 13, 184–87, 231; national identity, 183–84, 207–8, 215–16; refugees in, 189, 192–93, 212–14; with repressed guilt, 81, 91, 156, 201, 269n58, 294n14; Socialist Students of Austria, 155; student loans, 259n14; with tabooed past, 158–72; working class in, 165; with "working-through the past," 155–56, 158–61, 164–65, 169–72, 187–88, 201. *See also* far right, in Austria; FPÖ; *Und in der Mitte, da Sind Wir*

Austrian Freedom Party. *See* FPÖ

Austrian identitarian movement. *See* IBÖ

authoritarianism, 226, 256n20, 258n2, 269n64

Authoritarian Personality, The (Adorno), 33, 218, 244

Authoritarian Personality (AP) study, 9, 67–70, 82, 174, 190, 236, 251, 272n4

"Authoritarian Personality 2.0, The" (Weigel), 261n58

avant-garde, 152, 196, 208, 291n66

Azmanova, Albena, 18, 253n3, 258nn9–10, 290n40

Bannon, Stephen, 149, 152

Bazian, Hatem, 274n63

Bernhard, Thomas, 291n84

"beta males," 144–45, 148

Bewegung (movement), 192, 194, 197, 220

Billig, Michael, 153

birth-giving refusal (*Geburtenverweigerung*), 184

"black hand device," 191, 205, 209–10

Black Lives Matter movement, 236

body. *See* physical level; scars

bourgeois class, 17–20, 98, 100, 165, 250, 258n8, 260n45

Brameshuber, Sebastian, 157

Braune, Joan, 152, 234–36, 270n81, 276n2, 277n9, 278n10, 295n37

Breitbart (far-right news site), 125, 149, 152

bribing, with jokes, 130–35, 139, 145–46, 280n46

Brittain, Christopher C., 254n11

"brother horde," 79, 117, 148, 225, 288n7

Brown, Wendy, 21–22, 134, 135

Bruns, Julian, 198, 294n28

Burley, Shane, 149, 256n20

Butler, Judith, 262n8

"call-out culture," 152

capital, surplus value and, 25–29, 97

Capital, vampire, 25–27, 30, 32–33, 97–99, 102, 230, 240

capitalism: class hierarchy and, 258n12; culture industry and, 16–17, 34–37; digital, 261n58; humiliation and, 35; inhumanity of, 20; neoliberal, 18, 105, 154, 266n2; objective conditions of, 15, 16, 36; overthrow of, 248–52; pleasure and, 134; with shame, anger and hate, 258n11; "success" and, 2, 3, 17–20, 105–6. See also precarity capitalism

Capitalism on Edge (Azmanova), 258n9

Capitol, U.S., attack on, 7, 12, 110, 113, 115, 117, 151, 249

castration anxiety: alienated subject and, 30–34; with automation and labor, 25; culture industry and, 16–17, 34–37; declassing threat and, 16, 17–21; defined, 254n10; economic security and, 11, 15–21, 27; exploitation and subjectivity with, 16, 24–29; failure and, 3; gender and, 15, 16, 18, 20, 21; interpersonal relationships and, 11, 15, 16, 28–29, 144; nonwholeness and, 15, 16, 240; on physical level, 11, 15, 16, 24–29, 97–98, 144; precarity capitalism and, 18, 20, 24, 35, 131; race and, 15, 16, 18, 21; suffering and, 3, 19, 21, 36, 73; Tea Party and, 100; three forms of, 11, 15–18; white males with, 4; of whites, 16, 21–24

Catholic Church, 264n43

cell phones, 25, 260n42

Césaire, Aimé, 23

children: of bourgeois class, 18; in families with strict gender roles, 198–99, 225–26; fascist propaganda and, 13, 255n16, 272n4; parents and, 56, 164–80, 187–88, 238; primary envy in, 50; of working class, 19–20, 165, 259n14. See also families

Christianity: with aggression, 43, 50; evangelicals, 101, 254n11, 271n3; fascism and, 74, 141, 190, 206; leaders, 103

Chwe, Michael Suk-Young, 150

civilization: aggression and, 42; Freud and, 69; guilt and, 263n24; libidinal drives, aggression and, 262n13; "program of," 40, 48–49

Civilization and Its Discontents (Freud), 11, 38–39, 40, 41, 73, 263n19, 263n24; on aggression and superego, 265n66; jokes and, 128; satisfaction drives deprived, 63; on small cultural groups, 49, 264n56

Civil Rights Center and Museum, Greensboro, 294n16

class: alienation and, 260n45; bourgeois, 17–20, 98, 100, 165, 250, 258n8, 260n45; capitalism and hierarchy of, 258n12; castration anxiety and, 15, 16–21; declassing and, 16, 17–21, 30, 223, 254n11; middle, 21, 86, 97, 106, 122, 165; "up-classing," 19, 21, 78, 222–23; "upward mobility" and, 19–20, 258n8. See also working class

colonial classifications, 5, 229–30, 261n55

"colonial fascism," 23–24

coloniality of power, 22–23

colonial violence, 4–5, 24, 103, 137, 143, 214, 231, 285nn31–32

colonization: primal horde and, 266n101; race and, 80

Communist Workers Party (CWP), 232, 294n25

complete object love, 55, 57, 62, 109–10

dream state, 9, 258n3; culture industry
and, 270n83; far-right propaganda
technique and, 4, 8, 87–92; with
harmless psychosis, 90; sleep and, 12,
14, 65–66, 109, 132, 193, 196, 204,
224–25, 227–28, 239, 246, 247,
293n12; "success" and, 4

economy: alt-right with psychological
conditions and, 278n10; Austria, 156;
emotional self-interest and, 94–95;
fascism and, 17; hierarchy and
whites, 4, 16, 22, 24, 255nn12–13,
278n11; loss, 63, 106, 223, 228; race
and, 259n18; security, 11, 15–22, 27.
See also socioeconomics
"ecstatic high," 4, 14, 94–95, 101, 221,
225, 239, 241
Edelweiß (Maidens Group Edelweiss), 198
education, higher: children of working
class and, 19–20, 259n14; student
loans, 20, 259n14
ego, 38, 39, 52; ego ideal and, 12, 53–55,
59, 63–64, 73, 78, 105–7, 111–12, 132,
148, 150, 191, 193, 224, 229, 242, 247;
impoverished, 54, 57–58, 72, 107,
115, 284n15; jokes and, 126, 127, 131,
132, 138, 224–25, 278n19; superego
and, 41–43, 46, 58, 127, 193–94, 252,
263n34; unconscious and, 42, 44–45,
46. See also Group Psychology and the
Analysis of the Ego
ego ideal: ego and, 12, 53–55, 59, 63–64,
73, 78, 105–7, 111–12, 132, 148, 150,
191, 193, 224, 229, 242, 247; festival
and, 12, 53, 64; idealized leader and,
3, 7, 21; jokes and, 126; loss of, 180,
230; precarity capitalism and, 3,
123–24; propaganda and, 9;
replacement, 9, 11, 38, 51–56, 58,
72–73, 91, 102, 105, 107–9, 111,

116–17, 120, 150, 191, 259n15;
"success" and, 106; superego and, 5,
42, 52, 91, 131, 264n65, 265n90; of
Trump followers, 7
Ehemaligen, 180–83, 287n76
Eichmann, Adolf, 32
embodied reflective spaces, 14, 232,
237–38
emotional self-interest, 94–95, 113
empathy, 160–61, 167
employment, in Louisiana, 96–101,
273n21
environment: labor and, 96–98, 100–101,
108, 272n5; loss of clean, 103, 104
Eros (love drives): aggression and, 40,
41, 43; death and, 39–44, 262n3;
masses and, 48, 49–51
euphoria, 14, 192–99, 247
Eurocentrism, 22–23, 285n31
evangelicals, 101, 254n11, 271n3
exploitation: Amazon with robots and,
29; of natural resources, 23, 204;
precarity capitalism and, 28;
subjectivity and, 16, 24–29;
technology and, 25–27; vampire
Capital and, 25–27, 30, 32–33, 97–99,
230, 240; of working class, 20,
95–101, 273n21
"extinction anxiety," 203

fairy tales, 79, 114
Fallend, Karl, 121, 286n54
families: authoritarian, 226, 269n64;
children, 13, 18–20, 50, 56, 164–80,
187–88, 198–99, 225–26, 238, 255n16,
259n14, 272n4; with expenses of
higher education, 20; fathers, 60–62,
76–78, 80, 83–84, 89, 92, 112–13, 119,
172–80, 225–26, 231, 243, 269n70,
275n71; mothers, 136, 157, 166–75,
178–79, 202, 269n70; patriarchy and,

13, 172–80, 225–26, 255n16, 272n4.
See also primal horde

far right, 2, 6, 7, 18, 190; with anxieties,
258nn9–10; psychoanalysis and, 253n3;
violence, 14, 163–64, 189, 192–93,
212–14; women and, 198, 202–3,
288n1, 289n30. *See also* propaganda
techniques, far-right; resistance,
against far-right; *specific topics*

far right, in Austria: conspiracy theories,
183–84, 200, 202–3, 208, 216, 231,
287n77; with tabooed past, 158–72.
See also IBÖ

fascism: Adorno and, 2, 70–75, 80–83,
141, 190, 194–96, 227, 254n8, 267n25,
275n71, 276n1; aggression and, 39,
70–75; Christianity and, 74, 141,
190, 206; colonialism and, 23–24;
conspiracy theories and, 276n1;
economy and, 17; free-floating
aggression and, 269n64; Freud and,
70–71, 76; "incipient," 273n27;
masses, 70–75, 262n1; "On the
Historical Roots of US Fascism,"
259n18; propaganda, 2, 5, 13, 24, 33,
35, 65, 67, 190, 194–96, 255n16,
262n2, 272n4; protofascist elements
in U.S., 7, 38, 65; psychoanalytic
theory and, 9; resistance against, 66,
119–20; slogans, 107–8, 146, 163, 171,
174, 194, 212, 214, 218; small cultural
groups and, 264n56; Trump and,
282n92; violence and, 79–80. *See also*
neofascist groups

fathers: fascist leader as, 275n71;
patriarchal family structures and,
172–80, 225–26; primal, 60–62,
76–78, 80, 83, 89, 92, 112–13, 119,
225; threatening, 84, 113, 231, 243,
269n70

feminist theory, decolonial, 16

Ferenczi, Sandor, 269n70

Fernández, Johanna, 22, 259n18

festivals: ego ideal and, 12, 53, 64;
primal horde and, 12; Trump
followers and, 12, 119, 150

fetish: *Bewegung*, 192, 194, 197, 220;
indefatigability as, 86; military,
177–79, 211, 220; money, 99–100; of
"success," 2, 191, 223, 229, 240, 244,
248, 251; with wholeness, 256n23

Fichtelstein, Federico, 69

First Contributions to Psychoanalysis
(Ferenczi), 269n70

followers: identification and mass, 49–51,
53, 56, 72; libidinal drives between
leaders and, 38, 49–51, 53, 56–57; with
love, 233–34; mass leaders and, 56–59,
75–80, 83–87, 107–12, 116–19, 262n12;
phoniness of, 92–93, 119; primal
father and, 80; repression and, 79;
with unconscious, 7, 9, 46–47, 225

followers, far-right: agitators and, 5–6,
9, 75; ego ideal replacement and, 53,
72; IBÖ and enslavement of, 192;
with unconscious manipulated, 7, 9

followers, of Trump: ego ideal of, 7, 21;
emotional self-interest and, 94–95,
113; festivals, 12, 119, 150; "great
little man" device and, 116–19; as
"hypermasculine" men, 275n75; in
Louisiana, 94–105, 108, 110, 116–18,
128–29, 228–29, 271n1, 273n22;
manipulation of, 112–15;
melancholia/mania oscillation and,
94; from melancholia to mania,
101–7, 108, 229; with narcissistic love,
110–11; narcissistic regression and,
107–12; precarity capitalism and, 95,
96–101; recruitment, 255n19; threats
and fears motivating, 254n11; in U.S.
Capitol attack, 7, 113; violence of, 7

gays, as targets for blame, 22

Geburtenverweigerung (birth-giving refusal), 184

Gemeingeist (group spirit, or communal or social feeling), 50–51

gender, 4, 23, 281n88; castration anxiety and, 15, 16, 18, 20, 21; roles, 175, 198–99, 225–26

genocide: of indigenous populations, 103, 229, 230; of Jews, 81, 162, 205; of Ovaherero and Nama peoples, 162, 285nn30–31; of racial minorities, 121, 189; of Roma and Sinti peoples, 81, 156, 162, 163, 205; white, 121–22, 200, 203, 230

Germany, 155, 161, 207; guilt in postwar, 80–81, 158–59, 201; new right extremism in 1960s, 24–25

Goetz, Judith, 198

Goldstein, Alyosha, 103, 230

good and evil ("sheep and bucks") device, 73–74, 114

Gordon, Peter, 67–68, 69, 70, 76, 92

"great little man" device, 76–78, 96, 116–19, 295n45

"Great Replacement," 183–84, 200, 202–3, 208, 216, 231, 287n77

Green, Jon, 259n18

Greensboro Massacre (1979), 232, 294n16

Greensboro Truth and Reconciliation Commission (GTRC), 232, 235

Group Experiment (*Gruppenexperiment*), 253

Group Psychology and the Analysis of the Ego (Freud), 11, 38–39, 47, 73, 246–47, 264n56; ego ideal and, 53, 55, 265n90; fascism and, 70, 76; hypnotic regression and, 61; jokes and, 123, 132–33; masses and Eros in, 49–50; melancholia/mania and, 12; with

"primitive" mental activity and regression, 266n101; pure narcissism and, 57; sleep state and hypnosis in, 83–84

group spirit, or communal or social feeling (*Gemeingeist*), 50–51

Gruppenexperiment (Group Experiment), 253

GTRC (Greensboro Truth and Reconciliation Commission), 232, 235

guilt, 54, 61–62, 263n24; loss and, 8, 13, 43, 154, 156, 157, 159, 161–65, 168, 171, 176, 182–88, 207, 237–38, 241–43; mourning and, 159–61, 169; *The Politics of Repressed Guilt*, 156, 256n22, 269n58; in postwar Germany, 80–81, 158–59, 201; repressed, 81, 91, 156, 169, 185, 201, 256n22, 269n58, 294n14; unconscious, 13, 158, 159, 173, 263n36; violence and, 273n28

Guilt and Defense (Adorno), 1, 32, 38, 66, 253; defensive reactions of postwar Germans, 80–81, 158; past and, 155

guns, 148, 151, 177–78

Guterman, Norbert, 36, 114, 117, 257n26

Haider, Jörg, 181–82

hate, 12, 74, 79, 91, 258n11; crimes, 149, 150–51, 189; groups, 124, 199, 235–37, 243, 277n3; race and, 81–82; symbols, 137, 280n58; as unifying emotion, 49–50, 59

Hawley, George, 7, 149

Heldenplatz (Bernhard), 291n84

Herrenmenschen (master humans), 80–81, 204, 231

Hitler, Adolf, 32, 40, 46, 117, 159, 180–81, 230; with colonialism, 23; far-right propaganda and, 76–77; with "great little man" device, 116, 118

196, 208, 291n66; goals of, 189; growth of, 7–8; IBÖ and, 13, 190, 192–93; with immigrants as targets for blame, 289n35; left and, 294n28; "persecuted innocence device" and, 211–12, 214, 216–17, 219; women and, 288n1

identitarian movement of Austria. *See* IBÖ

identity: Austrian national, 183–84, 207–8, 215–16; avant-garde, 291n66; crisis, 201; German national, 207; masculine, 175, 178–79; nonidentity and, 1, 34; politics, 152; targeted groups with blurred, 114, 115; thinking, 34; whites, 242, 270n81

"if you only knew trick," 199–201

IM. *See* identitarian movement

immigrants, 28, 114, 260n38; as targets for blame, 22, 34, 122, 183, 201, 203, 215–17, 283n7, 289n35; violence against, 8

Inability to Mourn, The (A. Mitscherlich and M. Mitscherlich), 284n15

"incipient fascism," 273n27

incongruity theory, of humor, 125–26

"indefatigability" device, 8, 14, 85–86, 191–92, 195–97, 220, 289n14

indigenous populations: exploitation of, 23; in slavery, 4, 103, 124, 137, 204, 229, 230, 251; violence toward, 4, 293n13

inheritance, archaic, 76, 87

innuendo, 199–201

intellectual alienation, 33

interpersonal relationships, castration anxiety, 11, 15, 16, 28–29, 144

introjection: identification and, 268n28; *Verinnerlichung*, 53–54, 72

"irony poisoning," 142–43

"Is Art Lighthearted?" (Adorno), 135

Islamophobia, 182, 287n78

isolation, 1, 9, 15, 29, 190, 201, 208, 222–23

Jackson, James Harris, 135, 138

Jay, Martin, 69, 243, 267n17

jazz, 80

Jelinek, Elfriede, 212, 213–14

Jews, 50, 122, 183, 216; genocide of, 81, 162, 205; hostile jokes about, 136, 140. *See also* antisemitism; concentration camps

Johnson, Greg, 278n11

Johnson, Laurie M., 278n10

jokes: alt-right recruitment tactics with tendentious, 122–26, 128, 132–33, 136, 139–40, 143–44, 148–50, 153; bribing with, 130–35, 139, 145–46, 280n46; culture industry of, 121–23, 135, 138–41, 148, 153; ego and, 126, 127, 131, 132, 138, 224–25, 278n19; with external and internal obstacles, 279n32; gender norms and, 281n88; Holocaust, 136, 173–74, 286n54; hostile alt-right, 135–49; humor and, 44, 123, 125–30, 132, 139, 278n19; hypnosis and, 84, 132–33, 247–48; "irony poisoning" and, 142–43; left movements with, 152–53; neo-Nazis with, 125; pleasure from, 13, 126–28, 130, 133, 136, 139–40; psychological mass with humor and, 278n19; racist, 7, 124, 150, 240; sexist, 7, 124–25, 150, 240, 281n84; sexually aggressive alt-right, 128–31, 143–49, 279n25, 281n77; smut and, 146, 281n77; superego and, 126, 127, 131–32, 135, 138, 148, 278n19; Trump and alt-right, 149–51; unconscious and, 12–13, 41, 123, 126, 128–29, 132–34, 279n25, 280n46, 281n77; "unlaughter" with, 153–54

Capital, 102; of violent past, 156, 159, 173, 230. *See also* amnesia; mourning

Louisiana, U.S.: cancer rate in, 272n6; employment and exploitation in, 96–101, 273n21; Tea Party in, 94, 99–100, 272n13; Trump followers in, 94–105, 108, 110, 116–18, 128–29, 228–29, 271n1, 273n22

love, 41, 43, 49–50, 78; blindness of, 58, 115; complete object, 55, 57, 62, 109–10; followers with, 233–34; melancholic state and, 102, 103–4; narcissistic, 38–39, 55, 57, 59, 73, 108, 110–11, 159; narcissistic mass, 55–59, 73, 108; object and idealization, 56–57. *See also* Eros

Löwenthal, Leo, 36, 114, 117, 257n26

Lugones, Maria, 23

"Lulz" (laughter at the expense of another), 142

Luschan, Felix von, 161, 285n32

lynchings, in U.S., 81–82

Maidens Group Edelweiss (Edelweiß), 198

malaise, 36–37, 114–15

manhood, 20–21, 97, 100, 118

manic state, 102, 105–6, 108–9, 111, 115, 150, 229

Manosphere, 148

Marasco, Robyn, 68, 70, 272n4

Marcuse, Herbert, 6, 67, 134, 255n19, 257n26

Markovics, Alexander, 189

Marx, Karl, 8–9, 91, 256n23; alienation and, 31–33; on labor power, 26, 29, 260n29; revolutionary proletariat and, 248–51; vampire Capital and, 25–27, 30, 32–33, 97–99, 102, 230, 240

Marxism, cultural, 122, 276n2

masculinity, 20, 118, 175, 177–79

masochism, 262n3

Mason, Lilliana, 255n12

mass culture, 34, 71

masses: Catholic Church and army, 264n43; defined, 53, 72; Eros and, 48, 49–51; far-right, 3, 9, 38, 53, 64, 80, 224, 227–28; fascist, 70–75, 262n1; followers and identification, 49–51, 53, 56, 72; libido and aggression in, 48–51; narcissistic love, 55–59, 73, 108; primordial traits of, 94, 268n36; regression and leaders of, 83–84, 262n12; responsibility of hypnotized, 243–48; unconscious and, 263n42

mass media, 17, 34

mass psychology, 51, 263n42

master humans (*Herrenmenschen*), 80–81, 204, 231

"mastering of the past" (*Vergangenheitsbewältigung*), 155, 170

Matrix, The (film), 196

McElwee, Sean, 259n18

McIvor, David, 232–36, 273n28, 294n25, 294n27

media: FPÖ and, 182; IBÖ and, 288n5; mass, 17, 34; social, 34, 36, 71, 135–36, 140, 146, 275n69

melancholia/mania oscillation: ego ideal replacement and, 54; far-right propaganda techniques with, 12; psychological mass and, 105; Trump followers and, 94, 101–7, 108, 229

melancholic state, 12, 102–4, 106, 109

Melton, Neil, 118–19

Menillo, Gregory J., 270n83

"messenger" device, 116, 117

Mexicans, 22, 82, 110, 114, 273n21

Middle Ages, 50, 80

middle class, 21, 86, 97, 106, 122, 165

"migrantizing citizens," 249

noncitizens, 115, 249, 283n7

nonidentity, 1, 34

nonwholeness, 5, 14, 42, 52, 95, 222–24, 250–51; castration anxiety and, 15, 16, 240; precarity capitalism and, 10

NPI (National Policy Institute), 147

objective conditions: of capitalism, 15, 16, 36; of suffering, 11, 15, 16, 36, 71, 86

"On Narcissism" (Freud), 39, 51, 55, 57

"On the Historical Roots of US Fascism" (Fernández), 259n18

Others, 34, 79, 81, 114–15, 258n11, 274n63, 289n35

Ovaherero people, 162, 285nn30–31

Padmore, George, 23

Paluck, Elizabeth Levy, 150

"paranoid-schizoid position," 232, 234

paranoid stereopathy, 191, 211–12, 214–16, 220

patriarchy, 13, 20, 62, 172–80, 225–26, 255n16, 272n4

Pence, Mike, 110

Pensky, Max, 254n9

people of color, 22, 24, 203. See also racial minorities

"Pepe the frog," 137, 280n58

Pérez, Raul, 124

"persecuted innocence device," 211–19

persecution mania, 82–83, 215

Peter, Friedrich, 181

phoniness, 92–93, 119

physical (bodily) level: alienation on, 30–31; castration anxiety and, 11, 15, 16, 24–29, 97–98, 144

pleasure, 75, 129, 202, 219; of destructive action, 193–94; from jokes, 13, 126–28, 130, 133, 136, 139–40; principle, 45–47, 74, 127, 134

pogrom, 50, 74, 113, 142, 204–5, 214

"Politics and Psychoanalysis" (Fromm), 244

Politics of Repressed Guilt, The (Leeb), 156, 256n22, 269n58

populism, 6–7, 149, 256n20, 272n13

precarity capitalism, 1, 12, 14, 22, 25, 28, 34, 63, 157; castration anxiety with, 18, 20, 24, 35, 131; ego ideal and, 3, 123–24; far-right propaganda techniques and, 2, 4, 8; narcissism and, 64; scars of, 14, 221–28, 231, 239; "success" and, 137, 240–41, 251–52; suffering in, 3, 4, 10, 11, 16, 19, 131, 190–91; Trump followers and, 95, 96–101

preconscious, 44, 46, 132, 142, 227

"Preface to Capital" (Althusser), 26

primal father: followers and, 80; leader as, 61–62, 76–78, 83, 89, 112–13, 119, 225; primal horde and, 60–61, 77, 89, 92

primal horde, 62, 64, 75, 80, 266n101; "brother horde" and, 79, 117, 148, 225, 288n7; primal father and, 60–61, 77, 89, 92; regression and, 12, 76, 78–79

primary envy, 50, 79

"principled independence," 179

"program of civilization," 40, 48–49

projection, 81, 188, 212, 214–15, 217

proletariat: raced and gendered, 21, 230, 251–52, 276n79; revolutionary, 14, 99, 221, 248–51; vampire Capital and, 98. See also working class

propaganda: counterpropaganda, 219–20; ego ideal and, 9; fascist, 2, 5, 13, 24, 33, 35, 65, 67, 190, 194–96, 255n16, 262n2, 272n4; FPÖ, 8

propaganda techniques, far-right,
5, 16, 21, 31, 32, 70, 272n4;
dehumanization and, 80, 114–15,
280n66; dream state and, 4, 8, 87–92;
"great little man" device, 76–78, 96,
116–19, 295n45; hypnosis as, 2, 8, 28,
107, 227–28; "indefatigability"
device, 8, 14, 85–86, 191–92, 195–97,
220, 289n14; with language, 107–8,
275n69; "messenger" device, 116,
117; narcissistic regressions and,
75–80; psychoanalytic theory and,
68–69; psychologically oriented, 3–4,
258n2; "sheep and bucks" device,
73–74, 114; sleep state and, 4, 8, 12,
65, 83–87
Prophets of Deceit (Marcuse), 255n19
psychoanalysis, 1, 17, 37, 253n3; critical
theory and repression of, 66–70;
First Contributions to Psychoanalysis,
269n70; *New Introductory Lectures
on Psycho-Analysis*, 15, 39, 41, 46,
52, 263n34; "Politics and
Psychoanalysis," 244
psychoanalytic concepts: ego ideal
replacement and narcissism, 51–54;
Eros and death, 39–44; hypnotic
regression, 59–62; libido and
aggression in masses, 48–51;
narcissistic mass love, 55–59, 73, 108;
with socioeconomic dimension of
mass psychology, 47–48, 62–64;
unconscious, 44–48
psychoanalytic theory, 2, 9, 12, 65–70,
277n9
psychological, 1–4, 6–10, 253n1, 258n2,
278n10
psychological mass, 11, 47, 62, 105,
278n19; hypnosis and, 59, 265n93;
libidinal drives and, 38–39
psychological root technique, 222

*Psychological Technique of Martin Luther
Thomas' Radio Addresses, The* (Adorno),
74, 85, 87, 190, 275n71, 291nn74–75
Psychologie des Foules/Psychology of Crowds
(Le Bon), 263n42
psychology, 47–48, 62–64, 75, 225.
*See also Group Psychology and the
Analysis of the Ego*
pure narcissism, 55, 57, 62, 77, 109–10

Quijano, Annibal, 22–23

race, 103, 257n1, 259n18; Adorno,
fascism and, 80–83; castration
anxiety and, 15, 16, 18, 21; with
division of labor, 4, 23, 260n38
racial minorities, 5, 22, 24, 125, 236,
255n12; genocide of, 121, 189; hate
crimes against, 149, 150–51; jokes
targeting, 139–40, 224; as targets for
blame, 136, 225, 280n66; women, 4,
23, 28, 183, 203, 215–16, 255n13,
260n38
racial terrorism, 23
racism, 24, 34, 124, 140, 257n27; jokes,
7, 124, 150, 240; sexism and, 4, 5, 7
radio, culture industry and, 34, 74, 190
RamZPaul, 135
Rathgeb, Philip, 283n7
Rathkolb, Oliver, 184
reality, 45–47, 90
recruitment, 13, 255n19; of alt-right
with tendentious jokes, 122–26, 128,
132–33, 136, 139–40, 143–44, 148–50,
153; IBÖ tactics, 8, 190, 241
Reddit, 121
Reflections Upon Laughter (Hutcheson),
125
refugees, 114, 189, 192–93, 212–15
regression, 40, 70, 134, 266n101, 288n7;
archaic, 11, 66, 86–88, 107–8, 112,

193, 246; hypnotic, 59–62;
mass leaders with followers and,
83–84, 262n12; narcissistic, 75–80,
107–12; primal horde and, 12, 76,
78–79

Reinthaller, Anton, 181

Reiter, Margit, 180

relief theory, of humor, 125, 126

"Remembering, Repeating, and
Working-Through" (Freud), 227

Rensmann, Lars, 182, 237

repression, 52, 60, 74, 79, 88;
desublimation and, 134–35; of guilt,
81, 91, 156, 169, 185, 201, 256n22,
269n58, 294n14; past, 227–31;
pleasure with elimination of, 75; of
psychoanalysis in critical theory,
66–70

resistance, against far-right:
counterpropaganda, 219–20;
embodied reflective spaces, 14, 232,
237–38; fascism and, 66, 119–20;
hypnosis and, 92–93, 246; with
overthrow of capitalism, 248–52;
precarity capitalism and, 221,
222–27, 239; repressed past and,
227–31; on responsibility of
hypnotized masses, 243–48;
subject-in-outline and, 238–43,
250–51; "working-through the
past" and, 231–38

"Revidierte Psychoanalyse, Die"
(Adorno), 15, 17, 31–32, 225

revolutionary proletariat, 14, 99, 221,
248–51

right-wing populism, 7, 256n20

Rivers, Damian J., 275n69

robots, Amazon with, 29

Rodger, Elliott, 148

Roma people, 81, 156, 162, 163, 205

Rosenkranz, Walter, 186–87

Ross, Andrew S., 275n69

Ryan, Kathryn, 281n84

sadism, 262n3

Samudzi, Zoé, 80, 162, 285n31

scars: dream state without, 246; *Narben*,
222–25; of precarity capitalism, 14,
221–28, 231, 239; system of, 229–31,
238–41, 243, 250–51

Schaff, Mike, 97–98, 99

Schatz, Avery, 203, 258n11

Schuzbefohlenen, Die (wards, The), 212

self-hypnosis, 87, 198, 228, 245–47,
270nn81–82

Sellner, Martin, 83, 288n3, 288n5,
291n88; avant-garde and, 291n66;
IBÖ and, 13, 189–219, 290n65; terror
strategy and, 14, 191, 209

sexism, 4–5, 7, 23, 124–25, 150, 240,
281n84

sexual aggression: alt-right jokes,
128–31, 143–49, 279n25, 281n77;
against women, 281n84

sexual drive, 40–42, 48–49, 58–60, 63,
264n54

sexualization, of Jews, 216

sexual overvaluation, 55–56

shame, 129–30, 144–45, 185–86, 188,
258n11

"sheep and bucks" (good and evil)
device, 73–74, 114

Sherman, Lee, 96–97, 99, 100

"shiver down the spine device," 199,
202–3

shootings, mass, 148, 151

shrunk/cut-off/short phallus (*Stummel*),
261n59

silencing (*Verstummung*) of language, 35,
36, 261n59

Sinti people, 81, 156, 162, 163, 205

slave labor, Nazis with, 163

terror: "if you only knew trick," 199–201; "last hour device," 199, 204; mass shootings, 148, 151; racial, 23; "shiver down the spine device," 199, 202–3; strategy, 14, 74, 191, 199–205, 209; "unity trick," 191, 205–11, 290n65

Thomas, Martin Luther, 74, 85, 190, 206

"Thou shalt love thy neighbor as thyself," 43

threatening father, 84, 113, 231, 243, 269n70

time, unconscious and, 45, 263n36

Toscano, Alberto, 103

totalitarianism, 85

Totem and Taboo (Freud), 39, 53, 61–62, 157, 159, 266n101

totemic system, violence and, 61–62

transphobia, 143

troll culture, 121, 136, 142, 144, 149

Trump, Donald: with access to health care, 276n79; COVID-19 pandemic and, 12, 96, 117–19, 151, 271n1; death drive and rise of, 262n8; democracy and, 218; ego ideal, idealized leader and, 7, 21; with far-right propaganda techniques, 78, 79; fascism and, 282n92; with "great little man" device, 116–19; joking connection between alt-right and, 149–51; material and psychological sources of support for, 267n16; as narcissist, 110; noncitizens and, 249; as primal father, 112–13, 119; with race and economy, 259n18; rise of alt-right and, 6; with social media and language, 275n69; as threatening father, 113; on women, 13, 110, 125, 151, 274n63. *See also* followers, of Trump

Trumpism, 13, 125, 150, 255n12, 262n8

Tumblr, 152

Twitter, 140, 146, 275n69

Ukraine, 162

Unbehagen (discomfort), 43, 63, 263n24

Unbewusste Zeitgeschichte (Fallend), 121, 286n54

unconscious, 40, 70, 102, 143, 167, 263n42; Adorno on, 38, 68–69, 121, 173; ego and, 42, 44–45, 46; followers with, 7, 9, 46–47, 225; guilt, 13, 158, 159, 173, 263n36; id, 38, 39, 44–48, 126; jokes and, 12–13, 41, 123, 126, 128–29, 132–34, 279n25, 280n46, 281n77; manipulation of, 7, 9, 71, 257n27; preconscious, 44, 46, 132, 142, 227; time and, 45, 263n36

Und in der Mitte, da Sind Wir (And in the middle we are) (documentary film), 13, 286n38; closing books on past and authoritarian family structures, 175–80; patriarchal family structures and denied past, 172–75; with tabooed past, 157, 163–72

unemployment, 25, 27, 29, 108, 156, 190–91, 278n11

United States (U.S.), 24, 28, 217, 259n14, 259n18, 260n38; Capitol, 7, 12, 110, 113, 115, 117, 151, 249; lynchings in, 81–82; protofascist elements in, 7, 38, 65. *See also* alt-right; Louisiana

"unity trick," 191, 205–11, 290n65

"unlaughter," 153–54

"up-classing," 19, 21, 78, 222–23

"upward mobility," 19–20, 258n8

U.S. *See* United States

vampire Capital, 25–27, 30, 32–33, 97–99, 230, 240

Verbotsgesetz, 164, 285n35

Vergangenheitsbewältigung ("mastering of the past"), 155, 170

Verinnerlichung (introjection), 53–54, 72

GPSR Authorized Representative: Easy Access System Europe, Mustamäe tee
50, 10621 Tallinn, Estonia, gpsr.requests@easproject.com

www.ingramcontent.com/pod-product-compliance
Lightning Source LLC
Chambersburg PA
CBHW021850020426
42334CB00013B/263